Uncle Sam and You
Curriculum Package

How do elections work? What does the President do all day? Who decides where stop signs go? What is Labor Day? *Uncle Sam and You* is a one-year civics course that answers these questions and many more. Designed for students in grades five through eight, this curriculum guides you on an engaging tour of American government. Learn about elected leaders and everyday citizens who have important roles to fill in making our country work.

All of the instructions for how to use the course are included in *Part 1* and *Part 2*, so you do not need a separate teacher's manual. At the beginning of each weekly unit, an introductory page gives a list of the lessons and a list of the additional books the student will be using while studying that particular unit. Each unit has four daily lessons, followed by a holiday lesson you choose from the thirty holiday lessons included. If you have children younger than grade five, they can listen to the lessons and participate in the family activities.

The lessons are richly illustrated with full-color photographs and historic illustrations. At the end of each regular (non-holiday) lesson is a list of several supplemental activities. You may choose which activities to assign. *The Citizen's Handbook* is a collection of primary source documents and stories that are assigned after many lessons. Depending on how many activities you assign, most students will need 45-90 minutes to complete one lesson. One special family activity is assigned each week that corresponds with the holiday lesson you choose for that unit. These activities include craft and art projects, themed meals, and other multi-age activities.

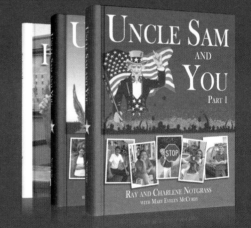

The full curriculum package includes:

- *Uncle Sam and You Part 1*
- *Uncle Sam and You Part 2*
- *The Citizen's Handbook*
- *Uncle Sam and You Answer Key*

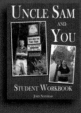 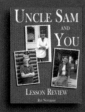

Eight works of literature are assigned in the *Uncle Sam and You* curriculum to give your child a richer perspective on the various topics studied. Two optional additional resources are the *Student Workbook* and *Lesson Review*, each of which provides a way to review material in each lesson. The *Answer Key* that comes with the curriculum package has all of the answers needed for grading.

For more information, visit notgrass.com or call 1-800-211-8793.

UNCLE SAM AND YOU

PART 1

Notgrass
company

Previous Page: Miami County (OH) Courthouse

Uncle Sam and You Part 1
by Ray and Charlene Notgrass
with Mary Evelyn McCurdy

ISBN 978-1-60999-046-6

Unless otherwise noted, scripture quotations taken from the
New American Standard Bible, Copyright 1960, 1962, 1963, 1971, 1972, 1973,1975, 1977, 1995
by the Lockman Foundation Used by permission.

Cover design by Mary Evelyn McCurdy
Interior design by Charlene Notgrass
with Mary Evelyn McCurdy

Printed in the United States of America

Notgrass Company
975 Roaring River Road
Gainesboro, TN 38562

1-800-211-8793
www.notgrass.com
books@notgrass.com

Table of Contents
PART 1

Presidential Campaign Items from 1888

Flag Made from Hay Bales

Introduction to the CURRICULUM

How do elections work? What does the President do all day? Who decides where stop signs go? What is Labor Day? This curriculum will answer these questions and many more. *Uncle Sam and You* guides your child on an engaging tour of American government. He or she will learn about elected leaders and everyday citizens, all of whom have an important role to fill in making our country work.

Uncle Sam and You Curriculum Package

The basic curriculum package for *Uncle Sam and You* includes:

★ *Uncle Sam and You, Part 1* — This book has seventy-five lessons, designed to be completed in one semester.

★ *Uncle Sam and You, Part 2* — This book has another seventy-five lessons, designed to be completed in one semester.

★ *The Citizen's Handbook* — This book is a collection of original letters, poems, songs, stories, and other writings related to civics.

★ *Uncle Sam and You Answer Key* — This book has all of the answers needed for the assignments included at the end of the lessons, the activities in the *Student Workbook*, and the questions and quizzes in the *Lesson Review*.

Additional Products

To make this curriculum a rich experience and to make it usable with children from grade five through grade eight, we offer three additional products:

Uncle Sam and You Student Workbook — This book has puzzles and other handwork activities which review information learned in the daily lessons. These are designed for younger students and for students whose learning style fits these kinds of activities.

Uncle Sam and You Lesson Review — This book has daily questions, literature review questions, and weekly quizzes, designed for older students. We expect that students will use either the *Student Workbook* or the *Lesson Review,* but your student can complete both if you prefer.

Uncle Sam and You Literature Package — This is a selection of eight literature titles that complement the lessons in *Uncle Sam and You.* These books can be purchased from Notgrass Company as a package or individually. You can also obtain them from another source such as the library, a bookstore, or an online source. You can use any unabridged edition of these books.

★ *Lincoln: A Photobiography* by Russell Freedman (Units 5-6)

★ *A Letter to Mrs. Roosevelt* by C. Coco De Young (Units 10-11)

★ *Brighty of the Grand Canyon* by Marguerite Henry (Units 12-14)

★ *Basher Five-Two* by Scott O'Grady (Units 16-17)

★ *Misty of Chincoteague* by Marguerite Henry (Units 18-19)

★ *The Long Winter* by Laura Ingalls Wilder (Units 22-24)

★ *The Wright Brothers: How They Invented the Airplane* by Russell Freedman (Units 25-26)

★ *Lost on a Mountain in Maine* by Donn Fendler (Units 29-30)

Notes for Parents on the Literature Selections

We carefully selected literature for *Uncle Sam and You* that is upbuilding and won't assault your faith or sense of decency. We intentionally excluded many titles that did not meet our criteria. Some of the ones we included have a few words or references that we want to tell you about before your child reads them. We want to let you know in case you want to do some editing or choose to read a book aloud to the student and skip over inappropriate words. We have listed here only the books in the literature list that have minor content issues.

Lincoln: A Photobiography by Russell Freedman — "As president he had been denounced, ridiculed, and damned by a legion of critics" (page 30).

Brighty of the Grand Canyon by Marguerite Henry — A few uses of dang/danged (pages 72, 88, 100, 124)

Basher Five-Two by Captain Scott O'Grady — Captain O'Grady discusses an article he read about "The Will to Survive." It told of two people lost in difficult circumstances. One had the will to survive and did for several days; the other gave up quickly and committed suicide. He shows how the latter was definitely the wrong course.

Lost on a Mountain in Maine by Donn Fendler — As he tells his story, Donn uses the word "Christmas" as an exclamation of surprise several times.

How to Use *Uncle Sam and You, Part 1* and *Part 2*

These two volumes are the core of the curriculum. They give you and your child all of the information you need in order to use *Uncle Sam and You* on a daily basis.

These two volumes contain fifteen units each for a total of thirty units. Your child can study *Part 1* during one half of the school year and *Part 2* during the other half. Each unit has four lessons. At the back of each book are fifteen lessons on America's patriotic holidays. If you want your child to do five lessons per week, the holiday lessons can be used as a fifth lesson; or they can be used on a family night so that Dad can join in.

At the beginning of each unit, an introductory page gives a list of the lessons in that unit and a list of the additional books the student will need while studying that unit. Following the introductory page are the daily lessons. Students can read these on their own, or you can read the lessons aloud. The lessons are richly illustrated. The student's learning experience will be greatly enhanced if he or she is encouraged to examine the illustrations closely. They have been carefully selected to be an integral part of the learning experience.

At the end of each lesson is a list of several activities. Students are not necessarily expected to complete all of these activities. You may choose which activities you wish to assign. Subjects of the activities vary from day to day, but they include:

★ Thinking Biblically assignments

★ Creative writing assignments

★ Vocabulary assignments

★ Short research assignments to look something up or ask a family member

★ Assignments to draw a picture or take a photograph

★ Reading assignments from *The Citizen's Handbook* or a literature title

★ Assignments in the *Student Workbook* or the *Lesson Review*

How to Use the American Holidays Lessons

An important part of civics is celebrating holidays with family, friends, and communities. Since families who homeschool can schedule their school year in many different ways, we designed *Uncle Sam and You* so that you can choose when to study the various holidays. If you start the curriculum in January, you don't want to study Thanksgiving in April! We arranged the holidays in chronological order from Independence Day to Inauguration Day in Part 1 and from Martin Luther King Day to Father's Day in Part 2. Each holiday lesson has a corresponding family activity. These are found in the section after the holiday lessons.

How to Use *The Citizen's Handbook* and Literature

At the end of many of the daily lessons, the student will be given a reading assignment. Some of the assignments are taken from *The Citizen's Handbook* and others are taken from the literature we recommend to go along with the course. Your child will know exactly what to read each day.

How to Use the *Student Workbook*

Students using the *Student Workbook* will complete Activity 1 after reading Lesson 1 and so on after each lesson. (There are no *Student Workbook* activities for the holiday lessons.)

How to Use the *Lesson Review*

Students using the *Lesson Review* will complete the questions for Lesson 1 after reading Lesson 1 and so on after each lesson. (There are no *Lesson Review* questions for the holiday lessons.) After finishing a book in the literature package, the student will answer questions on the book. At the end of each unit, the student will take a quiz.

Using a Three-Ring Binder Notebook for End-of-Lesson Activities

We recommend that each student have a three-ring binder notebook to use only for *Uncle Sam and You*. He or she will keep in this notebook the writing and art projects completed as part of the end-of-lesson activities.

Enjoying the Weekly Family Activities

A family activity is suggested at the end of each holiday lesson. Projects include art, crafts, recipes, games, and parties. The instructions for the family activities are found in the back of *Uncle Sam and You, Part 1* and *Part 2*. We recommend reading the instructions and gathering the supplies early each week. Then you can complete the activity the day you do the holiday lesson or on another day that is convenient for your family. Your supervision is required for your child's safety. See the box below.

Parental Supervision Required

The family activities are designed for parental involvement. Please review the activity and discuss with your child what he or she may do alone and what he or she needs your supervision to do. The family activities in this book include the use of sharp objects, the oven and stove, and a few Internet research suggestions. Notgrass Company cannot accept responsibility for the safety of your child in completing these activities. You are responsible for your child's safety.

Please Note: Be careful. Some children may be allergic to recipe ingredients or craft supplies.

Our family has long enjoyed a family night once each week. You could do the family activity on a family night so that more family members could take part in the fun and learning. Like all components of *Uncle Sam and You*, the family activities are optional. We offer them as extra learning experiences. You, the parent, are the best one to decide if you are able to schedule time to complete them.

How Much Time Does It Take to Complete Each Lesson?

Depending on how many activities you assign, most students will need forty-five minutes to an hour and a half to complete one lesson. More time will be needed on the day you do the family activity. This curriculum has one hundred and fifty lessons and is designed to be completed in one school year. Since a typical school year has about one hundred and eighty days, the student completes one lesson on most school days. However, some families may choose to spread the curriculum out over a longer period of time.

What Supplies Will My Student Need?

Students will need blank paper, notebook paper, a pencil, colored pencils, and a three-ring binder, plus the materials needed to complete the family activities. These materials are listed on the individual family activity instruction pages. You may also choose to use a camera for Picture This assignments at the end of certain lessons.

What Ages Can Use This Curriculum?

The curriculum is designed for students in grades five through eight. With parental help and supervision, younger children can participate in many activities and can benefit from hearing the lessons read aloud.

How Many Activities Should My Student Complete?

Parents know best what their children are capable of accomplishing. *Uncle Sam and You* is designed to be flexible. A variety of activities is included in each lesson. A parent may require an eighth grader who is academically gifted to read the daily lessons and complete every assignment at the end of each lesson independently. On the other hand, a parent with an academically-challenged fifth grader may decide to read aloud each lesson in *Uncle Sam and You* and the selections in *The Citizen's Handbook*, and help the student be successful with the other assignments. The variety of assignments is intended to make it easy for you to create a positive, rich, engaging learning experience for your student. You should not feel pressured to complete every activity suggestion.

As you look ahead to your school year or evaluate midway, consider how you might make your child's education less complicated and educationally richer by using *Uncle Sam and You* as a large part of his or her learning for this year. *Uncle Sam and You* is much more than civics and government. You can use *Uncle Sam and You* as part of your literature, writing, vocabulary, art, handwriting practice, and Bible learning. For example, you do not necessarily need a separate language arts curriculum. You may find that eliminating busy work in an entirely separate subject and allowing that subject to be incorporated into this study makes for a less stressful, more engaging, more memorable school year!

If you have more than one child in grades five through eight, you may enjoy reading the lessons aloud as a group. Afterward, you can give each child different assignments, depending on his or her age and skill level. If you have carefully observed your child and prayed about the direction to take, then you can look back at the end of the school year and know you have accomplished the goal of completing *Uncle Sam and You*.

Some Reminders So You Will Not Feel Overwhelmed

Remember that God gave you your children and your daily responsibilities. A homeschooling mother who has one child can complete more *Uncle Sam and You* activities than a homeschooling mother who has seven children and an elderly grandparent living in her home. God will use the efforts of both of these mothers. God does not expect you to do more than you can do. Be kind to yourself. He knows exactly what you and your children need this year. Remember that out of all the parents in the world to whom He could have given your children, He chose you. He is the one who put your family together. He knows what He is doing. Trust in His choice. God created you. He created your children. Relax and remember that this is the day that the Lord has made. Rejoice and be glad in it!

We are here to help you. If you have more questions or simply need some encouragement, send us an email (help@notgrass.com) or give us a call (1-800-211-8793).

Appreciation

Uncle Sam and You has been a family project. We have enjoyed working on it together. We appreciate our daughter Mary Evelyn for writing the holiday lessons and the family activities, and for her beautiful cover designs. We are thankful to our daughter Bethany for her excellent work editing *The Citizen's Handbook*, for choosing the literature, and for the lesson activities. We appreciate our son John for writing the *Student Workbook*, for all of his work in finalizing the project and getting the computer documents to the printer, and for his good example of Christian political involvement. We think they all did an excellent job.

We appreciate our proofreaders. If you find any typos, please blame us and not them. As Harry Truman said, "The buck stops here." Our chief proofreader was our longtime friend, homeschooling mother Dena Russell. Helping her were our longtime friend Olive Wagar, who has graduated her three homeschooled children, and our beloved son-in-law Nate McCurdy (ask him sometime at a homeschool conference why we call him that).

We appreciate each of the families who encourage us in our writing of homeschool curriculum. Thank you for giving us the opportunity to do what we love to do.

You could say that God used politics to bring us together. We met in the political science department at Middle Tennessee State University just a few months before Ray graduated. We were interested in politics even when we were children. Both of us campaigned for our favorite candidates when we were in high school, and both of us served as officers of (the same) political party's campus organization when we were in college. You'll have to guess which one.

We were both blessed by good history and government teachers in high school and in college. These teachers had a great influence on us and still do today. We would like to thank them by name:

★ The late Dr. Alvin Rose, Charlene's history teacher at Cheatham County High School, Ashland City, Tennessee

★ Wayne Darrow, Charlene's government teacher at CCHS

★ The late James M. Dressler, Charlene's political science and history professor at Cumberland College (now Cumberland University)

★ Curry Peacock, Charlene's professor, advisor, and Christian mentor at Middle Tennessee State University

★ Jerry Locke, Ray's history teacher at Central High School, Columbia, Tennessee

★ The late Dr. Bart McCash, one of Ray's history professors at Middle Tennessee State University

* The late Dr. Ernest Hooper, one of Ray's history professors at Middle Tennessee State University

* Dr. Robert Ireland, Ray's professor of Constitutional history in graduate school at the University of Kentucky

Ray began reading about politics, history, and government for fun while still in high school. He still does. In college, Ray had a weekly column in the campus newspaper, in which he wrote about political and social issues in the news at the time.

Charlene received many exciting opportunities while still a teenager. As a high school junior, she was part of a 4-H Congress that met in the Tennessee State Capitol. She also attended a mock United Nations at Middle Tennessee State University with students from many high schools. There the students pretended to be members of the U.N. She went to Cumberland College in Lebanon, Tennessee, for her first two years of college. One of the members of its Board of Directors was Congressman Joe L. Evins, who served in the U.S. House of Representatives from 1947 to 1977. Charlene was given the opportunity to serve as an intern in his office on Capitol Hill for one month.

We believe that an understanding of our government is important for every American citizen. We believe that Americans should understand both our history and the way government is organized today. We believe that our Founding Fathers provided a strong base for our country and that our country would do well to remember our dependence on God, the many benefits of freedom and limited government, and our responsibility to be good stewards of the blessings that come from living in our great country. We believe that we should honor what God teaches in His Word about respecting our government officials. We are grateful that our true King is the Creator of the heavens and the earth.

Now to the King eternal, immortal, invisible,
the only God, be honor and glory forever and ever. Amen
1 Timothy 1:17

Ray and Charlene Notgrass

UNIT 1 – WE THE PEOPLE

BOOKS USED IN UNIT 1

- The Citizen's Handbook

- Student Workbook (optional)

- Lesson Review (optional)

New citizens celebrate after a naturalization ceremony on Liberty Island in New York. The ceremony was part of a 2011 celebration of the 125th anniversary of the dedication of the Statue of Liberty.

Welcome HOME

Wesley Notgrass was working at a small town newspaper in Tennessee when World War II began in Europe and Asia. He had no plans to become a soldier. However, in 1941 Wes received a letter from Washington, D.C. The letter invited him to enlist in the U.S. Army and informed him that if he did not do so, he would be drafted.

Citizen Soldiers

Wes enlisted that summer and began training. See photos on page 3. In December Japan attacked Pearl Harbor and America entered the war. Two years later, Wesley and thousands of other soldiers sailed from New York City to England on giant ocean liners. After months of preparation there, Sergeant Notgrass was one of the American soldiers who landed in northern France in June of 1944 to help free people who had been terrorized and conquered by Nazi Germany.

In June of 1945, over a year and a half after leaving American soil, Notgrass boarded another ocean liner, again with thousands of other soldiers. This time they were coming back to America.

The soldiers looked forward to their first glimpse of the Statue of Liberty in New York harbor. As the ship drew closer, a line was painted down the middle of its deck. Officers told the men that half of them had to stay on one side of the line and half had to stay on the other. They knew that if all the men rushed to one side to see Lady Liberty, the ship might capsize!

Think about Wesley Notgrass (author Ray Notgrass' dad) and the other citizen soldiers of World War II. Few had ever left the United States before. Now they were returning home from a terrible war, while remembering their buddies who did not come home. As the Statue of Liberty came into view, they cheered and shed tears. They were back in America. Their families, friends, and fellow citizens were waiting to say, "Welcome home!"

Wesley Notgrass
Top Left: Private Citizen
Top Right: Young Recruit
Lower: With Fellow Veterans Fifty
Years After World War II
(Notgrass is second from left
in the second row.)

Honoring Our Country

God has given us a great country. He has provided us with abundant resources. We have used these gifts to care for our own people and to care for others. Americans have built schools and hospitals overseas, exported food around the globe, and shared technology that has brought opportunities to millions.

When wars have been fought to bring freedom to others, Americans have put on uniforms, helped to defeat people who wanted to hurt others, and then returned home to resume their lives as private citizens.

We can be thankful for what America stands for and what Americans have accomplished. We can show respect for our country and its leaders. Displaying our flag is one of the many ways that Americans show this respect. Look at the photo of Wesley Notgrass with fellow World War II veterans above. An American flag hangs behind them. Notice the flags in the photos on page 2. Read about where these photos were taken at right.

Flying the American Flag

(from top to bottom on page 2)

Putnam County Courthouse, Cookeville, Tennessee

Iowa State Capitol, Des Moines, Iowa

Ferry Between Bayfield, Wisconsin, and Madeline Island in Lake Superior

Plains, Georgia, Hometown of President Jimmy Carter

Pepin, Wisconsin, Birthplace of Laura Ingalls Wilder

A Place To Call Home

People around the world have seen America as a beacon of hope and a chance for a new start. Millions have come as immigrants, making the journey at great personal sacrifice. More than a century ago they arrived by ship. For those whose first stop was New York City, the Statue of Liberty gave them a greeting of "Welcome home!" just like she gave Mr. Notgrass.

Most Americans arrive in America as newborn babies who are blessed to call America home from their first breath. Their "Welcome home!" greeting comes from a family of people who love them.

Welcome Home, Little American!

Civics and Citizenship

Uncle Sam and You teaches about civics and about how to be a good citizen. Civics is a study about how citizens are involved in their communities and in their government. It is a study of citizens' rights and of their responsibilities. A citizen's rights are what his country owes him. These rights are sometimes called civil rights or civil liberties. A citizen's responsibilities are what he owes his country.

★ ★ ★
A citizen's rights are what his country owes him. A citizen's responsibilities are what he owes his country.
★ ★ ★

A person cannot have rights without responsibilities. It is selfish for people to insist on their rights without carrying out their responsibilities. This can cause a family, group, or nation to split apart. On the other hand, expecting people to carry out their responsibilities without respecting their rights treats people as though they are just parts of a machine.

While we hope that *Uncle Sam and You* will help you understand our system of government, we also want to help you learn ways that people are involved in their communities and states and their nation. We want to encourage you to make a difference for good where you live. We hope that your community and your nation will be better because you are a citizen of this great land.

The Right to Worship and to Pray

For Christians one of our most precious rights is the right to worship God freely. We can worship God in private and in public. This is an important right that is not granted to the citizens of every country. It is a right we should appreciate and hold dear.

From Maine to Alaska and Hawaii, American believers have built church buildings where they and their guests can worship God together. Seven of the thousands that have been built are pictured on pages 5 through 7. Following are some facts about these buildings and the congregations who have met in them.

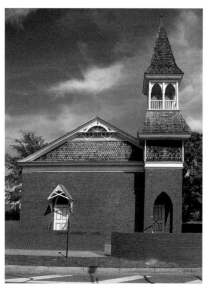
Auburn, Alabama
Auburn University Chapel

★ **Auburn University Chapel in Auburn, Alabama.** This chapel, built in 1851, first served as a Presbyterian church. Slaves made its bricks on a nearby plantation. It originally had one entrance for men and another for women. The building was used as a hospital during the Civil War. From 1926 until 1973, it served as Auburn's theater. It was then renovated and restored. In 1976 it reopened as University Chapel.

★ **Trinity Episcopal Church in Independence, Missouri.** This church was built in 1881. Here future President Harry Truman married his wife Bess in 1919. In 1956 their daughter Margaret married Clifton Daniel here. When the church added a new two-story wing in 1959, former President Truman gave a short address at its dedication.

Independence, Missouri
Trinity Episcopal Church

★ **St. Peter's Episcopal in Seward, Alaska.** Episcopal services were held in a tent and a railroad depot before St. Peter's Episcopal was built in 1906. Inside is a stylized painting by Dutch artist Jan Van Emple. The artist combined Jesus' resurrection and ascension with the landscape of nearby Resurrection Bay. He painted a Native American, a Native Alaskan, a fur trapper, a prospector, and a homesteader in the scene.

Seward, Alaska
St. Peter's Episcopal

- **Grace United Methodist Church in Harrisburg, Pennsylvania.** This church was completed in 1880. When the Pennsylvania state capitol burned seventeen years later, the state legislature used the building as their temporary capitol.

- **16th and Decatur Church of Christ in Washington, D.C.** Joe L. Evins served as a Tennessee Congressman for thirty years. He attended this church in Washington. Author Charlene Notgrass served as an intern in his office in 1974 and visited the church.

- **Maranatha Baptist Church in Plains, Georgia.** This is the home church of former President and Mrs. Jimmy Carter. People from around the world have visited here to participate in Carter's Sunday School class.

- **Grace Episcopal Church in Galveston, Texas.** This building, dedicated in 1895, survived the city's 1900 hurricane. In 1926 men used hand-operated jacks to raise the building four and one half feet to prevent future flooding. Nearby Trinity Episcopal Church was also raised four and one half feet with hand-operated jacks. A beating drum kept the workers in rhythm.

Harrisburg, Pennsylvania
Grace United Methodist Church (at far right)

Plains, Georgia
Maranatha Baptist Church

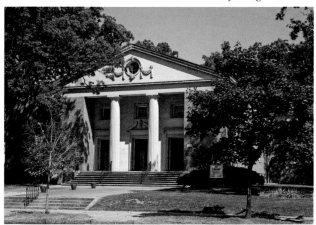

Washington, D.C.
16th and Decatur Church of Christ

Every American can pray for God's will to be done by our government leaders and by our citizens. We can pray for the safety of our nation and for His blessings on all the people of the world. We can ask God for greater faith and commitment on the part of our fellow citizens. Praying for our country and its leaders is a great right because we have the freedom to do so. It is a great responsibility because in prayer we can call on the One who can help our country the most.

Galveston, Texas
Grace Episcopal Church

First of all, then, I urge that entreaties and prayers, petitions and thanksgivings,
be made on behalf of all men, for kings and all who are in authority,
so that we may lead a tranquil and quiet life in all godliness and dignity.

1 Timothy 2:1-2

Lesson Activities

Thinking Biblically — Copy 1 Timothy 2:1-2 in your notebook, using the translation of your choice.

Literature — Read "My Country 'Tis of Thee" in *The Citizen's Handbook*, page 1.

Creative Writing — In your notebook, write one or two paragraphs about what you would want to do on your first day back in America if you had been away for a long time.

Picture This! — Take a photograph or draw a picture of the place your family meets with your church.

Student Workbook or Lesson Review — If you are using one of these optional books, complete the assignment for Lesson 1.

Fifty States
ONE NATION I

The fifty United States of America make up one nation. Each state has a unique geography. Florida, for instance, is surrounded by oceans on three sides and its highest elevation is 345 feet. Wyoming does not border an ocean and is home to the towering Grand Tetons. Its highest peak rises to almost 14,000 feet. See photos below.

Florida
Flamingos

Wyoming
Grand Teton National Park

Each state has a unique size. Rhode Island measures forty-eight miles from north to south and thirty-seven miles from east to west, while Alaska measures 1,400 miles by 2,700 miles. See photos on page 9.

Each state has a unique history. Delaware has a much longer history as a state than Hawaii. Delaware had been a state for over 170 years when Hawaii became one in 1959.

Each state has a unique government. The large state of Nebraska has a small legislature with just forty-nine legislators, while tiny New Hampshire has four hundred and twenty-four. Most states have a formal name that puts the words "State of" before the name of the state, as in State of Alabama. However, four states, Virginia, Massachusetts, Pennsylvania, and Kentucky, use the term "Commonwealth of," as in Commonwealth of Pennsylvania.

If you visited every state, you could experience many customs and traditions. You can buy hamburgers and hot dogs in any

Newport, Rhode Island
Rose Island Lighthouse

Alaska
Prince William Sound

state, but you can try a Hot Brown sandwich in Kentucky, a grinder in Connecticut, and a fluffernutter in Massachusetts. You can enjoy many musical styles in any state, but it would be fun to hear live country music in Tennessee, blues in Mississippi, and bluegrass in Kentucky.

When you see an American flag flying high above the United States Capitol, at your local courthouse, or on your front porch, you see a field of blue with fifty stars and thirteen stripes of red and white. You know that the thirteen stripes represent the thirteen original American colonies, and that the fifty stars represent America's fifty states, but do you know how the number of states grew from thirteen to fifty?

The First Thirteen States

Christopher Columbus discovered the New World in 1492. Soon Europeans began to claim land in what is now the United States. Spanish settlers moved into the Florida peninsula and into what is now California, Texas, and other western states. French settlers moved into areas around the Great Lakes and the Mississippi River. English settlers formed thirteen colonies along the Atlantic coast.

Spain, France, England, and other countries struggled over which country would be the most powerful in North America. At times they even fought one another. In 1707 England and Wales joined with Scotland to form Great Britain. In the mid-1700s, Great Britain and France fought a war called the Seven Years War in Europe and the French and Indian War in America. The war in America lasted nine years. British and American colonial soldiers, along with some Native American tribes, fought against French soldiers and other Native American tribes.

By the mid-1700s, some families had been in America for several generations. Though most residents of the colonies considered themselves to be British citizens, many had never even been to Great Britain. America was their home and they enjoyed its freedoms and opportunities. The British government wanted to make money from its American colonies. The king of Great Britain and the British Parliament treated the colonies harshly. Though American leaders worked to get them to stop, the British government refused.

In 1776 colonial leaders adopted the Declaration of Independence, in which they declared themselves to be independent of Great Britain. At that time, the thirteen colonies became the United States of America. Over the next few years, the two sides fought the American Revolutionary War. During the war, representatives of the thirteen states led the American government. They wrote and adopted the Articles of Confederation, a document that told how the states would work together.

States 1-13

1787
Delaware
Pennsylvania
New Jersey

1788
Georgia
Connecticut
Massachusetts
Maryland
South Carolina
New Hampshire
Virginia
New York

1789
North Carolina

1790
Rhode Island

A few years after the war, citizens representing twelve of the states (all except Rhode Island) met in Philadelphia to make improvements in the Articles. While there, they decided to write a new constitution. They completed the Constitution of the United States in September of 1787. The Articles of Confederation, the Declaration of Independence and the Constitution are discussed in Unit 2. Over the next several months, groups of leaders in each state voted on whether to ratify the Constitution. Three states ratified it before the end of the year, first Delaware, then Pennsylvania, and then New Jersey. The other ten states ratified it in 1788, 1789, and 1790. The chart at left gives the order of the first thirteen states.

Vermont, Kentucky, Tennessee, and Ohio

The treaty that ended the American Revolution gave America control of the land that was south of Canada, north of Florida, and east of the Mississippi River. The U.S. government set up guidelines for how new states could be formed. One requirement was that they write a state constitution. In 1791 Vermont was admitted as the fourteenth state. It was the first state that did not touch the Atlantic Ocean.

Great Britain had considered land west of the Appalachian Mountains to be Indian territory. In the years before the

Appalachian Mountains

Danville, Kentucky
Old Wilderness Road Street Sign

New Orleans, Louisiana
The French Quarter

American Revolution, only a few Europeans settled there. However, during and after the war, thousands of settlers crossed the mountains. Many traveled on the Wilderness Road through Cumberland Gap. One of the most famous was frontiersman Daniel Boone, who moved his family to Kentucky. It became the first state west of the Appalachians in 1792. An early settlement along the Wilderness Road was Danville, Kentucky. See one of its street signs at top right.

Tennessee, another "overmountain" state, joined the Union in 1796. Future President Andrew Jackson helped to write its state constitution. See a beautiful Appalachian scene above. Ohio became the first new state of the nineteenth century when it joined the Union in 1803. "Joining the Union" is a phrase that has the same meaning as joining the United States or becoming a state. See chart of states fourteen through seventeen at right.

Territories of France, Britain, and Spain

By 1800 France controlled over 800,000 square miles of land west of the Mississippi River. French territory spread from the headwaters of the Missouri River in the Rocky Mountains to the mouth of the Mississippi at the Gulf of Mexico. As seen above, French architecture can still be seen in New Orleans.

States 14-17
1791 Vermont
1792 Kentucky
1796 Tennessee
1803 Ohio

Spain controlled Mexico and the areas that are now Texas, California, New Mexico, and Arizona. The Spanish-built Mission San José, founded in 1720, is pictured below.

San Antonio, Texas
Mission San José y San Miguel de Aguayo

In 1803 France sold its land to the United States. This area, called the Louisiana Purchase, nearly doubled the size of America. President Thomas Jefferson chose Meriwether Lewis and William Clark to lead a team of men to explore these lands. In 1812 America added Louisiana, a small part of the Louisiana Purchase, its first state west of the Mississippi River.

In the decades before and after 1800, control of Florida swapped back and forth between Spain and Great Britain. Mexico rebelled against the Spanish government in 1810, just as the Americans had done against the British in 1776. Meanwhile, the British continued to harass America even though the American Revolution had ended. They fought the War of 1812 from 1812 to 1815.

Six New States in Six Years

While the war for Mexican independence continued to the south, the United States kept growing. In just five years, it added five states east of the Mississippi River and one to the west. Indiana joined in 1816, Mississippi in 1817, Illinois in 1818, Alabama in 1819, Maine in 1820, and Missouri in 1821.

Twenty-Five States and Counting

America was halfway to its total of fifty states when Arkansas became state number twenty-five in 1836. Michigan, with its upper and lower peninsulas bordering Lake Michigan, joined in 1837. Florida became a state in 1845 and so did Texas.

Manifest Destiny and War with Mexico

Mexico won its independence from Spain in 1821. That same year the Mexican government gave a group of American settlers permission to settle in the portion of Mexico called Texas. The settlers soon wanted to make Texas a new American state. In the 1840s many American leaders believed that the United States was destined to spread across the North American continent from the Atlantic Ocean to the Pacific. Belief in Manifest Destiny influenced President James K. Polk and members of Congress to allow Texas to become a state in 1845. The Mexican government opposed Texas statehood because they did not want to lose this large area. Mexican forces attacked Texans in May of 1846. American forces went to Texas to help. This began the Mexican War. Iowa became a state that year. See chart of states eighteen through twenty-nine at right.

A treaty ended the Mexican War in 1848. In addition to Texas, the United States gained the lands that are now California, New Mexico, Nevada, and Utah, plus portions of Arizona, Colorado, Oklahoma, and Wyoming.

Though Spain, England, France, Mexico, and the United States fought for control of land in North America, we should remember who is the actual owner.

The earth is the Lord's, and all it contains,
the world, and those who dwell in it.
Psalm 24:1

Lesson Activities

Vocabulary — Find each of these words in a dictionary: elevation, harsh, headwaters, harass, manifest. Copy each word into your notebook with the definition that corresponds to the way it is used in this lesson.

Literature — Read "We, the People of . . ." in *The Citizen's Handbook*, page 2.

Creative Writing — Imagine that you are serving on the committee to write a constitution for a new state. Write a preamble to the constitution describing what you think is important about the origins and goals of governments.

Find Out! — In what year was the most recent version of your state's constitution written?

Student Workbook or Lesson Review — If you are using one of these optional books, complete the assignment for Lesson 2.

States 18-29

1812 Louisiana
1816 Indiana
1817 Mississippi
1818 Illinois
1819 Alabama
1820 Maine
1821 Missouri
25 1836 Arkansas
1837 Michigan
1845 Florida Texas
1846 Iowa

Fifty States
ONE NATION II

Americans welcomed home the soldiers who had fought in the Mexican War. They were thankful that the war was over. However, disagreements between Americans were heating up over the issue of slavery and soon they would be fighting one another.

Tuscumbia, Alabama
Slave Quarters at Abernathy House

In the early years of the American colonies, English ships brought African slaves to America. See ruins of slave quarters above.

When America's leaders worked together to write the Constitution in 1787, they wrestled with the question of what to do about slavery. Some thought it should be outlawed while others believed it should continue.

In the mid-1800s, the question of slavery came to a head all over the country, causing divisions between states, neighbors, and even family members. By then northern states did not practice slavery, but southern states continued to do so. Both sides wanted new states to be like them. Southern states wanted slavery allowed in new states, but northern states did not. Southern states believed strongly that the issue was one that each individual state should decide and that the Federal government in Washington should leave them alone. People on both sides had strong opinions. Many people became angry about the question and sometimes fighting broke out.

While this controversy became more and more divisive, America continued to add new states. Wisconsin joined the Union in 1848. It was the last state formed east of the Mississippi River. That same year gold was discovered in California. Thousands of people from America and other

States 30-33
1848
Wisconsin
1850
California
1858
Minnesota
1859
Oregon

countries rushed there in the California Gold Rush of 1849. By 1850 California had enough people to form a state and join the Union. Minnesota joined as state thirty-two in 1858.

In 1836 thousands of Americans began moving west in covered wagons on the Oregon Trail. See statue at right. In 1859 Oregon became state thirty-three. See chart of states thirty through thirty-three on page 14.

Division and Reconciliation

By December of 1860, the conflict between northern and southern states was so serious that South Carolina declared itself to be independent and seceded from the Union (to secede is to pull away from). Early in 1861, six more southern states seceded. In February these seven states formed the Confederate States of America.

On March 4, Abraham Lincoln became the sixteenth President of the United States. On April 12, fighting began between Confederate and U.S. forces at Fort Sumter in Charleston, South Carolina. Flags fly at historic Fort Sumter at lower right. Soon President Lincoln asked the remaining U.S. states to provide 75,000 soldiers. By the end of June, eleven states had seceded (see box at right). Lincoln directed the U.S. Army to move into the Confederate states to force them to return to the Union.

The United States gained three new states during the Civil War. Kansas joined in 1861. One of the southern states that had seceded in 1861 was Virginia. Citizens in the western portion of the state did not agree with secession, so that area broke away from Virginia and became West Virginia, the thirty-fifth state, in 1863.

Salem, Oregon
"The Covered Wagon" at the Oregon State Capitol

The Eleven States of the Confederacy

People in the eleven states of the Confederacy still honor their ancestors who took part in it. Pictured below is a Confederate statue in Jasper, Alabama. At its base is a Confederate flag made of flowers. The Confederate states in the order of their secession were:

**South Carolina
Mississippi
Florida
Alabama
Georgia
Louisiana
Texas
Virginia
Arkansas
North Carolina
Tennessee**

Charleston, South Carolina
Fort Sumter

15

Look at scenes from the West Virginia town of Harpers Ferry below. From time to time in *Uncle Sam and You* we include information about an individual community to show ways that American government and civic life have affected that community. Often a town's geography plays a role in how government and civics have been involved in that place. This is certainly true of Harpers Ferry. Read part of its story below.

Civics at Harpers Ferry, West Virginia

In October of 1783, future President Thomas Jefferson visited the little village of Harpers Ferry, Virginia. A short walk from the village is the rock at right. Jefferson described the view from there as "perhaps one of the most stupendous scenes in Nature." The rock is now called Jefferson Rock.

The Shenandoah River flows into the Potomac River at Harpers Ferry. Two years after Jefferson's visit, future President George Washington visited the area to study ways to make the Potomac River and its tributaries more suitable for shipping and transportation. After becoming President, Washington chose Harpers Ferry as the location of the nation's second national armory. Construction of Harpers Ferry Armory and Arsenal began in 1799. By the time of the Civil War, workers at the arsenal had manufactured more than 600,000 muskets, rifles, and pistols.

Before leaving with William Clark and the Corps of Discovery to explore the Louisiana Purchase, Meriwether Lewis went to Harpers Ferry in the spring of 1803 to purchase supplies for the expedition. He bought rifles, powder horns, bullet molds, tools to repair guns, and a collapsible boat frame made of iron.

Harpers Ferry, Virginia, was the scene of fighting about the issue of slavery even before the Civil War began. Abolitionist John Brown and a band of twenty-one men captured Harpers Ferry Armory and Arsenal (an abolitionist was a person who wanted slavery to end). Brown had planned to give its 100,000 weapons to slaves so they could fight for their freedom. U.S. Army troops rushed to Harpers Ferry and captured Brown. He was tried in a Virginia court and found guilty of treason.

During the Civil War, both the Northern and Southern armies tried to control Harpers Ferry. It changed hands eight times. When West Virginia became the thirty-fifth state during the War, the town became Harpers Ferry, West Virginia. It is now part of the Harpers Ferry National Historical Park.

Nevada became the thirty-sixth state in 1864. The Civil War ended in 1865 when the Southern states surrendered. Over the next few years, they were allowed to return to the Union. In 1866 Tennessee became the first Confederate state to be readmitted to the Union. Georgia was the last in 1870. When you say the Pledge of Allegiance and speak the words, "one nation under God, indivisible," remember that these United States were once divided, but came back together again. The Civil War is remembered today by many monuments, as seen below.

States 34-36

1861
Kansas

1863
West Virginia

1864
Nevada

Sharpsburg, Maryland
Antietam Road Statues
Antietam National Battlefield

Manassas, Virginia
Union Veterans Memorial
Second Battle of Bull Run

Shiloh, Tennessee
Cannonball Monument
Battle of Shiloh

Near Chattanooga, Tennessee
Florida Monument
Battle of Chickamauga

Gettysburg, Pennsylvania
Hancock Monument
Battle of Gettysburg

Vicksburg, Mississippi
Illinois Monument
Battle of Vicksburg

New States From the Close of the Civil War to 1900

Nine western states joined the Union in the years between the Civil War and 1900. Nebraska joined in 1867 and Colorado in 1876. North and South Dakota came into the Union on the same day in 1889. Later that year Montana and Washington became states. Idaho and Wyoming joined in 1890 and Utah in 1896.

New States in the Twentieth Century

On April 22, 1889, the United States government began allowing settlers to claim land within an area called Indian Territory. An estimated eleven thousand people rushed in on that day and claimed free land. See photo at right. Just eighteen years later, in 1907, the area became the State of Oklahoma.

Oklahoma Land Rush, 1889

New Mexico became the forty-seventh state and Arizona the forty-eighth, both in 1912. The American flag had forty-eight stars for over four decades. In 1959 it gained two more. Neither of these states is connected to the other forty-eight geographically. Alaska, which is northwest of Canada, became state number forty-nine in January. The islands of Hawaii, which are in the Pacific Ocean, became the fiftieth state that August. The chart on page 19 lists states 37 through 50.

Out of Many, One

The envelope below was used sometime between 1861 and 1865. Though Americans were severely divided at that time, the phrase *E pluribus unum* printed at the upper left was a reminder of their former unity. *E pluribus unum* is a Latin phrase which means "out of many, one."

Envelope from Civil War Years

Fifty states joined together into one nation is an illustration of *E pluribus unum*. It is God's will that all people live together in harmony and respect for one another. It is His will for families, the church, nations, and the world.

To sum up, all of you be harmonious, sympathetic,

brotherly, kindhearted, and humble in spirit;

not returning evil for evil or insult for insult,

but giving a blessing instead;

for you were called for the very purpose

that you might inherit a blessing.

1 Peter 3:8-9

Lesson Activities

Thinking Biblically — Write a paragraph in your notebook or discuss with a parent: What are attitudes that encourage unity in a group of people?

Vocabulary — Write five sentences in your notebook, using one of these words in each: reconciliation, secede, stupendous, armory, treason. Check in a dictionary if you need help with their definitions.

Find Out! — What was the month, day, and year that your state joined the Union?

Picture This! — Take a photograph or draw a picture of your state flag.

Student Workbook or Lesson Review — If you are using one of these optional books, complete the assignment for Lesson 3.

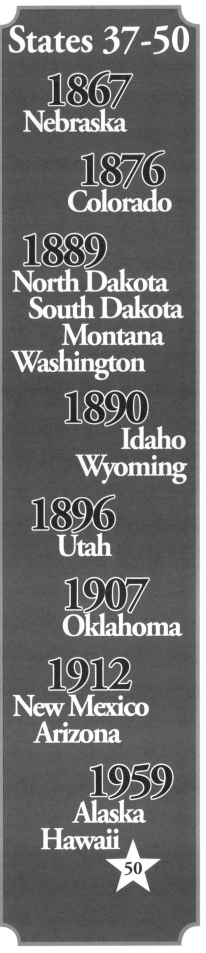

States 37-50

1867
Nebraska

1876
Colorado

1889
North Dakota
South Dakota
Montana
Washington

1890
Idaho
Wyoming

1896
Utah

1907
Oklahoma

1912
New Mexico
Arizona

1959
Alaska
Hawaii
50

Out of Many, ONE

Habeeb came alone to the United States from the Middle East when he was seventeen years old. After growing up in Lebanon in a Christian family, he came to America to attend a Christian college. Here he has stayed for almost forty years. Habeeb met and married a young woman from the Midwest. While still newlyweds, they helped his parents escape from a civil war in his native land. With joy and pride, Habeeb became an American citizen. He worked hard to become the president of a successful company. He is an active volunteer in his community, state, and country. Habeeb is proud of his Lebanese heritage and enjoys taking his family back for visits, but Habeeb is an American. He has a deep love for God, his wife, his children, his church, and his adopted country.

Wentworth, North Carolina
Family Reunion

Out of many, one. *E Pluribus Unum*. This phrase not only describes our one nation with its many states; it also describes the people of the United States. We come from all over the world, yet we are one people. The people pictured in the photo at top left are taking the oath of citizenship, the last step in the long process they completed to become U.S. citizens. Their ceremony took place at the rim of the Grand Canyon in September 2010. Think about

Madison, Wisconsin
Native Ceremony at State Capitol

New York City, New York
Sylvia's Soul Food in Harlem

the song "Jesus Loves the Little Children." Picture all the red, brown, yellow, black, and white children in the world. Now picture American children. They are red, brown, yellow, black, and white, too.

Like Habeeb, everyone in the world is an immigrant or the descendant of an immigrant. Since God scattered people at the Tower of Babel, they have been moving to new places. You or your parents or your grandparents or someone in your family moved to the area where you live.

The first immigrants to America were those we now call Native Americans or Indians. Europeans began arriving after 1492 and Africans after 1619. Immigrants and descendants of immigrants formed the United States after declaring themselves to be an independent nation in 1776.

Native Americans, African Americans, and Americans descended from Europeans are pictured on page 20. The Native Americans are participating in a ceremony on the grounds of the Wisconsin State Capitol in Madison. The African Americans stand outside Sylvia's Restaurant in Harlem in New York. It specializes in "soul food." Americans of European descent are gathered for a family reunion outside the log cabin where their ancestor was born in Wentworth, North Carolina.

In 1820 the government of the United States began keeping records of how many immigrants become legal permanent residents each year. The records show that people have emigrated to America from all over the world. According to the Department of Homeland Security, the largest numbers of legal permanent residents have come from fifteen regions. Mexico and Germany top the list. Look at the chart at right. Each large number represents how many millions of legal permanent residents have come from these places (some regions include two countries, such as Norway and Sweden, because in some years the records for these countries were combined).

Illegal immigrants who sneak into the United States without obeying our immigration laws are often in the news. However, America continues to welcome many legal immigrants each year. In the past, immigrants looked to America as a place where they could worship freely, live in peace, make a good living, and join family members who were already here. They still do.

Between 1820 and 2010, there were seventeen years when we granted permanent legal residence status to one million immigrants or more in a single year. Eight of those years were between 2001 and 2010!

Millions of Legal Permanent Residents from these Countries, 1820-2010

Mexico
Germany

Italy
United Kingdom

Ireland
Canada and
Newfoundland
Austria and
Hungary
Russia

Norway and
Sweden
Philippines

China
India
Cuba
Dominican
Republic
Korea

21

In 2010 immigrants from 201 countries became legal permanent residents of the U.S. Look at the names of these countries below. Use the chart at the bottom of the page to understand the meaning of the different colors.

People from These Countries
Became Permanent Legal Residents in 2010

Afghanistan
Albania   Algeria   American Samoa
Angola   Anguilla   Antigua-Barbuda   Argentina
Armenia   Aruba   Australia   Austria   Azerbaijan   Bahamas
Bahrain   **Bangladesh**   Barbados   Belarus   Belgium   Belize
Benin   Bermuda   Bhutan   Bolivia   Bosnia-Herzegovina   Botswana
Brazil   British Virgin Islands   Brunei   Bulgaria   Burkina Faso
Burma Burundi Cambodia Cameroon **Canada** Cape Verde Cayman Islands
Central African Republic   Chad   Chile   Colombia   Costa Rica   Cote d'Ivoire
Croatia   **Cuba**   Cyprus   Czech Republic   Democratic Republic of the Congo
Denmark Djibouti Dominica **Dominican Republic** **Ecuador** Egypt
El Salvador Equatorial Guinea Eritrea Estonia **Ethiopia** Federated States of Micronesia
Fiji Finland France French Guiana French Polynesia Gabon Gambia Georgia Germany
Ghana Greece Grenada Guadeloupe **Guatemala** Guinea Guinea-Bissau Guyana Haiti
Honduras Hong Kong Hungary Iceland India Indonesia **Iran** Iraq Ireland Israel
Italy Jamaica Japan Jordan Kazakhstan Kenya Kiribati Kosovo Kuwait Kyrgyzstan
Laos Latvia Lebanon Lesotho Liberia Libya Lithuania Luxembourg Macau Macedonia
Madagascar Malawi Malaysia Maldives Mali Malta Marshall Islands Martinique Mauritania
Mauritius Mexico Moldova Monaco Mongolia Montserrat Morocco Mozambique
Namibia Nepal Netherlands Netherlands Antilles New Caledonia New Zealand Nicaragua
Niger **Nigeria** Norway North Korea Oman Pakistan Palau Panama Papua New Guinea
Paraguay People's Republic of China **Peru** **Philippines** Poland
Portugal Qatar Republic of the Congo Romania Russia Rwanda Saint Kitts-Nevis Saint Lucia
Saint Vincent and the Grenadines Samoa Sao Tome and Principe Saudi Arabia Senegal
Serbia and Montenegro Seychelles Sierra Leone Singapore Slovakia Slovenia
Solomon Islands Somalia South Africa South Korea Spain Sri Lanka Sudan
Suriname Swaziland Sweden Switzerland Syria Taiwan Tajikistan Tanzania
Thailand Togo Tonga Trinidad and Tobago Tunisia Turkey Turkmenistan
Turks and Caicos Islands Uganda Ukraine United Arab Emirates
United Kingdom U.S. Virgin Islands Uruguay
Uzbekistan Venezuela **Vietnam** Yemen
Zambia Zimbabwe

Number of Immigrants Per Country			
Less than 10,000	blue	From 25,001 to 50,000	**purple**
From 10,000 to 15,000	**red**	From 50,001 to 75,000	gold
From 15,001 to 25,000	green	More than 135,000	turquoise

Something Old, Something New

American culture is a combination of traits from cultures around the world. These photos illustrate world cultures in our products, our food, and our architecture.

1. German apple pancakes are on the menu at this restaurant in Delavan, Wisconsin.

2. The Steinway piano factory in Queens, New York, was started by German immigrant Henry Steinway.

3. This chef is at one of the many Chinese restaurants in San Francisco.

4. This building in San Francisco's Chinatown has been used as a telephone company and as the Bank of Canton. It was built in 1891, destroyed in the 1906 San Francisco earthquake, and then rebuilt afterwards.

5. German, Swede, and Finn settlers brought the log cabin style of architecture to America. This one is in Cherokee, Alabama.

6. This dairy barn in Pennsylvania is built in a Swiss style.

Chinatown, Washington, D.C.
Chinese New Year Celebration

Rugby, Tennessee
Christ Church Episcopal

New York City
Little Italy Neighborhood

Words from Native American Languages

caribou – Mikmac
hickory – Algonquian
kayak – Inuit
moose – Algonquian
opossum – Algonquian
pecan – Illinois
persimmon – Algonquian
raccoon – Algonquian
skunk – Algonquian
squash – Narragansett
terrapin – Algonquian
toboggan – Algonquian

Though Americans share many traditions and customs from various cultures, we also enjoy traditions passed down to us from our own ancestors. Many immigrants even decide to live close to others who share their heritage. Some large cities have neighborhoods with nicknames like Chinatown or Little Italy. See photos at left.

Some American communities were started by immigrants of one nationality. English author Thomas Hughes established Rugby, Tennessee, in 1880. The Historic Rugby organization has restored the village and offers tours and special events. Rugby's Episcopal Church is pictured above.

Thirteen German Lutherans founded Frankenmuth, Michigan, in 1845. Their purpose was to encourage Germans living in the area and to evangelize members of the native Ojibwe tribe. Ninety more German immigrants joined them the following year. Now over a century and a half later, Frankenmuth continues to celebrate its German heritage and is a fun tourist destination.

Americans speak an American form of English which includes many words from other languages. Read the box at left for examples of common words that came from the languages of Native Americans. The box on page 25 lists words from the languages of non-English speaking immigrants.

The People of the United States

The number of people who live in the United States grows every day. If you write down the population of our country, in a few seconds that number will be incorrect. One service that the Founding Fathers provided in the Constitution was the requirement that a census or official count of the population be made every ten years. The first census was taken in 1790, and it has been taken every ten years since. The original purpose of the census was to insure that each state would have a fair number of representatives in the U.S. House of Representatives, but today it helps in many other ways.

The census is like a picture of a moving river. It tells us what the population of the United States was on a given day. We can tell how fast the population is growing, where the population is increasing or decreasing, and many other fascinating facts about our people. The census is an important civic activity in which everyone living in America can participate.

The United States Census Bureau determined that on April 1, 2010, the population of our country was 308,745,538. This was an increase of more than twenty-seven million people over the 2000 census. Our population was almost evenly divided between men and women.

The chart below illustrates what percentage of Americans are in different age groups. Out of every one hundred Americans, 24 are ages 17 and under; 37 are ages 18-44; 26 are ages 45-64; and 13 are ages 65 and over.

Percentages of People in Four Age Groups

Ages 0-17   Ages 18-44   **Ages 45-64**   Ages 65+

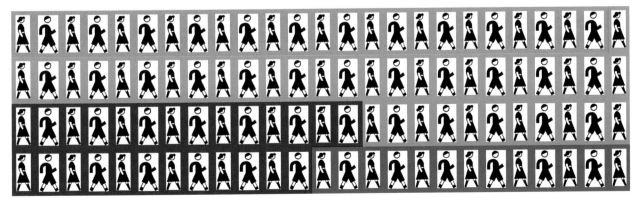

Free to Be Different

Americans are free to be different from one another. We can be rich or poor. Republicans, Democrats, or neither. Red, brown, yellow, black, or white. Our differences make us stronger. Anyone from any background can take part in the government and in society and can achieve his or her dreams. Together we can help other Americans overcome difficulties and achieve their dreams. We are many, but we are one.

Every person is descended from the first man God created. Therefore, we should have respect and love for all people.

> And He made from one man every nation of mankind to live on all the face of the earth, having determined their appointed times and the boundaries of their habitation.
>
> Acts 17:26

New York City, New York
These rooms in the Tenement Museum illustrate life for new immigrants in the early 1900s.

Lesson Activities

Thinking Biblically — Read Luke 10:25-37 to learn Jesus' teaching on loving others, even those who are different from us.

Vocabulary — In your notebook, write each of these words and the letter of the definition that goes with each word: evangelize, census, bureau, gingham, moped.

a. an administrative division of the government
b. fabric with small checks in white and one other color
c. to preach the gospel to a person or group
d. a count of the population
e. a small motorcycle that sometimes also has pedals

Chicago, Illinois
This German business, Berghoff Cafe, advertises as Chicago's oldest restaurant.

Literature — Read "You Dreamed Dreams of What America Was to Be" in *The Citizen's Handbook*, pages 3-4.

Creative Writing — In your notebook, write a short story of at least one page about an American family making a new immigrant welcome.

Find Out! — Does your family know anyone who became an American citizen as an adult?

Picture This! — Take a photograph or draw a picture of something in your house that originates from another culture.

Student Workbook or Lesson Review — If you are using one of these optional books, complete the assignment for Lesson 4.

★ Remember to choose an American Holiday to study this week! ★

UNIT 2 – AMERICA'S FOUNDING DOCUMENTS

BOOKS USED IN UNIT 2

- The Citizen's Handbook

- Student Workbook (optional)

- Lesson Review (optional)

"Reading the Declaration of Independence" by Edwin Austin Abbey, hangs in the chamber of the state House of Representatives in the Pennsylvania State Capitol.

The National ARCHIVES

Washington, D.C.
Constitution Avenue Entrance to the National Archives

The Declaration of Independence, the Constitution of the United States, and the Bill of Rights are America's most treasured documents. They outline much of what the word America means to its own citizens and to people around the world. In a short span of only thirteen years, America's Founding Fathers wrote these documents that continue to form the basis of our American government and our way of life. They completed the Declaration of Independence in 1776, the Constitution of the United States in 1787, and the Bill of Rights in 1789. Government workers keep them safe in the National Archives.

More than one million people visit the Archives each year. It is located along the National Mall in Washington, D.C. The Mall is a rectangular-shaped open space. Scattered within the Mall and lining it on all four sides are some of America's most famous landmarks and monuments, including the United States Capitol, the White House, the Smithsonian, and the Washington and Lincoln Memorials. The Archives stands mid-way between the Capitol and the White House. It is across from the Mall's outdoor ice skating rink.

History of the National Archives

Since its beginning, the Federal government of the United States has kept records; but for over 150 years, it did not have a central location to keep them together and safe. Finally, in 1926 Congress decided to build a National Archives. Site work began on the land in 1931. This work became difficult because the ground was marshy and there was even an underground stream running beneath the property.

Architect John Russell Pope planned the massive limestone and granite National Archives. It fills two city blocks. Pope included areas where employees would work to protect the records, places for the records to be stored, and public areas where special documents could be displayed. When President Hoover laid the cornerstone in 1933, he said, "This temple of our history will appropriately be one of the most beautiful buildings in America, an expression of the American soul."

Constitution Avenue Entrance, 1935

One hundred twenty staff members began working in the unfinished Archives in late 1935. In the photo at right, an Archives employee checks a humidity recorder to make sure that the air in the Archives has the correct moisture level. By the late 1960s the building's 900,000 square feet of storage space was filled and the government began renting more storage space. In 1993 a second building called Archives II was completed in nearby College Park, Maryland.

Mrs. Adelaide Minogue checks the humidity level in stacks at the National Archives in 1942.

A Walk Around the National Archives

Let's begin our walk around the exterior of the National Archives at the Constitution Avenue entrance. The statues, "Guardianship" and "Heritage," flank its staircase. They were designed by James Earl Fraser. "Guardianship" is a male figure with a helmet, a lion skin, and a sword. The statue symbolizes that the historical record must be protected for future generations. On its pedestal are the words: "Eternal Vigilance is the Price of Liberty." "Heritage" is a female figure. She holds a child and a sheaf of wheat, which symbolize growth and hope. On its pedestal are the words: "The Heritage of the Past is the Seed that Brings Forth the Harvest of the Future."

Look at the photo on page 28 and imagine that you are climbing these stairs. At the top are some of the Archives' seventy-two Corinthian columns. Each one is fifty-three feet high, five feet eight inches in diameter and weighs ninety-five tons. Behind the columns are massive bronze doors. At thirty-eight feet tall and almost ten feet across, they are largest bronze doors in the world. Above the columns is a pediment. Fraser also designed this pediment, which is entitled "Recorder of the Archives." Its mythological figures depict a man holding the keys to the Archives while he receives and catalogs America's most precious documents. An inscription above the pediment tells why the Archives was constructed: "The ties that bind the

Pennsylvania Avenue Entrance to the National Archives

Details of the Pennsylvania Avenue Entrance

Rooftop View of Washington, D.C., from the National Archives with One of Its Twelve-Foot Eagles

"The Future," Designed by Robert I. Aitken

"The Past," Designed by Robert I. Aitken

lives of our people in one indissoluble union are perpetuated in the archives of our government and to their custody this building is dedicated."

As you circle the building to the right, look up at the words carved on the eastern side: "This building holds in trust the records of our national life and symbolizes our faith in the permanency of our national institutions."

Turn the corner to see the Pennsylvania Avenue entrance of the Archives, pictured above. Here historians, genealogists, government workers, lawyers, scholars, students, veterans, and other citizens enter to do research. The pediment at this entrance is entitled "Destiny." It was designed by Adolph A. Weinman. Its mythological figures illustrate that progress is based on knowledge of the past. Atop both the Constitution Avenue and Pennsylvania Avenue pediments are two twelve-foot eagles with their wings extended. See one of the eagles at left above.

Robert I. Aitken designed the statues, "The Future," and "The Past," to the left and right of this entrance. They are pictured at left. "The Future" is a young female who is looking up from an open book to see into the future. On its base are the words, "What is Past is Prologue." "The Past" is an elderly man holding a scroll and a closed book as he "stares down the corridors of time." The words on its base read, "Study the Past." Like the statues, "Heritage" and "Guardianship," each was cut from a single block of limestone weighing 125 tons.

Continue around the western side of the building to read its inscription: "The glory and romance of our history are here preserved in the chronicles of those who conceived and builded the structure of our nation."

Rotunda for the Charters of Freedom

In the center of the National Archives is a beautiful rotunda, rising seventy-five feet high. The Declaration of Independence, the Constitution, and the Bill of Rights are displayed with American flags in this Rotunda for the Charters of Freedom. The documents are encased in glass to protect them from deteriorating. See close-up photos of the Declaration of Independence and the Constitution at right.

On either side of these "Charters of Freedom" are murals entitled "The Declaration" and "The Constitution." Each is approximately thirteen by thirty-four feet. Artist Barry Faulkner painted them in oil at his studio in Grand Central Station in New York City. Both are imaginary scenes which include portraits of some of the real men who helped found our American government. The murals are pictured below.

Rotunda for the Charters of Freedom

The Declaration of Independence

The Constitution of the United States

Murals by Barry Faulkner
Left: "The Declaration"; Right: "The Constitution"

Attorney General Robert Kennedy speaks at the opening of the Emancipation Proclamation Exhibit, January 4, 1963.

From Left to Right: Vincent Viola, General Raymond T. Odierno, and Retired Captain Anthony K. Odierno, 2011

The Rotunda for the Charters of Freedom is a fitting location for ceremonies honoring individuals and events. At left Attorney General Robert F. Kennedy, brother of President John Kennedy, speaks at the opening of an exhibit displaying the Emancipation Proclamation. This document freed the slaves in Confederate states during the Civil War. Father and son soldiers, Army Chief of Staff General Raymond T. Odierno and his son, retired Captain Anthony K. Odierno, receive the first Marine Gunnery Sergeant John Basilone Award for Distinguished Military Service. See lower photo. The honor was bestowed by the National Italian American Foundation in October of 2011.

NARA Facilities Around the Country

The Archivist of the United States heads the National Archives and Records Administration (NARA). The NARA is responsible for protecting and storing millions of records of the Federal government. In addition to the National Archives facility in Washington, D.C., and Archives II in College Park, Maryland, the NARA has other facilities around the country. Locations are listed on page 33, as are photos of three of them. Notice that the one in Lee's Summit, Missouri, is underground. Each location specializes in certain kinds of records or in records from specific regions of the country. Many facilities also have programs and displays of interest to the public. Presidential libraries and museums for each American President since Herbert Hoover are also part of the National Archives system. Franklin Roosevelt was the first President to begin a presidential library. At its dedication in June of 1941, Roosevelt spoke these words which are printed on the poster on page 32:

> *To bring together the records of the past and to house them in buildings where they will be preserved for the use of men and women in the future, a Nation must believe in three things. It must believe in the past. It must believe in the future. It must, above all, believe in the capacity of its own people so to learn from the past that they can gain in judgment in creating their own future.*

Wise government leaders keep records. Again and again the Old Testament books of 1 and 2 Kings mention the chronicles of the kings of Israel and Judah.

Now the rest of the acts of Hezekiah and all his might, and how he made the pool and the conduit and brought water into the city, are they not written in the Book of the Chronicles of the Kings of Judah?

2 Kings 20:20

Lesson Activities

Vocabulary — Look up each of these words in a dictionary and read their definitions: archives, marshy, humidity, pedestal, pediment.

Literature — Read "The Archivist's Code" in *The Citizen's Handbook*, pages 5-6.

Creative Writing — Ask a parent about the ways and places that your family keeps records. Make a list in your notebook, titled "Our Family Archives."

Find Out! — Which National Archives and Records Administration facility is closest to your home?

Picture This! — Take a photograph or draw a picture of an important document preserved in your household.

Student Workbook or Lesson Review — If you are using one of these optional books, complete the assignment for Lesson 6.

NARA Locations

Anchorage, Alaska
Atlanta, Georgia
Boston, Massachusetts
Chicago, Illinois
College Park, Maryland
Dayton, Ohio
Denver, Colorado
Ft. Worth, Texas
Kansas City, Missouri
Laguna Niguel, California
Lee's Summit, Missouri
Lenexa, Kansas
New York City, New York
Philadelphia, Pennsylvania
Pittsfield, Massachusetts
Riverside, California
San Francisco, California
St. Louis, Missouri
Seattle, Washington
Suitland, Maryland
Valmeyer, Illinois

College Park, Maryland
Archives II

Atlanta, Georgia
Southeast Region

Lee's Summit, Missouri
Central Plains Region

The Declaration of INDEPENDENCE

Philadelphia, Pennsylvania
Independence Hall

After many years under the rule of Great Britain, representatives of the thirteen British colonies met at Carpenters' Hall in Philadelphia from September 5 to October 26, 1774. They formed the Continental Congress. Their purpose was to find ways to persuade Great Britain to treat them fairly. Their efforts failed.

In April of 1775, British soldiers and colonists fought two battles in Massachusetts, the Battles of Lexington and Concord. This was the start of the Revolutionary War. In May the colonies sent representatives to Philadelphia again. This Second Continental Congress met in the State House of the Province of Pennsylvania in Philadelphia. The building, now known as Independence Hall, is pictured above. Colonial representatives continued to try to reconcile differences between the colonies and Great Britain, but the mother country would not change how it treated them.

Finally on June 7, 1776, Richard Henry Lee, a delegate from Virginia, made a motion that the thirteen colonies declare themselves to be independent of Great Britain. Lee said that:

> . . . these United Colonies are, and of right ought to be, free and independent States, that they are absolved from all allegiance to the British Crown, and that all political connection between them and the State of Great Britain is, and ought to be, totally dissolved.

On June 11, the Congress assigned two future Presidents, Thomas Jefferson and John Adams, along with Roger Sherman, Benjamin Franklin, and Robert Livingston, the task of writing a document declaring to the world the reasons that the colonies should be independent. The Committee of Five set to work while the rest of the members of the Congress recessed (took a break). On June 28 the committee brought its first draft to the Continental Congress. Artist John Trumbull illustrated the scene. Read about the artist and his painting below.

Using Talents to Serve: Artist John Trumbull

"The Declaration of Independence" hangs in the Rotunda of the United States Capitol. It depicts Thomas Jefferson handing a draft of the Declaration of Independence to John Hancock (seated at right), who served as president of the Second Continental Congress. Standing by Jefferson are other members of the Committee of Five. Forty-one other members of the Continental Congress are watching.

In 1817 the U.S. Congress commissioned sixty-one year old artist John Trumbull to paint four scenes from the time of the American Revolution. He completed this one the following year. Trumbull based this 12 x 18 foot painting on a smaller 21 x 31 inch one he had created decades earlier. The artist began planning the smaller version in 1786, just ten years after the historic event took place. He decided to portray the individuals accurately, so he only included men whom he could paint from life or paint from other portraits that had been painted from life. He used a sketch Thomas Jefferson had created from memory to know how to paint the room. This painting was exhibited in New York City, Boston, Philadelphia, and Baltimore before being brought to the Capitol in 1819. It was sometimes displayed in various rooms and sometimes stored until 1826. At that time, it was hung in the Rotunda, along with three other paintings by Trumbull. When he was seventy-two years old, Trumbull applied wax to the backs and new varnish to the fronts to protect his paintings.

John Trumbull was the son of a colonial governor of Connecticut and was a graduate of Harvard. He was a patriot who served as an aide-de-camp to General George Washington during the American Revolution. His artistic works included patriotic scenes, portraits, and religious scenes.

Independence is Declared

On July 2 members of the Second Continental Congress voted to approve Richard Henry Lee's motion. Late on the morning on July 4, they voted to approve the final version of the Declaration of Independence. The document informed Great Britain that the colonies would no longer submit to its authority and announced to the world America's beliefs about freedom. In these words it declares faith in God, the equality of all people, and the rights of citizens:

> *We hold these Truths to be self-evident, that all Men are created equal, that they are endowed, by their CREATOR, with certain unalienable Rights, that among these are Life, Liberty, and the Pursuit of Happiness.*

The Declaration of Independence refers to "Nature's God" and to "the Supreme Judge of the World." It declares a "firm Reliance on the Protection of DIVINE PROVIDENCE."

The document states that people are more important than government when it says, "Governments are instituted among Men, deriving their just Powers from the Consent of the Governed." John Hancock and Continental Congress secretary Charles Thomson signed the Declaration. That day the Committee of Five took Thomas Jefferson's handwritten manuscript to John Dunlap, who was the official printer of the Continental Congress. He printed it that night. Members of the Congress sent copies to the states and to commanders of the Continental Army. Twenty-six copies still survive. The copy pictured at right is in the holdings of the National Archives.

Signing the Declaration

On July 19, Congress declared that the Declaration of Independence be copied on parchment and signed by each member. Most members signed the parchment copy on August 2. Other signatures were added later that year. One member, Thomas McKean, signed it five years later in 1781. This is the copy on display in the Rotunda for the Charters of Freedom. It is pictured on page 37. Another early printing of the Declaration of Independence is described in the box below.

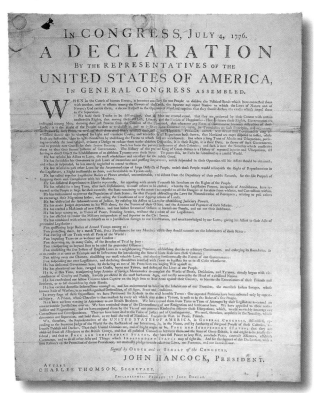

First Printed Copy of the Declaration of Independence, Printed by John Dunlap of Philadelphia on July 4, 1776

Using Talents to Serve: Printer Mary Katherine Goddard

Members of the Second Continental Congress kept the list of signers secret at first out of fear of the British government, but in January of 1777, they ordered that "an authentic copy of the Declaration of Independencey, with the names of the members of Congress subscribing to the same, be sent to each of the United States, and that they be desired to have the same put upon record."

At this time the Second Continental Congress was meeting in Baltimore, Maryland. Baltimore newspaper editor Mary Katherine Goddard printed fourteen of these "authentic" copies.

The words of the Declaration were printed in two columns. Below it were four columns, listing the name of each signer by state. Along the bottom edge were these words: Baltimore, in Maryland: Printed by Mary Katharine Goddard.

The Continental Congress continued to govern the United States throughout the American Revolution. It was followed by the Confederation Congress. Charles Thomson served as secretary of these congresses for fifteen years, from 1774 to 1789. During this time, he kept the original signed copy of the Declaration of Independence in his possession. During the

American Revolutionary War, the fighting made it necessary for him to move it from place to place several times.

From the Department of State to the National Archives

In the spring of 1789, the First Congress under the Constitution convened in New York City, America's temporary Capital. In July new President George Washington ordered Thomson to give the original signed Declaration to the Deputy Secretary of Foreign Affairs.

In March of 1790, Thomas Jefferson returned to America from France where he had been serving as U.S. Ambassador. The Department of Foreign Affairs was renamed the Department of State and Jefferson was its first Secretary. At that time, Jefferson became the caretaker of the document he had written.

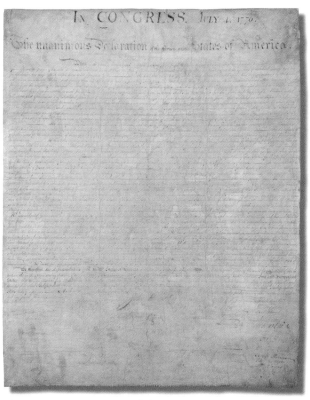

The original signed copy of the Declaration of Independence was embossed on parchment in July 1776. It is on display in the Rotunda for the Charters of Freedom at the National Archives in Washington, D.C.

The Federal government moved from New York to Philadelphia before moving permanently to the new Capital of Washington, D.C., in 1800. The Declaration of Independence moved with the government.

The British attacked Washington, D.C., during the War of 1812. Before the attack, Secretary of State James Monroe told a State Department clerk about the imminent danger. The clerk purchased linen, which was made into bags to carry the Declaration, Constitution, and other records away from danger. They were taken to a private home in Leesburg, Virginia, where they remained for several weeks.

In 1841 the Declaration of Independence was mounted on a wall opposite a window in the U.S. Patent Office Building. Here it hung for thirty-five years while its ink grew fainter and the parchment deteriorated.

When America celebrated the 100th anniversary of the Declaration of Independence in 1876, President Ulysses S. Grant gave temporary custody of the document to the mayor of Philadelphia. Richard Henry Lee's grandson read the Declaration of Independence there. See illustration at the top of page 38.

After the Declaration was brought back to Washington, it was placed in what is now the Eisenhower Executive Office Building. This turned out to be a blessing because the interior of its former home, the U.S. Patent Office, burned a few months later. In 1921 President Harding ordered that the Declaration of Independence and the Constitution be moved to the Library of Congress. On September 30, the Librarian of Congress carried them in a Model T Ford truck.

Illustrated London News *Drawing of Richard Henry Lee's Grandson, also Named Richard Henry Lee, Reading the Declaration in Philadelphia on July 4, 1876*

The Library of Congress Receives the Declaration of Independence, 1921

President and Mrs. Coolidge with the Librarian of Congress at the Dedication of the Shrine, 1924

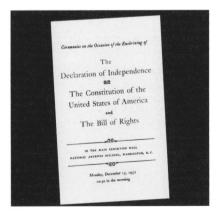

An appropriate shrine was constructed and President Calvin Coolidge dedicated it in 1924. See photos at left. Guards protected the documents there twenty-four hours a day.

When America entered World War II, the Declaration and other important documents were carried by train to Fort Knox for safekeeping. They were met by members of the Secret Service and a troop of soldiers. The Declaration stayed in the Bullion Depository for the remainder of the war, except for one special trip back to Washington, D.C. The Declaration was displayed during the dedication of the new Jefferson Memorial in April of 1943 and then returned to Fort Knox where it stayed until it was returned to its shrine in the Library of Congress in 1944.

On December 13, 1952, the Declaration of Independence and the Constitution were moved to the National Archives, which already had the Bill of Rights. On December 15, a formal enshrining ceremony was held with President Harry Truman as the featured speaker. See ceremony program at left below.

Transfer of the Declaration of Independence and the Constitution to the National Archives, 1952

The Declaration of Independence often found in history books is actually a copy authorized by the U.S. Department of State in 1823. Read about it at right.

The principle of the equal value of all people found in the Declaration of Independence is in keeping with what Jesus taught about God's salvation for "whoever believes."

> For God so loved the world,
> that He gave His only begotten Son,
> that whoever believes in Him
> shall not perish, but have eternal life.
>
> John 3:16

Lesson Activities

Thinking Biblically — Discuss with a parent or write a paragraph in your notebook: Do you think that the idea that "all men are created equal" is a Biblical concept? Why or why not?

Vocabulary — Copy these words in your notebook, each on a separate line: allegiance, varnish, providence, consent, imminent. Look up each word in the dictionary. Next to each word, write what part or parts of speech it is according to the way the word is used in the lesson.

Literature — Read "Response to an Invitation from the Citizens of Washington" in *The Citizen's Handbook*, page 7.

Creative Writing — Choose any one person from the illustrations in this lesson. In your notebook, write a letter of at least one-half page from that person to a family member describing what it was like to experience the event occurring in the illustration.

Student Workbook or Lesson Review — If you are using one of these optional books, complete the assignment for Lesson 7.

Using Talents to Serve: Engraver William Stone

Around 1820 Secretary of State John Quincy Adams commissioned engraver William Stone to create a new official copy of the Declaration of Independence and the signatures. He completed it in 1823 and sold it to the State Department. The State Department had 200 copies engraved on parchment. The U.S. Congress passed a resolution that the engravings be stored in official locations and be given to certain government officials and to the original signers who were still living. Two members of the Committee of Five, Thomas Jefferson and John Adams, received copies. Only a few dozen of these original prints survive. In 1888 Stone's widow gave one to the Smithsonian Institution. The engraving below is in the holdings of the National Archives.

The United States CONSTITUTION

When the thirteen former colonies declared themselves independent of Great Britain on July 4, 1776, members of the Second Continental Congress were already talking about a government for their new nation. Their experience as colonies had made them afraid of a strong central government, so they chose to keep government power in the thirteen individual states. However, they did decide to unite in a confederation. A confederation is an alliance of independent countries or states that join together to support each other. In November of 1777, the Continental Congress adopted America's first constitution, called the Articles of Confederation. They decided that it would go into effect when all thirteen states ratified it.

The fighting of the Revolutionary War was almost over by the time Maryland became the thirteenth state to ratify the Articles of Confederation on March 1, 1781. The name of the Second Continental Congress then became the Congress of the Confederation. See Articles of Confederation below.

Original Articles of Confederation

The Continental and Confederation Congresses led our new country to victory in the American Revolution. The Confederation Congress created a good plan for the land west of the Appalachians that America received after the Revolution. Their plan was called the Northwest Ordinance.

Article III of the Articles of Confederation said that this organization of states had "a firm league of friendship with each other." However, American leaders worried about the strength of their new country. Future Presidents George Washington and James Madison were among those who were concerned. Washington wrote to Madison: "Wisdom and good examples are necessary at this time to rescue the political machine from the impending storm." Madison and New York lawyer Alexander Hamilton (who later became the first Secretary of the Treasury) asked the Confederation Congress to call delegates from all states together to revise the Articles. The Confederation Congress agreed to do so.

The Constitutional Convention

Delegates slowly trickled into Philadelphia in May of 1787. Among them were Washington and Madison representing Virginia and Hamilton representing New York. Madison brought strong ideas about how the United States government should be organized. Earlier he had written to Washington: "[I have] formed in my mind some outlines of a new system, I take the liberty of submitting them without apology, to your eye." Throughout the convention, Madison provided capable leadership and kept careful notes.

Finally, on May 25, delegates from a majority of the states arrived and meetings began in Independence Hall. The first act of the proceedings was to elect a president for the Constitutional Convention. Delegates chose General George Washington by unanimous vote.

Soon a majority of the delegates decided not simply to make changes but to write a new constitution. They decided that the United States needed a strong national government that could act when needed, while protecting the rights of states and of individual citizens.

Delegates faced controversial issues, especially about how to make the new government fair to large states and small ones. They learned to compromise and to work through differences. They worked in secret through the summer and finally, in September, a majority agreed on the document that governs America today. Fifty-five delegates participated in the Convention. Of those, thirty-nine signed the Constitution of the United States on September 17, 1787. See painting below and read about its artist.

Using Talents to Serve: Artist Albert Herter

Albert Herter lived from 1871 to 1950. He painted this 9 x 18.5 foot mural of the signing of the Constitution for the Wisconsin Supreme Court Hearing Room in the Wisconsin State Capitol in Madison. Herter's son Christian later became the Governor of Massachusetts. His son also served as U.S. Secretary of State under President Dwight D. Eisenhower.

Delegates held a farewell banquet and then returned to their home states, where most delegates worked to convince their states to ratify the Constitution. The original signed Constitution is pictured on page 42.

The Constitution of the United States

The Original Four-Page Handwritten Copy of the Constitution of the United States

With its opening words, "We the People," the Preamble to the Constitution restates a principle from the Declaration of Independence: the power of government comes from the consent of the people being governed.

We the People of the United States, in Order to form a more perfect Union, establish Justice, insure domestic Tranquility, provide for the common defence, promote the general Welfare, and secure the Blessings of Liberty to ourselves and our Posterity, do ordain and establish this Constitution for the United States of America.

Harrisburg, Pennsylvania
Pennsylvania State House
"The Creation and Preservation of the Union—
George Washington at the Constitutional Convention"
by Violet Oakley

Washington's Leadership

Washington had led his troops well in the American Revolution, and he provided strong leadership during the convention. The painting at left illustrates Washington rising to speak, and saying, "If to please the people we offer what we ourselves disapprove, how can we afterward defend our work? Let us raise a standard to which the wise and the honest can repair; the event is in the hand of God." When New Jersey-born artist Violet Oakley painted a series of sixteen murals for the state senate chamber of the Pennsylvania State Capitol in Harrisburg, she included a portion of that quote along the top border of the mural at left.

A Time of Transition

Delegates had written in Article VII of the Constitution that it would go into effect when state conventions in nine states had ratified it. Meanwhile the Confederation Congress continued to operate the United States government. In late September, it directed state legislatures to organize ratification conventions in each state.

As you learned in Unit 1, all thirteen states eventually ratified the Constitution; but it took four years. Delaware was first. Acting quickly, it ratified the Constitution on December 7, 1787, less than three months after it was signed. By January 9, 1788, Pennsylvania, New Jersey, Georgia, and Connecticut had also ratified it. Still, the people in many states were divided about what to do. The main objections were fears that the Constitution made the Federal government too strong and that it did not protect the rights of individual citizens adequately.

The Federalist Papers

Soon after the Convention, the proposed Constitution was published in newspapers. People began to write essays opposing it. James Madison and Alexander Hamilton joined New York attorney John Jay to write essays supporting it. Jay was not a member of the Constitutional Convention, but he had held important government positions during the American Revolution and during the time America was governed by the Articles of Confederation. Madison, Hamilton, and Jay published their essays anonymously in New York State newspapers during 1787 and 1788. They used the pen name "Publius." Each essay was called "The Federalist" and they were numbered one through eighty-five. The essays were published together in book form in 1788. They are now referred to as *The Federalist Papers*. Thomas Jefferson later called the essays the "best commentary on the principles of government ever written."

A New Government

The Constitution went into effect on June 21, 1788, when New Hampshire became the ninth state to ratify it. Virginia and New York soon followed. In September the Confederation Congress passed an election ordinance which told the states when they should select electors for an Electoral College which would then elect the first President. Electors in each state met to cast their votes on February 4, 1789. Each elector could vote for two people. The person who received the most votes would become President and the person who received the second highest number would become Vice President (electors and the Electoral College are explained in Lesson 44).

State legislatures chose Senators and elections were held for members of the House of Representatives. The new Senators and Representatives began gathering in New York City in the spring of 1789. When enough arrived to achieve a quorum, they convened the first Congress (a quorum is a minimum number of people who must be present for a meeting to be official). A quorum was achieved in the House of Representatives on April 1, 1789, and in the Senate on April 6.

Congress officially counted the ballots of the Electoral College, which included electors from ten states (New York had not chosen their electors in time and North Carolina and Rhode Island had not yet ratified the Constitution). George Washington received the most votes because every elector cast a vote for their beloved Revolutionary War hero. John Adams received the second highest number of votes. He began acting as Vice President on April 21. Washington was inaugurated on April 30. John Jay, co-writer of *The Federalist Papers*, became the first Chief Justice of the Supreme Court. North Carolina and Rhode Island ratified the Constitution in 1789 and 1790, and then they also sent representatives to the First Congress.

James Madison, Father of the Constitution

In the years after the Constitution took effect, Americans began to honor James Madison as the Father of the Constitution. His able leadership helped bring it into existence and his hard work helped convince reluctant states to ratify it. Madison planned that his notes from the Constitutional Convention not be published until the last delegate to the convention had died.

This turned out to be Madison himself. His notes were published after his death.

In 1980 a fitting memorial was dedicated to Madison, the James Madison Memorial Building at the Library of Congress. At right are a nine-foot statue of Madison and one of the eight quotes by Madison which are inscribed on the teak wood walls inside the building's Memorial Hall. See the sculptor at work on page 45.

The Enduring Constitution

All of American government in our cities and towns, our states, and our nation is based on the Constitution of the United States. It is our most important document, a blueprint for what our government can do and what it cannot do and a standard that each citizen

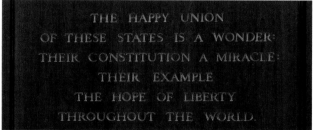

Washington, D.C.
Memorial Hall, James Madison Memorial Building,
Library of Congress
Above: Statue of James Madison by Walker K. Hancock
Below: Words Penned by Madison in 1829

Sculptor Walker K. Hancock at Work in 1974

and government official must obey. When a new President or Senator or Representative is elected to serve in Washington, D.C., he or she must take an oath to support and defend our Constitution.

Government officials should reread the Constitution often to remind them of the foundation of our laws. When God spoke to the Israelites about the responsibilities of their king, who would be their highest government official, He commanded that the king write his own copy of the Law of Moses. He told them:

> It shall be with him and he shall read it all the days
> of his life, that he may learn to fear the Lord his God,
> by carefully observing all the words of this law and
> these statutes, that his heart may not be lifted up above
> his countrymen and that he may not turn aside from the
> commandment, to the right or the left, so that he and his sons
> may continue long in his kingdom in the midst of Israel.
> Deuteronomy 17:19-20

Lesson Activities

Thinking Biblically — Copy Deuteronomy 17:19-20 into your notebook, using the version of your choice.

Literature — Read "The First Prayer of the Continental Congress" in *The Citizen's Handbook*, page 8.

Find Out! — Does your local library have a copy of The Constitution of the United States? What are the call numbers (shelf location)?

Picture This! — Draw a picture of one of the men involved in the creation of the Constitution mentioned in this lesson. Find a portrait to copy.

Student Workbook or Lesson Review — If you are using one of these optional books, complete the assignment for Lesson 8.

The Bill of RIGHTS

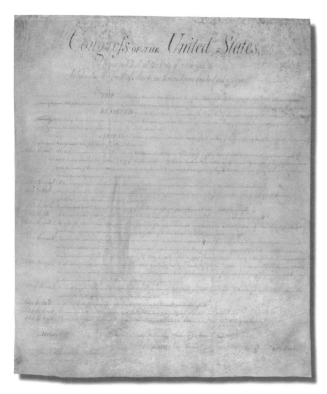

Original Bill of Rights

The writers of the Constitution realized that American leaders would sometimes want to amend (or change) the Constitution, so they included instructions about how that could be accomplished.

People in many states believed that the Constitution should give more rights to individual citizens. President George Washington mentioned this in his first inaugural address. Citizens were concerned that the new Federal government might become too strong and take away the rights that Americans enjoyed. They remembered how the British government denied certain rights to the colonists, and they did not want their government ever to do the same thing.

While state conventions were meeting to decide about ratifying the Constitution, they came up with suggestions for about 350 amendments they believed would guarantee the rights of individual American citizens. Many of the proposed amendments were similar.

James Madison gathered these suggestions, blended them together, and proposed twelve amendments for the First Congress to consider. Congress passed them and sent them to President Washington on September 25, 1789. The President sent them to the individual states, which voted on each of these amendments individually. The Constitution requires ratification by three-fourths of the states before an amendment becomes part of the Constitution.

Ratification of the Bill of Rights by the State of New York

Three-fourths of the states ratified ten of the amendments. They became known as the Bill of Rights. The original handwritten copy is pictured on page 46.

The official handwritten ratification by the State of New York is also pictured on page 46. It begins: "We the People of the State of New York, By the Grace of God, Free and Independent."

The First Amendment

> I. *Congress shall make no law respecting an establishment of religion, or prohibiting the free exercise thereof; or abridging the freedom of speech, or of the press; or the right of the people peaceably to assemble, and to petition the Government for a redress of grievances.*

When the Constitution was written, many countries in Europe had official state churches. In England it was the Church of England. In France it was the Roman Catholic Church. The First Amendment states that the United State Congress cannot choose a church as the official church of the United States.

When Congress passed the First Amendment and the states ratified it, they were not saying that government officials could not mention God or Jesus. They did not mean that prayers could not be said at official government functions. They did not mean that the Ten Commandments could not be posted on government property. Congress was trying to prevent the United States from having the kinds of problems that happened in Europe. There the leaders of the official religion sometimes persecuted those who believed differently. Sometimes a country that had one official religion went to war against a country that had another official religion, just because of that religious difference. Some of the individual states in America had official churches and they continued to do so for several years after the Constitution was ratified. However, the national government could not do this for the entire United States.

The First Amendment also says that Congress cannot pass laws "prohibiting the free exercise" of religion. It cannot make it hard for people to practice their religion.

Americans cannot persecute people of a particular group. The First Amendment also protects the rights of people in government who want to exercise their religion. Because Americans believe that individuals are important, they believe that people should be able to think and believe as they wish. The Girl Scouts at right are worshipping at a Freewill Missionary Baptist church.

Montgomery, Alabama
Freewill Missionary Baptist Church

Columbia, Tennessee
The Daily Herald *Newspaper*

Madison, Wisconsin
Protester with Signs at the State Capitol

The First Amendment also states that Congress cannot pass laws that would prevent people from saying what they want to say. It cannot tell people or organizations, like the small town newspaper, pictured above, what they can write either.

Before the United States was founded, people in other countries were sometimes put in jail or even executed for criticizing the king. Americans believed that kings and governments can sometimes be wrong and that people are too valuable to have to suffer when their leaders are wrong. They wanted Americans to be free to change the government for the better if they saw a need to do so. See a woman protesting at the Wisconsin State Capitol above.

The First Amendment also makes it illegal for Congress to pass laws that keep groups of American citizens from getting together as long as the groups gather peacefully.

The Second and Third Amendments

> II. *A well regulated Militia, being necessary to the security of a free State, the right of the people to keep and bear Arms, shall not be infringed.*

> III. *No Soldier shall, in time of peace be quartered in any house, without the consent of the Owner, nor in time of war, but in a manner to be prescribed by law.*

The Second and Third Amendments protect American citizens from an army that is too powerful. A militia is an organization of citizens who serve as temporary soldiers to defend their families and property from attack. The First Congress realized that if the government and its army are the only ones who have weapons, such an arrangement can potentially put the people at risk of losing their freedom. They realized that citizens should have the right to keep and bear arms so that they could protect their country and their own lives, families, and property. They wanted them to be able to engage in peaceful activities such as hunting.

During the colonial period, the British government required colonists to house British troops stationed in America. This was a violation of the private property rights of the colonists. The government needs to provide for the housing of troops without invading private homes to do so. The photo at right shows the interior of a barracks at Lackland Air Force base in San Antonio. All airmen go through basic training at this base.

San Antonio, Texas
Barracks at Lackland Air Force Base

The Fourth Through Eighth Amendments

IV. The right of the people to be secure in their persons, houses, papers, and effects, against unreasonable searches and seizures, shall not be violated, and no Warrants shall issue, but upon probable cause, supported by Oath or affirmation, and particularly describing the place to be searched, and the persons or things to be seized.

V. No person shall be held to answer for a capital, or otherwise infamous crime, unless on a presentment or indictment of a Grand Jury, except in cases arising in the land or naval forces, or in the Militia, when in actual service in time of War or public danger; nor shall any person be subject for the same offence to be twice put in jeopardy of life or limb; nor shall be compelled in any criminal case to be a witness against himself, nor be deprived of life, liberty, or property, without due process of law; nor shall private property be taken for public use, without just compensation.

VI. In all criminal prosecutions, the accused shall enjoy the right to a speedy and public trial, by an impartial jury of the State and district wherein the crime shall have been committed, which district shall have been previously ascertained by law, and to be informed of the nature and cause of the accusation; to be confronted with the witnesses against him; to have compulsory process for obtaining witnesses in his favor, and to have the Assistance of Counsel for his defence.

VII. In Suits at common law, where the value in controversy shall exceed twenty dollars, the right of trial by jury shall be preserved, and no fact tried by a jury, shall be otherwise re-examined in any Court of the United States, than according to the rules of the common law.

VIII. Excessive bail shall not be required, nor excessive fines imposed, nor cruel and unusual punishments inflicted.

The Fourth through Eighth Amendments guarantee that the government will not bully private citizens. They are mainly about protecting the rights of people who have been accused of committing a crime. They express a belief that every human being is valuable and has rights, even people who have been accused of breaking the law. Someone accused of committing a crime has the guarantee that the American court system will be fair when deciding whether he is guilty or innocent.

Hillsboro, Texas
Sheriff's Vehicle

People who were in favor of the Bill of Rights did not want the government to have too much power. They only wanted the government to help people be able to live in freedom, peace, and security. They did not want the government to be able to arrest someone or put him in prison simply because he disagreed with government decisions or because he was of a different race or religion than the people running the government. The government cannot go into someone's home and search for evidence of a crime unless there is a good reason to do so. The Eighth Amendment even protects people who have been found guilty of committing crimes from having to pay fines that are too big. It also protects people from "cruel and unusual punishment."

The Bill of Rights guarantees that a person accused of a crime will not have to go to trial over and over again for the same crime once he has been declared innocent by a court. People accused of certain crimes must not have to wait a long time before they go to court. They must be allowed to have a jury decide whether they are guilty or innocent. They must be able to talk to the people who are accusing them.

The last portion of the Fifth Amendment says that the government cannot take a citizen's private property to build something like a road or a school unless it pays the property owner fairly. The government cannot simply take a person's home or possessions just because it has enough power to do so.

The Ninth and Tenth Amendments

IX. *The enumeration in the Constitution, of certain rights, shall not be construed to deny or disparage others retained by the people.*

X. *The powers not delegated to the United States by the Constitution, nor prohibited by it to the States, are reserved to the States respectively, or to the people.*

The last two amendments in the Bill of Rights are general statements that protect the rights of the people and the rights of individual states. They are meant to limit the powers of the Federal government. The Ninth Amendment says that the listing of certain rights in the

Constitution does not mean that people do not have other rights just because the Constitution does not mention them.

The Tenth Amendment says that the states or the people have all rights that the Constitution does not specifically give to the Federal government. This means that the authors of the Constitution wanted the Federal government to have limits on what it could do. The Tenth Amendment also says that states or the people cannot do something that the Constitution specifically says they cannot do. For example, the Constitution says that no state can make a treaty with a foreign country.

Many Americans have memorized portions of the Constitution, especially its Preamble. However, one man in the 1930s performed an amazing feat of memorization. Read about him at right.

We can thank God that we live in a country where the government is based on the recognition of the worth of every person. This enables us to live in freedom, safety, and security. Those of us who believe in the worth of every person in the eyes of God must take part in the civic life of our country so that these rights and freedoms can continue.

Freedoms that Americans enjoy today are laid out in the Bill of Rights. Long before these were written, God gave Christians freedom in Christ. God wants us to use the freedom He gives us to bless other people.

For you were called to freedom, brethren;
only do not turn your freedom into an
opportunity for the flesh,
but through love serve one another.
Galatians 5:13

Using Talents to Serve: Harry E. Wilhelm

Forty-three-year-old Harry E. Wilhelm is reciting the Constitution from memory. In 1937 the Constitution was 150 years old. By then it had been amended a total of twenty-one times. At that time, the document included 6,757 words. On September 13 of that year Harry Wilhelm visited Congressman Sol Bloom, a member of the U.S. House of Representatives. Bloom was then serving as the Chairman of the United States Constitutional Sesquicentennial Commission. Wilhelm told Bloom that he was the only person in the world who could recite the Constitution from memory. Bloom told Wilhelm that if he could perform this feat, he would give him a job on the commission. Wilhelm recited as Bloom checked the words. Wilhelm did indeed quote the entire Constitution and its twenty-one amendments. Wilhelm got the job.

Lesson Activities

Thinking Biblically — In your notebook, write down ways you practice your faith with freedom and without fear of punishment. Consider with thankfulness the freedom of religion as promised in the Bill of Rights.

Vocabulary — Write five sentences in your notebook, using one of these words in each: amend, petition, function, accusation, sesquicentennial. Check in a dictionary if you need help with their definitions.

Creative Writing — Using your freedom of speech, design a poster that protests something you think should be changed in your town, state, or country. Include the reasons for your opinion and how you think the change could be made.

Find Out! — What is the name of your local newspaper, or a newspaper published nearby?

Picture This! — Draw a picture or take a photograph of someone exercising a freedom guaranteed in the Bill of Rights.

Student Workbook or Lesson Review — If you are using one of these optional books, complete the assignment for Lesson 9.

★ Remember to choose an American Holiday to study this week! ★

UNIT 3 – HOW AMERICA WORKS

BOOKS USED IN UNIT 3

- The Citizen's Handbook

- Student Workbook (optional)

- Lesson Review (optional)

Colorado State Capitol in Denver

Government on
THREE LEVELS

American government is organized on three levels: national, state, and local. The address on the envelope below illustrates them. Kathleen is an American girl who received a letter from Melita, her English pen pal. Notice that Kathleen lives in Franklin, Kansas, in the U.S.A. Her national government is the United States of America. Her state government is the

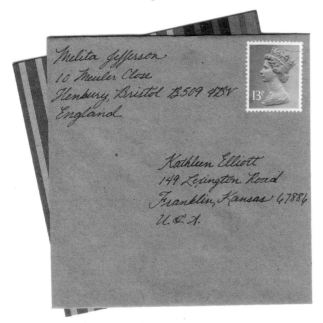

State of Kansas. Her local government is the town of Franklin.

The Constitution of the United States outlines how our government is organized on the national level. Another term used for our national government is Federal government. Both terms are used in *Uncle Sam and You*. Each state has a state constitution that outlines the organization of that state and the local governments within that state. American citizens can serve in a variety of ways at the national, state, and local levels.

The National Level

The headquarters of our national government is in our Capital City of Washington, D.C. The United States Capitol is there. Notice that the building is spelled capitol and the city is spelled capital. In addition to the Capitol, our Federal government has many other facilities in Washington, D.C. Examples are the U.S. Department of Commerce, the U.S. Department of Agriculture (USDA), and the National Aeronautics and Space Administration (NASA), all pictured at the top of page 55. The Federal government also has facilities in thousands of other places around the country. Federal facilities in Idaho, Iowa, Maine, and Washington are also pictured on page 55.

The National Level in Washington, D.C.

United States Capitol

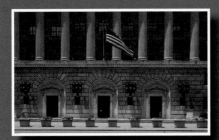

Herbert C. Hoover Building
Department of Commerce

Woodsy Owl and Smokey
Bear at the U.S. Department
of Agriculture

Headquarters of the National
Aeronautics and Space
Administration (NASA)

The National Level Around the Country

Prairie City, Iowa
Neal Smith National Wildlife Refuge

Arco, Idaho
*Visitor Center, Craters of the Moon
National Monument and Preserve*

Owl's Head, Maine
*Owl's Head Light, Operated by
the United States Coast Guard*

Carson, Washington
Carson National Fish Hatchery

The State Level

The headquarters of each of the fifty state governments is the state capitol in its state capital. In some states, the capitol building is called a state house (and some states use the spelling "statehouse"). Notice the similarities and differences in the state capitols pictured below. Please note that the old capitols of Arizona and Florida are pictured. These are now museums.

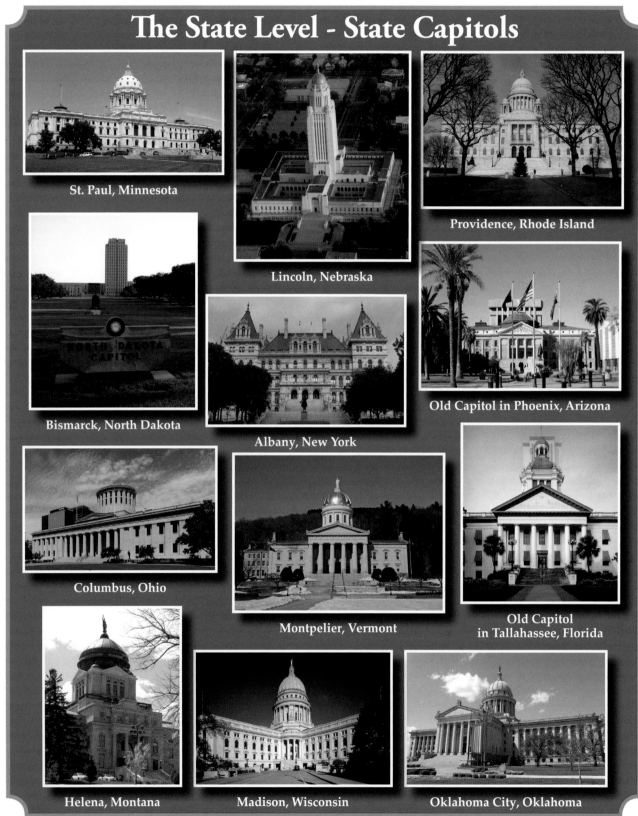

The State Level - State Capitols

St. Paul, Minnesota

Lincoln, Nebraska

Providence, Rhode Island

Bismarck, North Dakota

Albany, New York

Old Capitol in Phoenix, Arizona

Columbus, Ohio

Montpelier, Vermont

Old Capitol
in Tallahassee, Florida

Helena, Montana

Madison, Wisconsin

Oklahoma City, Oklahoma

The State Level in Capital Cities

Madison, Wisconsin
Wisconsin Historical Museum

Harrisburg, Pennsylvania
Statue of Abraham Lincoln in Library of the Matthew J. Ryan Legislative Office Building

Sacramento, California
California Firefighters Memorial in Capitol Park

Like the Federal government, each state government has other facilities in its capital city. See examples above. They also have facilities around the state. The photos below include a Department of Transportation building in Oregon, a welcome center in Michigan, and the historic Alamo in Texas. In the welcome center photo are statues erected in honor of workers who have died while working on road construction.

The State Level Around the State

Bend, Oregon
Department of Transportation Offices

Clare, Michigan
Welcome Center with Transportation Worker Memorial

San Antonio, Texas
The Alamo historic site is owned by the State of Texas but managed by a private organization, the Daughters of the Republic of Texas.

The Local Level

States have a variety of local governments. Let's think about counties first. All states are divided into counties, except Louisiana, which has parishes, and Alaska, which has boroughs. The headquarters of a county government is in one of its towns, called the county seat. The main offices of a county are often in a county courthouse.

Towns and cities also have local governments. Their main offices are in town halls or city halls. Other local governments include townships and special districts. Examples of special districts include school, library, electric, water, and sewer districts. Pictured below are various local government facilities.

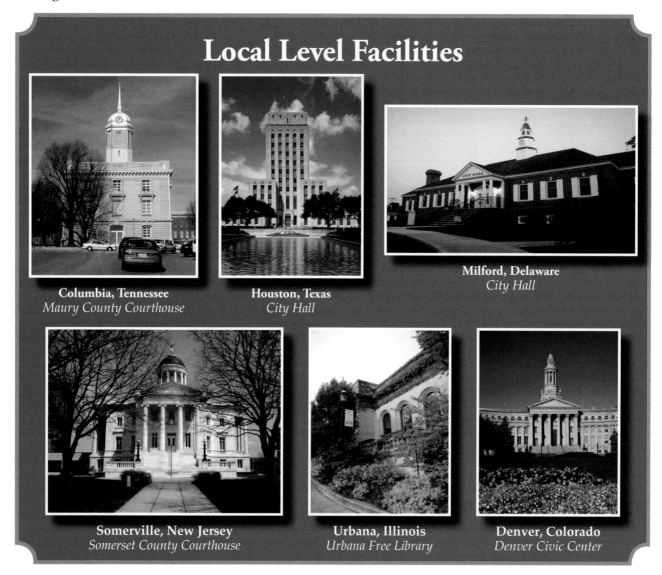

Local Level Facilities

Columbia, Tennessee
Maury County Courthouse

Houston, Texas
City Hall

Milford, Delaware
City Hall

Somerville, New Jersey
Somerset County Courthouse

Urbana, Illinois
Urbana Free Library

Denver, Colorado
Denver Civic Center

Three Levels and You

As you study *Uncle Sam and You*, you will learn what governments do at the national, state, and local levels. Today let's look at a few ways local, state, and Federal governments affect your daily life.

Transportation. If you live in a city, the street in front of your house is probably owned by the local city government. If you travel to another city several miles away, you might ride on a state or Federal highway or on an Interstate. Interstates are examples of one way that the Federal government works with state governments. These roads are owned by whatever state they are in, yet most of the money to pay for Interstates has come from the Federal budget.

Taxes. Americans pay taxes to local and state governments and to the Federal government. Look at the sales receipt at right. Notice that the sales tax rate is 9.75%, so the sales tax due on the purchase of a $15.00 game is $1.46. Since both local and state governments sometimes collect sales tax, this hypothetical sales tax could include a 9% state sales tax of $1.35 and a local sales tax of $0.11 (or .75%). Your parents must pay Federal income tax based on their yearly income. Depending on where you live, they might also pay local and/or state income taxes.

Parks. Your family might enjoy outings at local, state, and national parks. Perhaps your soccer team plays games at a local city park. Your grandparents may organize a family reunion at a county park. In the fall, your family may rent a state park cabin for a weekend getaway. Your family could also travel to Grand Canyon National Park for a vacation in the summer.

| Ralph's |
| Department Store |
| 212 Austin |
| Catawba, New Mexico 88785 |

Stuffed Shirts Game	$15.00
Subtotal	$15.00
Sales Tax (rate: 9.75%)	$1.46
Total	$16.46

Number of Items Sold: 1
Receipt # 0980981
Date 11/11/11 Time 2:37

As Christians, we are subject to the authority of our government at the local, state, and Federal levels. As Paul wrote to the Christians in Rome:

Every person is to be in subjection to the governing authorities.

For there is no authority except from God, and those which exist are established by God.

Romans 13:1

Lesson Activities

Thinking Biblically — Discuss with a parent: Why do you think God created government?

Creative Writing — In your notebook, write a short story of 2-3 paragraphs about a person interacting with all three levels of government on a single day.

Find Out! — What is your local sales tax rate?

Picture This! — Take a photograph or draw a picture of a local government building or vehicle. Be sure you don't get in the way of government workers doing their jobs.

Student Workbook or Lesson Review — If you are using one of these optional books, complete the assignment for Lesson 11.

Government in THREE BRANCHES

When America's Founding Fathers wrote the U.S. Constitution, they decided to create a Federal government with three branches. They based this idea on a philosophy that began in Europe. In the 1700s European philosophers were thinking about new ways for governments to be organized. Frenchman Baron de Montesquieu (MON-tes-kew), pictured at right, was one of them. Montesquieu wrote that the power of government should be divided into three branches. He thought people working in each branch should take care of one set of responsibilities. Montesquieu

Baron de Montesquieu

suggested that governments have a legislative branch which would make laws, an executive branch which would make sure the laws were enforced, and a judicial branch which would make decisions when the laws were disobeyed or questioned. Montesquieu believed that separating government responsibilities into three areas would keep the people who worked in any one area from getting too powerful. This idea is called separation of powers.

America's Federal government is divided into legislative, executive, and judicial branches, as illustrated in the blue box. The Federal legislative branch makes laws and is called the U.S. Congress. It includes two parts called houses: the Senate and the House of Representatives. Members of the Senate are Senators; members of the House of Representatives are called Congressmen, Representatives, or members of the House. Congress meets in the U.S. Capitol.

The Federal executive branch makes sure that laws passed by Congress are enforced. The executive is headed by our President, who lives and works in the White House. The President oversees the people who work in the executive branch.

The Federal judicial branch makes decisions about laws passed by Congress. It includes the U.S. Supreme Court and other Federal courts across the country. The Supreme Court meets in the Supreme Court Building.

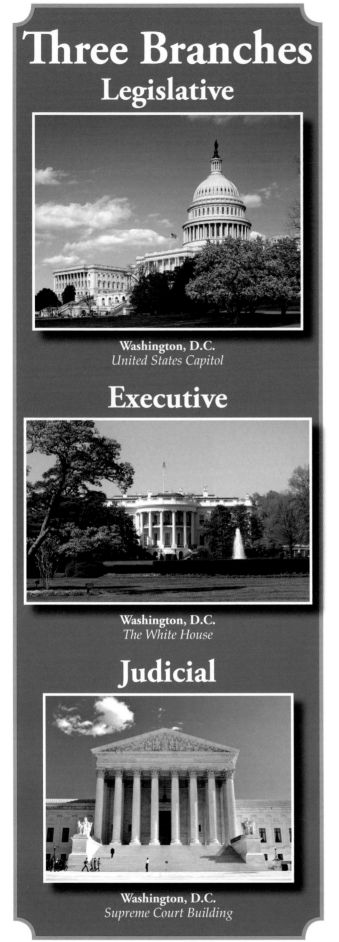

Three Branches

Legislative

Washington, D.C.
United States Capitol

Executive

Washington, D.C.
The White House

Judicial

Washington, D.C.
Supreme Court Building

Checks and Balances

The three branches of government are not only separate, but each branch also limits and balances the powers of the other two branches so that no branch becomes too powerful. This arrangement is called checks and balances. Here are some examples:

★ Congress passes laws, but the President can veto (or reject those laws. However, if two-thirds of both the House and the Senate vote to do so, Congress can reject (or override) the President's veto.

★ After a President is elected and inaugurated he serves as President for four years. However, Congress can remove him from office if he is found guilty of serious crimes.

★ Congress and the President share power during times of war. Congress has the power to declare war, but the President has authority to act as the Commander in Chief of the Army, Navy, Air Force, and Marines.

★ The President decides who he wants to appoint as judges in Federal courts, but the Senate must approve the people he appoints before they can serve.

★ Once they are appointed and approved by the Senate, Federal judges can serve in their positions for the rest of their lives. However, Congress can remove those found guilty of serious crimes.

Working Together

Families work best when each member cooperates and works for the good of each family member. Likewise the Federal government works best when the three branches work together. When George Washington was inaugurated, New York City served as our Capital City. All three branches were housed in New York's City

New York City, New York
*Statue of President George
Washington in Front of Federal Hall*

Washington, D.C.
*House Speaker Carl Albert,
President Richard Nixon, and
Chief Justice Warren Burger
at the National Archives
on July 4, 1971*

Hall. The building, now known as Federal Hall, is pictured above. When the Capital City moved briefly to Philadelphia, all three branches met in Independence Hall.

Nevada
*Ash Meadows National Wildlife Refuge is home to at least
twenty-four plants and animals found nowhere else on earth.*

Austin, Texas
J. J. Pickle Federal Building

Washington, D.C.
Meeting in the Longworth House Office Building, 2012

Urbana, Illinois
Federal Courthouse

As illustrated in Lesson 11 and the lower photos on page 62, the Federal government has grown greatly since then. Though this growth makes cooperation harder, it is still necessary.

The photograph at top right on page 62 records a time when leaders of the three branches of the Federal government were together for a ceremony at the National Archives. Speaker of the House of Representatives Carl Albert, a leader in the legislative branch; President Nixon, our 37th Chief Executive; and Warren Burger, Chief Justice of the U.S. Supreme Court, were photographed prior to Fourth of July speeches in 1971.

Three Branches in State and Local Governments

Each of the fifty state governments is also organized into legislative, executive, and judicial branches. A state legislative branch is called the state legislature. The legislature of every state except one has two parts, a senate and a house of representatives, which is sometimes called a state assembly. The one exception is Nebraska, which has only a senate. A term used for a two-part legislature is bicameral. The Nebraska legislature is unicameral. The mosaic below represents Moses, the lawgiver, and the legislature of Wisconsin, the law-making body of Wisconsin state government.

Madison, Wisconsin
This mosaic made of thousands of pieces of colored glass adorns the Rotunda of the Wisconsin State Capitol.
Artist Kenyon Cox intended for the mosaic to remind viewers of Moses.

The head of a state executive branch is called a Governor. Just as leaders in each of the three branches must cooperate, government leaders on various levels must cooperate as well. In the photo at left below, Secretary Tom Vilsack, head of the U.S. Department of Agriculture, speaks with Montana Governor Brian Schweitzer at a breakfast for Federal officials and Governors of western states.

Each state also has a state judicial system, including a state supreme court and a system of circuit courts. At right below is the supreme court chamber in the Iowa State Capitol.

Local governments have three branches, too. Town, city, and county names for these vary widely; but for now, we'll just mention the following as examples. A city legislative branch may be called a city council; a city executive, a mayor; and a local judicial branch, a city court.

Washington, D.C.
U.S. Department of Agriculture Secretary Tom Vilsack (left) meets with Montana Governor Brian Schweitzer in the Lincoln Room at the Headquarters of the U.S. Department of Agriculture on February 26, 2012.

Des Moines, Iowa
Supreme Court Chamber in the Iowa State Capitol

Three Branches and You

You will also learn details about what the three branches of government do as you study *Uncle Sam and You*, but today let's look at one example of how the three branches of government may affect your daily life. Imagine that your town's city council (legislative branch) passes a law that all dogs must be kept on a leash and that people who violate that law must pay a $25 fine. If your family owns a dog, you will have to obey the law. The mayor (executive branch) is responsible for making sure that the city police force does its job. If your family repeatedly lets your dog run around without a leash, the police are required to give your parents a citation to appear in court (judicial branch) because they are not obeying the law.

64

God's Word teaches us that we should honor and obey the people who serve in our government. In this passage, the apostle Peter instructs Christians to obey the Roman government, which was in authority over Israel during the time of the New Testament.

Submit yourselves for the Lord's sake to every human institution,

whether to a king as the one in authority, or to governors as sent by him

for the punishment of evildoers and the praise of those who do right.

1 Peter 2: 13-14

Lesson Activities

Vocabulary — In your notebook, make a simple drawing for each of these words that illustrates what it means: philosophy, legislative, executive, judicial, veto. Write the word under the drawing. Check in a dictionary if you need help with their definitions.

Literature — Read "Three Branches—Excerpts from the Constitution" in *The Citizen's Handbook*, page 9.

Find Out! — Where is the Federal courthouse nearest to you?

Picture This! — Take a photograph or make a drawing that illustrates a law your family must obey.

Student Workbook or Lesson Review — If you are using one of these optional books, complete the assignment for Lesson 12.

America's FOUNDING FATHERS

Our nation did not just happen. God raised up a remarkable group of about one hundred individuals who brought about the founding of the United States of America. Among them were the men who wrote and signed the Declaration of Independence, those who served in the Continental Congress, those who wrote and signed the Constitution, and those who boldly and courageously helped and encouraged these leaders. By the 1820s, politicians were calling these men "the founders" or "the fathers." In a 1916 speech at the Republican National Convention, Senator (and later President) Warren Harding of Ohio used the term "Founding Fathers" to describe them. The term has been used ever since. Look at illustrations of the Founding Fathers below and on page 67.

Most of the Founding Fathers were born in the American colonies, but some were born in foreign countries, including Ireland, England, and Scotland. One, Alexander Hamilton, was born in the West Indies. Almost all believed in Jesus Christ. Most were Protestants; two were Roman Catholic.

As boys and young men, some were educated at home, some had tutors, and others attended local or private schools. At a time when only a small percentage of Americans received a college education, about half of these men attended college and some were college graduates.

Harrisburg, Pennsylvania
Sculptors carved some of our Founding Fathers on the entrance doors of the Pennsylvania State Capitol Rotunda.
At left are men involved in writing and signing the Declaration of Independence,
and at right are men involved in writing and signing the Constitution.

In adulthood they worked in various professions. Some were merchants and others invested in business. Many were planters (a term used for people who owned and managed large farming operations). Some were lawyers or physicians. Almost all were fairly well-off, and a few were considered wealthy. Some inherited wealth from their families, but others had worked hard for their material possessions. Some owned slaves.

Before the American Revolution, many had been elected to offices in their local communities or their colonies. During the War, many served as officers in the Continental Army. After the Constitution was adopted, the Founders continued to have considerable influence. Among the most prominent were four future Presidents, George Washington, John Adams, Thomas Jefferson, and James Madison; the first Secretary of the Treasury, Alexander Hamilton; the first Chief Justice of the Supreme Court, John Jay; and inventor, diplomat, and statesman Benjamin Franklin. Numerous others served as U.S. Senators and Congressmen, diplomats, judges, state Governors, or members of a President's Cabinet. Many of their descendants served in government also. In this lesson we will look at two of the remarkable men who helped to found our great nation, but whose names are not quite so well known.

The Federal Works Progress Administration created this poster c. 1940. Notice the Founding Father and American flag behind the men who are studying democracy.

Roger Sherman's Early Life

Only two men signed all three of these founding documents: the Declaration of Independence, the Articles of Confederation, and the United States Constitution. They were Roger Sherman of Connecticut and Robert Morris of Pennsylvania. Roger Sherman was born in 1721 in Massachusetts. His father was a farmer and a cobbler. As a boy, Roger worked alongside his father. He helped him on their farm and learned his trade. Roger went to the local school, but he gained much of his knowledge through his great love of reading. When he grew up, he kept an open book with him while he was working, so that he could turn to the book when his eyes were not needed for the other work he was doing.

When Roger was twenty-two years old, his father died. After helping to settle his father's estate, Roger moved with his family to New Milford, Connecticut, near his elder brother. There he worked hard and continued to study. Sherman became a justice of the peace and was elected to serve in the legislature of the Connecticut colony. Though he was never trained at a law school, his self-education made him able to pass the bar exam and become a lawyer.

New Haven, Connecticut
Roger Sherman's Home

New Haven, Connecticut
Old Yale Library

Washington, D.C.
Statue of Senator Roger Sherman in the Statuary Hall Collection in the United States Capitol

Roger Sherman in New Haven

Sherman eventually settled in New Haven. At left is a drawing of his home, which is no longer standing. In New Haven, he became a judge and again served in the colony's legislature. He later became the town's first mayor, serving in that office for the rest of his life. Roger Sherman operated a store near Yale College (now Yale University). He was also elected treasurer of Yale. The college gave him an honorary Master's degree in 1768 to show appreciation for his service. At left is a photo taken on the Yale campus around 1900.

Sherman Serves His Country

Beginning in 1774, Sherman represented Connecticut in the First Continental Congress. In 1776 he served on the Committee of Five, along with Thomas Jefferson, John Adams, Benjamin Franklin, and Robert Livingston, that drafted the Declaration of Independence. Sherman later served on the committee that drafted the Articles of Confederation.

When the Constitutional Convention met in Philadelphia in 1787, Sherman again served his state and his country. American patriot Patrick Henry called him one of the greatest men at the convention. When representatives had a difficult time deciding how many representatives each state would have in the new American government, Sherman proposed an idea now called the Great Compromise (also called the Connecticut Compromise). He proposed that Congress be made up of two parts or houses. The number of members each state would have in the House of Representatives would be based on population, while the Senate would have two Senators from each state. This compromise helped the representatives work through their differences and speed up the work of writing the Constitution. Sherman wrote letters to the *New Haven Gazette* encouraging his fellow Connecticuters to ratify the new Constitution. The letters were titled, "To the People of Connecticut from A Countryman."

When the first U.S. Congress under the Constitution met in New York City in 1789, Sherman was one of Connecticut's first five members of the House of Representatives. He later became a U.S. Senator. Sherman died in 1793 at the age of 72. On page 68 is a statue of Sherman that the State of Connecticut placed in his honor in the United States Capitol.

The Faith, Family, and Legacy of Roger Sherman

Six years after moving from Massachusetts to Connecticut, Roger Sherman returned to the town of his birth to marry Elizabeth Hartwell, whom he had known in his youth. Together they had seven children. Elizabeth died when Roger was about forty years old and he remarried three years later. His second wife Rebecca gave birth to eight more children.

Roger Sherman's daughter Martha married Jeremiah Day, a Congregationalist minister who became president of Yale University. Sherman's youngest daughter Sarah married Samuel Hoar who became a Congressman from Massachusetts. Another daughter Rebecca married Simeon Baldwin who became a Congressman from Connecticut. After Rebecca died, Simeon Baldwin married Elizabeth, another of Roger Sherman's daughters. Sherman's descendants continued to serve their country for generations as seen in the chart below.

Roger Sherman was a man of deep and humble faith in God. He wrote sermons which revealed details of his faith. In his late sixties he published "A Short Sermon on the Duty of Self-Examination Preparatory to Receiving the Lord's Supper." Thomas Jefferson once said of Roger Sherman that he "never said a foolish thing in his life." John Adams described him as "honest as an angel." See Sherman memorial below.

New Haven, Connecticut
Memorial to Roger Sherman

Descendants of Roger Sherman Serve Their Country

Grandsons

William Maxwell Evarts, Senator from New York, Secretary of State under President Rutherford B. Hayes

Roger Sherman Baldwin, Senator from Connecticut, Governor of Connecticut

George Frisbie Hoar, U.S. Congressman and Senator from Massachusetts

Ebenezer Rockwood Hoar, U.S. Congressman from Massachusetts

Great-Grandsons

Rockwood Hoar, U.S. Congressman from Massachusetts

Sherman Hoar, U.S. Congressman from Massachusetts

Simeon Eben Baldwin, Governor of Connecticut

Great-Great-Grandson

Henry Sherman Boutell, U.S. Congressman from Illinois

Benjamin Harrison, Ancestor of Presidents

Benjamin Harrison V was a signer of the Declaration of Independence. Two of his descendants rose to the highest office in the land, President of the United States. Benjamin Harrison V was born in 1726 in Virginia into a family that had been deeply involved in civic life. He attended William and Mary College, but left without graduating so that he could oversee his family's plantation following the death of his father.

Harrison was elected to the Virginia House of Burgesses when he was twenty-three years old and served there until 1775. At first he was reluctant to see the colonies separate from Great Britain; but when tensions between the colonies and the mother country increased, Harrison became a strong supporter of the revolution. Beginning in 1774, Harrison represented Virginia in the First Continental Congress. He later served as Governor of the State of Virginia. When a convention was held in Virginia to decide whether Virginia would ratify the Constitution, Harrison served as a delegate to the convention.

The record of public service in the Harrison family is remarkable. See chart at right to see ways they served.

**Descendants of Benjamin Harrison V
Serve Their Country**

Sons

Carter Bassett Harrison, U.S. Congressman from Virginia

William Henry Harrison, U.S. Congressman from Ohio, U.S. Senator from Ohio, President of the United States

Grandsons

John Scott Harrison, U.S. Congressman from Ohio

Great-Grandson

Benjamin Harrison, U.S. Senator from Indiana, President of the United States

Great-Great-Great Grandson

William Henry Harrison, U.S. Congressman from Wyoming (his mother's father was Alvin Saunders, U.S. Senator from Nebraska)

President Benjamin Harrison, Great-Grandson of Benjamin Harrison V

The Faith of Harrison's Great-Grandson and Namesake

Harrison's great-grandson and namesake, President Benjamin Harrison, pictured at left, was a devout believer in Jesus Christ. He served as a church elder for forty years and also taught Sunday School. While serving in the Civil War, he held nightly prayers in his tent. During the War, he wrote to his wife, asking her to pray for him so that God would enable him to be a good soldier of Jesus Christ and give him valor and skill so that he would honor his country and his friends. When he became President, he prayed daily before the day's work began. After his death, his wife donated a Tiffany stained glass window, "Angel of the Resurrection," to their church in his honor. It is now in the Indianapolis Museum of Art.

What the Founders Gave Us

The Founding Fathers were intelligent men who saw a need and responded to it. They felt strongly about the cause of freedom and were willing to risk their lives to bring it about. They were not perfect. They had failings and they had conflicts among themselves at times over certain issues. But as a group they sensed that the time had come to change the way nations govern themselves. They created a remarkable system that has worked well for over two hundred years. It has allowed and encouraged people to live up to their God-given potential and enjoy the blessings of freedom better than any man-made system of government in the history of the world. Our nation's government has served as the model and inspiration for many other countries.

Americans must remember the foundations that our Founding Fathers laid down for us. Foundations are important. Jesus taught about the importance of building our lives on a firm foundation when He told the parable of the wise and foolish builders.

Therefore everyone who hears these words of Mine and acts on them,
may be compared to a wise man who built his house on the rock.
Matthew 7:24

Lesson Activities

Thinking Biblically — In your notebook, write a paragraph about ways a civil servant's faith should influence the way he or she serves in government.

Vocabulary — In your notebook, write your own definition for each of these words: politician, merchant, diplomat, cobbler, tension. Look in the lesson for clues for their meanings. When you are finished writing your definitions, look in a dictionary for comparison.

Literature — Read "Letter to the Governor of Connecticut" in *The Citizen's Handbook*, pages 10-11.

Creative Writing — In your notebook, make a list that answers the question, "What did the Founding Fathers give to me?"

Picture This! — Take a photograph or draw a picture of a place or street named for a Founding Father or a President.

Student Workbook or Lesson Review — If you are using one of these optional books, complete the assignment for Lesson 13.

Uncle Sam Wants *YOU*

Uncle Sam has been a nickname for the United States since the War of 1812. During World Wars I and II, artists drew pictures of Uncle Sam on posters. The posters encouraged Americans to help their country. Read the ones at left. Many men and women joined the military, while other citizens collected scrap metal and rubber, worked in factories to make supplies for the military, grew food for soldiers far away, or did countless other things to help. They did these things to fulfill their civic responsibilities as American citizens, just as the Founding Fathers had done.

We are using "Uncle Sam Wants You!" as the title of this lesson to teach you ways citizens can serve and to encourage you to fulfill your civic responsibilities. American citizens have the freedom — and the responsibility — to be involved in their communities, states, and country. In the words of President John F. Kennedy:

Ask not what your country can do for you—ask what you can do for your country.

Citizens can help in many ways. Some choose a government career. Many work hard and pay taxes. Sometimes local, state, and Federal governments ask specific citizens to do certain things and sometimes governments require them to do so. Some citizens run for an elected office. Many citizens vote and many volunteer.

Working for the Government or Working in the Private Sector

What do you want to be when you grow up? Do you want to be a barber, a mechanic, a pharmacist, a Marine, an engineer, a plumber, or a law enforcement officer? Some of these occupations, like Marine and law enforcement officer, are obviously government jobs. A Marine works for the Federal government, but people trained in law enforcement can work in any level of government. Here are a few possibilities. They can be police officers for the local government, highway patrol officers for the state, or agents of the Federal Bureau of Investigation. Marines, law enforcement officers, and millions of other government employees work in the public sector. They receive government paychecks.

Workers who do not have government jobs work in the private sector. A plumber who works for a small business owner, a mechanic working for a car dealer, a barber who owns his own barber shop, a pharmacist who owns his own drugstore, and an engineer who works for a corporation, all work in the private sector.

However, people in each of those professions could also choose a job in the public sector. Government at each level uses the services of plumbers. A mechanic could repair school buses for a city or, as seen in the photo below, he could refurbish planes for the U.S. Air Force. A barber or a pharmacist could work in a Federal veterans hospital. A pharmacist could also do research for the government. In the photo at left below is William R. Carter, who worked as a government pharmacist for forty years.

Engineers work in many government agencies. One example is the National Aeronautics and Space Administration (NASA). A NASA engineer is pictured at the top of page 74.

William R. Carter worked for the Federal government as a pharmacist for forty years. Carter worked in a laboratory where he helped test whether bandages were sterile.

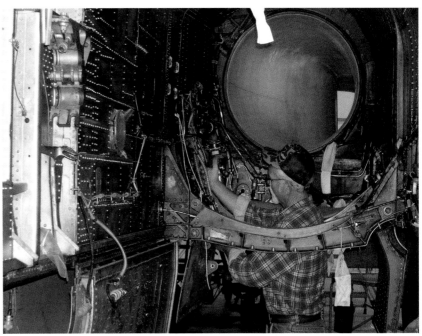

This mechanic is inspecting a plane that is being refurbished at an Air Force base in Arizona.

While many Americans believe that our government is too large and too expensive, there are many government jobs that few of us would want eliminated. If we have an accident, we want a police officer in a hurry. When we see a traffic light that isn't working, we want it to be repaired. When a child is born, we want our state to issue a birth certificate. When

Huntsville, Alabama
NASA Engineer Examines Space Telescope at the Marshall Space Flight Center

we go to government offices to get a marriage license, a license plate for our car, or a driver's license, we want them to have enough employees so that we do not have to wait long.

Below the license plates on page 75 is a photo of the first woman in Washington, D.C. to obtain a motorcycle license. In the box below, read details about a birth certificate and a marriage license from the late nineteenth century.

Legal Documents That Families Need

Marriage is a legal relationship between a man and a woman, so states require them to get a marriage license. When a baby is born, his or her birth is recorded in the child's birth state. Here are examples of each from the late nineteenth century.

At top right is the birth certificate of Bessie Bland, who was born in New York City in 1899. Her mother was Rose Hannah Moonay Bland, who was seventeen years old when Bessie was born. Rose, too, was born in New York City. Bessie's father was Andrew Bland. He was twenty-two when Bessie was born. Andrew was born in Ireland.

At lower right is the marriage license of future President William Howard Taft and Helen Herron, married in Hamilton County, Ohio, in 1886. The license required Taft to state that he was over twenty-one years old and that Helen was over eighteen and that they were "not of nearer relation to each other than that of second cousin". The license was signed by the groom, a probate judge, a deputy clerk, and the minister who performed the marriage. The minister referred to himself as "a minister of the gospel."

For our system of government to work, we need citizens who are willing to work in government jobs. However, private sector jobs help Americans, too, because it is the private businesses in America that make our economy strong. Our government could not operate without the money earned in the private sector, because taxes paid on income earned in the private sector pays for our government.

One way that you can serve your community, state, and country is by becoming a responsible citizen who works to earn a living, whether your job is a public one or a private one. Another way to serve is to be the parent in a family who takes care of the home and children so that the other parent has time to work and earn a living.

Serving When Appointed to Serve

Some positions in government are filled by people who are appointed. Sometimes they are paid and sometimes they are not. A mayor may appoint a citizen to serve on the board of a city-owned hospital. A Governor may appoint someone to serve on a committee to improve the quality of a state's water. A President may appoint a citizen to serve as an Ambassador to a foreign country. See photos of two Ambassadors at right. People are not required to say yes when appointed to a position, but our government needs people who are willing to serve.

Running for Office and Voting

America needs citizens who are willing to make the sacrifices necessary to be elected to various offices, from a seat on the town council to the President of the United States. When a candidate decides to run, he knows that his many hours of work and sacrifice may be rewarded with victory, but he also knows that he could lose. See photo on page 76 of presidential candidate John McCain and vice presidential candidate Sarah Palin. After working hard to get elected in 2008, they lost to Barack Obama and Joe Biden.

Collectible License Plates

Washington, D.C.
In 1937 Mrs. Sally Halterman became the first woman in Washington, D.C., to be granted a license to drive a motorcycle. She was 4 feet 11 inches tall and weighed only 88 pounds.

Joseph Kennedy, father of future President John F. Kennedy, served as U.S. Ambassador to Great Britain.

In 2010 President Barack Obama appointed Terence McCulley as U.S. Ambassador to Nigeria.

Each American citizen can consider whether he should become a candidate himself. If not, he can appreciate those who are willing to run, and he can help those he supports to get elected. Citizens can also vote for the candidates they believe will do the best job. In Units 5-9, we learn about the American election process and about leaders who have been elected.

Vice Presidential Candidate Sarah Palin (behind microphones) and Presidential Candidate John McCain (to her left), 2008

Serving When Our Government Says We Must

Let's look at some examples of times that our government requires us to serve.

Jury Duty. When an American is accused of breaking a law, he or she has the right to be treated fairly. Sometimes a citizen must stand trial so that a court can decide if he or she is innocent or guilty. In some cases a judge makes the decision. In other cases a jury decides. A jury is made up of citizens, usually twelve.

First All-Female Jury in California, 1911

Cleveland, Ohio
Jury Box in the East Courtroom at the Howard M. Metzenbaum U.S. Courthouse

When an American citizen receives a letter in the mail saying that he or she has been chosen for jury duty, that citizen must follow the instructions in the letter. He or she may be required to show up at a courthouse on a certain day. Sometimes a person chosen for jury duty must be available for several weeks and must postpone other responsibilities while serving as a juror. While this may be inconvenient, people who serve on juries are important to our court system. The jury may help decide whether someone accused of drunk driving can keep his driver's license or whether an accused thief is innocent or guilty. Serving on a jury is an important service to the community. Look at the photos at left. The place where a jury sits in court is called a jury box.

Subpoenas. When a person has witnessed a crime, he may receive a document called a subpoena, commanding him to appear in court as a witness. On rare occasions, a citizen may be subpoenaed to appear before a committee of a state legislature or the U.S. Congress. See example at right.

Selective Service. Most males living in the United States must register with the Selective Service System within thirty days of reaching eighteen years of age. This even includes males who are not American citizens and those who are conscientiously opposed to fighting in a war. This registration helps the Federal government know who would be available to serve in the military in case of a national emergency. If an emergency occurs, men who are registered with Selective Service may be drafted into the military. Those conscientiously opposed to war may be required to serve in an alternative service program. At right is a photo of men standing in line to register around 1918.

General Motors President William Knudsen signs a subpoena on December 6, 1938.

Men register for the draft c. 1918.

Volunteering

America's leaders often encourage its citizens to become involved in helping other people. At right President Bill Clinton gives a speech about national service at Rutgers University.

America is strongest when many citizens serve their fellow man. In addition to working for the government, serving when required or appointed, running for office, and voting, American citizens can make a positive impact in the lives of individuals and in their communities, states, and country by volunteering.

In *On the Banks of Plum Creek*, Laura Ingalls Wilder told about a time her father served by giving $3.00 to help purchase a bell for his church instead of buying a much-needed pair of boots. As you can see in the photo at right, his gift is still blessing the people of Walnut Grove, Minnesota, well over a century later.

New Brunswick, New Jersey
President Clinton speaks at Rutgers University on March 1, 1993.

Walnut Grove, Minnesota
Charles Ingalls, father of Laura Ingalls Wilder, gave $3.00 to help pay for this church bell.

The best list of ways to volunteer is the one given by our Savior:

For I was hungry, and you gave Me something to eat;

I was thirsty, and you gave Me something to drink;

I was a stranger, and you invited Me in;

naked, and you clothed Me;

I was sick, and you visited Me;

I was in prison, and you came to Me.

Matthew 25:35-36

Lesson Activities

Thinking Biblically — Write a paragraph in your notebook or discuss with a parent: What are some ways that a Christian can be a positive influence while serving his or her country?

Vocabulary — Copy the sentences below into your notebook, filling in each blank with one of these words: sector, aeronautics, refurbish, juror, conscientious.

1. My cousin is majoring in mechanical engineering because he wants to work in the _____ industry.
2. Alvin C. York was a _____ objector at the start of WWI, but he later changed his mind and became a national war hero.
3. Dad said there is no reason to buy a new flashlight when we can easily _____ our old one.
4. My aunt served as a _____ in a trial that made big news across our state.
5. Three of my close relatives work in the public _____; one is a mayor, one is a policeman, and one is in the Air Force.

Literature — Read "Mascot of the Marines" in *The Citizen's Handbook*, page 12.

Creative Writing — In your notebook, copy the quote by John F. Kennedy on page 72, and underneath write ten ways that you can serve your country.

Find Out! — Has anyone in your family held a job in the public sector?

Student Workbook or Lesson Review — If you are using one of these optional books, complete the assignment for Lesson 14.

★ Remember to choose an American Holiday to study this week! ★

UNIT 4 — PATRIOTIC SYMBOLS AND AMERICAN IDEALS

BOOKS USED IN UNIT 4

- The Citizen's Handbook

- Student Workbook (optional)

- Lesson Review (optional)

A special tactics parachutist delivers American flag during ceremony of Air Mobility Rodeo at Joint Base Lewis-McChord, Washington, July 24, 2011.

The Story of the
STARS AND STRIPES

LESSON 16

Pearl Harbor, Hawaii
Sailors honor a veteran who survived the attack on Pearl Harbor.

Washington, D.C.
Some of the Fifty American Flags that Surround the Washington Monument

New York City, New York
New York Harbor

In Washington, D. C., in state capitals, and in cities across the land, Americans proudly fly the Stars and Stripes. The Red, White, and Blue. Old Glory. Our soldiers and sailors raise, lower, carry, and fold it respectfully. So do our Boy Scouts and our veterans. We hang it over our streets and on our houses. A spotlight shines on our flag when a horse and rider bring it into view at the rodeo. We carry it proudly in our parades. We display it on our vehicles and hang it from construction sites.

Americans hold their hands over their hearts and pledge allegiance to it. Our military personnel and first responders salute it. We sing about it at ceremonies and at ball games.

The Official Birth of the Stars and Stripes

While the Second Continental Congress was busy fighting the American Revolution against the British, it formed a Marine Committee. On June 14, 1777, that committee adopted a resolution which read: "Resolved that the flag of the United States be thirteen stripes, alternate red and white; that the union be thirteen stars, white in a blue field representing a new constellation."

The committee did not say specifically how the stars would be arranged. Therefore, the lineup of stars of early American flags varied. Some had rows of stars, others had scattered stars, and on others the stars were arranged in a circle. The resolution did not say how many points would be on the stars.

Some flags had six-point stars and some had stars with eight points. We do not know for sure who suggested the five-point star, but it may have been Francis Hopkinson, a member of the Second Continental Congress from New Jersey. Hopkinson was also a signer of the Declaration of Independence.

Fifteen Stripes and Fifteen Stars

After Kentucky and Vermont became states, a 1794 resolution changed the design of the flag to one with fifteen stars and fifteen stripes. This remained the official flag until 1818. It was the flag that inspired the writing of what became our national anthem, "The Star-Spangled Banner."

From Twenty Stars to Fifty

A captain in the U.S. Navy suggested to Congress that the flag be changed. He proposed that the flag have thirteen stripes to represent the original colonies and that a new star be added to the field of blue for each new state. Congress passed a law requiring that the flag have thirteen stripes and twenty stars, which was the number of states at the time. President James Monroe signed the law in 1818. The bill stated that a new star would be added to the flag on the first Fourth of July that fell after a state was admitted. The fifty-star flag was flown for the first time at 12:01 A.M. on July 4, 1960 at Fort McHenry National Monument in Baltimore, Maryland. Why Fort McHenry? Read on.

"The Star-Spangled Banner"

The national anthem of the United States was written during the War of 1812. Lawyer, poet, and devout Christian Francis Scott Key began writing the words on the morning of September 14, 1814. Seventeen months before, Major George Armistead had taken command of Fort McHenry, which guarded the entrance to Baltimore. Armistead soon made arrangements with local flag maker Mary Pickersgill to make two flags for the fort, a seventeen by twenty-five foot flag to be

New York City, New York
Yankee Stadium

Indianapolis, Indiana
Indiana War Memorial Museum

Denver, Colorado
Dozens of people display the flag during a Denver Broncos game at Mile High Stadium.

Boston, Massachusetts
Old Glory hangs from the Senate Chamber in the Massachusetts State House.

81

Delaware, Ohio
Fourth of July Parade

New York City, New York
New York Stock Exchange

Montana
A U.S. Forest Service Honor Guard salutes the flag.

Soccer Match Between the U.S.A. and Spain

Gainesboro, Tennessee
Christmas Parade

used in wet weather and a much larger and more impressive thirty by forty-two foot garrison flag. Major Armistead wanted a "flag so large that the British will have no difficulty in seeing it from a distance."

Pickersgill was an experienced flag maker, who had learned the craft from her mother. She had four assistants in her flag making business. Three were thirteen years old: her daughter Caroline, her niece Eliza Young, and an African American indentured servant named Grace Wisher. Her niece Margaret Young was fifteen. Mary and her assistants, who may have also included her elderly mother, spent between six and eight weeks making the flags. It is no wonder that the task took so long. Each cotton star of the garrison flag was two feet across, as was each of the fifteen stripes. The seamstresses pieced together the field of blue and the red and white stripes by hand, stitching together individual wool pieces that were only about twelve or eighteen inches wide! When the entire flag was sewn together, they had created a flag that was about one quarter the size of a modern basketball court.

On the morning of September 14, Francis Scott Key was on a ship in Baltimore harbor. Early in September, he had gone to a British prisoner-exchange ship to request that an elderly friend be released. The British relented, but Key and his friend were required to stay on a nearby ship while the British attacked the fort. Key agonized as he watched his countrymen bombarded by cannon fire for twenty-five hours. On the morning of the 14th, Key realized that the British had stopped firing at the fort. He looked to see if the American flag still flew above it. About that time, American soldiers raised the huge garrison flag. Key took a letter from his pocket and began a poem to express what he felt. He completed it later that day in a rented room in a nearby tavern.

On September 17, a young apprentice at the *Baltimore American* newspaper printed the poem as a large poster. Its title was "Defence of Fort McHenry." Copies were distributed around town; each of Fort McHenry's soldiers received a copy. Within the first month, more than a dozen newspapers in the East had published it. Early in November it was set to music and named "The Star-Spangled Banner."

Years after Francis Scott Key wrote the song, he spoke to a group in his hometown of Frederick, Maryland. He said:

> *"I saw the flag of my country waving over a city — the strength and pride of my native State . . . . I witnessed the preparation for its assaults. I saw the array of its enemies as they advanced to the attack. I heard the sound of battle; the noise of the conflict fell upon my listening ear, and told me that 'the brave and the free' had met the invaders . . . . Let the praise, then, if any be due, be given, not to me, who only did what I could not help doing, not to the writer, but to the inspirers of the song!"*

"The Star-Spangled Banner" became a popular patriotic song during the 1800s, especially during the Civil War. By the 1890s, the U.S. military was requiring that it be played when the flag was raised and lowered. In 1916 President Woodrow Wilson ordered that it be played at military ceremonies.

Around this time, Congressman John Charles Linthicum of Maryland and many patriotic groups began working to make the song America's official national anthem. However, many opposed the idea. Some thought the song was too hard to sing. Some wanted "Yankee Doodle," "America the Beautiful," or some other patriotic song. More and more patriotic organizations pushed for the adoption of "The Star-Spangled Banner," and finally on March 3, 1931, President Herbert Hoover signed an act of Congress that made the song our official national anthem.

The family of Lieutenant Colonel Armistead kept the flag that had flown that day over Fort McHenry as a family heirloom for ninety years. In 1907 a descendant of Armistead loaned the flag to the Smithsonian Institution. In 1912 he made it a permanent gift.

Boston, Massachusetts
John Fitzgerald Kennedy Presidential Library

Minnesota

Georgia and American Flags, 1941

Savannah, Georgia

By 1912 the Star-Spangled Banner was much smaller than when it flew over Fort McHenry. In the late 1800s, people collected souvenirs of famous people and events. Many asked the Armisteads for a piece of the flag. Though they gave them only to people they thought should be especially honored, like veterans and government officials, by the time they donated it to the Smithsonian, more than two hundred square feet had been removed, including one star. The Smithsonian now has more than a dozen of these pieces that the Armisteads gave away.

In the box below, read the stories of what two grandchildren said about their flag maker grandmothers.

Vernona, New Jersey
A young woman sews stripes on an American flag at the Annin Flag Company in March of 1943.

Vernona, New Jersey
An Italian-American woman clips threads on an American flag at the Annin Flag Company in March of 1943. Her two sons were serving in the U.S. Army.

Using Talents to Serve: Two Grandmothers

People who made flags during the American Revolution included John Shaw of Maryland and Cornelia Bridges, Rebecca Young, and Elizabeth (Betsy) Ross of Pennsylvania. The most famous is Betsy Ross, a flag maker for fifty years. She became famous after 1870, the year that her grandson William J. Canby read a paper at a meeting of the Historical Society of Pennsylvania. In it he told the story that his grandmother had told to him and a dozen or more others when he was a little boy. He said that General George Washington and two others visited his grandmother, telling her that they were a committee of Congress. He said that General Washington brought his grandmother a drawing and that after she made certain suggestions, the General redrew it in pencil in her back parlor. Canby said that this incident happened before independence was declared in July of 1776.

In 1876, Caroline Pickersgill Purdy, daughter of Mary Pickersgill, sent a letter to Georgiana Armistead Appleton, daughter of George Armistead. She wrote about her mother's work on the Fort McHenry flag and of her own role in helping her mother. Caroline said that Mary Pickersgill was an "exceedingly patriotic woman." She said that her mother's mother was Rebecca Young. She wrote, "My grandmother, Rebecca Young, made the first flag of the Revolution under George Washington's directions."

The home where Betsy Ross lived in Philadelphia and the home where Mary Pickersgill made the famous Fort McHenry flag in Baltimore are both historic landmarks.

In 2010 Congress passed the Star-Spangled Banner Commemorative Coin Act. It requires the U.S. Mint to issue gold $5 coins and silver $1 coins to celebrate the bicentennial of the writing of The Star-Spangled Banner. The Maryland War of 1812 Bicentennial Commission is to use a portion of the money earned from sales of these coins to pay for bicentennial activities and improvements of historic sites.

State Flags

Each of the fifty states also has a state flag. The Avenue of Flags at the Mount Rushmore National Memorial in Keystone, South Dakota, displays each of the state flags, plus the flags of each of America's six territories. These include the District of Columbia; the Territories of Guam, American Samoa, and the Virgin Islands; and the Commonwealths of Puerto Rico and the Northern Mariana Islands. The Avenue of Flags is pictured below.

The Pledge of Allegiance

I pledge allegiance to the flag of the United States of America and to the Republic for which it stands, one nation, under God, indivisible, with liberty and justice for all.

With these words American citizens honor the United States of America and its flag. The word *allegiance* means loyalty and commitment. When Americans say the Pledge of Allegiance, they declare their loyalty to their country and to its flag. Loyalty is a trait that God desires us to have.

Keystone, South Dakota
Avenue of Flags at Mount Rushmore National Memorial

He who pursues righteousness and loyalty
finds life, righteousness, and honor.
Proverbs 21:21

Lesson Activities

Thinking Biblically — Flags have been used for thousands of years to represent families and nations. Read Numbers 2:1-2 for an example.

Vocabulary —Write a paragraph using all of these words: resolution, anthem, devout, agonize, heirloom. Consult a dictionary if you need help with their definitions.

Literature — Read "The Flag Goes By" in *The Citizen's Handbook*, page 13.

Creative Writing — In your notebook, write one or two paragraphs about times you have honored the flag of the United States.

Picture This! — Take photographs or draw pictures of United States flags around your community.

Student Workbook or Lesson Review — If you are using one of these optional books, complete the assignment for Lesson 16.

The Great Seal of the
UNITED STATES

President Wilson speaks at his inauguration with the Great Seal of the United States displayed before the lectern, March 4, 1913.

Governments have used official seals for thousands of years. In the photo at left, President Woodrow Wilson stands behind the Great Seal of the United States while giving his inaugural address. The designs on a government seal represent ideals that are important to that nation. The symbols on the Great Seal of the United States represent ideals that were important to the Founding Fathers and that continue to be important to Americans today. Its history began on the same day that the United States of America was born.

A seal is a hard device, designed to make an impression in a softer material, such as wax or thick paper. Seals have designs engraved on them. These designs can include letters, words, or phrases, as well as objects, people, symbols, and pretty flourishes. The word *seal* is also used for the image that is produced when a seal is pressed into a soft material.

In ancient times, kings and men of wealth or status often wore a piece of jewelry called a signet ring which included a seal. They were made of pottery or metal. Impressions made by these rings served the same purpose as a modern signature. A drawing of the signet ring of a European king who lived in the 400s is pictured below. Other ancient seals were pieces of gems like garnet or amethyst engraved with a design. A cylinder seal was carved around a stone cylinder. See reproduction at right.

At Left: Illustration of a Gold Signet Ring Found in the Grave of Childeric, a King Who Lived in the 400s in What is Now Belgium
At Right: A Replica of an Ancient Cylinder Seal and an Impression Created by It

Seals in the Bible

Seals and signet rings are mentioned many times in the Bible. Pharaoh put his signet ring on the hand of Joseph (Genesis 41:42). When God gave instructions for how the high priest's clothing was to be made, He told the workers to engrave stones "as a jeweler engraves a signet" (Exodus 28:11, 21, 36 and 39:6, 14, 30). When the Israelites donated objects for use in the construction of the Tabernacle and its furnishings, their donations included signet rings (Exodus 35:22).

Queen Jezebel wrote letters in the name of her husband King Ahab and sealed them with his seal (1 Kings 21:8). The signet ring of King Ahasuerus was used to seal decrees (Esther 3:10-12). When his signet ring sealed a document, it could not be revoked (Esther 8:8-10). When King Darius issued an injunction making it illegal for people to pray to anyone besides the king, Daniel defied it by praying to God three times a day in front of an open window. When he was thrown into a den of lions as punishment, the king sealed the stone which was placed over the mouth of the den with his own signet ring and those of his nobles (Daniel 6, especially verse 17).

A seal was placed on the stone that closed the tomb of Jesus (Matthew 27:66), but God ignored the seal and raised Him from the dead!

History of the Great Seal of the United States

When the members of the Second Continental Congress declared that the thirteen colonies were independent of Great Britain on July 4, 1776, they immediately began making decisions about the new nation. Before adjourning for the day, they adopted this resolution:

> *Resolved, that Dr. Franklin, Mr. J. Adams and Mr. Jefferson, be a committee, to bring in a device for a seal for the United States of America.*

Benjamin Franklin, John Adams, and Thomas Jefferson were all members of the Committee of Five who had written the Declaration of Independence. Now they took on the responsibility for coming up with a design for the seal. They asked Swiss artist Pierre Eugene du Simitiere to help them. The committee submitted a design to the Second Continental Congress in August of 1776, but Congress put off a decision. It would take six years and the work of eleven more men before a final decision was made.

In March of 1780, the Continental Congress appointed a new committee to work on the design of the seal. They were James Lovell, a delegate from Massachusetts who had once been an educator; John Morin Scott, a delegate from New York who was also a lawyer; and William Churchill Houston, a delegate from New Jersey who had once served as a professor at Princeton College. This committee sought the help of Francis Hopkinson from Philadelphia (see page 81). Hopkinson had designed the Great Seal of the State of New Jersey. The second committee submitted its design, but Congress did not approve it either.

In 1781, the Continental Congress passed the Articles of Confederation. In May of 1782, the new Confederation Congress appointed yet a third committee, including John Rutledge, a delegate from South Carolina who later became an Associate Justice of the U.S. Supreme Court; Arthur Middleton, another delegate from South Carolina who was also a very wealthy plantation owner; and Elias Boudinot, a representative from New Jersey who was also a lawyer and later became the first president of the American Bible Society. The committee asked for the help of William Barton, an artistic lawyer from Philadelphia. Barton quickly drew up two designs, which the committee submitted to Congress just five days after their work began. Congress rejected these designs, too.

However, in June the Confederation Congress gave each design that had been submitted since 1776 to Charles Thomson, who was then serving as Secretary of Congress. Thomson examined them, chose the elements that he liked best from each one, and added some ideas of his own. On June 20, 1782, Thomson presented a written description of his new design to the Confederation Congress. They adopted it that day.

A Description of the Great Seal

The most prominent symbol on the Great Seal of the United States is the American bald eagle. The eagle holds an olive branch in one talon and thirteen arrows in the other. These represent the powers of peace and war. The thirteen arrows represent the original thirteen states.

Andrew B. Graham produced this lithograph of the front of the Great Seal of the United States more than one hundred years ago.

In front of the eagle is a shield in the colors of the American flag. In his description of the Great Seal, Charles Thomson gave these meanings for the colors: "White signifies purity and innocence; red, hardiness & valour; and blue . . . signifies vigilance, perseverance & justice." The shield's thirteen red and white stripes also represent the first thirteen states. The blue area at the top of the shield represents Congress.

The motto on the ribbon in the eagle's mouth is *E Pluribus Unum*. A constellation above the eagle's head represents the United

States as a new nation taking its place among all the nations of the world. The constellation's thirteen six-pointed stars also represent the original thirteen states.

Read more about the American eagle below.

Making Dies of the Great Seal

Soon after the Confederation Congress decided on the official Great Seal, a brass seal was made of the final design. The first time it was used was on a document that authorized George Washington to work out an agreement with the British about Revolutionary War prisoners.

The Federal government used this seal until it was too worn to make a clear impression. In 1841 an engraver was hired to make a new steel seal. This engraver engraved only six arrows in the eagle's talon and made the stars with only five points. Another engraver made a third seal in 1877. He carefully copied the second one, which meant that it had the same mistakes.

In the early 1880s Tiffany and Company of New York was hired to make a new steel seal. Their top designer read the original description by Charles Thomson and designed a beautiful and accurate seal. This designer gave the olive branch thirteen leaves and thirteen olives. The Tiffany seal was completed in 1885.

The Bureau of Engraving and Printing made a master die in 1986. Any seals that are made in the future are to be made from this master die so that future seals will always look the same.

Using the Great Seal

Since 1789, the Secretary of State of the United States has been the official keeper of the Great Seal. A member of his staff affixes the Great Seal

The American Eagle

The eagle is a popular government symbol around the world. William Barton suggested including an eagle on the Great Seal. He suggested a small, crested, white, Imperial eagle; but Charles Thomson recommended the American bald eagle instead because it is native to North America. Notice the eagles in the photos below. At top left is an eagle in the Great Hall of the Thomas Jefferson Building of the Library of Congress in Washington, D. C. It holds arrows and an olive branch. Below it is a bald eagle in a National Wildlife Refuge in Oregon. At right below is a bald eagle I photographed near our home.

Charlene Notgrass

Mrs. Helen S. Bru, a clerk in the Department of State, affixes the Great Seal of the United States to a document, January 8, 1938.

to between 2,000 and 3,000 documents per year. Today he or she does this in a special glass room in the Exhibit Hall of the Department of State building in Washington, D.C. The room is always kept locked, even when the staff person is using the Great Seal. First he glues a 3 3/4 inch circle of off-white linen paper with a scalloped edge onto the document. Sometimes he glues ribbons under this paper "wafer." At left is clerk Mrs. Helen S. Bru who had this responsibility in the late 1930s.

The seal design is also used on money, postage stamps, government stationery, public buildings, and military uniforms. A gold seal is on U.S. passports. A Great Seal is above the door of each U.S. embassy around the world.

The most common place to see the Great Seal is on the back of the one dollar bill. The Charles Thomson design included a reverse side, but an official engraving of the reverse side has never been created for official use by the Secretary of State. However, there have been official drawings of the reverse, like the one that is on the back of the one dollar bill.

Examine the reverse side of the Great Seal on the dollar bill pictured below. At the top of the reverse side of the Great Seal is the Latin phrase *Annuit Coeptis*, which means "He [God] has favored our undertakings." In the center is a pyramid with thirteen steps. The pyramid represents strength and duration. At its top is the Eye of Providence. Thomson wanted to include the Eye because he believed Providence had many times worked "in favor of the American cause." At the base of the pyramid are the Roman numerals for 1776, the year the thirteen colonies declared independence from Great Britain. Thomson said that the year signifies the "beginning of the New American Era." The Latin phrase *Novus Ordo Seclorum* at the bottom means "a new order of the ages."

The President of the United States, state governments, Federal departments, and many government agencies in the United States also have seals. Examples of state seals are pictured on page 91.

The two sides of the Great Seal are printed on the back of the one dollar bill.

A government seal makes a document official. Jesus told His listeners that God had placed His seal on Him.

Do not work for the food which perishes, but for the food which endures to eternal life, which the Son of Man will give to you, for on Him the Father, God, has set His seal.

John 6:27

Lesson Activities

Thinking Biblically — Choose one of the Bible references in the lesson that refers to a seal or signet. Read the reference, and then draw a design in your notebook of what you think that seal or signet might have looked like.

Vocabulary — In your notebook, write your own definition for each of these words: impression, cylinder, talon, vigilance, scalloped. Look in the lesson for clues for the meaning of the words. When you are finished writing your definitions, look in a dictionary for comparison.

Find Out! — What does the seal of your state look like? Does your town or city have an official seal?

Picture This! — Take a photograph or draw a picture of the official seal of your town, your state, or the United States.

Student Workbook or Lesson Review — If you are using one of these optional books, complete the assignment for Lesson 17.

Great Seals of Ohio, California, Arkansas, Oklahoma, and Mississippi

More Treasured Symbols
OF AMERICA

Wimberley, Texas
Fourth of July Parade

Morro Bay, California
Fourth of July Bike Parade

Since the Founding Fathers adopted the American flag and the Great Seal, American citizens have come up with many other symbols to represent America.

Uncle Sam

One of those symbols inspired the title of this curriculum. Uncle Sam was born in 1813 when a meatpacker from Troy, New York, began stamping U.S. on barrels of pork and beef he shipped to American soldiers fighting in the War of 1812. When soldiers saw the U.S. on the barrels, they began saying that Uncle Sam was sending them gifts.

Today Uncle Sam is a tall, thin, old man with a white beard. He wears red and white striped trousers, a blue jacket, and a top hat. However, before the Civil War, he was sometimes fat and sometimes thin and he was pictured in a variety of clothes, even pajamas!

Many people dress up like Uncle Sam for parades and other events. Sometimes Uncle Sam can be a balloon, a pumpkin, or even a moose! See photos on pages 92-93. In the black and white photo on page 93, an employee of the National Archives sits with a drawing of Uncle Sam. Both are encouraging people to be careful what they say during World War II, so they won't give secrets away to the enemy.

Delaware, Ohio
Fourth of July Parade

Uncle Sam and an Employee
of the National Archives

Lady Liberty

Her real name is Liberty Enlightening the World, but she is usually called the Statue of Liberty. The people of France gave her to the people of America as a gift of friendship. American citizens were responsible for building the pedestal. Read about how they did that below.

Citizens Volunteer for Lady Liberty

American citizens needed to provide a pedestal for the Statue of Liberty. Eight years before she was delivered, volunteers formed the American Committee for the Statue of Liberty to raise money to build the pedestal. They hired American architect Richard Morris Hunt to design it. In 1884 the committee ran out of money. The following year the 300 copper pieces that make up the statue were placed into 214 crates and transported by ship from France. The pieces arrived in New York on June 17, ready to be assembled on an island in New York Harbor. Since the pedestal was not completed, they had to stay in storage. *New York World* newspaper publisher Joseph Pulitzer stepped in to help, using his newspaper to request donations. In six months the newspaper collected enough to finish the work on the pedestal. The Committee hired a construction company to reassemble the statue. Most of the crew were immigrants. The Statue of Liberty was unveiled on October 28, 1886, and dedicated by President Grover Cleveland. In the photo at right, Marines man the rails of the USS *Iwo Jima* on May 24, 2011.

Columbia

By the time of the American Revolution, America was sometimes called Columbia in honor of Christopher Columbus. Columbia is a feminine form of Columbus. It has been common for countries to have a feminine nickname. For example, Great Britain is called Britannia; Germany, Germania; and France, Marianne. In 1775 African American poet Phillis Wheatley wrote a poem entitled "To His Excellency General Washington" and sent it to George Washington. In it she spoke of America as "Columbia's state."

On April 21, 1789, George Washington rode through Trenton, New Jersey, on his way to his inauguration as first President of the United States. While he was in Trenton, a band played "President's March," also called "Washington's March," in his honor. The tune was written by German immigrant Philip Phile. A few years later Joseph Hopkinson, son of Francis Hopkinson (see pages 81 and 87), wrote a poem to go with the music. The song was sung in public for the first time at Philadelphia's New Theater in 1798. It received many encores and the audience began to sing along. A few nights later President John Adams, the second President of the United States, came to hear it performed. Joseph Hopkinson wrote to the retired President Washington about his new song and Washington replied. The song eventually became known as "Hail Columbia" and was often used as a sort of national anthem before "The Star-Spangled Banner" became the official national anthem. Today it is the song played when the Vice President of the United States makes an official entrance.

By the 1850s, newspaper cartoonists were drawing a goddess-like woman named "Miss Columbia" to represent equality, liberty, and justice. As you can see below, her image varied just as Uncle Sam's did. Around 1900 women dressed like Miss Columbia for Fourth of July parades. The Columbia Pictures movie studio chose her as their symbol in 1924. Images of Miss Columbia became less common after the middle of the 1900s, and she is rarely seen today.

Columbia

The Liberty Bell

The Speaker of the colonial legislature of Pennsylvania ordered a bell to celebrate the fiftieth anniversary of the colony. The bell was hung in the tower of the colony's State House in Philadelphia (later renamed Independence Hall) and was used to notify Philadelphians of public announcements. On July 8, 1776, it announced the first public reading of the Declaration of Independence. In the 1830s, abolitionists (people who wanted to end slavery) adopted the bell as a symbol of liberty for slaves and began to call it the Liberty Bell. After the Civil War, the Liberty Bell traveled by train to fairs around the country, helping to remind Americans who had suffered during the Civil War that they had once been united in the cause of liberty. It returned to Philadelphia in 1975.

Philadelphia, Pennsylvania
The Liberty Bell

Today the Liberty Bell is on display in Liberty Bell Center, near its original home at Independence Hall. It is a symbol of liberty for all Americans and for the many world visitors who come to see it each year.

The Oak, the Official National Tree

In December of 2004, President George Bush signed a bill which made the oak the official national tree of the United States. The oak was chosen by American citizens of all ages, who voted on the website of the National Arbor Day Foundation. Voters could choose between the state trees of each of the fifty states and the District of Columbia. Since many states have the same state tree as other states, the total number of trees considered was twenty-one. Voters could also write in their own choice. The oak received more than 101,000 votes. The nearest competitor was the redwood tree with almost 81,000. The other trees in the top five were the dogwood, maple, and pine.

The Rose, the Official National Flower

During the presidency of Ronald Reagan, Congress passed a resolution asking the President to issue a proclamation declaring the rose to be the official flower of the United States. President Reagan signed the resolution in a ceremony in the White House Rose Garden in October of 1986 and made the official proclamation on November 20.

Patriotic Songs

In addition to "The Star-Spangled Banner" and "Hail Columbia," Americans enjoy many other patriotic songs. Read the stories of ten of them on pages 96-97. Read each column from top to bottom.

1767

"Yankee Doodle, keep it up,
Yankee Doodle Dandy.
Mind the music and the step . . . ."

No one knows for sure when "Yankee Doodle" was written, but it was mentioned in one of America's first operas, *The Disappointment*, written in 1767. The author of some of its verses may have been Dr. Richard Schackburg, a British army surgeon who served in the French and Indian War. Perhaps he wrote it to make fun of colonial soldiers. Colonists enjoyed the song and became proud of it. Americans still love "Yankee Doodle."

1879

"Eternal Father, strong to save, '
Whose arm hath bound the restless wave . . . ."

In 1879 Lieutenant Commander Charles Jackson Train began a tradition of singing the first verse of "Eternal Father, Strong to Save" at the end of Sunday worship at the U.S. Naval Academy in Annapolis. Train was then serving as the director of the Midshipmen's Choir. The song came to be called "The Navy Hymn." It was written by two English ministers in the early 1860s and is also popular in the British and French Navies.

1831

"My country 'tis of thee,
Sweet land of liberty, of thee I sing."

Seminary student Samuel Francis Smith wrote the words to "My Country 'Tis of Thee," also known as "America." The tune was first published in 1744 in England and has been used as the national anthem of Prussia, Liechtenstein, and Great Britain, where it is called "God Save the Queen (or King)." The first public performance of the words was on July 4, 1831.

1895

"O beautiful for spacious skies,
For amber waves of grain . . . ."

Schoolteacher Katharine Lee Bates wrote "America the Beautiful" while on a lecture trip to Colorado. It was a quick gaze from the top of Pike's Peak that inspired its opening lines. The poem was first published in *The Congregationalist* newspaper on July 4, 1895. It is sung to a melody written by Samuel Augustus Ward, a church organist and choirmaster.

1862

"Mine eyes have seen the glory
of the coming of the Lord . . . ."

Julia Ward Howe wrote "Battle Hymn of the Republic" in 1861. It was first published in the *Atlantic Monthly* in February 1862. Howe based the song on a folk song that first became popular at Methodist camp meetings (a type of revival) and at churches of free blacks in the area around Charleston, South Carolina. By the time Howe wrote her version, the tune had become popular with the American public and was used as an army marching song.

1906

Anchors Aweigh, my boys, Anchors Aweigh.
Farewell to college joys, we sail at break
of day-ay-ay-ay . . . ."

"Anchors Aweigh" is the official song of the Navy. It was first sung publicly on December 1, 1906 at an Army-Navy football game. The Navy team won the game 10 to 0. Lieutenant Charles A. Zimmermann wrote the music and Midshipman Alfred H. Miles wrote the words.

♫ ♫ ♫ 1908 ♫ ♫ ♫

"Over hill, over dale,
As we hit the dusty trail,
And those caissons go rolling along . . . ."

Brigadier General Edmund Louis "Snitz" Gruber wrote "The Caissons Go Rolling Along" in 1908. He was a descendant of Franz Gruber who wrote "Silent Night." He and other soldiers wrote the tune together. The song became popular throughout the Army. In the early 1950s it was modernized by Dr. H. W. Arberg. In 1956 the modern version, "The Army Goes Rolling Along," became the official Army song.

♫ ♫ ♫ 1938 ♫ ♫ ♫

"God bless America, land that I love.
Stand beside her and guide her
Through the night with a light from above."

"God Bless America" was first performed by singer Kate Smith on a CBS radio program broadcast from the New York World's Fair on November 10, 1938. The song was written by Irving Berlin, a Jewish immigrant from Russia. See Irving Berlin and his wife below. Berlin gave the money he earned from the song to charity. Irving Berlin lived to be 101 and wrote more than 1,000 songs.

♫ ♫ ♫ 1919 ♫ ♫ ♫

"From the halls of Montezuma,
To the shores of Tripoli,
We will fight our country's battles
In the air, on land, and sea . . . ."

The tune of the "Marine's Hymn" dates from a comic opera presented in 1859. No one knows for certain when the first words were added to the tune, but Colonel Henry C. Davis may have written one or two verses in the early 1900s. The first printed version appeared in 1919 in *The Leatherneck*, a Marine Corps magazine published in Quantico, Virginia.

♫ ♫ ♫ 1939 ♫ ♫ ♫

"Off we go into the wild blue yonder
Climbing high into the sun . . . ."

In the late 1930s, *Liberty* magazine sponsored a contest for a new song for the U.S. Army's Air Corps. The winner, chosen by airmen's wives, was amateur pilot Robert Crawford. Crawford sang the song at its first public performance at the Cleveland Air Races in 1939. The U.S. Air Force was established as a separate military service in 1947. Crawford's song eventually became "The U.S. Air Force Song." Astronauts took the first page of Crawford's original score to the moon in 1971.

Mr. and Mrs. Irving Berlin

When the Speaker of the Pennsylvania colonial legislature ordered the Liberty Bell, he asked that this verse be placed on the bell:

Proclaim Liberty throughout all the Land

Unto all the inhabitants thereof.

Leviticus 25:10 KJV

Superior, Wisconsin
Fourth of July Parade

Delaware, Ohio
Fourth of July Parade

A Children's Fourth of July Parade

Lesson Activities

Vocabulary — Copy the sentences below into your notebook, filling in each blank with one of these words: enlighten, feminine, encore, caisson, corps.

1. I am proud of my uncle who is serving in the United States Marine _____.
2. The artillery unit was slowed down in the rocky terrain that was damaging the _____ wheels.
3. Samuel, can you _____ me on why there are no more cookies in the jar?
4. Roberta is the _____ form of the boy's name Robert.
5. Sara didn't know what to do when her dad yelled, "_____!" after she finished her piece in the piano recital.

Literature — Read "Newspaper Timeline of the Statue of Liberty" and "Proclamation Number 5547" in *The Citizen's Handbook*, pages 14-17.

Creative Writing — In your notebook, write a short story of at least one page about Uncle Sam.

Find Out! — Find and read the complete lyrics of one of the patriotic songs introduced in this lesson.

Picture This! — Draw a picture of one of the treasured symbols of America mentioned in this lesson.

Student Workbook or Lesson Review — If you are using one of these optional books, complete the assignment for Lesson 18.

American I**DEALS**

Our loving God established governments to protect people. According to God's teaching in Romans 13:1-7, a government should encourage what is good and punish what is wrong. If we did not have government, everyone would risk being the victim of the sinful actions of others. Government limits those sinful actions by enforcing laws that protect all the people. The citizens of a nation have the responsibility to respect the government's authority and to live under it.

The Founders of our nation organized our government with certain ideals or principles. It is the duty of American citizens to commit themselves to living up to these ideals.

One Nation Under God

The most important American ideal is faith in God. From the time that our country was founded, Americans have understood that our country is "one nation under God." We have confessed that "in God we trust." In fact, it is our national motto. See monument and coin at right.

The Declaration of Independence, which established our nation, states that all men are created equal and that we are given certain rights by our Creator which cannot be taken away. Notice that the Founders acknowledged that we were created and did not say that we had evolved. All of the Founders believed

Hillsboro, Texas
In God We Trust Monument
on the Grounds of the Hill County Courthouse

99

Harrisburg, Pennsylvania
Words from a Quote Circling the Rotunda of the State Capitol

Near the Entrance of the Pennsylvania State Capitol

Decoration in the Rotunda

in the God who created the world and who sustains life. Many had a strong personal faith in Jesus Christ. They believed that God gives value to human beings, that He guided the formation of our country and continued to guide it, and that everyone must answer to Him for how we live.

Evidence of the founding principle of faith in God can be seen in many public places around the country. Each of the examples on this page are at the Pennsylvania State Capitol in Harrisburg, Pennsylvania.

The picture at top left shows a portion of a quote from Pennsylvania founder William Penn. His words surround the interior of the beautiful capitol dome. The entire quote is:

> *"There may be room there for such a holy experiment. For the nations want a precedent. And my God will make it the seed of a nation. That an example may be set up to the nations. That we may do the thing that is truly wise and just."*

The pediment at center left is near the entrance to the capitol. The circular painting in the picture at lower left is one of four medallions that decorate the capitol dome.

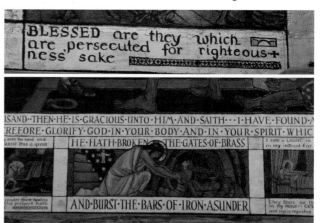

Inside the Hall of the House of Representatives

These medallions painted by Edwin Austin Abbey represent four forces of civilization: Religion, Art, Justice, and Science. This photo also shows a portion of the quote from William Penn.

Freedom of Religion

As a nation we express faith in God; however, we believe in God's power and love so much that we do not require everyone to believe the same way. The United States does not have and has never had an official religion. Our country does not endorse, protect, or support one particular religion or denomination, nor does it persecute the members of any faith just for believing that faith. The United States protects every person's right to believe as he or she wishes.

The Founding Fathers expected that faith would be a part of public life. Many of them were committed to praying personally, and they prayed together as they founded our nation and as they began our Federal government under the Constitution. Notice the Ten Commandments monument on the grounds of the Missouri State Capitol at right.

Personal and Political Freedom

Another American ideal is freedom, specifically personal and political freedom. The people of the United States are free to believe as they wish, say what they want, go where they desire, live where they would like, work where they want,

Jefferson City, Missouri
Ten Commandments on the Grounds of the Missouri State Capitol

and do many other things without being arrested or fined. An American citizen is free to start a business, to vote for the candidate of his or her choice, and to own a gun. Our ideal of freedom has enabled Americans to use their talents and labor to make life better for themselves and for the nation and the world.

We must understand, however, that freedom is never absolute. Our freedoms are guaranteed within certain reasonable limits. A person who misuses a gun, for instance, loses the right to own one. A person's speech in public cannot be false about another person or promote rebellion against the United States.

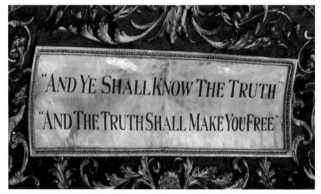

The engraving at right is on the ceiling in the Hall of the House (of Representatives) in

Harrisburg, Pennsylvania
Engraving on the Ceiling in the Hall of the House of Representatives in the Pennsylvania State Capitol

the Pennsylvania State Capitol. It quotes words of Jesus from John 8:32. Spiritual freedom in Christ is the greatest freedom anyone can have. The truth of Christ makes us free from the bondage of sin. As long as our nation stands on the basis of the truth that is freely communicated, we will be free from the bondage that comes as a result of ignorance and of depending on others to tell us what they think we need to know.

Equality

Another national ideal is equality. The Declaration of Independence says that "All men are created equal." This means that every American has the same worth before the law. The United States does not have royalty or an aristocracy, or a certain class of people who get special treatment before the law. The person who cannot read has the same right to a fair trial as someone with a college degree. Citizens of any race or national heritage have the same right to vote and to start a business.

We must admit that the United States has not always protected the ideal of equality for every citizen. For instance, for many years and in many places, Native Americans, African Americans, and Asian Americans did not have rights that were equal to those enjoyed by white Americans. Since the mid-1960s, the United States has taken great strides to correct this situation.

Opportunity

Freedom and equality provide the basis for another national ideal, opportunity. The poor immigrant who comes to the United States with nothing may start a business and become wealthy—and many immigrants have done just that. Someone who has broken the law has the opportunity to regain a place in society. Regardless of his or her past, an American citizen has the opportunity for a better future. This ideal of opportunity has given millions of people the hope for a better life. The only limit on what people can accomplish is the limit of what they are willing and able to work for.

Unity

America was also founded on the ideal of unity. We come from a wide range of ethnic and national groups, such as Native Americans, English, Scots-Irish, German, Italian, Chinese, Scandinavian, Polish, Hispanic, Vietnamese, and many more. Notice the group of immigrants at Ellis Island, New York, at top right on page 103. Many immigrants who came to America between 1892 and 1954 stopped first at Ellis Island. At top left on page 103, Vietnamese-Americans march in a Fourth of July parade in Washington, D.C., in 2008. Many Vietnamese immigrants began coming to America in the 1970s after the Vietnam War.

Washington, D.C.
Vietnamese-Americans march in a Fourth of July parade.

New York City, New York
Immigrants at Ellis Island

We are influenced by the different parts of the country in which we live: New England, the Mid-Atlantic region, the South, the Midwest, the Southwest, the West Coast, and Alaska and Hawaii. Americans are Protestants, Catholics, Jews, and people of other faiths. In politics we are liberals, conservatives, and moderates. We are Republicans, Democrats, supporters of minor political parties, and Independents. With all of these differences, we can find many reasons to be divided. But the American ideal is unity.

Our common identity as Americans makes us able to live and work together. Citizens from all backgrounds serve together in the military. People from all different faiths can help a community recover from a natural disaster. Your political party membership shouldn't matter when the country faces a threat from beyond our borders. Benjamin Franklin expressed the need for unity as the Continental Congress signed the Declaration of Independence and took on the role of traitors to the British king. Franklin said, "We must, indeed, all hang together, or most assuredly we shall all hang separately." A divided country is a weaker country, while a united country is a stronger one.

New York City, New York
An Italian woman learns citizenship and English at the Hudson Park Library, 1943.

In the photo at right, a teacher helps an Italian immigrant learn citizenship and English. When people who are new to the U.S. learn these, it makes us more unified. Because many Americans believe that God created all people equal, we respect one another and help one another. When we are unified and living in peace with one another, we can more easily influence others for Christ. This can lead to the even greater unity of being one in Christ.

The Purpose of Our Ideals

An ideal is a goal, a statement of how we think things ought to be. The American ideals of faith, freedom, equality, opportunity, and unity are principles that help America be strong and that help Americans have peace and well-being. Our ideals help us to become more of what we should be. We would be a poorer, weaker nation if we did not hold these ideals. We would not be a beacon of hope to millions around the world without these ideals. Holding to these ideals, defending them, and growing in them are essential to what it means to be a citizen of the United States.

American ideals help citizens live better on earth, but Christians have eternal goals. Paul encouraged Christians in Philippi with these words:

> I press on toward the goal for the prize of the upward call of God in Christ Jesus.
>
> Philippians 3:14

Lesson Activities

Thinking Biblically — Read Romans 13:1-7.

Literature — Read "Civility, Courage, Compassion, and Character" in *The Citizen's Handbook*, pages 18-19.

Creative Writing — Write a poem of at least 2-3 stanzas about America's ideals.

Find Out! — Ask each person in your family, "What is one American ideal?"

Picture This — Take a photograph or draw a picture of an American living out one of the ideals discussed in this lesson.

Student Workbook or Lesson Review — If you are using one of these optional books, complete the assignment for Lesson 19.

★ Remember to choose an American Holiday to study this week! ★

UNIT 5 — AMERICA'S LEADERS

BOOKS USED IN UNIT 5

- Lincoln: A Photobiography

- The Citizen's Handbook

- Student Workbook (optional)

- Lesson Review (optional)

*The Hermitage in Nashville, Tennessee,
Home of Andrew Jackson, America's 7th President*

Choosing People to LEAD

As we learned in Lesson 11, residents of each of America's fifty states live under a local government, a state government, and the Federal government. People do the work of government. For America to work as the Founding Fathers intended, we must have people who are willing to serve and to lead. Jesus taught His disciples about serving and leading in Luke 22:25-26:

> *And He said to them, "The kings of the Gentiles lord it over them; and those who have authority over them are called 'Benefactors.' But it is not this way with you, but the one who is the greatest among you must become like the youngest, and the leader like the servant."*

In America some government workers are hired, others are appointed, and others are elected. In this lesson, we learn about those who are elected and about important characteristics voters should look for in these elected officials. In the remaining lessons in Unit 5, we learn about the leaders who have served in America's highest elected office.

Elected Offices in America

State governments vary on which officials the people elect and which ones are appointed or hired, but voters vote for the Governor of their state and for state senators and state representatives to represent them in their

Arizona
Campaign Signs, November 2010

Ohio
Campaign Signs, Summer 1938

106

own state's legislature. The State of Nebraska is an exception (see page 63). Nebraska voters choose only state senators, since Nebraska does not have a state house of representatives.

Which officials are elected and which are appointed or hired also varies from one local government to another. Some examples of local elected officials include county mayor, city mayor, alderman, county commissioner, and so forth. Look for a variety of elected offices in the campaign posters and signs on page 106.

Voters in Federal elections choose people to represent them in the U.S. Congress. They also vote for the presidential candidates of their choice. When a voter votes for a certain presidential candidate, he is automatically voting for the vice presidential candidate running with him.

The President and Vice President are the only elected officials who represent every American. The presidential election is the only election in which every voter across the country can participate. It is the most talked about election in the country and the one that gets the most attention from the news media. Many Americans consider it the most important election in the United States.

Requirements for Elected Offices

To serve in an elected office, a candidate must meet certain basic requirements. He cannot be guilty of certain crimes, he must live in a certain area, and he must be a certain minimum age. The U.S. Constitution describes the specific requirements people have to meet to hold Federal offices. Requirements for those holding state and local offices are described in individual state constitutions or state laws.

Federal Offices. Voters in each state elect two U.S. Senators who represent all of the people of that state. Senators serve for six years before they must run for re-election.

Each state has one or more congressional districts. The number of districts each state has depends on the number of people living in that state. This is explained in more detail in Lesson 29. The total number of congressional districts in all of the United States is 435. Voters in each congressional district select one U.S. Congressman to represent the people living in their district. A Congressman does not have to live in the congressional district that he represents, but he must live in the

Burlington, Vermont
Vermont Senator Patrick Leahy, his wife, and Vermont Congressman Peter Welch (all three on the right) welcome Navy Admiral Mike Mullen and his wife (left) who have arrived for a ceremony honoring members of the Vermont National Guard who are about to be sent overseas, January 8, 2010.

state where the congressional district is located. Congressmen serve for two years before they must run for re-election.

The President serves for four years before he must be re-elected. Presidents can only be elected to two four-year terms. Read the chart below to see the requirements the Constitution outlines for Presidents, Senators, and Congressmen. Notice that the requirements for President are greater than those for Senators and Congressmen.

Requirements for Presidents and Members of Congress

Residency	Age	Citizenship
The President must have lived in the U.S. for fourteen years or more.	President - 35	The President must be a natural-born citizen of the United States.
A Senator must live in the state he represents.	Senator - 30	A Senator must have been a citizen of the United States for at least nine years.
A Congressman must live in the state where his congressional district is located.	Congressman - 25	A Congressman must have been a citizen of the United States for at least seven years.

State and Local Offices. Some states require that citizens be at least eighteen or twenty-one to hold any elected office. Most states have minimum age requirements for Governors, state senators, and state representatives.

Maturity

Most candidates in state and Federal elections run for office when they are middle-aged. In 2015, according to the National Conference of State Legislatures, the average age of state legislators was 56 and the average age of members of Congress was 59. By the time a person reaches his fifties, he or she has had many years of experience in handling family and work responsibilities and in handling money. He has also built a reputation that voters can examine.

The Founding Fathers and other American leaders of the past have seen the importance of elected officials reaching a certain age. The two major candidates in the 2016 election were sixty-nine (Hillary Clinton) and seventy (Donald Trump).

John McCain campaigns for President.

President Barack Obama

When Donald Trump was elected, he became the oldest person elected to a first term as President.

In 1984 Republican candidate Ronald Reagan, who was running for a second term, was seventy-three years old. Some people were concerned about his age and health. Reagan made a joke of people's concerns by saying that he would not make age an issue. He said that he would not exploit Democratic candidate Walter Mondale's youth and inexperience. Mondale was then fifty-six.

While some voters have worried about a presidential candidate being too old, other voters have worried about candidates being too young. Many voters thought that thirty-six-year-old Democrat William Jennings Bryan was too young when he ran against Republican William McKinley in 1896. Bryan's nickname was the "Boy Orator of the

Political Cartoon about Candidates William McKinley and William Jennings Bryan on the Cover of the August 29, 1896 Issue of Harper's Weekly

Platte" (the Platte is a river in Bryan's home state of Nebraska). Read the cover of the issue of *Harper's Weekly* above. Some thought forty-three-year-old Democrat John F. Kennedy was too young when he ran against Republican Richard Nixon in 1960. Bryan lost his election, but Kennedy won his.

Experience

Governors, Senators, and one Congressman have all been elected as Presidents. Almost one-third of Presidents previously served first as Vice President. Others served first in appointed government positions. Twelve Presidents had previously been generals. The most recent general to become President was Dwight D. Eisenhower. The aircraft carrier at right was named for him. Donald Trump had a long career in business. He is the first President who has not have previous government or military experience.

USS Dwight D. Eisenhower

Reputation

The work of being elected to an office actually begins many years before the campaign. Historically people have needed a good reputation in order to be elected to office. A reputation is built over many years. Each decision that a person makes from his youth up determines his reputation. If someone makes bad decisions early in life, voters often find out about it while he or she is running for office. It is important that we guard our good name.

Colossians 4:5 teaches people in God's kingdom to conduct themselves with wisdom toward outsiders. Of course, people may misunderstand our actions sometimes, but a person who conducts himself with wisdom will usually build a good reputation.

When Paul wrote to Timothy about men who desired to be overseers in the church, he said that they should have a good reputation with those outside the church (1 Timothy 3:7). Later in 1 Timothy, he wrote about widows who were worthy of support from fellow Christians. They, too, were to have a reputation for good works. Christians should be careful that the candidates they support are people with a good name. As you grow up, be careful about your own reputation.

Grand Rapids, Michigan
Boy Scouts gather at the Gerald R. Ford Presidential Museum. Those in the two lower photos are members of the Gerald R. Ford Council of Michigan. As a boy, President Ford was an Eagle Scout. As an adult, he had a reputation of being a man of maturity, experience, and integrity.

> *It is by his deeds that a lad distinguishes himself*
> *If his conduct is pure and right. Proverbs 20:11*

One way to protect your reputation is by being careful about your companions.

> *He who walks with wise men will be wise,*
> *But the companion of fools will suffer harm. Proverbs 13:20*

Integrity

A good reputation is built on integrity. Psalm 15 teaches about a person who walks with integrity. Candidates would do well to follow its teachings.

O Lord, who may abide in Your tent?
Who may dwell on Your holy hill?
He who walks with integrity, and works righteousness,
And speaks truth in his heart.
He does not slander with his tongue,
Nor does evil to his neighbor,
Nor takes up a reproach against his friend. Psalm 15:1-3

People who seek elected offices often face difficult temptations and find it hard to walk with integrity. They may be tempted to behave dishonestly in order to be elected. They may slander other candidates to make themselves look better. Sometimes they are even tempted to betray their friends in their efforts to get elected.

Candidates who fall to these temptations get much publicity about their wrongdoings. However, many candidates and elected officials serve honorably, walk in integrity, honor others with their speech, and remain true to their friends. It is these kinds of people that voters should choose.

A righteous man who walks in his integrity—
How blessed are his sons after him.
Proverbs 20:7

Lesson Activities

Thinking Biblically — Read Titus 2:2. Think of a person you admire who is over sixty years old and has the traits described in this verse. Write a paragraph about him in your notebook, telling how he shows these traits in his life, or discuss this person with a parent.

Vocabulary — Copy these words in your notebook, each on a separate line: characteristic, alderman, media, reputation, maturity. Look up each word in the dictionary. Next to each word, write what part or parts of speech it is according to the way the word is used in the lesson.

Literature — Read chapter 1 in *Lincoln: A Photobiography*.

Creative Writing — Write a prayer for American candidates and officials who are already serving in elected offices. Pray that they will speak and act kindly and honorably. Pray that they will not fall into the temptations that are particularly dangerous for people who seek political office.

Find Out! — Ask your parents for whom they have voted in past presidential elections and why they chose those candidates.

Student Workbook or Lesson Review — If you are using one of these optional books, complete the assignment for Lesson 21.

Presidents Make Peaceful TRANSITIONS

Since 1788 Americans have held a presidential election every four years. Because the United States is a major leader in the world, its President has one of the most powerful jobs on earth. Units 11 and 12 of *Uncle Sam and You* describe what the President does. As we begin to study elections for the next few weeks, let's take some time in this unit to learn some facts about the individuals Americans have chosen to serve as their top leaders. Before we begin, read aloud the Timeline of American Presidents between pages 112 and 128.

Head of State

Our President is our head of state. In this case, the word state refers to a country and not to one of the fifty individual states that make up the United States of America. Throughout most of the history of the world, the head of state of most countries was a king, or sometimes a queen. The king was a ruler—he made the rules and the people had to follow them. The citizens of these countries were simply subjects of the king. If citizens did not like what the king did, they had little power to change it. If a king did not like what a citizen did, he could banish him, put him in prison, or even execute him.

Timeline of American Presidents

George Washington   John Adams   Thomas Jefferson

Most kings ruled until they died. In many cases a member of his family became the new ruler in his place. However, change from one king to a new one was often far from peaceful. Sometimes family members fought one another to become the new ruler. Sometimes one or more of the king's advisors tried to take his place.

When a New President is Elected

The Founding Fathers of the United States created a different kind of government, a government ruled not by kings or dictators, but by the people. American citizens choose their own leaders, from the mayor of a small town to the Governor of a state to the President of the country. Change of leadership happens peacefully and in an orderly way. If American citizens do not like the way a leader is doing his job, they can choose a new leader at the next scheduled election.

President-Elect Woodrow Wilson with Outgoing President William Howard Taft on Inauguration Day, March 4, 1913

On a certain date after an election, the current elected official steps down (this is called leaving office), a new leader is sworn in, and he or she begins to do the job. Since 1797, when our first President, George Washington, stepped down and our second President, John Adams, took his place, America has enjoyed peaceful transitions from one leader to another.

Rutherford B. Hayes began the tradition of the President-elect visiting the outgoing President at the White House before the Inauguration Day ceremonies. In the photo above, President-

James Madison   James Monroe   John Quincy Adams

elect Woodrow Wilson visits President William Howard Taft. An usher who worked in the White House for forty-two years described in detail what happened during the photography session when this photo was taken. He said that when Wilson joined Taft for the first photos, Taft remarked that four years before he had stood in that same place to have his photo taken

Arlington, Virginia
President George W. Bush was honored with an Armed Forces farewell tribute on January 6, 2009. Secretary of Defense Robert M. Gates (left) awarded the President the Department of Defense Medal for Distinguished Service.

with then-President Theodore Roosevelt. While photographers took pictures, President Taft and Mr. Wilson walked around the room arm in arm. The photo on page 113 was taken on a porch. Taft and Wilson were asked to stand with their toes on a line which had been drawn on the floor with face powder supplied by a female photographer.

In some countries the military tries to take control of the country, but this has never happened in the United States. Look at the picture at left. Here the American military

honors President George W. Bush about two weeks before he leaves office in January 2009. The peaceful transition from one President to another can happen because of the good plan of government our Founders created and because of the character of the men who have served.

Taking the Oath of Office to Become President

After someone has been elected to become President of the United States, he is called the President-elect until the time that he takes the oath of office. The words of the oath are written in the Constitution. Most Presidents have taken the oath on Inauguration Day, which has been held every four years since George Washington became the first President in 1789. All Presidents who have begun a full four-year term as newly-elected Presidents have taken the

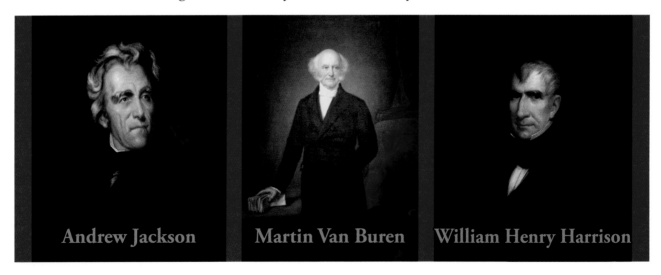

Andrew Jackson   Martin Van Buren   William Henry Harrison

oath in Washington, D.C., except the first two, who were inaugurated in temporary capitals before the U.S. Capital City was built. George Washington was inaugurated in New York City for his first term and in Philadelphia for his second; John Adams was also inaugurated in Philadelphia.

Inauguration Day is now celebrated every four years on January 20. If the 20th falls on a Sunday, the President takes the oath privately on the 20th and then publicly on the 21st. Eisenhower did this in 1957 and Reagan did so in 1985. Inaugurations are great celebrations where Americans observe the transfer of the presidency from one citizen to another. Many events are held around Washington, but the oath of office is usually taken at the U.S. Capitol. Details about the celebrations held on Inauguration Day are described in the Inauguration Day lesson beginning on page 479. When a sitting President is elected for a second four-year term, he begins his second term with another grand inaugural celebration.

However, several Presidents have died in office and their Vice Presidents have had to replace them. One Vice President had to become President after a President resigned. These men have taken the oath of office in some very unusual circumstances. Only four of them took the oath in Washington. Two of these were in hotels. William Henry Harrison had been President just over one month when he became the first President to die in office. Vice President John Tyler took the oath on April 6, 1841, in Brown's Hotel. Following Abraham Lincoln's assassination in 1865, Andrew Johnson took the oath at the Kirkwood Hotel. After Franklin Roosevelt died while vacationing in Georgia in 1945, Harry S. Truman took the oath in the Cabinet Room of the White House. Gerald R. Ford took the oath of office in the East Room of the White House after President Nixon resigned in 1974.

Two Presidents, in addition to Washington, have taken the oath in New York. Chester A. Arthur took it privately in his own home in New York City, following the assassination of James A. Garfield in 1881. When William McKinley was assassinated in Buffalo in 1901, Theodore Roosevelt hurried to Buffalo and took the oath in the home of a friend.

John Tyler   James K. Polk   Zachary Taylor

One oath was taken in Texas. When John F. Kennedy traveled to Dallas in November, 1963, Vice President Lyndon Johnson and others traveled with him. After Kennedy was assassinated, Johnson took the oath on Air Force One, the airplane that is assigned specifically to transport the President. For the first time, a woman, Federal Judge Sarah T. Hughes, administered the oath.

When a President takes the oath of office, a government official administers it. This means that the government official asks the President-elect to repeat the oath after him. A judge, usually the Chief Justice of the Supreme Court, has administered every presidential oath except for one. One Vice President became President after the oath was administered by his dad.

Calvin Coolidge and his wife were vacationing at his father's home in Plymouth Notch, Vermont, in August of 1923. In the early morning hours of August 3, Coolidge's father received word that President Harding had died of an illness during the night. Mr. Coolidge went upstairs to his son's room to awaken his son and daughter-in-law and tell them the news. Coolidge knelt to pray and then went downstairs. John Coolidge was a notary public in his small town, so he administered the oath to his son in the family living room by the light of a coal oil lamp while Mrs. Coolidge watched. See father and son at right.

President Calvin Coolidge (left) and His Father John

Fun Oath Facts

Bible. Presidents take the oath of office with one hand on a Bible. Franklin Roosevelt took the oath with his hand on a Bible that had been in his family since around 1686. It is in the Dutch language and is the oldest Bible used by a President while taking the oath.

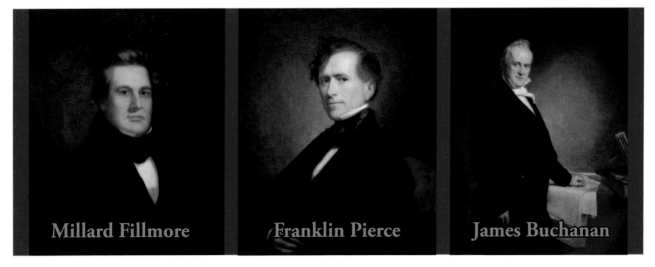

Millard Fillmore   Franklin Pierce   James Buchanan

Long Pants. John Quincy Adams was the first President to take the oath of office wearing long trousers instead of knickers that came just below the knee.

Images of the President. The first known drawing of a presidential inauguration to be printed in a newspaper was that of James K. Polk. The drawing was published in *The Illustrated London News.* James Buchanan's was the first to be photographed. William McKinley's inauguration was the first to be recorded by a movie camera.

Technology. The inauguration of James K. Polk was the first inauguration to be reported to other parts of the nation by telegraph. Warren G. Harding's was the first to make use of loudspeakers. The inauguration of Calvin Coolidge in 1925 was the first to be broadcast to the nation by radio. Harry S. Truman's inauguration in 1949 was the first to be broadcast on television. The inauguration of Bill Clinton in 1997 was the first to be broadcast live on the Internet.

When a President-elect visits the outgoing President, he is giving him the honor that is due him. God is pleased when people honor those in authority. In Romans He teaches us:

> *Render to all what is due them . . . custom to whom custom;*
> *fear to whom fear; honor to whom honor.*
> *Romans 13:7*

Lesson Activities

Thinking Biblically — Write a paragraph in your notebook or discuss with a parent: Why do you think Presidents take the oath of office with their hand on a Bible?

Vocabulary — Look up each of these words in a dictionary and read their definitions: banish, execute, transition, resign, knickers.

Literature — Read "Letter from Elizabeth E. Hutter" in *The Citizen's Handbook*, page 20 and chapter 2 in *Lincoln: A Photobiography*.

Creative Writing — If you were an incoming President visiting an outgoing President, what questions would you like to ask him? Write at least five questions in your notebook.

Find Out! — What is the first presidential inauguration your parents remember?

Picture This! — Take a photograph or draw a picture of the Bible you would use if you were taking the presidential oath of office.

Student Workbook or Lesson Review — If you are using one of these optional books, complete the assignment for Lesson 22.

Presidents' Home
SWEET HOMES

Each American President must meet the constitutional requirement of being a natural-born citizen. Our first through seventh Presidents and also our ninth were born in America, but they were born before the Declaration of Independence was signed in 1776. The eighth President, Martin Van Buren, was born during the time that the Confederation Congress led America (after the end of the American Revolution, but before the writing of the Constitution in 1787). John Tyler was the first U.S. President to be born after the U.S. Constitution was written. He was born in Virginia two years after that state ratified the Constitution.

Abraham Lincoln was the first President born west of the Appalachian Mountains. Study the map on page 119 to learn where our Presidents were born. Which states have been the birthplace of more than two Presidents? Which states have had the most Presidents born there? How many Presidents were born west of the Mississippi River?

Some Presidents have been born in very humble homes. Andrew Jackson, Abraham Lincoln, Millard Fillmore, James Buchanan, and James Garfield were born in log cabins. Franklin Roosevelt, on the other hand, was born in a large mansion. The birthplaces of Presidents John Adams, John Quincy Adams, Woodrow Wilson, Herbert Hoover, and Richard Nixon are pictured on pages 120-121.

Abraham Lincoln   Andrew Johnson   Ulysses S. Grant

Birth States of America's Presidents

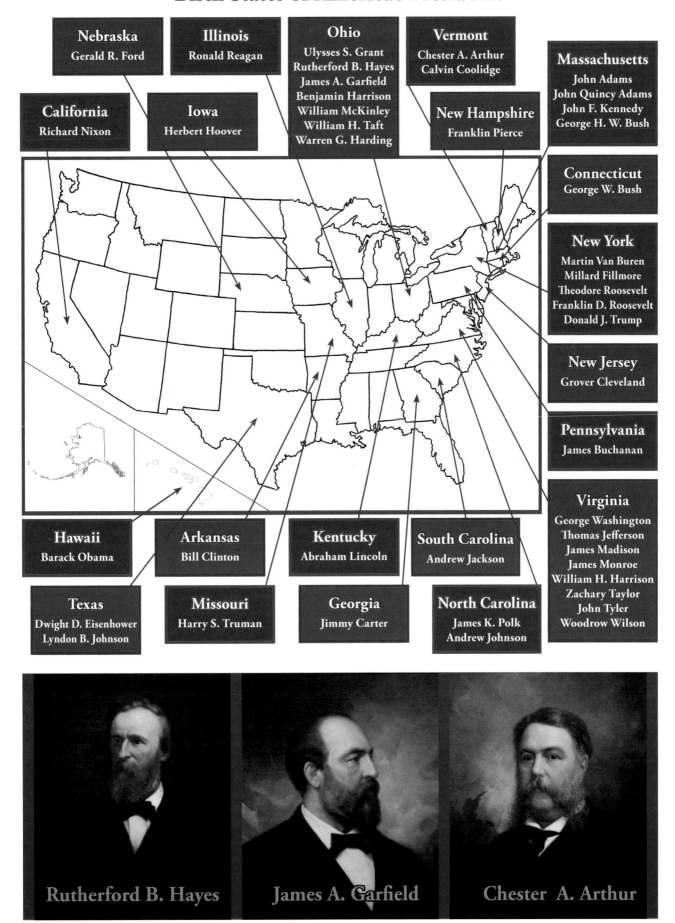

Nebraska
Gerald R. Ford

Illinois
Ronald Reagan

Ohio
Ulysses S. Grant
Rutherford B. Hayes
James A. Garfield
Benjamin Harrison
William McKinley
William H. Taft
Warren G. Harding

Vermont
Chester A. Arthur
Calvin Coolidge

Massachusetts
John Adams
John Quincy Adams
John F. Kennedy
George H. W. Bush

California
Richard Nixon

Iowa
Herbert Hoover

New Hampshire
Franklin Pierce

Connecticut
George W. Bush

New York
Martin Van Buren
Millard Fillmore
Theodore Roosevelt
Franklin D. Roosevelt
Donald J. Trump

New Jersey
Grover Cleveland

Pennsylvania
James Buchanan

Virginia
George Washington
Thomas Jefferson
James Madison
James Monroe
William H. Harrison
Zachary Taylor
John Tyler
Woodrow Wilson

Hawaii
Barack Obama

Arkansas
Bill Clinton

Kentucky
Abraham Lincoln

South Carolina
Andrew Jackson

Texas
Dwight D. Eisenhower
Lyndon B. Johnson

Missouri
Harry S. Truman

Georgia
Jimmy Carter

North Carolina
James K. Polk
Andrew Johnson

Rutherford B. Hayes

James A. Garfield

Chester A. Arthur

Quincy, Massachusetts
Birthplaces of Presidents John Quincy Adams (left) and John Adams (right)

Staunton, Virginia
Birthplace of President Woodrow Wilson with His Car

West Branch, Iowa
Birthplace of President Herbert Hoover

Grover Cleveland   Benjamin Harrison   Grover Cleveland

Yorba Linda, California
*Birthplace of President Richard Nixon with
First Lady Pat Nixon's Rose Garden*

Dixon, Illinois
Boyhood Home of President Ronald Reagan

Home States of U.S. Presidents Who Moved From Their Birth States

California	New Jersey
Herbert Hoover Ronald Reagan	Woodrow Wilson

New York

Chester A. Arthur
Grover Cleveland
Dwight Eisenhower

Illinois

Abraham Lincoln
Ulysses S. Grant
Barack Obama

Ohio

William Henry
Harrison

Indiana

Benjamin Harrison

Louisiana

Zachary Taylor

Tennessee

Andrew Jackson
James K. Polk
Andrew Johnson

Massachusetts

Calvin Coolidge

Texas

George H. W. Bush
George W. Bush

Michigan

Gerald Ford

American citizens often move from one state to another. This has been true for almost half of our Presidents. Look at the chart above. It shows the home states of Presidents who moved away from the state of their birth. Some were pioneers who crossed the Appalachian Mountains when they were young. Zachary Taylor was born in Virginia, but his family moved to the Kentucky frontier when he was a child. Andrew Jackson was born in South Carolina

William McKinley

Theodore Roosevelt

William Howard Taft

and James K. Polk and Andrew Johnson were born in North Carolina, but all made Tennessee their permanent homes. Jackson moved there as a young man to work as a lawyer. James K. Polk's father moved his family across the mountains when the future President was ten years old. Andrew Johnson moved to Tennessee with his mother and step-father when he was a teenager.

Springfield, Illinois
Home of Abraham and Mary Todd Lincoln and Their Family

Lincoln was born on the frontier of Kentucky, but his family moved to Indiana when he was a child. He later settled in Illinois. The home at right is the one he purchased for his wife Mary Todd Lincoln and their family.

After the frontier years, Presidents moved away from their birth state for a variety of reasons. Like Polk and Johnson, some moved as children with their families while others moved for college or to start a career.

Many Presidents' homes have been restored and are open for tourists. Four years after Kennedy's death in 1963, his mother restored his birthplace to the way she remembered it looking in 1917, the year of his birth. The home is now part of the National Park Service. On page 123 are photos of his home and of objects that belonged to Kennedy when he was a child.

Let your father and your mother be glad,
And let her rejoice who gave birth to you.
Proverbs 23:25

Woodrow Wilson   Warren G. Harding   Calvin Coolidge

Brookline, Massachusetts
Birthplace of John Fitzgerald Kennedy

*Kennedy's Childhood Bowl, Spoon, and Napkin Ring at the
John Fitzgerald Kennedy National Historic Site*

Lesson Activities

Literature — Read "Vermont Is a State I Love" in *The Citizen's Handbook*, page 21, and chapter 3 in *Lincoln: A Photobiography*.

Creative Writing — If you became President, what special artifacts from your childhood should be in your birthplace museum? Make a list in your notebook of at least 10 items.

Find Out! — Were any Presidents born in your state or did any Presidents move to your state as their long-term home? Find out the city where they were born and if there is a home open for tourists.

Picture This! — Take a photograph or draw a picture of the first home where you lived.

Student Workbook or Lesson Review — If you are using one of these optional books, complete the assignment for Lesson 23.

Presidential Birthdays
AND FAMILIES

All Presidents have met the minimum age requirement of thirty-five, as set forth in the Constitution. The youngest man to become President was Theodore Roosevelt, who took office when President McKinley was assassinated. Roosevelt was forty-two. The youngest person to be elected was John F. Kennedy, who was elected at age 43. On page 125 is an illustration showing the ages of our Presidents when they took office. Notice that by far most of them were in their fifties.

Presidential Birthdays

Only two American Presidents share a birthday. James K. Polk was born on November 2, 1795 and Warren G. Harding was born on that date seventy years later. November 2 happened to be Election Day in 1920, so Harding was elected on his birthday. Calvin Coolidge was the only President born on the Fourth of July. He was born in 1872. The only President whose birthday is an official Federal holiday is George Washington. Though many people today call it President's Day, the official holiday is still Washington's Birthday.

President Franklin Roosevelt sometimes used his birthday as a way to raise money to help people who had a disease called infantile paralysis or polio. As an adult, Roosevelt himself

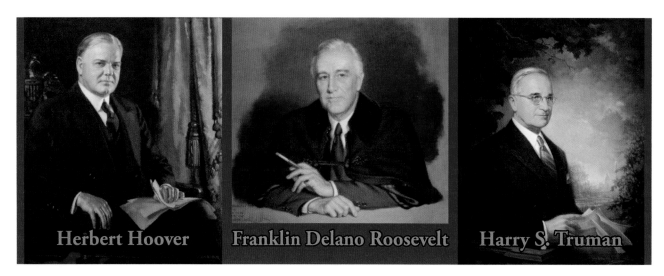

Herbert Hoover   Franklin Delano Roosevelt   Harry S. Truman

had become handicapped as a result of the disease. See the photo at right of a New York Senator and his wife celebrating Roosevelt's birthday on January 29, 1938. Below the photo is a poster inviting people to one of the fundraisers to fight polio.

Senator Royal S. Copeland and his Wife at an Event Celebrating the Birthday of President Franklin Roosevelt

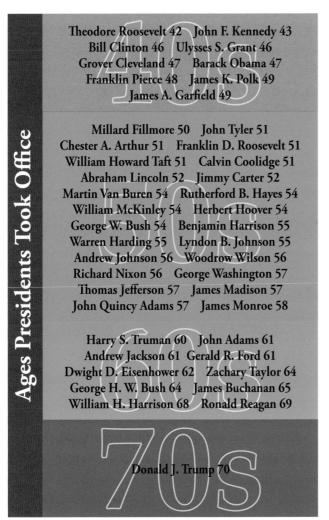

Ages Presidents Took Office

40s

Theodore Roosevelt 42   John F. Kennedy 43
Bill Clinton 46   Ulysses S. Grant 46
Grover Cleveland 47   Barack Obama 47
Franklin Pierce 48   James K. Polk 49
James A. Garfield 49

50s

Millard Fillmore 50   John Tyler 51
Chester A. Arthur 51   Franklin D. Roosevelt 51
William Howard Taft 51   Calvin Coolidge 51
Abraham Lincoln 52   Jimmy Carter 52
Martin Van Buren 54   Rutherford B. Hayes 54
William McKinley 54   Herbert Hoover 54
George W. Bush 54   Benjamin Harrison 55
Warren Harding 55   Lyndon B. Johnson 55
Andrew Johnson 56   Woodrow Wilson 56
Richard Nixon 56   George Washington 57
Thomas Jefferson 57   James Madison 57
John Quincy Adams 57   James Monroe 58

60s

Harry S. Truman 60   John Adams 61
Andrew Jackson 61   Gerald R. Ford 61
Dwight D. Eisenhower 62   Zachary Taylor 64
George H. W. Bush 64   James Buchanan 65
William H. Harrison 68   Ronald Reagan 69

70s

Donald J. Trump 70

The President's BIRTHDAY BALL

FIGHT INFANTILE PARALYSIS

"So we may DANCE AGAIN"

JAN. 30 - 8:30 P.M. - ADMISSION $1.00
PRESIDENT HOTEL
ON THE BOARDWALK
WPA FEDERAL ART PROJECT DI/4

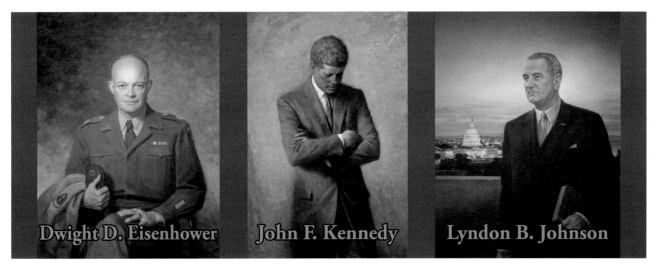

Dwight D. Eisenhower   John F. Kennedy   Lyndon B. Johnson

College Station, Texas
Birthday Party for Former President George H. W. Bush and His Wife Barbara at the George Bush Presidential Library and Museum, June 2011

College Station, Texas
President George H. W. Bush parachutes in tandem onto the grounds of his presidential library in celebration of his 80th birthday.

The birthday of President George H. W. Bush is June 12. His wife Barbara was born on June 8. At left are photos of their 2011 birthday party at the George Bush Presidential Library and Museum in College Station, Texas. President Bush was 87 and Mrs. Bush was 86. President Bush celebrated his 75th, 80th, 85th, and 90th birthdays by parachuting. He said this about his jump for his 80th birthday: "Don't just sit around watching TV, talking to it. Get out there and realize at 80 years old you still got a life. And that is what this was about." After the jump for his 85th, he said: "Just because you're an old guy, you don't have to sit around drooling in the corner. Get out and do something. Get out and enjoy life."

Presidential Relatives

An American President can come from a poor family or a rich one. Our country does not have royalty and it does not have a nobility. As mentioned in Lesson 22, the presidency is not passed down from father to son or within certain families. However, some of the Presidents that American citizens have chosen have been closely related. George H. W. Bush

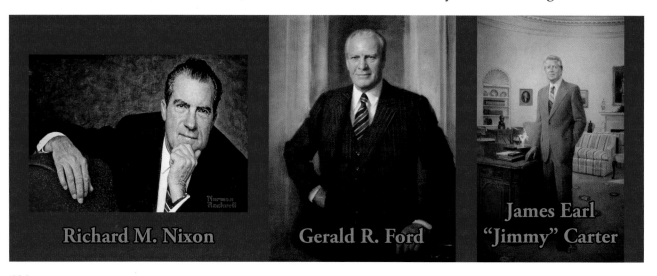

Richard M. Nixon   Gerald R. Ford   James Earl "Jimmy" Carter

was the 41st President; his son George W. Bush was the 43rd. They are pictured at right. John Adams was the second President and his son John Quincy Adams was the sixth. John Adams moved his family from the birthplace of John Quincy Adams, shown on page 120, into "Peacefield," when John Quincy was a young man. From 1788 to 1927, it was the family home of four generations of Adams. "Peacefield," also called the Old House or Peace field, is pictured below.

William Henry Harrison was the ninth President and his grandson Benjamin Harrison was the 23rd. James Madison was the fourth President; his second cousin Zachary Taylor

Arlington, Texas
Former Presidents George W. Bush and George H. W. Bush throw out the first pitch of Game Four of the World Series, 2010.

Quincy, Massachusetts
Adams National Historical Park is home to three Adams Homes: Peacefield and the two Adams birthplaces.

Atlantic Ocean
Former Presidents Bush and Bush attend a reenlistment ceremony aboard the new aircraft carrier USS George H. W. Bush.

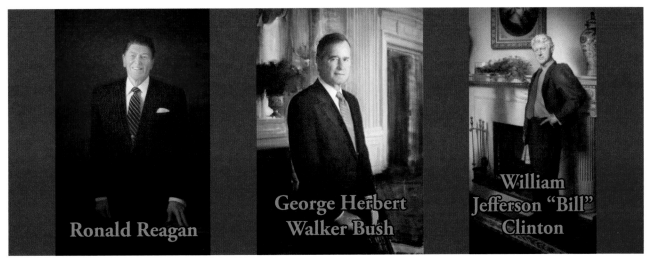

Ronald Reagan

George Herbert Walker Bush

William Jefferson "Bill" Clinton

Presidential Relatives

Fathers and Sons
Adams and Adams
Bush and Bush

Grandfather & Grandson
Harrison and Harrison

Second Cousins
Madison and Taylor

Fifth Cousins
Roosevelt and Roosevelt

was the twelfth. Theodore Roosevelt was the 26th President; his fifth cousin Franklin Delano Roosevelt was the 32nd. In fact, Franklin Roosevelt was distantly related by blood or marriage to ten other Presidents! See list of presidential relatives at left.

Most Presidents have come from large families, and no President has been an only child. Several Presidents and First Ladies have come from families in which the father was a minister. Presidents Chester A. Arthur, Grover Cleveland, and Woodrow Wilson were all the sons of ministers. Presidents John Adams, Millard Fillmore, Franklin Pierce, Benjamin Harrison, and Woodrow Wilson each married the daughter of a minister.

Two White House pets have even been related. George W. Bush's dog Spotty was the offspring of George H. W. Bush's dog Millie! Millie and her puppies are pictured below taking a walk with the President.

Presidential Names

Almost half of our Presidents have shared a first name with another President. See list on page 130. Each pair of father and son Presidents—the Adamses and the Bushes—even shared both first and last names! In fact the two Bushes' names are almost exactly alike: the father is George Herbert Walker Bush and the son is George Walker Bush.

President George H. W. Bush walks with Millie and her puppies on the lawn of the White House.

George W. Bush   Barack Obama   Donald J. Trump

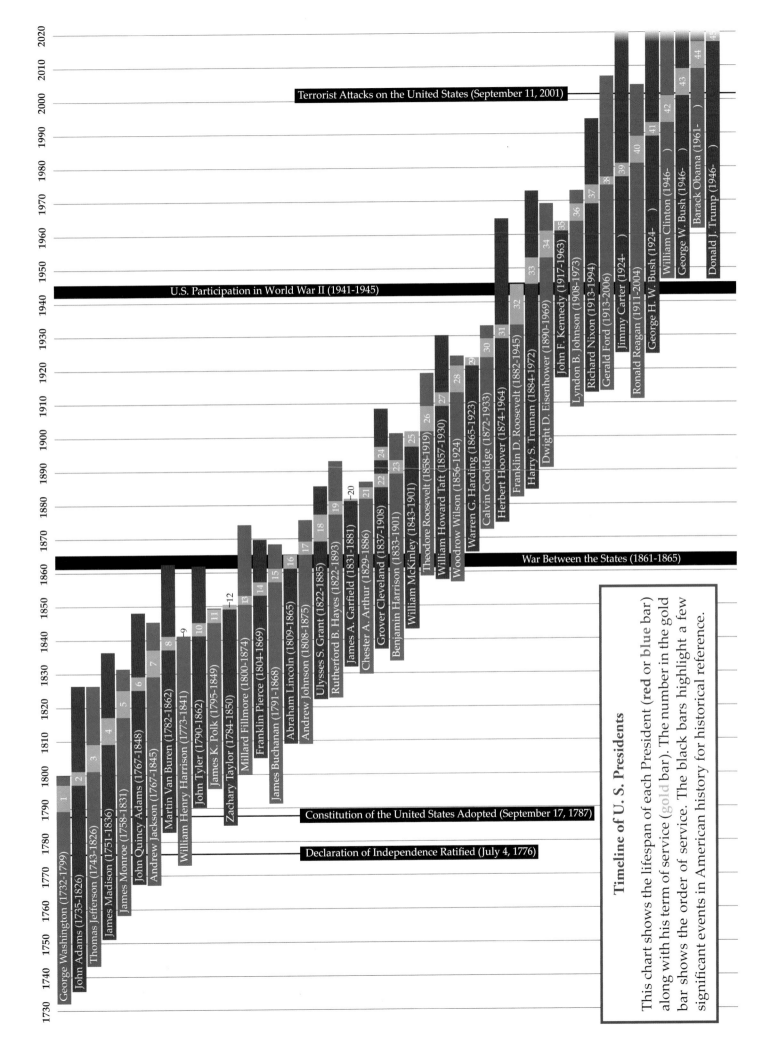

Terrorist Attacks on the United States (September 11, 2001)

U.S. Participation in World War II (1941-1945)

War Between the States (1861-1865)

Constitution of the United States Adopted (September 17, 1787)

Declaration of Independence Ratified (July 4, 1776)

Timeline of U. S. Presidents

This chart shows the lifespan of each President (red or blue bar) along with his term of service (gold bar). The number in the gold bar shows the order of service. The black bars highlight a few significant events in American history for historical reference.

George Washington (1732-1799)
John Adams (1735-1826)
Thomas Jefferson (1743-1826)
James Madison (1751-1836)
James Monroe (1758-1831)
John Quincy Adams (1767-1848)
Andrew Jackson (1767-1845)
Martin Van Buren (1782-1862)
William Henry Harrison (1773-1841)
John Tyler (1790-1862)
James K. Polk (1795-1849)
Zachary Taylor (1784-1850)
Millard Fillmore (1800-1874)
Franklin Pierce (1804-1869)
James Buchanan (1791-1868)
Abraham Lincoln (1809-1865)
Andrew Johnson (1808-1875)
Ulysses S. Grant (1822-1885)
Rutherford B. Hayes (1822-1893)
James A. Garfield (1831-1881)
Chester A. Arthur (1829-1886)
Grover Cleveland (1837-1908)
Benjamin Harrison (1833-1901)
William McKinley (1843-1901)
Theodore Roosevelt (1858-1919)
William Howard Taft (1857-1930)
Woodrow Wilson (1856-1924)
Warren G. Harding (1865-1923)
Calvin Coolidge (1872-1933)
Herbert Hoover (1874-1964)
Franklin D. Roosevelt (1882-1945)
Harry S. Truman (1884-1972)
Dwight D. Eisenhower (1890-1969)
John F. Kennedy (1917-1963)
Lyndon B. Johnson (1908-1973)
Richard Nixon (1913-1994)
Gerald Ford (1913-2006)
Jimmy Carter (1924-   )
Ronald Reagan (1911-2004)
George H. W. Bush (1924-   )
William Clinton (1946-   )
George W. Bush (1946-   )
Barack Obama (1961-   )
Donald J. Trump (1946-   )

More important than what a President's parents named him at birth is the good name he has because of his reputation. A good name helps him get elected and a good name helps him be remembered and honored by his country.

A good name is to be more desired than great wealth,
Favor is better than silver and gold.
Proverbs 22:1

Lesson Activities

Thinking Biblically — Copy Proverbs 22:1 into your notebook, using the version of your choice.

Vocabulary — Find each of these words in a dictionary: minimum, polio, parachute, royalty, nobility. Copy each word into your notebook with the definition that corresponds to the way it is used in this lesson.

Literature — Read "Our Presidents" in *The Citizen's Handbook*, page 22, and chapter 4 in *Lincoln: A Photobiography*.

Find Out! — Look at the Timeline of U.S. Presidents on page 129. Each President's life span is represented by a red or blue bar. The gold portions of the bars show their years of service as President. Answer these questions:

1. Who was the first President born after 1900?
2. Which pairs of Presidents were born in the same year?
3. Which Presidents were born after World War II?
4. What other interesting facts did you learn from the chart?

Picture This! — Design your own "presidential portrait." Dress in a nice outfit and choose a background. You might want your background or an object in the portrait to express something about you. Have someone in your family take your photograph.

Student Workbook or Lesson Review — If you are using one of these optional books, complete the assignment for Lesson 24.

★ Remember to choose an American Holiday to study this week! ★

Presidents Who Share a Name

Andrew
Andrew Jackson
Andrew Johnson

Franklin
Franklin Pierce
Franklin D. Roosevelt

George
George Washington
George Herbert Walker Bush
George Walker Bush

James
James Madison
James Monroe
James K. Polk
James Buchanan
James A. Garfield
James Earl (Jimmy) Carter

John
John Adams
John Quincy Adams
John Calvin Coolidge
John Tyler
John F. Kennedy

Thomas
Thomas Jefferson
Thomas Woodrow Wilson

William
William Henry Harrison
William McKinley
William Howard Taft
William Jefferson (Bill) Clinton

UNIT 6 — VOTING IN AMERICA

BOOKS USED IN UNIT 6

- Lincoln: A Photobiography

- The Citizen's Handbook

- Student Workbook (optional)

- Lesson Review (optional)

Maryland Governor Martin O'Malley votes in the Democratic primary election on March 29, 2012.

What Is VOTING?

When people need to make a decision that affects a group, they often try to find out what the majority wants to do. If a dad wants his family to choose which park to visit, he can simply ask each member of the family which park he or she likes best. A group of boys deciding whether to play a game may use the thumbs up or thumbs down method. At the word, "Go!" boys who want to play the game stick their thumbs up and boys who do not want to play put their thumbs down. Larger groups decide by other voting methods.

People like to be with other people who have similar interests. They often form clubs where they can be with others who enjoy what they enjoy. The top photo on page 133 shows three young women in a social club called Daughters of the House. The club was organized in 1937 and included daughters, daughters-in-law, nieces, and unmarried sisters of members of the U.S. House of Representatives. The group met regularly at the U.S. Capitol, except during World War II, and disbanded in the 1950s. They enjoyed biking, swimming, skating parties, teas, picnics, luncheons, and charitable work. The ladies in the photo are the daughters of Congressmen from Wisconsin and Georgia and the niece of a former Oklahoma Congressman.

Club members have many opportunities for voting. A club president may ask for a show of hands when the club needs to make a simple decision about a certain idea. He will first give the members who approve the idea an opportunity to raise their hands and then do the same for those who disapprove.

At other times, a club president may call for a voice vote. First he will say, "All in favor say, 'Aye.'" Then he will say, "All opposed say, 'Nay.'" Aye means yes and nay means no.

Sometimes a club votes secretly by paper ballot. If, for example, the club is voting on a new president, each member may write the name of his or her preference on a piece of paper and drop it into a container. Then someone counts the paper ballots. The person whose name is on the most ballots becomes the new club president.

Members of some social clubs vote on whether to accept someone as a new member. They may use a voting method involving small white balls and black balls. When the name of a potential member is put before the group, each current member drops either a white ball or a black ball into a container. Dropping a white ball means, "I want this person"; a black ball means "I do not." This is the origin of the term "blackballed."

Washington, D.C.
Members of the Daughters of the House at a Luncheon Meeting, March 13, 1940

Consent of the People

Philosophers in the 1600s and 1700s taught that citizens should be free to participate in their governments. They believed that government leaders received their authority from the consent of the people they led. When America's Founding Fathers set up the United States government, most of them agreed with this idea and wanted citizens to be able to choose leaders who would carry out their wishes. They decided that American citizens would be given the right to vote.

Majority Rule

The concept of doing what most people want to do is one of America's founding principles. It is called majority rule. The main way that we find out what the majority wants is by voting. The opportunity to vote is one of the rights Americans enjoy; it is also one of our responsibilities.

What Decisions Do Citizens Make by Voting?

When we think of voting in America, we usually think of voting for candidates to fill elected offices; but Americans sometimes vote about issues, as well. Examples of issues are questions about whether to allow liquor to be sold in local restaurants and whether it is okay to raise taxes to pay for a new school. A vote about an issue like these is called a referendum.

Our Federal government does not hold referenda (plural of referendum), but some state governments and many local governments do. In addition to major elections, citizens of many towns in New England hold town meetings to make some decisions. Look at the photos on pages 134 and 135 that illustrate one New England town meeting in 1940.

Civics at Woodstock, Vermont

Townspeople gather.

During the time that Franklin Roosevelt was serving as President of the United States, photographers working for the Farm Security Administration traveled around the country taking photographs of average citizens living their daily lives. In March of 1940, photographer Marion Post Wolcott took photos of local citizens who were participating in a town meeting in Woodstock, Vermont. The townspeople were considering whether to allow the sale of alcoholic beverages in Woodstock. They also discussed aid to the poor.

A moderator leads the townspeople in a discussion of important issues.

Town Hall

Townspeople participate in the meeting.

A lifelong Vermonter and one of Woodstock's oldest residents listens to discussion.

Townspeople enjoy visiting while together for the town meeting.

This man is casting a vote.

*When these ladies gave this selectman his ballot,
they told him: "If you vote yes for liquor, you'd
better put it in a box in a different town.
We won't let you stay around here long."*

*The former sheriff guards the ballot boxes
during the town meeting's noon lunch recess.*

*Woodstock town treasurer works in his office
on the day of the town meeting.*

*At night movies are shown in the Woodstock town hall. Notice that
the movie advertised at right stars future President Ronald Reagan.*

Washington, D.C.
Statue of Moses in the Main Reading Room
of the Thomas Jefferson Building of the Library of Congress

Washington, D.C.
Oil Painting of Moses in a Stairway
in the Great Hall of the
U.S. Department of Justice

A Story From Ancient Israel

Though we have no examples of voting in the Bible, we do read about times when people chose some of their own leaders. Moses led the nation of Israel during the years recorded in the books of Exodus, Leviticus, Numbers, and Deuteronomy in the Old Testament. Moses had been personally selected by God to lead His chosen people out of slavery in Egypt. In the first chapter of Deuteronomy, Moses records a speech that he gave to the Israelites on the first day of the eleventh month of the fortieth year after their journey out of Egypt began. In his speech, he talked to them about what God had done for them during the last forty years. He reminded them of something he had told them one day during their journey. That day he had said to them:

> *I am not able to bear the burden of you alone. The Lord your God has multiplied you, and behold, you are this day like the stars of heaven in number. May the Lord, the God of your fathers, increase you a thousand-fold more than you are and bless you, just as He has promised you! How can I alone bear the load and burden of you and your strife? Choose wise and discerning and experienced men from your tribes, and I will appoint them as your heads. You answered me and said, "The thing which you have said to do is good." So I took the heads of your tribes, wise and experienced men, and appointed them heads over you, leaders of thousands and of hundreds, of fifties and of tens, and officers for your tribes. Deuteronomy 1:9-15*

See the statue and painting of Moses in the photographs on page 136. Both are in Federal buildings in Washington, D.C. The cards at right are in the collection of the Library of Congress. Cards like these were once given to children in Sunday School.

As American citizens vote, we should also remember to:

> Choose wise and discerning
> and experienced men . . .
> Deuteronomy 1:13

Lesson Activities

Thinking Biblically — Reflect on the scripture you read in this lesson, Deuteronomy 1:9-15. Write a paragraph in your notebook or discuss with a parent: How can you know if a person is wise and discerning and experienced and would make a good leader?

Sunday School Cards Teaching About the Life of Moses, Published by the American Baptist Publication Society Between 1900 and 1913

Vocabulary — Write a paragraph using all of these words: potential, consent, majority, method, strife. Consult a dictionary if you need help with their definitions.

Literature — Read "The Constitution is Yours" in *The Citizen's Handbook*, page 23, and chapter 5 in *Lincoln: A Photobiography*.

Student Workbook or Lesson Review — If you are using one of these optional books, complete the assignment for Lesson 26.

Women Gain the
RIGHT TO VOTE

In families and clubs and among boys playing together, each individual usually gets the opportunity to vote. However, most countries restrict the right to vote to people who have certain characteristics and who meet certain requirements. The city-state of Athens in ancient Greece gave freeborn males over eighteen years of age the right to vote. Ancient Rome also gave the right to vote to certain citizens.

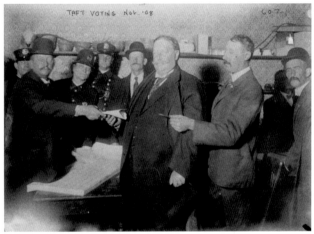

William Howard Taft votes in the November 1908 election in which he won the presidency.

Our government has always placed certain limits on who could vote. Today any citizen of the United States who is eighteen years old or older may vote, unless he or she has been convicted of certain crimes and has not been declared mentally incompetent by a court.

The U.S. Constitution left to the states the responsibility of deciding who could vote. At first, most states required that voters be white, twenty-one years old or older, and owners of property. Some of the first thirteen states banned people from certain religious groups from voting. However, when Vermont became the fourteenth state in 1791, it allowed all white males to vote, regardless of their religious preference and whether or not they owned property. Gradually other states did the same.

Though America was founded on the belief in the equality of all people, many Americans have experienced discrimination because of their race, the nation where they or their ancestors were born, or the color of their skin. Discrimination is treating people unjustly based on certain characteristics. One way citizens were not treated equally involved the right to vote.

However, our form of government allows citizens to work together to make changes. Through the years, groups of Americans who were concerned about discrimination in voting have worked together to bring suffrage to various groups who did not already have that right. The word suffrage means "the right to vote." It comes from the Latin word *suffragium*.

Look at the photo on page 138. When William Howard Taft voted in the November 8, 1908 election in which he won the presidency of the United States, many American women and many minorities could not vote. Reformers worked for many years to obtain suffrage for more American citizens. Eventually the United States Congress and a majority of state legislatures passed amendments to the Constitution, that gave more Americans the right to vote. No longer were states allowed to make all the decisions on who could vote and who could not.

Women Lose the Right to Vote

Before the American Revolution, members of the Quaker religion believed that women should have the right to vote. Patriotic writer Thomas Paine thought so, too. Before the thirteen original colonies declared their independence from England, several colonies allowed women to vote. However, during the American Revolution, one by one states began taking away their right to vote. By the time the U.S. Constitution was ratified, only New Jersey allowed women to vote. They allowed women who owned property to vote, as long as the women were not married. In 1807 New Jersey stopped allowing even those women to vote.

The Women's Suffrage Movement

In America citizens can work to change laws they believe to be unfair. In the early 1800s, citizens who believed in women's suffrage began working to gain women the right to vote. Women in this movement were called suffragettes. Some famous suffragettes were Lucretia Coffin Mott, Elizabeth Cady Stanton, and Susan B. Anthony. The statue at right is in the U.S. Capitol. Famous men who supported

Lucretia Mott, Elizabeth Cady Stanton, and Susan B. Anthony

them included author Ralph Waldo Emerson and preacher Henry Ward Beecher. Beecher was a brother of Harriet Beecher Stowe, who wrote *Uncle Tom's Cabin*. American citizens were divided in their thinking on this issue.

Many who believed that women should be able to vote lived in the West. When Wyoming organized as a territory in 1869, it gave the approximately 1,000 women who lived there the right to vote. One by one several western states and territories began giving suffrage to women. In 1913 Illinois became the first state east of the Mississippi River to give women suffrage (since New Jersey had taken away that right in 1807). Soon other states followed.

New York City, New York
Suffragettes march in a parade, with a banner which reads, "President Wilson Favors Votes for Women," c. 1916.

Cleveland, Ohio
Supporters of women's suffrage stand outside a Woman Suffrage Headquarters in Ohio. The "Amendment No. 23" in the sign refers to an amendment to the Ohio state constitution and not to the U.S. Constitution.

The chart below tells when individual states and territories gave women the right to vote. The photos at left show activities in support of women's suffrage.

One supporter of women's right to vote was the great-great-grandson of Founding Father Roger Sherman (see pages 67-69). Read about him below.

Votes for Women!

1869 — **Wyoming Territory**
1870 — **Utah Territory**
1893 — **Colorado**
1896 — **Utah, Idaho**
1910 — **Washington**
1911 — **California**
1912 — **Oregon, Kansas, Arizona**
1913 — **Illinois, Alaska Territory**
1914 — **Nevada, Montana**
1917 — **Arkansas, Nebraska, New York, North Dakota, Rhode Island**
1918 — **Michigan, Oklahoma, South Dakota, Texas**
1919 — **Indiana, Iowa, Maine, Minnesota, Missouri, Ohio, Tennessee, Wisconsin**

Suffragist Roger Sherman Hoar

Roger Sherman Hoar was the great-great-grandson of Founding Father Roger Sherman. Hoar was twenty-eight years old when the *New York Times* newspaper did an article on him in 1910. He had just become the youngest person ever to be elected to the Massachusetts state legislature. Hoar described himself as a "militant suffragist." He believed that politics would be less corrupt if women were voters.

The article was entitled, "The Busiest Man of His Age in the World," and described Hoar's accomplishments. At the time the article was written, he had already invented a waterproof blanket. At twenty-eight years of age, he was a Harvard law student, a professional cartoonist, and secretary of the town committee of Concord, Massachusetts. He played trumpet in a Harvard musical group and was writing a law book in which he wanted to prove that the Bible was valuable as a textbook for lawyers.

The Nineteenth Amendment

In May of 1919 the United States Congress passed a Constitutional amendment making it illegal for any state to restrict voting rights based on a person's sex. Thirty-six state legislatures had to ratify this amendment before it could become part of the Constitution. In the photo at right, Governor Frederick Gardner of Missouri signs the resolution that made Missouri the eleventh state to ratify it.

Jefferson City, Missouri
Governor Frederick Gardner of Missouri signs the resolution, making Missouri the eleventh state to ratify the Nineteenth Amendment.

The Power of One Vote

Thirty-five states had approved the amendment when the Tennessee legislature considered it in August of 1920. Citizens for the amendment and citizens who opposed it gathered at the state capitol in Nashville. See photos at right.

The controversy came to be called the "War of the Roses," because legislators who favored the amendment wore yellow roses on their lapels and those who opposed it wore red ones. On August 18, 1920, the Tennessee legislature voted on whether to ratify the amendment. In the first two roll call votes that day, the legislature was tied with 48 votes for the amendment and 48 against it.

Harry Burn, a 24-year-old state representative, voted nay the first two times. However, in his pocket was a note from his widowed mother. It read:

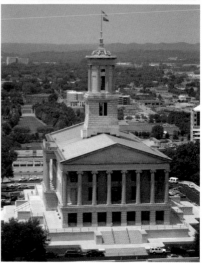

Nashville, Tennessee
State Capitol, 1934 and 2011

> Dear Son:
>
> Hurrah, and vote for suffrage! Don't keep them in doubt. I notice some of the speeches against. They were bitter. I have been watching to see how you stood, but have not noticed anything yet.
>
> Don't forget to be a good boy and help Mrs. Catt put the "rat" in ratification.
>
> Your Mother.

When legislators voted the third time, Burn voted aye and the amendment passed by just one vote. The Governor of Tennessee signed it on August 24. The Nineteenth Amendment was officially added to the U.S. Constitution on August 26, 1920.

Leslie's Illustrated Newspaper, *1920*

Chicago, Illinois
*Original Board of Directors, League of Women Voters
Chicago Convention, February 1920*

Look at the cover of *Leslie's Illustrated Newspaper* dated October 2, 1920, just weeks after the passage of the Nineteenth Amendment. The American symbol Columbia is urging voters to vote for the good of the nation. Notice the cover story, "How I Felt When I Was Nominated," by Republican presidential candidate Senator Warren G. Harding and Democratic candidate Governor James M. Cox. Harding beat Cox in the election that November.

League of Women Voters

Suffragette Carrie Chapman Catt founded the League of Women Voters in Chicago just six months before the Nineteenth Amendment was passed (Mrs. Catt, pictured at lower left, is the woman referred to in Mrs. Burn's note to her son). The League's purpose was to help the twenty million new American women voters with their new responsibility. In the photos on page 143, members of the Mississippi League of Women Voters celebrate the ninetieth anniversary of the organization. The League continues to encourage citizens to be active in their communities, states, and nation.

While young Harry Burn was serving in the Tennessee legislature in 1920, many people tried to influence him. At an important moment, he decided to honor his mother, as wise Solomon had encouraged in Proverbs.

Hear, my son, your father's instruction and do not forsake your mother's teaching.

Proverbs 1:8

Lesson Activities

Vocabulary — In your notebook, write each of these words and the letter of the definition that goes with each word: incompetent, discrimination, suffrage, favor, influence.

a. give support to

b. the right to vote

c. affect the beliefs or behavior of someone

d. not able to function properly; inadequate

e. unjust treatment based on race, sex, or any other characteristic

Literature — Read "Women Here Rejoice Over Right to Vote" in *The Citizen's Handbook*, pages 24-25, and chapter 6 in *Lincoln: A Photobiography.*

Creative Writing — Imagine that you have a relative serving as a state or U.S. Representative. Write a letter in your notebook expressing your hopes of how they will vote on a certain issue.

Find Out! — On average do more men or women vote in presidential elections?

Picture This! — Draw a picture of a suffragette casting her first vote.

Student Workbook or Lesson Review — If you are using one of these optional books, complete the assignment for Lesson 27.

Jackson, Mississippi
Members of the Mississippi League of Women Voters celebrate the ninetieth anniversary of the organization at the Mississippi State Capitol, 2010.

Minorities Gain the
RIGHT TO VOTE

Throughout much of the history of the United States, most citizens were white. Therefore, white citizens were in the majority and groups of people whose skin was darker were in the minority. For many years, minorities did not have the same voting rights as whites.

The first minority group to gain the right to vote were African Americans. After the Civil War, whites and African Americans had to learn how to live in a new society where all African Americans were free. As former slave Houston Hartsfield Holloway wrote: "For we colored people did not know how to be free and the white people did not know how to have a free colored person about them."

Former slaves had no homes, no land, and no ways of supporting themselves and their families. Churches, missionary groups, and teachers, both black and white, worked hard to educate former slaves to help them learn how to live their lives in their new free state.

The U.S. Congress passed laws to help whites and blacks live together in a new society where there was no slavery. It passed the Thirteenth Amendment in January 1865, which outlawed slavery in the United States. The required number of states ratified it that December. In 1866 Congress passed the Fourteenth Amendment, which included five sections, some of which punished the former Confederate states. However, Section 1 stated that every person born in the United States was a U.S. citizen. Thus former slaves were given citizenship. The Fourteenth Amendment was ratified in 1868.

In February of 1869, Congress passed the Fifteenth Amendment. It was ratified the following February. The Fifteenth Amendment states that voting could not be denied to people because of their race, the color of their skin, or their "former condition of servitude" (meaning that a person could not be kept from voting because he had once been a slave).

On page 145 is the cover of the November 16, 1867, issue of *Harper's Weekly*. In Alfred R. Waud's illustration entitled "The First Vote," four men line up to cast their first vote: a poor laborer, a businessman, and a Union soldier. The man at back is perhaps a farmer. It illustrates ways that African Americans became involved in the American economy.

HARPER'S WEEKLY.
A JOURNAL OF CIVILIZATION.

VOL. XI.—No. 568.] NEW YORK, SATURDAY, NOVEMBER 16, 1867. [SINGLE COPIES TEN CENTS.
[$4.00 PER YEAR IN ADVANCE.

Entered according to Act of Congress, in the Year 1867, by Harper & Brothers, in the Clerk's Office of the District Court for the Southern District of New York.

"THE FIRST VOTE."—Drawn by A. R. Waud.—[See next Page.]

State and local officials in many places tried to find ways to keep African Americans from voting. They passed laws that required citizens to take a literacy test before they could vote. Literacy is the ability to read. Literacy tests were given to make sure a person could read. The drawing at right was published on January 18, 1879, in *Harper's Weekly*. It illustrates the problem of literacy tests which already existed by 1879, just ten years after the passage of the Fifteenth Amendment. In the drawing Uncle Sam is writing this: "Eddikashun qualifukashun. The Black man orter be eddikated afore he kin vote with us Wites, signed Mr. Solid South." The spelling and grammar were meant to ridicule uneducated Southern whites. Here is a translation: "Education qualification. The black man ought to be educated before he can vote with us whites, signed Mr. Solid South."

Cartoon by Thomas Nast in Harper's Weekly *Newspaper, January 18, 1879*

In some places, officials passed laws that required voters to pay a poll tax. A poll is a place where people vote and a poll tax was a fee that had to be paid before voting.

The literacy and poll tax laws were often enforced for blacks but not for whites. Many poor and illiterate whites (illiterate means unable to read) were allowed to vote anyway, even if they could not pass the literacy test or pay the poll tax. Officials in some places passed "grandfather clauses," which stated that a poor and illiterate person could vote if his grandfather could vote when he was alive. Since the grandfathers of most African Americans living in these places had not been allowed to vote, their grandchildren could not vote either.

During the 1950s and 1960s, Americans concerned about civil rights for all their fellow Americans worked for better laws and greater equality for every citizen. They helped to pass the Twenty-fourth Amendment, which made poll taxes illegal. It was ratified in 1964. The next year Congress passed the Voting Rights Act of 1965. It outlawed literacy tests and other forms of discrimination based on race, color, and language.

Voting Rights for Native Americans

Though the Fifteenth Amendment granted all U.S. citizens the right to vote regardless of race, Native Americans were kept from voting in many places. In the cartoon by Thomas Nast at right, a policeman tells a Native American to "move on" away from the polls where immigrants from foreign countries are voting. In 1924 Congress passed the Indian Citizen Act. President Calvin Coolidge signed it on June 2. The Act stated plainly and specifically that all Native Americans born in the United States were citizens. Calvin Coolidge's great-grandmother was part Native American. Coolidge was sympathetic to the hardships Native Americans faced. He was made an honorary member of the Hopi tribe in 1924 and a Sioux Chief in 1927. In the photo at right, he meets with the Indian Republican Club of Sioux Indians from the Rosebud Reservation in South Dakota.

Even after the Indian Citizen Act, many states continued to keep Native Americans from voting. At one time, North Dakota would only allow a Native American to vote if he were "civilized" and had stopped being a part of his tribe. In Utah officials once said that Native Americans were not residents of the state but of their own reservations. Native Americans in New Mexico, Washington, Maine, Mississippi, and Idaho had to pay a tax before they could vote. In 1962 New Mexico became the last state to give full voting rights to Native Americans.

Cartoon by Thomas Nast in Harper's Weekly *Newspaper, April 22, 1871*
The caption reads: "Move on!" Has the Native American no rights that the naturalized American is bound to respect?

Washington, D.C.
Indian Republican Club of Sioux Indians from the Rosebud Reservation meets with President Calvin Coolidge on the White House lawn in 1925. Coolidge is fifth from right on the front row.

Fort Rucker, Alabama
Dakota tribesman and former U.S. Army soldier Richard Greybull, salutes the American flag at a Native American Heritage Celebration in 2010.

Voting Rights for Asian Immigrants and Their Descendants

Millions of immigrants have come to America because of its great freedoms and opportunities. However, like many countries of the world, the U.S. has limited how many people can come. White Americans have often been reluctant to welcome non-white immigrants.

Earlier in our history, many whites were prejudiced toward Asians and did not

Puck *Magazine, March 12, 1879*

want them to move here. The Naturalization Act of 1790 stated that only free white people could become citizens of the United States. When many Chinese immigrated to the U.S. during the mid-1800s, some whites believed that they kept whites from getting jobs. In 1882 the U.S. Congress passed the Chinese Exclusion Act. It said that Chinese people could not move to the United States and that those already here could not become U.S. citizens. Just three years before, *Puck* magazine published the above cartoon that suggested that if the Chinese voted they would give many votes to Democratic candidates.

Congress passed laws that kept other Asians from immigrating here, too. For many years, even children born in America to Chinese immigrants could not become citizens. California passed a law stating that "no native of China" could vote. In 1926 the U.S. Supreme Court overturned that law. In 1943, the U.S. Congress passed the Magnuson Act. It allowed Chinese people to immigrate to America and gave Chinese immigrants the right to become citizens. After they became citizens, they could vote.

Voting Rights for Non-English Speakers

Some minorities find voting difficult, because they do not speak and read English very well. In 1975 Congress passed another Voting Rights Act. Places with a large number of Native American, Native Alaskan, or Hispanic citizens must provide printed election material and voting assistance in the language of their particular minorities.

What language people speak is controversial in America today. In the past, immigrants to America accepted the fact that they would need to learn English to get along well in their new land. Many Americans believe that people who want to live in the United States should learn English instead of demanding that our local, state, and Federal governments provide information and government services in their native languages. However, others believe that special consideration should be given so that non-English speakers find it easier to participate in America's democracy.

The Twenty-Sixth Amendment Lowers the Voting Age to Eighteen

In the 1960s many American men younger than age twenty-one were being drafted into the military and required to fight in the Vietnam War. Many thought it was unfair to make a person fight when he was not allowed to vote. In 1971 the Twenty-sixth Amendment lowered the minimum voting age to eighteen for all Americans voting in Federal elections.

It is sad that our country with its foundations on Biblical principles has not always regarded others with the respect that they deserve. We should all remember:

Opening his mouth, Peter said:

"I most certainly understand now that God is not one to show partiality,

but in every nation the man who fears Him and does what is right is welcome to Him.

Acts 10:34-35

Lesson Activities

Thinking Biblically — Copy Acts 10:34-35 into your notebook, using the version of your choice.

Creative Writing — The debate about who should be allowed to vote continues. Some people believe that all adults living in the U.S. should be allowed to vote whether they are citizens or not. Some believe voting age should be lowered to sixteen. In your notebook, write two or three paragraphs about what you believe about these issues.

Literature — Read "We Are Not Ready for That in Mississippi" in *The Citizen's Handbook*, pages 26-28.

Find Out! — Find out the minimum voting age in two other countries.

Student Workbook or Lesson Review — If you are using one of these optional books, complete the assignment for Lesson 28.

Rules About VOTING

Voters can vote in local, state, and Federal elections. All Federal elections are held in even-numbered years on the first Tuesday in November that falls after a Monday. In some states voters also choose state and local officials that day. However, various state and local elections are held in various months in both even- and odd-numbered years.

U.S. Citizens Can Vote in Federal Elections

A citizen of the United States can vote for a President and his vice presidential running mate, two U.S. Senators who will represent his home state, and one member of the U.S. House of Representatives who will represent his congressional district. Pictured at right are U.S. Representative Michael McCaul from Texas and U.S. Senator Jerry Moran from Kansas.

The United States is divided into 435 congressional districts. According to the Constitution, each district must have approximately the same number of people. Since people live close together in some places and far apart in others, congressional districts vary greatly in size.

The map on page 151 shows the congressional districts of the state of Indiana during the years 2011-2020. The congressional districts are numbered 1 through 9 and shown in different colors. The smaller areas shown

Kabul, Afghanistan
U.S. Representative Michael McCaul visits U.S. troops, November 2011. McCaul was elected from Texas' 10th congressional district and was appointed a member of the House Committee on Homeland Security.

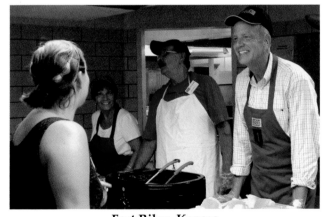

Fort Riley, Kansas
U.S. Senator Jerry Moran (right) serves food at a dinner for military families at Fort Riley in 2009. Senator Moran served in the U.S. House of Representatives from Kansas' 1st congressional district for fourteen years before he was elected to the U.S. Senate in 2010. As Senator he continued his practice of returning to Kansas each weekend.

Indiana Counties and Its Nine U.S. Congressional Districts
2011-2020

Source: National Atlas of the United States of America, United States Department of the Interior

on the map are counties. Find District 7, which includes the large city of Indianapolis. Notice that it is very small geographically. District 9 is much larger because it is a farming area.

Of course, states with small numbers of citizens have fewer congressional districts than states with large populations. The populations of Alaska, Delaware, Montana, North Dakota, South Dakota, Vermont, and Wyoming were so small that they each had only one congressional district in 2011-2020. See map of Wyoming below. By contrast, the population of California was so large that it had fifty-three districts.

Wyoming Counties and Its One U.S. Congressional District 2011-2020

Source: National Atlas of the United States of America, United States Department of the Interior

The Federal government takes a census every ten years to count the people living in the United States. If a state loses a certain number of people, its number of congressional districts is reduced and, if it gains enough people, the number is increased. However, the total number of districts remains at 435. When the number of districts within a state changes, the shape of one or more remaining districts must be redrawn. This is called redistricting and is the responsibility of the state's legislature.

U.S. Citizens Can Vote in State Elections

Citizens of each of the fifty states can vote for a Governor and for other statewide officials in their own state. If a voter is a citizen of Montana, he can vote for the Governor and other state officials for Montana, but he can't vote for the Governor or state officials of Florida, Nevada, or any other state.

Just as each state is divided into U.S. congressional districts, it is also divided into districts for its own state legislature. States are divided into state senate districts and into smaller state house of representative (sometimes called state assembly) districts. The one exception is Nebraska, which has only a state senate. At right is a photo of Colorado State Senator Scott Renfroe receiving the 2011 Statesman of the Year Award from Christian Home Educators of Colorado.

Denver, Colorado
Colorado State Senator Scott Renfroe receives award from homeschoolers.

The state senate and state house of representatives districts for the State of Montana are shown on the map below. Each senate district is outlined and labeled in pink. In Montana, each senate district is divided into two house of representatives districts. On the map, house districts are outlined and labeled in blue. A citizen votes for a state senator to represent him in the state senate and for a representative to represent him in the state house of representatives.

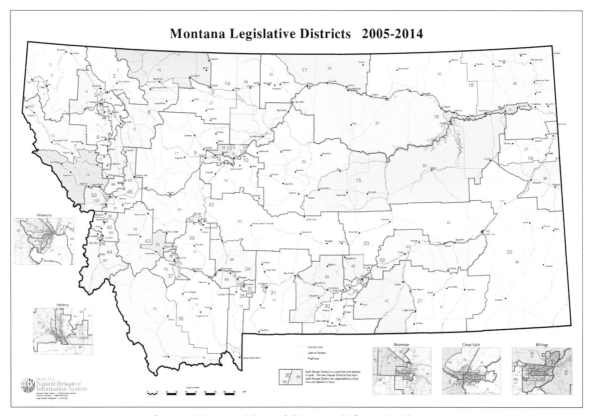

Source: Montana Natural Resource Information Systems

Examples of
Local Elected Officials

Charter Township of
West Bloomfield, Michigan

Clerk
Supervisor
Treasurer
Trustees

Town of Owl's Head, Maine

Assessors
Harbor Master
Assistant Harbor Master
Overseers of the Poor
Road Commissioner
Regional School Unit #13 Director
Selectmen
Town Council Members

City of Oakland, California

City Attorney
City Auditor
Mayor

Salt Lake County, Utah

Assessor
Auditor
Clerk
Council Members
District Attorney
Mayor
Recorder
Sheriff
Surveyor
Treasurer

(Officials Listed in Alphabetical Order)

U.S. Citizens Can
Vote in Local Elections

How local governments are organized varies from state to state. Some states have townships and others do not. County governments have more responsibilities in some states than in others. Governments of large cities are different from those in small towns. At left are examples of local elected officials in various places.

Voters must live within the boundaries of a local government in order to vote for its officials. For example, all of the voters in a county can vote for its county officials. However, voters who live outside the city limits of the county's municipalities cannot vote in city elections (a municipality is another word for a town or a city). Just as states are divided into U.S. congressional districts and state legislative districts, many cities are divided into wards and counties into districts. Sometimes the voters in each ward or district choose officials to represent them on a city or county council. These operate in a similar way to the U.S. Congress and state legislatures.

New Orleans, Louisiana
Voters line up to vote at the designated polling place for New Orleans Ward 10, Precinct 11, 2008.

Where Do Voters Vote?

Counties, cities, towns, and wards are divided into voting precincts. Voters living within a precinct vote at a certain place, called a polling place or poll. The voters in the photo on page 154 are lined up to vote at their polling place.

Fullerton, California
Attendees at a political rally are encouraged to register to vote.

Voter Registration

When a person goes to the polls to vote in an election, voting officials must make sure that the person is eligible to vote. They must be certain that the person votes only one time and that the voter is eligible to vote in that location. One way to do this is to require that voters register (or sign up) with a local official who is responsible for registering voters.

Fairfax, Virginia
George Mason University students are encouraged to register to vote.

Registration policies vary from state to state. Many states try to make voter registration easy by putting applications in public libraries, county election offices, post offices, schools, and other government locations. In the photos above, citizens are being encouraged to register to

vote. Some states allow a citizen to register to vote when he or she obtains a driver's license. Some states require voters to register as many as 30 days before an election, but some allow voters to register and vote on Election Day.

The first state to require its citizens to register was Massachusetts in 1800. After the Civil War, many states began to register voters. The main reason for the change was to make elections more honest. At the time, some people came to the polls and voted more than one time and others cast more than one ballot. Sometimes people even voted under the names of people who had died! Registration is an attempt to keep this dishonesty from happening. On the cover of an edition of *Frank Leslie's Illustrated Newspaper* from 1882, Chester A. Arthur registers to vote.

Chester A. Arthur registering to vote, 1882.

In most places, a voter registers just one time and does not have to do so again unless he or she has experienced a life change, like changing names (as when a woman gets married) or changing addresses. However, some places, especially cities, require voters to reregister periodically, so that their list of voters stays accurate and up-to-date. The Federal government requires each state to have a website where voters can be sure that they are registered to vote, can know where they are registered, and can find the location of their polling place.

Some states require that voters register as Democrats, Republicans, Independents, or members of some other political party. Lesson 31 teaches about political parties. In some states, voters receive a voter registration card. Examine the card below. Imaginary voter John M. Doe lives at 618 Memory Lane which is in Precinct 7 of Ward 2 in Anytown, which is in Lincoln County in the State of Maryland. He registered to vote two days after he turned eighteen. Mr. Doe votes at Chester Arthur School.

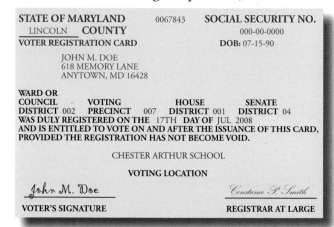

Though not for the purpose of voting, the government where Jesus' earthly parents lived once required them to register.

Joseph also went up from Galilee, from the city of Nazareth, to Judea, to the city of David which is called Bethlehem, because he was of the house and family of David, in order to register along with Mary, who was engaged to him, and was with child.

Luke 2:4-5

Lesson Activities

Vocabulary — In your notebook, write your own definition for each of these words: statesman, municipality, ward, eligible, ballot. Look in the lesson for clues for the meaning of the words. When you are finished writing your definitions, look in a dictionary for comparison.

Literature — Read "To Do Well and Wisely with the Ballot" in *The Citizen's Handbook*, page 29, and chapter 7, "A Lincoln Sampler," and "In Lincoln's Footsteps" in *Lincoln: A Photobiography*.

Find Out! — Are your parents and any siblings age 18 or over registered to vote? How, where, and when did they register?

Picture This! — Take a photograph or draw a picture of the polling place where your family members who are over 18 can vote.

Student Workbook or Lesson Review — If you are using one of these optional books, complete the assignment for Lesson 29.

★ Remember to choose an American Holiday to study this week! ★

UNIT 7 — POLITICAL PARTIES AND THEIR CANDIDATES

BOOKS USED IN UNIT 7

- The Citizen's Handbook

- Student Workbook (optional)

- Lesson Review (optional)

Georgia, Indiana, Louisiana, North Carolina, Oregon, and Texas delegates gather at the 2008 Republican National Convention in St. Paul, Minnesota.

American
POLITICAL PARTIES

Haley Barbour, Former Governor of Mississippi and Former Chairman of the Republican National Committee (right) at an Annual Mississippi Central Park Picnic in New York City

In many countries, including the United States, people have joined together to form political parties. The word political comes from politics, which means activities involved in the government of a country or area. A political party is an organization which seeks to encourage voters to support its ideas about government and to elect its candidates.

Founding Father Views

George Washington and other Founding Fathers did not like political parties. Washington invited men of various opinions to work in his administration. In politics the word administration means the people who work with a government official like a President or a Governor. When Washington gave his Farewell Address after his second four-year term as President, he said that a party spirit:

> ". . . serves always to distract the public councils and enfeeble the public administration. It agitates the community with ill-founded jealousies and false alarms; kindles the animosity of one part against another; foments occasionally riot and insurrection."

In *Federalist* No. 10, James Madison wrote that "the public good is disregarded in the conflicts of rival parties."

Government leaders after Washington ignored his advice and began to form factions that became political parties.

158

One-, Two-, and Multi-Party Countries

Most countries in Western Europe have multi-party systems, with between three and six major political parties. When no party wins a majority in a multi-party system, two or more parties often join together. Together they form a coalition government.

The United States has usually had a two-party system, although the parties have changed. In a two-party system, government power goes back and forth between political parties depending on which one wins the most elected offices in the most recent election.

Some governments have only one party. China is an example. One-party systems give citizens the least opportunity for changing their government.

Two Parties — Federalists and Democratic-Republicans

The first major political parties in the United States were Federalists, who wanted the United States to have a strong Federal government, and the Democratic-Republicans, who wanted state governments to be strong. Two early Federalist leaders were the first Secretary of the Treasury Alexander Hamilton and second President John Adams. The Federalist Party was popular with business leaders. For many years, Federalists elected many state leaders, but John Adams was our only Federalist President. In relations with foreign governments, the Federalists favored Great Britain.

Our third and fourth Presidents, Thomas Jefferson and James Madison, were early Democratic-Republican leaders. They wanted the Federal government to be small and they did not believe that it should have any power over the economy. Economy means the wealth and resources (like timber, metals that can be mined, crops grown, etc.) of a country or area. Economies have to do with things that can be made to sell or buy. In relations with foreign governments, the Democratic-Republican Party favored France. This party was the most powerful party for about forty years, beginning around 1800. At right is a list of Federalist and Democratic-Republican Presidents.

Political Parties of Presidents 1789-1829

Black-No Party
Purple - Federalist
Teal - Democratic-Republicans

George Washington
John Adams
Thomas Jefferson
James Madison
James Monroe
John Quincy Adams

Two Parties — Whigs and Democrats

During the presidential campaign of 1828, the Democratic-Republicans split into two parties. President Andrew Jackson was the leader of those who became the Democrats. The members of the party that did not follow him organized the National Republican Party, which lasted only a short time. The main difference between the two parties involved beliefs in how the Federal government should be involved in the economy.

In 1834 former members of the National Republican Party, plus other people opposed to Andrew Jackson, formed a new party called Whigs. Daniel Webster and Henry Clay were major leaders of the Whigs. Webster served as a Representative from New Hampshire, a Senator from Massachusetts, and Secretary of State under three Presidents. Clay served as a Representative and a Senator from Kentucky and as Secretary of State under President John Quincy Adams.

The Whigs and Democrats were the two main political parties in the U.S. for several years. At right is a chart showing Democrat and Whig Presidents from 1829 through 1861.

**Political Parties
of Presidents
1829-1861**

Blue-Democrat
Gold - Whig

Andrew Jackson
Martin Van Buren
William Henry Harrison
John Tyler
James K. Polk
Zachary Taylor
Millard Fillmore
Franklin Pierce
James Buchanan

Two Parties — Democrats and Republicans

The Democrats and Republicans have been the two major political parties in the United States since the mid-1850s. Since the election of Franklin Pierce in 1852, every U.S. President has been either a Democrat or a Republican. See chart on page 161. Cartoonist Thomas Nast, who drew illustrations for the *Harper's Weekly* newspaper, was the first person to symbolize Democrats with a drawing of a donkey and Republicans with a drawing of an elephant.

Mrs. Bess Truman (second from left) meets with Democratic women. She was the wife of President Harry Truman.

A Short History of the Democrats. The father of the American Democratic Party is Andrew Jackson. From the presidency of Jackson to the end of the 1800s, Democrats stood for a small Federal government. They believed that the Federal government should stay out of state business and that states should stay out of the business of local governments.

Because of their belief in states' rights, the Democratic Party supported the spread of slavery into western states. This caused many Democrats from northern states to leave and join the Republican Party before the start of the Civil War.

Look at the chart at right. Notice that only two Democrats, Cleveland and Wilson, were elected President between the end of the Civil War and the beginning of the Great Depression (Andrew Johnson was not elected). After the War, most voters in northern states were Republicans and most voters in the South were Democrats. Northern states had many more people than southern states.

When Franklin Roosevelt ran as a Democrat against Republican President Herbert Hoover in 1929, he promised Americans a "New Deal." The New Deal was a major change in the way Democrats had believed in the past. Under the leadership of Roosevelt, they began to support a larger Federal government. They also supported government involvement in the economy and in welfare programs. Welfare programs are government programs to help people in need. Before the New Deal, most Americans believed that helping people in need was the responsibility of individuals, families, churches, and volunteer organizations and not the responsibility of government.

A Short History of the Republicans. Northern Democrats, Whigs, and members of the smaller Know-Nothing (also called American) Party joined together to form the Republican Party in the 1850s. A meeting held in a schoolhouse in Ripon, Wisconsin, in 1854 is considered to be the first meeting of the Republican Party. It is pictured at right.

The nickname of the Republican Party is the G.O.P. The letters are usually seen as standing for "grand old party," but it originally meant "gallant old party."

Political Parties of Presidents 1861-2013
Blue-Democrat Red - Republican
Abraham Lincoln
Andrew Johnson
Ulysses S. Grant
Rutherford B. Hayes
James A. Garfield
Chester A. Arthur
Grover Cleveland
Benjamin Harrison
Grover Cleveland
William McKinley
Theodore Roosevelt
William Howard Taft
Woodrow Wilson
Warren G. Harding
Calvin Coolidge
Herbert Hoover
Franklin Delano Roosevelt
Harry S. Truman
Dwight D. Eisenhower
John F. Kennedy
Lyndon B. Johnson
Richard M. Nixon
Gerald R. Ford
Jimmy Carter
Ronald Reagan
George H. W. Bush
Bill Clinton
George W. Bush
Barack Obama
Donald J. Trump

At Right: Ripon, Wisconsin
Location of First Meeting of the Republican Party

Springfield, Pennsylvania
Michael Puppio, Chairman of the
Springfield Republican Party, July 4, 2010

Active Third Parties in the 21st Century

Constitution Party

Several independent parties joined together in 1992 to form the Constitution Party. The party believes that American government needs to follow the Constitution more closely.

The Green Party of the United States

In 2001, the Association of State Green Parties joined together to form the Green Party of the United States. It supports protection of the environment and is committed to non-violent ways of settling problems between nations.

The Libertarian Party

The Libertarian Party was founded in 1961. It supports an economy that is not regulated by government and believes that the United States should not get involved directly in what happens in other countries.

The first successful presidential candidate from the Republican Party was Abraham Lincoln, who was elected in 1860. The party grew in numbers during the Civil War.

After the Civil War, Americans built many industries. Owners of these industries became wealthy and were major supporters of the Republican Party. Republicans continue to be supporters of private business. Just as the Great Depression changed the Democratic Party, it changed the Republican Party, too. Republicans began to be against the Federal government being involved in the economy. In the late 1900s and into the 21st century, Republican candidates began to make public statements in support of traditional morals and values.

"Third Parties"

Since America has a two-party political system, new parties that form are often called "third parties" or minor parties. Third parties have been important in American life. They have emphasized certain concerns that voters have had and have offered an alternative to citizens who are not satisfied with either the Democrats or the Republicans. The box at left tells about some of America's third parties that have been active in the 21st century.

People enjoy being around others who think like they do. It is easy to think that our opinions are better than those of people who think differently than we do. It is essential that we study the Scriptures to find out what God teaches about various ideas and form our own ideas based on what He says. It is also important that we are kind and patient with those who have different opinions.

Be of the same mind toward one another;

do not be haughty in mind, but associate with the lowly.

Do not be wise in your own estimation.

Romans 12:16

Lesson Activities

Thinking Biblically — Write a paragraph in your notebook or discuss with a parent: How can and should the Bible influence our political views?

Vocabulary — Look up each of these words in a dictionary and read their definitions: politics, animosity, faction, economy, symbolize.

Creative Writing — Most churches are considered non-profit organizations by the Federal government. Therefore, they cannot endorse a candidate for office. They can educate voters about issues and about candidates, encourage them to vote, and pray for the elections. Write a paragraph in your notebook explaining what you think about these rules.

Find Out! — What do your parents believe is the role of government in the economy?

Picture This! — The Republican symbol is the elephant and the Democratic symbol is the donkey. Draw a symbol for the Constitution, Green, and Libertarian parties.

Student Workbook or Lesson Review — If you are using one of these optional books, complete the assignment for Lesson 31.

Fairfax, Virginia
Donkey encourages students to come to Democratic Party meeting at George Mason University.

Pasadena, California
Republican Headquarters

Man poses with Reagan and Bush cutouts at Pasadena Republican Headquarters.

Jumping into THE RACE

A citizen must do much soul searching before deciding to run for office. Does he or she have time? Has he lived in such a way that he has a good reputation? Can he take time from his current job while campaigning for this new one? Does she have enough experience to do a good job? Are there people who would be willing to volunteer to help him? Can he raise enough money? Is her family willing to make the necessary sacrifices, both during the campaign and while she serves in office? One by one, thousands of people say yes to those questions and jump into the race. Pictured on these two pages are some of the people who said yes to jumping into the race for President in 2008, 2012, and 2016.

Candidates Who Jumped Into the Race for President in 2008, 2012, 2016

Fmr. Congresswoman Michele Bachmann
Republican Candidate, 2012

Former Governor Mitt Romney
Republican Candidate, 2008, 2012

Senator John McCain
Republican Candidate, 2008

Senator Marco Rubio
Republican Candidate, 2016

Former Governor Gary Johnson
Libertarian Candidate, 2012, 2016

Dr. Ben Carson
Republican Candidate, 2016

Carly Fiorina
Republican Candidate, 2016

Former Senator Joe Biden
Democratic Candidate, 2008

Former Mayor Rudy Giuliani
Republican Candidate, 2008

Former Congressman Newt Gingrich
Republican Candidate, 2012

Former Senator Rick Santorum
Republican Candidate, 2012, 2016

Herman Cain
Republican Candidate, 2012

Former Secretary Hillary Clinton
Democratic Candidate, 2008, 2016

Governor Rick Perry
Republican Candidate, 2012, 2016

Former Governor Mike Huckabee (left)
Republican Candidate, 2008, 2016
With Talk Show Host Sean Hannity

Former Senator John Edwards (right),
Democratic Candidate, 2008
Edwards also sought the presidency
in 2004 as did Senator John Kerry
(left). Kerry won the nomination
of the Democratic Party and chose
Edwards as his vice presidential
running mate. They lost to
Republicans George W. Bush
and Dick Cheney.

Dr. Jill Stein
Green Party Candidate, 2012, 2016

Former Congressman Ron Paul
Republican Candidate, 2008, 2012

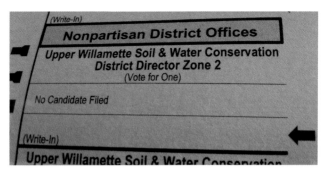

Columbus, Ohio
*Judge Mary Jane Trapp fills out paperwork
to become a candidate for Associate Justice of the
Ohio Supreme Court, 2011.*

As discussed in Lesson 14, America needs people who are willing to run for office from the mayor of a tiny town to the President of the United States. Look at the portion of a ballot from Oregon above. Notice that no one is running for Director of Zone 2 of the Upper Williamette Soil & Water Conservation District. What happened? Was no one willing to take the steps necessary to get on the ballot? Did no one care?

Taking the First Steps

Once a citizen has said yes to the questions on page 164, it is time to jump into the race. Exact requirements vary from state to state and from one office to another. By way of example, read the checklist on page 167 for a person running for certain county offices in Wisconsin. Two of the necessary steps are

*Judge Mary Jane Trapp turns in a stack of petitions
with her collected signatures.*

also illustrated in the photos of an Ohio candidate above.

When voters go to the polls to vote, they choose from candidates whose names are already printed on a paper ballot or some type of voting machine. Steps like those listed for Wisconsin and those pictured for Ohio are requirements a candidate must perform to get his name on an official ballot.

During most of the 1800s, state governments did not print ballots for voters to use on Election Day. At first the most common way to vote was for voters to simply speak their choice to an election official. Soon political parties began making their own ballots, which were called "tickets." See example on page 167. These tickets listed the party's candidates for offices. On Election Day, voters could bring these tickets to the polling place and drop them in the ballot

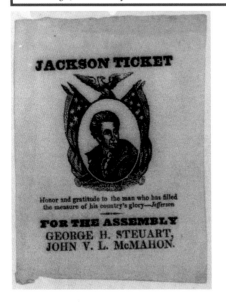

box. They could also write in changes or simply write out their choices on a piece of paper.

This is the origin of the terms Democratic ticket and Republican ticket. Today the terms simply refer to who a party's candidates are and not to an actual piece of paper. When it is said that someone "votes a straight party ticket," it means that he does not look at the merits of each candidate individually. Instead, he is so loyal to his political party that he votes for everyone from that party who is running.

Incumbents, Challengers, and Term Limits

Many political races are between an incumbent and one or more challengers. An incumbent is the candidate who currently holds the office that he is seeking. In the case of presidential elections, Bill Clinton ran as an incumbent in 1996, as did George W. Bush in 2004 and Barack Obama in 2012.

When an incumbent is running for office, the person who runs against him is called the challenger. Ronald Reagan was the challenger when he ran against Jimmy Carter in 1980 and Bill Clinton was the challenger when he ran against George H. W. Bush in 1992.

When a citizen is elected to a Federal office, he serves for a set number of years. This set number of years is called a term of office. A Congressman serves for two years, a President and a Vice President for four, and a Senator for six. Elected state and local officials also serve for a set term. The lengths of those terms vary, but they are usually from two to four years. Some political offices have a fixed number of terms that one person can serve in that office or a certain number of terms he can serve consecutively. This is called term limits. The only Federal office with term limits is the presidency with a limit of two terms.

Campaign Finance

At the local level in a small community, a candidate may be able to do much of his campaigning personally. He can knock on doors and ask for people's votes. He can attend public and social events where he can meet potential voters. Even then, he must give a great deal of time. Often his family and close friends give a great deal of time, as well.

The photos on this page were taken on a Saturday morning in March 2012 when volunteers were hitting the streets to campaign for a group of Republican candidates. Their office that morning was the hood and tailgate of State Representative Woody Burton's minivan "mobile office." Representative Burton is the Indiana legislator who pushed for Indiana's "In God We Trust" license plate.

When someone runs for a big city, state, or national office, the costs are multiplied many times, both in terms of money and time. Whether they are the winners or the losers, some national candidates end their campaigns in debt.

Candidates who want to become President spend many months trying to get the support of voters. They travel around the country giving speeches and attending meetings. They make advertisements for television, radio, and the Internet. They send mail directly to voters. They create websites. All of this costs money—lots of money. Presidential candidates spend millions of dollars on their campaigns.

Franklin, Indiana
Republican volunteers get ready for a Saturday morning of campaigning.

Individuals and groups donate money to help candidates. Federal and state governments have passed laws that limit how a candidate can raise money and how he can spend it. The Federal government offers funds to presidential candidates who accept extra rules about how to spend campaign dollars. The Federal Election Commission (FEC) enforces Federal election laws and oversees giving funds to candidates. These funds are called matching funds. When a candidate receives a donation of less than $250, he can apply to the FEC for the same (or matching) amount.

Special Interest Groups and Political Action Committees

People who share similar interests often support candidates who say they will work for those interests. For example, homeschooling families often support candidates who have stated publicly that they support the right of parents to teach their children at home. Homeschooling families are one special interest group. Trucking companies support candidates who say they will work for lower taxes on fuel. America has thousands of special interest groups.

Some special interest groups organize a political action committee or PAC so that they can help elect political candidates. PACs must register with the FEC. Phyllis Schlafly organized a conservative, pro-family organization called Eagle Forum in 1972. It is an organized special interest group. The group later formed the Eagle Forum PAC which endorses candidates for political races around the country.

Washington, D.C.
Eagle Forum President Phyllis Schlafly at CPAC, 2012

In the photo at right, Mrs. Schlafly is on stage at the Conservative Political Action Conference (CPAC) in February of 2012. This year's CPAC was sponsored by The American Conservative Union and TeaParty.net. The American Conservative Union is a special interest group that was organized in 1964. It supports liberty, personal responsibility, traditional values, national security, lower taxes, and less government spending. The Union has an American Conservative Union PAC which supports candidates for office.

The Tea Party movement includes many special interest groups that are not connected to a particular political party. People in the

Rick Santorum and Family at CPAC, 2012

St. Paul, Minnesota
Tea Party Rally Opposing Health Care Reform, 2010

movement support a smaller Federal government, individual freedoms for all citizens, and a return of more political power to states and the people of America. The organization has held "tea parties" across the country.

Candidates jump into political races with the intention of winning. God encourages us to live our lives as if we are running a race.

Therefore, since we have so great a cloud of witnesses surrounding us,

let us also lay aside every encumbrance and the sin which so easily entangles us,

and let us run with endurance the race that is set before us.

Hebrews 12:1

Lesson Activities

Vocabulary — In your notebook, write your own definition for each of these words: origin, merit, social, enforce, conservative. Look in the lesson for clues for the meaning of the words. When you are finished writing your definitions, look in a dictionary for comparison.

Literature — Read "I was born Feb. 12, 1809 . . ." in *The Citizen's Handbook,* pages 30-31.

Creative Writing — Pretend that you are living in the 1800s and can make up your own ballot. In your notebook, list these offices down one side of a piece of paper: President, Vice President, Senator, Congressman, Governor, Mayor. Beside each office, write the name of a person you know whom you think would be qualified.

Picture This! — Look at the Libertarian campaign bus on page 164. Draw a design for a campaign bus.

Student Workbook or Lesson Review — If you are using one of these optional books, complete the assignment for Lesson 32.

Winning Delegates Through CAUCUSES & PRIMARIES

LESSON 33

Many local elected offices are non-partisan, which means that candidates run as individuals and not as representatives of any political party. However, political parties matter a great deal in some local elections and in most state and Federal elections, especially presidential elections. Individuals may run for President or any other office as an Independent, but a candidate is more likely to be elected if he or she is part of a political party whose members support him.

Political parties choose nominees for many offices. The two main ways that parties do this are by caucuses and primaries. In some states, parties use a caucus or meeting of party members to choose candidates. Other states use primaries. A primary is a preliminary election for the public in which candidates from the same party run against each other. The winner of a primary runs against the nominees of other parties in the general election a few weeks or months later. Some states have closed primaries, in which a voter may vote only if he is registered in that party. In other states, a voter can choose in which primary he wants to vote on Election Day. A voter can only vote in one party primary.

The Democratic and Republican parties choose their presidential and vice presidential nominees at national party conventions, based on results of state caucuses and primaries. State parties (as well as parties in the District of Columbia and U.S. territories) send delegates to the national conventions. At right is a photo of Jimmy Carter at a meeting of the Illinois Democratic Party that took place after the 1976 Democratic National Convention and a few weeks before Carter defeated President Ford in the general election.

Though every elected official and the members of every political party are important, in Lessons 33 and 34 we will concentrate on the process of choosing the presidential and vice-presidential nominees of America's two major parties, the Democrats and the Republicans.

Candidate Jimmy Carter (left) with Mayor Richard Daley (right) at a meeting of the Illinois Democratic Party, 1976.

Campaigning Before the Caucuses and Primaries

A year or more before Election Day, presidential candidates file statements of candidacy with the Federal Election Commission and announce to the public that they want to become President. They begin to travel and to raise money for their campaigns. The major television networks, ABC, CBS, and NBC; cable news stations, like FOX News, CNN, MSNBC, and C-SPAN, and other news organizations, such as the Associated Press (AP), follow the candidates and share information about the candidates and what is happening in various campaigns. Radio and television talk show hosts, Internet news websites, and newspapers do the same.

Beginning in January of an election year, states start to hold caucuses and primaries. Their dates vary from one election year to another. Let's keep it simple. We will use the Republican caucus and primary schedule for 2016 as an example. The way caucuses and primaries are held varies from state to state, too. We will use the first caucus in Iowa and the first primary in New Hampshire as examples of the ways that caucuses and primaries are conducted.

The Iowa Caucus

On Monday, February 1, 2016, Republican voters from each voting precinct in Iowa gathered at 7:00 p.m. They gathered in churches, city halls, community centers, courthouses, libraries, and hundreds of schools, plus American Legions, fire halls, telephone companies, businesses, golf courses, senior centers, hotels, nature centers, auditoriums, memorial halls, an opera house, private homes, and more. The groups listened to information about various candidates and voted. Only citizens who were registered as Republicans could vote, but attendees were allowed to register that evening.

In 2016, for the first time, a Microsoft app helped to tally the results. The state Republican party released vote count results to the media. That night over 180,000 Republicans cast votes in the Republican caucuses. Caucus attendees chose Texas Senator Ted Cruz for their choice for the Republican nomination. Democrats also met in caucuses that evening. Secretary of State Hillary Clinton narrowly won over U.S. Senator Bernie Sanders of Vermont in this first contest of the 2016 election process.

Left: Donald Trump campaigns in Muscatine, Iowa, one week before the Iowa caucuses. Right: Ted Cruz Campaign Bus

The New Hampshire Primary

New Hampshire held the nation's first presidential primary election for the 2016 race eight days later on February 9. The New Hampshire primary is an open primary. There voters, regardless of their party preference, can choose to vote in either the Democratic or the Republican primary. A large percentage of voters in New Hampshire are Independents.

As in years past, candidates had campaigned vigorously in the state in hopes of winning and receiving the media attention that comes with a victory in the first primary. The Republican primary winner in 2016 was Donald Trump and the Democratic winner was Senator Bernie Sanders.

When New Hampshire became the first-in-the-nation primary in 1920, primaries were new in America. It is so important to New Hampshire citizens that theirs is first, that the New Hampshire legislature passed a law in 1999 giving its secretary of state authority to move their primary seven days or more ahead of those in other states.

Democratic voters from one Iowa precinct caucus in an elementary school gym in 2016.

Ted Cruz campaigns in New Hampshire on February 3rd, 2016.

Scene from the 2008 New Hampshire Primary

Though they were bitter rivals during the New Hampshire primary, Senator Bernie Sanders later campaigned for former Secretary of State Hillary Clinton to encourage voters to vote for her on Election Day.
Photo from Portsmouth, New Hampshire, July 12, 2016.

173

Not only is it important to New Hampshire that it be the first state, tiny Dixville Notch enjoys the distinction of being the first place in New Hampshire where citizens can vote. Their polls opened at midnight on February 9. Eight voters of this tiny village voted and the polls closed less than one minute later. By 12:05 the votes were counted.

Gaining Convention Delegate Votes Through Caucuses and Primaries

Republican Party organizations in each state, each territory, and the District of Columbia can choose a certain number of voting delegates to send to the national convention. This is also true for the Democratic Party, but to keep this discussion simple, we will discuss mainly the Republican Party.

In some states, caucuses and primaries are binding, meaning that the state's delegates must go to the convention committed to voting for the candidate chosen in their caucus or primary. However, in some states the primary or caucus is only to let the party know who voters prefer and does not require the delegates to vote in a certain way. Some binding state primaries are winner-take-all, meaning that the candidate who receives the most votes in the primary will get all of that state's delegate votes. Other binding primaries are proportional, meaning that if Candidate A gets 40% of the vote and Candidate B gets 20%, Candidate A will receive 40% of a state's delegate votes and Candidate B will get 20%.

As the various caucuses and primaries are held during the winter, spring, and summer, the news media report the numbers of delegates that must vote for a certain candidate at the convention because of the results of binding primaries. When a candidate reaches the number of delegates required for nomination at the convention, his nomination is guaranteed. As the caucuses and primaries progress, candidates who have not gotten many votes drop out of the race. At a certain point, they decide that it is not worth the time and money to continue because they know they will not be successful.

Listed on pages 175 and 176 are the dates of the 2016 caucuses, primaries, and conventions and the number of delegates that each place was allowed to send to the Republican National Convention. Notice that March 1 was Super Tuesday. The date when the largest number of states hold primaries is, of course, a very important one to candidates; and it has been nicknamed Super Tuesday.

174

2016 Republican Convention Delegate Selection

Date	Event	# of Convention Delegates
February 1	Iowa Caucuses	30 Delegates
February 9	New Hampshire Primary	23 Delegates
February 20	South Carolina Primary	50 Delegates
February 23	Nevada Caucuses	30 Delegates
	--- SUPER TUESDAY ---	
March 1	Alabama Primary	50 Delegates
	Alaska Caucuses	28 Delegates
	Arkansas Primary	40 Delegates
	Georgia Primary	76 Delegates
	Massachusetts Primary	42 Delegates
	Minnesota Caucuses	38 Delegates
	Oklahoma Primary	43 Delegates
	Tennessee Primary	58 Delegates
	Texas Primary	155 Delegates
	Vermont Primary	16 Delegates
	Virginia Primary	49 Delegates
March 5	Kansas Caucuses	40 Delegates
	Kentucky Caucuses	46 Delegates
	Louisiana Primary	46 Delegates
	Maine Caucuses	23 Delegates
March 6	Puerto Rico Primary	23 Delegates
March 8	Hawaii Caucuses	19 Delegates
	Idaho Primary	32 Delegates
	Michigan Primary	59 Delegates
	Mississippi Primary	40 Delegates
March 12	District of Columbia Convention	19 Delegates
	Wyoming Convention	29 Delegates
March 15	Florida Primary	99 Delegates
	Illinois Primary	69 Delegates
	Missouri Primary	52 Delegates
	North Carolina Primary	72 Delegates
	Ohio Primary	66 Delegates
March 22	Arizona Primary	58 Delegates
	Utah Caucuses	40 Delegates
April 3	North Dakota Convention	28 Delegates
April 5	Wisconsin Primary	42 Delegates
April 9	Colorado Convention*	37 Delegates
April 19	New York Primary	95 Delegates
April 26	Connecticut Primary	28 Delegates
	Delaware Primary	16 Delegates
	Maryland Primary	38 Delegates
	Pennsylvania Primary	71 Delegates
	Rhode Island Primary	19 Delegates

Some Colorado delegates were selected at earlier meetings.
List continued on next page.

Boston, Massachusetts
Former Governor Mitt Romney speaks at Romney Headquarters on Super Tuesday, March 6, 2012.

Maryland
Maryland Governor Martin O'Malley is interviewed in March 2012 after casting his ballot during early voting before the Maryland primary.

Berkeley, California
Congressman Ron Paul speaks on the campus of the University of California at Berkeley on April 5, 2012.

May 3	Indiana Primary	57 Delegates
May 10	Nebraska Primary	36 Delegates
	West Viriginia Primary	34 Delegates
May 17	Oregon Primary	28 Delegates
May 24	Washington Primary	44 Delegates
June 7	Californnia Primary	172 Delegates
	Montana Primary	27 Delegates
	New Jersey Primary	51 Delegates
	New Mexico Primary	24 Delegates
	South Dakota Primary	29 Delegates

Primary Pollworkers

Primaries and caucuses give American voters a chance to declare their choices. Every individual makes choices every day. After Joshua led the Israelites into the land of Canaan, he talked to them about choosing. He said:

. . . choose for yourselves today whom you will serve

. . . but as for me and my house, we will serve the Lord.

Joshua 24:15

Lesson Activities

Vocabulary — In your notebook, make a simple drawing for each of these words that illustrates what it means: candidacy, precinct, chairman, attendee, proportional. Write the word under the drawing. Check in a dictionary if you need help with their definitions:

Literature — Read "Candidate Cards" in *The Citizen's Handbook*, page 32.

Creative Writing — Think about your family and how each member could help you if you ever ran for a political office. Include not only your immediate family, but grandparents, aunts, uncles, and cousins, too. Make a list of their names and then list the character traits and abilities they could use to help you.

Find Out! — When was the most recent primary or caucus held in your state? Do you have to be a registered voter to participate?

Student Workbook or Lesson Review — If you are using one of these optional books, complete the assignment for Lesson 33.

Democratic and Republican CONVENTIONS

St. Paul, Minnesota
*Former Mayor of New York Rudy Giuliani speaks
at the 2008 Republican National Convention.*

Denver, Colorado
*Former President Bill Clinton speaks
at the 2008 Democratic National Convention.*

Every four years the Democratic and Republican Parties hold national conventions to nominate presidential and vice-presidential candidates. The convention is also an opportunity to put on a show for the American public. With all the glitz, glamour, and balloons, national conventions look like parties.

Convention History

Democrats held their first national convention in 1832. There they nominated Andrew Jackson. The Republicans held their first convention in 1856.

Conventions today are calm compared to those in the 1800s. In 1860 Democrats met for ten days while trying to pick a candidate. They finally gave up and came back together six weeks later in another city to finish. From 1832 until 1936, Democratic Party rules required that two-thirds of delegates vote for a candidate before he could be chosen. In 1924 they voted 103 times before one candidate finally got two-thirds of the votes. Even though Republicans only required a simple majority, they voted thirty-six times in 1880 before they finally nominated James Garfield.

Future President Dwight D. Eisenhower (second from left) and his wife Mamie watch the Republican National Convention, 1952.

National conventions began to be covered by television networks in 1952. In the photo at left, Dwight and Mamie Eisenhower watch coverage of the Republican National Convention held in Chicago that summer. Before 1952 important convention events happened in the daytime. When television news began to cover conventions, the most exciting events were moved to the evenings, so that television networks could broadcast them.

The Democratic Convention of 1968 occurred at a time when the United States was fighting a war in Vietnam. Many opposed America being involved in the war. American citizens watched television in disbelief as they saw Democrats arguing with one another inside the convention while violence broke out in the streets outside. After that disastrous convention, the Democratic and Republican Parties began to change how they chose candidates. Both began to rely more and more on the votes in primaries and caucuses to help them choose.

Planning a Convention

National party conventions are held in the summer before a November presidential election. The party who does not have a President in office has their convention first. Both the Democratic and Republican parties receive funds from the Federal government to help pay for them. Preparations begin many months before. Conventions bring many millions

St. Paul, Minnesota
CNN Building Set Up for Press and Convention Parties During the 2008 Republican National Convention

of dollars to a host city, so businessmen and government officials from various cities try to convince convention planners to choose their location. About eighteen months before the convention, the national committees of both parties issue a "call." The call tells the location and dates of the next convention. The chart on page 179 shows where conventions have been.

Convention planners and host cities must work out many details. They plan for the safety of everyone involved. They make arrangements for delegates and the thousands of other people who come to town, including several thousand people working for television stations, radio stations, newspapers, magazines, and news websites. Notice the CNN building at the 2008 Republican convention above. Modern convention planners always keep television coverage in mind. They hire people to make professional films that are a cross between a documentary and a commercial for the political party and its candidate. They oversee the designing and building of an elaborate stage. Notice the 2008 stages on page 177.

Cities Hosting the Democratic and Republican National Conventions By State, 1832-2016

CALIFORNIA	ILLINOIS	MARYLAND	MISSOURI	OHIO
Los Angeles	**Chicago**	**Baltimore**	**Kansas City**	**Cincinnati**
Democratic 1960	Republican 1860	Democratic 1832	Democratic 1900	Democratic 1856
Democratic 2000	Democratic 1864	Democratic 1835	Republican 1928	Republican 1876
	**Republican 1868	Democratic 1840	Republican 1976	Democratic 1880
San Francisco	Republican 1880	Democratic 1844		
Democratic 1920	Republican 1884	Democratic 1848	**St. Louis**	**Cleveland**
Republican 1956	Democratic 1884	Democratic 1852	Democratic 1876	Republican 1924
Republican 1964	Republican 1888	^Democratic 1860	Democratic 1888	Republican 1936
Democratic 1984	Democratic 1892	*Republican 1864	Republican 1896	Republican 2016
	Democratic 1896	Democratic 1872	Democratic 1904	
San Diego	Republican 1904	Democratic 1912	Democratic 1916	**PENNSYLVANIA**
Republican 1996	Republican 1908			
	Republican 1912	**MASSACHUSETTS**	**NEW JERSEY**	**Philadelphia**
COLORADO	Republican 1916			Republican 1856
	Republican 1920	**Boston**	**Atlantic City**	Republican 1872
Denver	Republican 1932	Democratic 2004	Democratic 1964	Republican 1900
Democratic 1908	Democratic 1932			Democratic 1936
Democratic 2008	Democratic 1940	**MICHIGAN**	**NEW YORK**	Republican 1940
	Republican 1944			Republican 1948
FLORIDA	Democratic 1944	**Detroit**	**New York City**	Democratic 1948
	Republican 1952	Republican 1980	Democratic 1868	Republican 2000
Miami Beach	Democratic 1952		Democratic 1924	Democratic 2016
Republican 1968	Democratic 1956	**MINNESOTA**	Democratic 1976	
Democratic 1972	Republican 1960		Democratic 1980	**SOUTH CAROLINA**
Republican 1972	Democratic 1968	**Minneapolis**	Democratic 1992	
	Democratic 1996	Republican 1892	Republican 2004	**Charleston**
Tampa				^Democratic 1860
Republican 2012		**St. Paul**	**NORTH CAROLINA**	
		Republican 2008		**TEXAS**
GEORGIA			**Charlotte**	
			Democratic 2012	**Dallas**
Atlanta				Republican 1984
Democratic 1988				
				Houston
LOUISIANA				Democratic 1928
				Republican 1992
New Orleans				
Republican 1988				

Notes:
^ The Democratic National Convention began in Charleston in 1860, but adjourned without choosing a candidate. It reconvened in Baltimore a few weeks later.
** The Republican Party used the name National Union Party in 1864.*
***The Republican Party used the name National Union Republican Party in 1868.*

Convention Delegates

Each party has a complicated system of choosing delegates to attend their national conventions and determining how many delegates each state can send. Some are chosen by voters in primaries, some by presidential candidates, and some at state party conventions. The number of delegates who attend a national convention has grown a great deal in the last several decades, especially for the Democratic Party. In 1952 Democrats had 1,230 delegates at their convention; Republicans had 1,206. Republican delegates have doubled since then and Democratic delegates have quadrupled.

Democratic. The Democratic Party assigns each state a certain number of delegates that the state parties can send to the national convention. Numbers are based on how many votes

Presidential candidate Senator Barack Obama and vice presidential candidate Senator Joe Biden greet well-wishers during the Democratic National Convention, 2008.

Democratic candidates have received in that state in the past and how many electoral votes the state has (electoral votes are explained in Lesson 44). Additional delegates include former Democratic Presidents and Vice Presidents, former chairmen of the Democratic National Committee, current Democratic Governors, the chairman and vice-chairman of each state Democratic Party, and all Democrats currently serving in the U.S. Senate and House of Representatives.

1912 Republican National Convention Delegates from Pennsylvania (top), Texas (middle), and Oklahoma (lower)

Republican. Republican Convention delegates include three delegates for each congressional district in every state, plus six at-large delegates from each state. State parties can send extra delegates if the states meet certain characteristics. They may be rewarded with extra delegates if a Republican presidential candidate won the state's electoral votes in the previous presidential election; if the state elected a Republican Governor or Senator since the last presidential election; if half of the state's members of the House of Representatives are Republican; or if the state holds its primary or caucus after March 15. Above are delegates from three states who attended in 1912.

Daily Schedules

Both Democratic and Republican National Conventions usually last for four days. On the first day, the party's national chairman calls the convention to order. A roll is taken of state delegations. The mayor of the host city gives a welcome speech, and often the Governor of the state does as well.

Keynote Address. Party leaders invite a prominent person, or someone they believe may become a prominent leader in the future, to deliver a keynote address. Former Mayor Rudy Giuliani gave the keynote address at the 2008 Republican National Convention. See picture at right.

Former New York City Mayor Rudy Giuliani speaks at the 2008 Republican National Convention.

Party Platform. Convention delegates adopt a party platform, which is a document that states the party's stands on various issues. Individual parts are called planks.

Nominating the Presidential Candidate. In a club, when a person's name is placed before the members so that they can consider electing him to an office, a club member nominates him. Another club member who agrees then says, "I second." This procedure is followed at conventions. Prominent members of the party officially nominate candidates for President. They give speeches telling about the candidates' strengths. Others give speeches to second their nominations.

The Roll Call of States. The roll call of the states follows the nominating and seconding speeches. The clerk of the convention calls on the chairman of each state's delegates (called a delegation) to announce that delegation's vote for the party's presidential nominee. Delegates pay attention as the number of votes rises. When a candidate receives the number of votes he must have to win the nomination, the entire convention breaks out into a loud celebration, or "spontaneous demonstration." When delegates have quieted down, the roll call continues. Afterwards, the convention chairman often asks all the delegates to make the decision unanimous by all voicing their approval.

Senator Joe Biden accepts the nomination for Vice President at the 2008 Democratic National Convention.

Nominating the Vice Presidential Candidate. The presidential nominee chooses a vice presidential running mate. He or she is nominated on the last day of the convention. His nomination happens in a similar way to that of the presidential candidate with speeches and a vote, though the chairman often has everyone voice their approval at once, instead of conducting a roll call of each state.

Acceptance Speeches. After the vice presidential candidate is nominated, he gives an acceptance speech. See photos at right. The presidential candidate follows with his acceptance speech. This is a convention highlight.

Governor Sarah Palin accepts the Republican vice presidential nomination at the 2008 Republican National Convention.

Democratic Nominee Barack Obama and Family at the 2008 Democratic National Convention

Grand Finale at the 2008 Republican National Convention

Grand Finale. After his speech, the presidential candidate and his family and the vice presidential candidate and his family come to the stage for a grand finale to the convention. They are joined by the candidates they defeated and leaders of the party. The purpose of this show of unity is to let the country know that everyone is now united in purpose and ready to win the election. After a joyous celebration, often accompanied by the dropping of balloons, the convention is adjourned.

National party conventions end with rejoicing and hope for America. Rejoicing is something Christians can do every day because of their hope.

> Rejoice in the Lord always;
> again I will say, rejoice!
> Philippians 4:4

Lesson Activities

Thinking Biblically — Think about some "planks" in a party platform that should be particularly important to Christians. Write down 5-10 Bible verses in your notebook that would influence you if you were writing a party platform.

Literature — Read "Prepare for the Coming Battle of the Ballots" in *The Citizen's Handbook*, page 33.

Creative Writing — Imagine that you are on the planning committee for a major party political convention. Make a list of tasks that need to be done and a list of items you would need to purchase.

Picture This! — Draw a picture of a presidential candidate accepting his or her party's nomination, or take a photograph of a family member pretending to do this.

Student Workbook or Lesson Review — If you are using one of these optional books, complete the assignment for Lesson 34.

★ Remember to choose an American Holiday to study this week! ★

UNIT 8 — FROM THE CONVENTION TO ELECTION DAY

LESSONS IN UNIT 8

Lesson 36 — Putting Together a Campaign

Lesson 37 — Advertising Your Candidate

Lesson 38 — Traveling the Campaign Trail

Lesson 39 — The Presidential Debates

Lesson 40 — Choose an American Holiday

BOOKS USED IN UNIT 8

- The Citizen's Handbook

- Student Workbook (optional)

- Lesson Review (optional)

Historic campaign posters at the DC office of the Washington Post, *Election Day, 2012.*

Putting Together a
CAMPAIGN

When the national conventions close, it is time for members of each party to lay down their differences and work together to elect the party's new presidential and vice presidential nominees in the upcoming general election. Candidates who opposed the presidential nominee in the primaries and caucuses usually announce their support after the convention.

Jimmy Carter (left) works with his chief speechwriter Pat Anderson during the 1976 campaign.

Senator Hattie Caraway looks at an artist's portrait of herself to see if she would like to use it in her campaign.

Each pair of running mates and their campaign workers join forces with their party to form a powerful campaign team. They plan. They raise money. They study what the opposing campaign team is doing. They conduct surveys to find out what voters are thinking around the country. They use this information to help them choose priorities.

Hiring a Staff

Campaign teams hire staff members: managers, advertising experts, volunteer coordinators, researchers, speechwriters, fundraisers, personal assistants, a press secretary, transportation directors, event organizers, security personnel, and more. At top left is former Governor Jimmy Carter with his chief speechwriter.

Campaigns sometimes hire artists to help with campaign advertising. A Los Angeles artist painted a campaign portrait of Barack Obama for his 2008 campaign. The original now hangs in the National Portrait Gallery in Washington, D.C. A poster print of the painting hangs in the campaign office pictured at left below. Though these were not created for presidential candidates, look at the Senate campaign portrait at lower left on page 184 and the design for a campaign trinket to help elect a mayor at right.

Design for a Campaign Advertisement

Volunteers

The best campaign teams have volunteers who work at the national, state, and local levels. Campaign teams work with state organizations, which work with local ones. See campaign volunteers below.

Volunteering in a campaign is a way that many citizens can participate in the civic life of their city, state, and nation. Because American citizens have freedom of speech, they can show support for the candidates they believe will do the best job. Citizens can donate money, put signs in their yards, volunteer to stuff envelopes for mailing, make phone calls, talk to their neighbors, and campaign door-to-door. When a candidate comes to their hometown, they can be part of the crowd that greets him, while holding up signs and cheering to show their support.

Campaign Volunteers

Media Attention

After the convention, campaign teams of each party quickly host kickoff events meant to get as much attention from the media as possible. Receiving media attention is important because anytime a news program talks about a candidate in a positive way, it is like free advertising. Campaign teams coach candidates on what to say and how to say it. News programs often broadcast only a few words from what a candidate has said, thus turning his words into what is called a "sound bite." Campaigns sometimes give out brief quotations from their candidate, hoping the words will sound good in the media.

Campaigns also pay for radio, television, newspaper, magazine, and online advertisements. When General Dwight D. Eisenhower ran for President in 1952, he became the first candidate to spend a great deal on television advertising. He spent almost $2 million.

Campaign Appearances

Campaign teams schedule places for the presidential and vice presidential nominees to appear in person and on television. Candidates give speeches, attend picnics, tour factories, visit schools, shake hands, sign autographs, and get their pictures taken.

Teams make schedules for the candidates' families, too. For most presidential candidates, and for many candidates for other elected offices, families take on important roles during the election process. Family members may work in the spotlight or behind the scenes. In 1975 Jimmy Carter and his family traveled throughout the United States meeting people, so that it would be easier for him to get elected in 1976. In 1988 George W. Bush moved to Washington, D.C., with his family, so he could help his father in his presidential campaign.

Warren G. Harding and his wife make a campaign appearance in 1920.

Mitt Romney makes a campaign speech on Super Tuesday, 2012.

Barack Obama makes a campaign speech, 2008.

Vice presidential nominee Sarah Palin makes a campaign speech, 2008.

Vice presidential nominee Joe Biden makes a campaign speech, 2008.

President Bill Clinton makes a campaign appearance in Minnesota to support the campaigns of presidential candidate Barack Obama and senatorial candidate Al Franken, 2008.

Cindy McCain, wife of John McCain, campaigns on his behalf during the New Hampshire primary before he received the nomination that summer, 2008.

Campaign teams also schedule appearances by well-known politicians who are willing to speak on behalf of a candidate. Teams not only plan where candidates go, they also pay careful attention to when they go. They plan events at times news programs are more likely to report about them. Teams also try to get many people to come to events, so that their candidate looks popular. Look at the photos above and on page 186 to see examples of candidate, family, and celebrity appearances in both the primary and general elections.

Focusing on Groups

Experienced campaign leaders understand that not every voter will vote for their candidate. They know that voters have varied concerns, like education, the rights of people who are members of labor unions, the rights of illegal immigrants, the rights of minority groups, or the strength of America's military. Candidates try to meet with members of many groups and gain their support. Their teams study what members of different special interest groups, ethnic groups, and religious groups think about the candidate and try to share their ideas with the ones they think are most likely to support them. They work hard trying to convince voters

Milwaukee, Wisconsin
Laborfest and Obama Rally, 2008

they believe will agree with them. In the photos above, people concerned with the rights of members of labor unions gather in Milwaukee, Wisconsin, for a Laborfest and Obama Rally on September 1, 2008.

Getting Out the Vote

Campaign teams work to register voters. They also try to "get out the vote" (GOTV) because it doesn't matter how many people like a candidate if they do not go to the polls and vote for him.

Arlington, Virginia
Volunteer at the Young Democrats
Get Out the Vote Rally, 2010

Front Porch and
Rose Garden Campaigns

Today's candidates travel from coast to coast. Presidential candidates have not always campaigned this way. Many candidates in the 1800s and the early 1900s stayed close to home, while their supporters traveled the country. They received visitors at their homes, made occasional statements that were reported in newspapers, and made a limited number of appearances.

When Warren G. Harding ran for President in 1920, his campaign team organized a "front porch campaign," which they ran from his home in Marion, Ohio. His campaign staff worked out of a little house on the property. Popular singer Al Jolson toured the country, singing songs that compared Harding to Abraham Lincoln. The campaign worked. Harding won in thirty-seven states. See photos of Al Jolson and of Harding's home and front porch on page 189.

Marion, Ohio
Home of Warren G. Harding and Detail of His Front Porch

Washington, D.C.
Mrs. Calvin Coolidge, John Drew,
President Coolidge, Al Jolson

Sometimes when an incumbent President is running for re-election, he will limit his campaign appearances and let his party do more of the work for him than he would if he were not serving as President. These campaigns are called Rose Garden campaigns. They are named for the Rose Garden on the grounds of the White House.

Change is good if people are changing to become more like God wants them to be. However, change is not good if it is a change from righteousness to modern ideas that are man-made and not based on the principles God has laid out in His Word. Each individual is responsible for changing to be the way God wants us to be.

Truly I say to you, unless you are converted and become like children,

you will not enter the kingdom of heaven.

Matthew 18:3

Lesson Activities

Thinking Biblically — Read Matthew 18:1-5. Discuss with a parent or write a paragraph in your notebook: What kind of changes is Jesus talking about in verse 3?

Vocabulary — Write a paragraph using all of these words: convention, conduct, priorities, speechwriter, convince. Consult a dictionary if you need help with their definitions.

Find Out! — Ask your parents about experiences they have had receiving campaign phone calls and door-to-door campaigners.

Picture This! — Take a photograph or draw a picture of a place in your community that would be a perfect spot for a presidential candidate to hold a rally.

Student Workbook or Lesson Review — If you are using one of these optional books, complete the assignment for Lesson 36.

Advertising Your CANDIDATE

*Top: Lincoln Campaign
Button from 1860
Lower: Campaign Button from 1864*

GET SMARTER
VOTE FOR
JIMMY CARTER
IN '76

Design for 1976 Campaign Button

Campaign teams have found imaginative ways to get voters' attention. Let's look at ways they have done that through old fashioned advertising—advertising that is not electronic, but is actually something you can touch.

Buttons and Ribbons

When George Washington was inaugurated for his first term in 1789, he and his supporters wore the first American political buttons. Today "buttons" are actually pins, but Washington's was really a brass button that was sewn onto his coat. In the center were his initials. Around the center were the words, "Long Live the President." Around the words were symbols of each of the first thirteen states.

The first buttons that actually showed a candidate's likeness were produced during the 1860 election. Campaign buttons are made with the technology that is available at the time. The Lincoln buttons were possible because of the invention of tintype photos. The campaign button was actually a sort of medallion that hung from a ribbon and was attached to a lapel. The top button at left was from the 1860 campaign and the lower one from 1864. Notice that Lincoln grew a beard after the first photo was taken.

The type of button seen in today's campaigns were first used during the campaigns of Republican William McKinley and his opponent William Jennings Bryan in 1896. The button was a metal disc, topped first by a photo and then by a piece of transparent celluloid. Celluloid was an early kind of plastic that is still used to make table tennis balls and guitar picks. On the back was a pin. These pins were invented by the Whitehead and Hoag Company of New Jersey. About twenty years later, button makers began to make buttons with the image printed directly on the metal.

Buttons for Republican Nominees, 2008

Similar to campaign buttons are campaign ribbons. During the 1844 presidential campaign, James K. Polk's supporters wore silk campaign ribbons with drawings of Polk and his running mate. A lapel decoration for the first Republican presidential candidate, John C. Fremont, had white ribbons with a picture of the candidate riding a horse.

Banners, Posters, and Billboards

Early candidates used elaborate campaign banners, like those at right below. Notice how "busy" the Cleveland and Thurman poster is compared to the more modern ones at left. Some early banners were on fabric, like the one for Lincoln. Today's posters and banners come in many sizes from ones people can hold to billboard size.

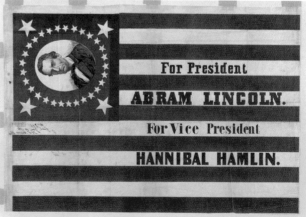

Campaign Symbols

Today's political campaigns hire advertising specialists to invent clever symbols to print on a variety of objects. In 2012 Barack Obama used a rising sun. Others use artistic styles of lettering like the "R" in Romney at right. Symbols were used in earlier elections, too. Theodore Roosevelt and others have used Uncle Sam. Theodore Roosevelt also used a moose. When Franklin Roosevelt was challenged by Kansas Governor Alf Landon, Landon used his state symbol, the sunflower.

William Henry Harrison used the log cabin. Editor Horace Greeley printed a newspaper called *The Log Cabin* to help William Henry Harrison get elected, even though Harrison had been born into a wealthy Virginia family.

Some candidates have had memorable nicknames. Andrew Jackson was "Old Hickory" and Abraham Lincoln was "Honest Abe." Some Presidents and candidates have become known by their initials, either by accident or by choice. George W. Bush used "W" and Barack Obama used "O." Others known by their initials include LBJ (Lyndon Baines Johnson), JFK (John Fitzgerald Kennedy), FDR (Franklin Delano Roosevelt), and TR (Theodore Roosevelt).

Campaign Slogans

Campaigns use catchy slogans to print on campaign advertisements. Here are a few:

Vote Yourself a Farm – *Abraham Lincoln*

A Full Dinner Pail – *William McKinley*

Keep Cool with Coolidge – *Calvin Coolidge*

A Chicken in Every Pot and a Car in Every Garage – *Herbert Hoover*

Don't Swap Horses – *Herbert Hoover*

I Like Ike – *Dwight D. Eisenhower*

A Time for Greatness – *John F. Kennedy*

"Click with Dick" Nixon for President – *Richard Nixon*

The Stakes Are Too High for You to Stay at Home – *Lyndon B. Johnson*

Nixon Now – *Richard Nixon*

A Leader for a Change – *Jimmy Carter*

It's Morning Again in America – *Ronald Reagan*

Renew America's Strength with Great American Values – *Ronald Reagan*

Bumper Stickers

When Senator Fred Thompson announced his plans to seek the Republican presidential nomination on a late night television show in 2007, the host held up a Thompson bumper sticker. The first bumper decorations were made of metal or cardboard and looked more like a license plate than a modern bumper sticker. They were secured with wire, which was wrapped around the bumper. After sticky-backed paper became available in the mid-1940s, Forest Gill from Missouri decided that the paper could be useful in making signs to attach to car bumpers. The first large use of bumper stickers was as souvenirs. When people went on vacation, they often came home with a bumper sticker showing where they had been. Politicians realized the potential of bumper stickers and began to order them. Gill-line of Lenexa, Kansas, is still a major supplier of bumper stickers. Today's bumper stickers are usually made of vinyl. The images below are based on real bumper sticker designs.

Presidential Campaign Bumper Sticker Slogans

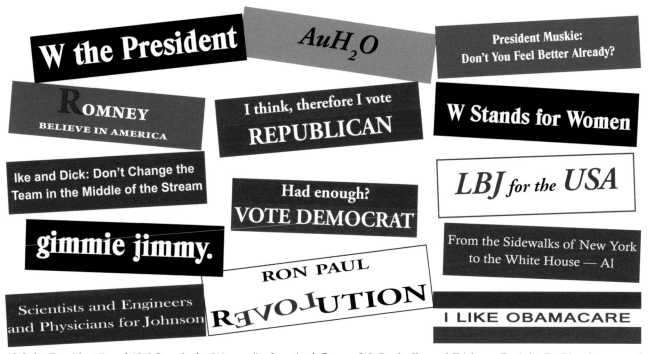

"W the President" and "W Stands for Women" advertised George W. Bush. Ike and Dick are Dwight D. Eisenhower and Richard Nixon who were elected President and Vice President in 1952 and 1956. Edmund Muskie sought the Democratic nomination in 1972. "jimmy" is Jimmy Carter. LBJ is President Lyndon Baines Johnson. AuH$_2$O stands for Barry Goldwater, Republican nominee in 1964. "Al" is Al Smith, who ran against President Herbert Hoover. The Romney, Obama, and Paul slogans are from 2012.

Campaign This and That

One way Americans show their fellow citizens how they feel about something important to them is by wearing a T-shirt with a slogan or symbol. T-shirts have become popular political advertisements.

Americans have invented many other ways to advertise their favorite candidates and to celebrate them after they have been elected. Sometimes American companies join in the fun by putting political slogans and images on their products. Here are some of the most unusual:

* ★ A James Monroe top hat.

* ★ An Andrew Jackson hairpin.

* ★ A paper lantern with an image of Ulysses S. Grant.

* ★ A James Garfield oil lamp.

* ★ A William McKinley parasol.

* ★ A red, white, and blue Theodore Roosevelt bandana.

* ★ A tin plate with William Howard Taft and his running mate James Sherman in the center with the other ten Republican nominees since 1856 around the edge.

* ★ A Herbert Hoover sewing kit.

* ★ A Vote for Hoover cigar band.

* ★ A blue enamel Hoover/Curtis lapel pin.

* ★ A Hoover pencil box.

* ★ A Franklin D. Roosevelt campaign button with Roosevelt's picture. A red, a white, and a blue ribbon and a tiny donkey hung below the button.

* ★ A "Pull for President, Wendell Willkie" matchbook. Wilkie was Roosevelt's opponent in 1940.

* ★ A green Harry Truman for President pendant.

* ★ "I Like Ike" gloves.

* ★ "I Like Ike" socks.

* ★ A box of Kellogg's Corn Flakes with pictures of Eisenhower and his opponent Adlai Stevenson and the slogan, "Vote As You Please, But Remember to Vote."

T-Shirts from the 2008 Campaigns

* A paper dress advertising John Fitzgerald Kennedy.

* A Good Humor Kennedy Ice Cream Bar and a Good Humor Nixon Ice Cream Bar.

* A can of Johnson Juice: A Drink for Healthcare. It was decorated with a kicking donkey and the "I" in Juice was dotted with a star.

* A six-pack of Goldwater: The Right Drink for the Conservative Taste. Barry Goldwater ran against President Lyndon Johnson.

* A dress emblazoned with blue stars and the name NIXON printed in red.

* A Richard Nixon bubble gum cigar.

* A "Nixon-Think Republican" pencil.

* A Gerald Ford matchbook which read, Betty for First Lady (Betty was his wife).

* A Gerald Ford matchbook which read, Win with Betty's Husband: Republican National Convention, August 1976.

* A Jimmy Carter walking stick.

* A Lillian Carter postcard ("Miss Lillian" was Jimmy Carter's mother).

* A pair of Ronald Reagan slippers.

* Jelly bean postcards with Reagan's photo in the center (Reagan liked jelly beans).

* A George H. W. Bush balloon. See picture below.

* A Bill Clinton can of soda with the imprint, "1 Taste 2 Come Back 4 More."

A Child Dressed Up as a Voting Booth

Today's campaigns sell merchandise to raise money. They sell bumper stickers, signs, T-shirts, sweatshirts, buttons, and baseball caps. They sell some unusual items, too. An Obama website in 2008 listed these items for sale: car flags ($25), golf balls (3 for $15), tote bags ($30), water bottles ($12), an umbrella ($45), a windshield shade ($18), a plastic bracelet ($4), car and refrigerator magnets ($5), and a cardboard hand fan ($3). An

President George H. W. Bush speaks to a crowd beside the Ohio River during the 1988 campaign.

Obama website in 2012 listed these: Obama-Biden iPhone Case ($40), an Obama Soy Candle ($20), Obama Glassware Set ($85), I Meow for Michelle Cat Collar ($12), Obama Dog T-Shirt ($30), Obama 2012 Grill Spatula ($40), State Lapel Pin Collector's Set ($450), Obama Cufflinks ($40), and Obama Tube Socks ($15).

Campaign "ThunderStix"

A John McCain website in 2008 listed these items: an ice scraper ($10), a travel bag ($25), a beach towel ($35), a fleece blanket ($40), an embroidered sports towel ($15), a door mat ($70), a mouse pad ($25), a wall clock ($50), and a license plate holder ($25). A Mitt Romney website in 2012 listed only a few items besides bumper stickers, signs, T-shirts, sweatshirts, buttons, and caps. Other items included: Believe in America Water Bottle ($15), "I'm a Mom for Mitt" window decal ($8), and Romney 2012 Canvas Tote Bag ($20).

The purpose of advertisements for presidential candidates is to imprint a short phrase or an impression about the candidate on the minds of voters. God has given us many short phrases in His Word that help us quickly remember His power and how much He loves us. Just a few words can make us remember so much about our Heavenly Father. Here is an example:

In the beginning, God created the heavens and the earth.
Genesis 1:1

Lesson Activities

Vocabulary — In your notebook, write these vocabulary words and the letter of the sentence that each word completes: lapel, slogan, souvenir, emblazon, embroidered.

a. My dad's work shirts have his name _____ above the pocket.

b. The Nike _____ is "Just do it."

c. I had to wear a white carnation on the _____ of my tuxedo in my sister's wedding.

d. David bought a T-shirt as a _____ of the Grand Canyon.

e. Wait, guys! Mom said she doesn't want us to _____ "garage sale" on the side of the house!

Literature — Read "Campaign Songs" in *The Citizen's Handbook*, pages 34-35.

Creative Writing — In your notebook, write a campaign song for a real or imagined candidate.

Picture This! — Design a campaign poster in color advertising a real or imagined candidate.

Student Workbook or Lesson Review — If you are using one of these optional books, complete the assignment for Lesson 37.

Traveling the CAMPAIGN TRAIL

As mentioned in Lesson 36, many early presidential candidates let others campaign for them. Andrew Jackson was the first who tried to get citizens to vote for him by traveling and speaking to them directly. When he traveled for his campaign, he road horses and he traveled in boats. Jackson and his wife Rachel took a riverboat to New Orleans during the campaign. Another candidate who traveled on horseback to campaign was Abraham Lincoln. See artwork at right.

Whistle Stop Campaigns

Jackson was the first President to ride on a train while in office, but later candidates used trains a great deal. The first to travel considerable distances by train while campaigning was William Jennings Bryan in 1896. In 1932 Governor Franklin Roosevelt visited thirty-six states, traveling 13,000 miles by train. When President Harry S. Truman

Springfield, Illinois
The caption reads: Abraham Lincoln's Return Home After His Successful Campaign for the Presidency of the United States, in October, 1860.

Independence, Missouri
Harry S. Truman ended his whistle-stop campaign at this train depot in 1948.

campaigned for the presidency in 1948, he went on what was called a whistle stop tour by train. That means he stopped at small communities, that were only a whistle stop. He gave speeches from the back of the train. After 32,000 miles and 201 stops, his whistle-stop tour ended at the depot in his hometown of Independence, Missouri, pictured above.

From Coast to Coast

Richard Nixon ran for President against John F. Kennedy in 1960. He made campaign appearances in all fifty states, even Alaska and Hawaii which had just become the 49th and 50th states the year before. Most candidates do not visit every state, but they do travel from coast to coast.

Campaign Buses

Today's candidates make some campaign trips on campaign buses. In his 2004 campaign, President George W. Bush rode in a 45-foot blue bus with the slogan, "Yes, America Can." On a trip to Michigan during the primary season, his bus was hard to miss. It was followed by seven more buses, plus Secret Service vehicles and Michigan state police cars. In 2008 John McCain's bus was inscribed with the words, "Straight Talk Express." In 2012 President Obama toured in a black bus decorated simply with the presidential seal. Mitt Romney's bus in 2012 read, "Conservative. Businessman. Leader." Among the pictures posted inside were pictures of Romney's father when he ran for the Republican nomination for President in 1968.

Top: President Barack Obama (right) with Principal Deputy Press Secretary Josh Earnest Aboard Air Force One
Lower: View of Air Force One

Campaign Planes

The main form of transportation for modern candidates is planes. When an incumbent President campaigns for re-election, he travels on Air Force One, which the Federal government supplies for him to use while he is in office. Each time the President uses Air Force One for campaign purposes, his campaign must reimburse the government for the cost of a first class airline ticket for the President and for each of his political advisors. Though it may seem unfair for the President to get to use Air Force One, he is required to fly on it so that he will be safe.

Jimmy Carter's campaign plane in the 1976 campaign was called "Peanut One." In 2008 Barack Obama's campaign plane was a white Boeing 757 decorated with his campaign motto, "Change We Can Believe In."

Intense Travel Schedules

Candidates have only a few weeks after the national conventions to get their message across to voters. Often their travel schedule is intense. The photographs below and on page 200 illustrate the kind of schedule candidate Jimmy Carter kept during one seven-day period in September of 1976. At right is the train depot in Plains, Georgia, the headquarters for Jimmy Carter's successful campaign for President in 1976.

Plains, Georgia
Jimmy Carter Campaign Headquarters, 1976

Carter Campaign — September 7-13, 1976

Tuesday, September 7

Pittsburgh, Pennsylvania
Carter speaks to a crowd.

Brooklyn, New York
Carter speaks at Brooklyn College.

Avoco, Pennsylvania
Carter disembarks from Peanut One at the Wilkes Barre/Scranton Airport.

Wednesday, September 8

Wednesday, September 8 or Thursday, September 9

Thursday, September 9

West Miflin, Pennsylvania
Carter disembarks from Peanut One at the Pittsburgh-Allegheny County Airport.

Columbus, Ohio
Carter shakes hands during a campaign stop.

Chicago, Illinois
Torchlight Parade with Mayor Richard Daley

Carter leaves a church in Jacksonville, Florida.

Carter holds an informal press conference aboard Peanut One.

Carter visits his brother Billy and hometown neighbors in Billy's gas station in Plains, Georgia.

Monday, September 13

Hitting the Campaign Trail Again!

When President Gerald Ford ran in 1976, he was an incumbent, but he was not running for re-election. How could that be? Ford had been Speaker of the House of Representatives, when Richard Nixon's Vice President Spiro Agnew resigned after being accused of participating in illegal activity. President Nixon appointed Congressman Ford to take Agnew's place. Less than a year later, Nixon resigned when it came to light that he had participated in illegal activities in a different matter. Gerald Ford became President of the United States without being elected to either the presidency or the vice presidency. This is the only time in U.S. history that this has happened.

When Ford took office, he spoke these words to the American people on television:

> *I am acutely aware that you have not elected me as your President by your ballots. So I ask you to confirm me as your President with your prayers.*

President Ford decided to run for office himself in 1976. While it is rare for an incumbent President to be seriously challenged by other members of his party, Ford was challenged, especially by former California Governor Ronald Reagan. When the Republican National Convention met that summer, Ford barely got the nomination. A look at his presidential diaries from September of 1976 shows that he decided to stay mainly at the White House to run a Rose Garden campaign. In September he fulfilled his duties as President, spent time with his wife, and, through telephone calls and visits, stayed in close contact with his adult children. In the photo at right, he is giving a press conference.

President Ford Giving a Press Conference at the White House

Ford spent a small percentage of his time working on his campaign. He filmed television commercials, studied for his televised debates with Carter, and took three short campaign trips. On September 15 Ford flew by helicopter to Andrews Air Force Base. From there, he flew to Michigan on the "Spirit of '76." Presidents Nixon and Ford used this name for Air Force One in honor of the country's bicentennial in 1976. Ford traveled by motorcade to Ann Arbor, where he spoke at his alma mater, the University of Michigan. He also attended several activities with the U of M football team and athletic staff before returning to Washington late that evening. On September 20, he met with Farmers for Ford at the White House. He campaigned in the South from September 23 through 27. See photos below and on page 202.

Ford Campaign — September 23-27, 1976

Thursday, September 23 & Friday, September 24, While In Philadelphia for 1st Debate

Philadelphia, Pennsylvania

President Ford greets voters as his motorcade goes through the streets. Notice the Secret Service agents. President Ford toured the Italian market area on the south side of Philadelphia.

Ford pilots the SS Natchez. He and his wife Betty toured on the Mississippi River, stopping at several ports.

Ford campaigned in New Orleans and traveled by motorcade to Bay St. Louis, Gulfport, Biloxi, and Pascagoula in Mississippi, and to Mobile, Alabama. He then flew on the "Spirit of '76" to Miami. From Miami, he flew to Andrews AFB, and then back to the White House by helicopter.

As candidates travel from place to place, they can get weary of hotels and restaurants, but sometimes they are received warmly into someone's home where they enjoy the family's hospitality. Jesus knew what it was like to enjoy a welcoming home in the midst of travel.

Now as they were traveling along, He entered a village;

and a woman named Martha welcomed Him into her home.

Luke 10:38

Lesson Activities

Literature — Read "And, Folks, Here's My Mamie!" in *The Citizen's Handbook*, pages 36-37.

Creative Writing — Imagine that you are a newspaper reporter in a small town visited by a major presidential candidate. In your notebook, write a one-page article about his or her visit to your town.

Find Out! — Have your parents ever seen a presidential candidate in person?

Picture This! — Design a bumper sticker in color advertising a real or imagined candidate. Use a catchy slogan.

Student Workbook or Lesson Review — If you are using one of these optional books, complete the assignment for Lesson 38.

The Presidential DEBATES

In the weeks before Election Day, candidates prepare for some of the most important events of the campaign, the presidential debates. For most voters, the debates are their only opportunity to see candidates side by side. This helps them to make a decision about which one they believe has the ability and the character to do a good job for the country.

Debate planners have tried various formats. Usually there has been one person who serves as a moderator. It is the moderator's job to ask the candidates questions and to make sure they follow the rules laid out ahead of time, especially the rules about how long they can speak and how well they stay on the subject. In addition to questions from a moderator, debaters sometimes receive questions from a panel of journalists or from the audience.

Jim Lehrer, long time journalist for PBS, has served as moderator at more debates than any other person. He has written a book about his experiences. Its title, *Tension City: Inside the Presidential Debates, from Kennedy-Nixon to Obama-McCain*, was inspired by President George H. W. Bush, who said that television debates were like an evening in "tension city." In the photo at right, Lehrer tells about his book at the University of Virginia's Miller Center for Public Affairs.

Charlottesville, Virginia
Jim Lehrer at the Miller Center for Public Affairs, October 2011

Political debates have a long history in America. Among the most famous were the debates between two candidates running for Illinois Senator. In 1858 senatorial candidates Abraham Lincoln and Stephen Douglas debated seven times. Each debate was three hours long. One candidate spoke for an hour, then the other spoke for an hour and a half, and then the first candidate spoke for another half hour. The main topics were slavery and whether the states would remain united.

The first presidential debates were between two Republican candidates trying to win the Oregon primary in 1948. New York Governor Thomas Dewey and former Minnesota Governor Harold Stassen debated for one hour. The debate was broadcast on radio and heard by over forty million people. Their main topic was whether the Communist Party should be outlawed in the United States. The first televised presidential debate was in 1956 between candidates Adlai Stevenson and Estes Kefauver who were seeking the Democratic nomination, but it was not broadcast nationwide.

The real beginning of modern televised presidential debates was in 1960 when Vice President Richard Nixon, the Republican nominee, debated Senator John F. Kennedy, the Democratic nominee. The NBC, CBS, and ABC television networks sponsored them. One was in September and three were in October. Over 60 million people watched each debate.

It was 1976 before another series of presidential debates would take place. In each of the presidential elections in between, one candidate did not want to debate. Incumbent Democratic President Lyndon Johnson did not want to debate in 1964. Richard Nixon did not want to debate in 1968 when he ran as the Republican candidate nor in 1972 when he ran as the incumbent President.

Du Page County, Illinois
Poster for Reenactment of Lincoln-Douglas Debate, c. 1938

Debates Sponsored by The League of Women Voters

Debates have been held during each presidential campaign since 1976. The League of Women Voters, discussed on page 142, sponsored them in 1976, 1980, and 1984.

In 1976 they sponsored three debates between the incumbent President Gerald R. Ford, Republican nominee, and the challenger Jimmy Carter, Democratic nominee. The photos at right and at the top of page 205 are from the first presidential debate that year. The League also sponsored a debate between their vice presidential running mates, Senator Bob Dole and Senator Walter Mondale. A Mondale poster is pictured on page 205.

Washington, D.C.
On September 23, 1976, President Gerald R. Ford prepares for a presidential debate in his office at the White House.

Philadelphia, Pennsylvania
Left: Supporters greet President Gerald R. Ford before his debate on September 23, 1976.
Top Right: Carter and Ford debate on television. Lower Right: TV anchorman Walter Cronkite comments.

In 1980 incumbent President Jimmy Carter was the Democratic nominee and Governor Ronald Reagan was the Republican. The League of Women Voters decided that Congressman John Anderson, who was running as an Independent, should be included in the debates. When President Carter refused to participate in a debate that included Anderson, the League sponsored a debate between Anderson and Reagan in September and between Carter and Reagan in October.

In 1984 the League of Women Voters again sponsored debates, two between incumbent President Ronald Reagan and his challenger Walter Mondale, and one between Republican vice presidential nominee Vice President George H. W. Bush and his Democratic challenger Congresswoman Geraldine Ferraro.

New York City, New York
Supporters hang giant poster of Walter Mondale at the Democratic National Convention in 1976.

The Commission on Presidential Debates

The Democratic and Republican parties wanted to control presidential debates. In February of 1987, the Democratic National Chairman Paul G. Kirk Jr. and Republican National Chairman Frank J. Fahrenkopf held a news conference announcing the creation of the Commission on Presidential Debates. They also announced that the Commission would sponsor the 1988 debates. When questioned about third party candidates being included, Kirk said that he did not believe that third party candidates should be included and Fahrenkopf said that he did not think the commission would be favorable about including them.

The president of the League of Women Voters held a news conference to respond. She stated publicly that the commission was trying to steal the debates from American voters. She said that third party candidates who had good support from American voters should be included in the debates.

Debates Sponsored by the Commission on Presidential Debates

The Commission on Presidential Debates has sponsored presidential and vice presidential debates during every election year since 1988.

In 1992 the Commission decided to allow an Independent candidate into the debates. Democratic candidate Governor Bill Clinton, Republican candidate President George H. W. Bush, and Independent candidate Ross Perot participated in the three debates they held that year. It also sponsored one vice presidential debate between Democratic Senator Al Gore, Republican Vice President Dan Quayle, and Independent James Stockdale.

Universities have become popular sites for presidential debates. Hosting them gives the universities prestige and publicity, but the financial costs are high. In 2008 each

Presidential and Vice Presidential Debate Locations Since 1988

Arizona
Arizona State University
Tempe

California
University of California
at Los Angeles
University of San Diego

Colorado
University of Denver

Connecticut
Bushnell Performing Arts Center
Hartford

Florida
Mahaffey Theater
St. Petersburg
University of Miami
Coral Gables
Lynn University
Boca Raton

Georgia
Georgia Tech
Atlanta

Kentucky
Centre College
Danville

Massachusetts
University of Massachusetts
Boston

Michigan
Michigan State University
East Lansing

Mississippi
University of Mississippi
Oxford

Missouri
Washington University
St. Louis

Nebraska
Omaha City Auditorium

Nevada
University of Nevada-Las Vegas

New York
Hofstra University
Hempstead

North Carolina
Wake Forest University
Winston-Salem

Ohio
Case Western
Reserve University
Cleveland, Ohio

Tennessee
Belmont University
Nashville

Virginia
University of Richmond
Longwood University
Farmville

university spent at least $3 million, including a $1.35 million production fee charged by the Commission.

Even people who do not get tickets to attend a debate in person come to the debate site to campaign for their favorite candidates, to report on what is happening there, or to watch what everyone else is doing. The photos below were taken in Oxford, Mississippi, when the first presidential debate of the 2008 campaign was held there in September.

Scenes from Outside the Debate at the University of Mississippi in Oxford

At top left is the Lyceum, completed in 1848. It was the first building constructed at "Ole Miss" (nickname for the University). The Lyceum served as a hospital during the Civil War. One soldier wrote to his wife: "This is a beautiful place, and the Sick Souldiers have enjoyed themselves very Well." Its bell is believed to be the oldest college bell in America. On its front columns are bullet marks from when the campus experienced racial violence in 1962 when the school's first African American student enrolled. The Lyceum sits on "The Circle," a green space surrounded by other historic buildings. On September 26, 2008, "The Circle" became the gathering place for political campaigners and events held in connection with the debates. At top center is a booth manned by Concerned Women of America. At top right is a concert. The three lower photos were taken at the League of Women Voters booth, where members encouraged people to register to vote.

People working for the media must fill out an application in order to attend a debate. They must fill out a form giving the name of their organization along with its address. They must state the media organization type: university, radio, local television, network television, news agency, photo agency, print newspaper, print magazine, or online. If people working for the media are going to use microphones, in-ear monitors, two-way radios, video links, intercoms, wireless cameras, remote controls, or other wireless devices, they must submit a request so that frequencies can be coordinated between the various media. Each must also supply his name, e-mail address, and the date, city, state, and country of his birth. U.S. citizens must supply a

Social Security number, and foreign visitors must supply a passport number and tell their country of citizenship. They must also supply a photograph.

The wisest debater looks to God's Word for truth. To make sure he is not a foolish debater, he conforms his words to God's.

> Where is the wise man? Where is the scribe?
> Where is the debater of this age?
> Has not God made foolish
> the wisdom of the world?
> 1 Corinthians 1:20

Philadelphia, Pennsylvania
Reporters in a press room watch the first Ford-Carter debate on September 23, 1976.

Lesson Activities

Thinking Biblically — Read Acts 15:1-35 about a debate in the early church and its resolution.

Vocabulary — In your notebook, write your own definition for each of these words: journalist, moderator, favorable, prestige, online. Look in the lesson for clues for the meaning of the words. When you are finished writing your definitions, look in a dictionary for comparison.

Creative Writing — In your notebook, write a list of at least five questions for candidates to discuss in a presidential debate.

Student Workbook or Lesson Review — If you are using one of these optional books, complete the assignment for Lesson 39.

Pasadena, California
Republicans watch the third 2008 debate at party headquarters.

Fairfax, Virginia
Students at George Mason University watch a 2008 debate.

★ Remember to choose an American Holiday to study this week! ★

UNIT 9 — THE VOTERS SPEAK

BOOKS USED IN UNIT 9

- The Citizen's Handbook

- Student Workbook (optional)

- Lesson Review (optional)

Cameramen and Photographers Record the Celebration of Republican Wins in Nevada, 2010

Getting Ready for ELECTION DAY

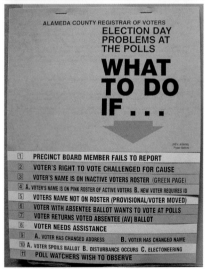

Alameda County, California
Election Materials

Preparations for Election Day begin long before the first Tuesday after the first Monday of November during every even-numbered year. Elections take many election officials, part-time workers, and volunteers. Each of the fifty states is responsible for holding elections for its own voters. In most states, the person in charge of elections is that state's secretary of state. State and local governments also have groups of people who work on elections. These groups are called by titles like Board of Elections, Board of Election Commissioners, Department of Elections, or Election Commission.

Local election officials are responsible for the practical work at the local level. The following is a partial "to do" list for these public servants:

★ Register voters.

★ Purchase supplies and equipment.

★ Design ballots.

★ Print ballots or have them printed.

★ Hire and train people to work in each precinct on Election Day.

★ Prepare polling places.

★ Make sure that elections are fair and that all election laws are obeyed.

At left are photos illustrating work election officials do before Election Day. Notice the boxes of printed ballots. These are sealed with "tamper evident" tape, so that no one can steal ballots and use them illegally. The instruction booklet for the Registrar of Voters of Alameda County, California, helps to prepare him or her for Election Day.

Equipment and Supplies

Officials purchase election equipment and supplies from private companies which specialize in these products. Many items are available for purchase—some are necessary and others make elections more patriotic events. Officials can buy name badges, lanyards, smocks, and patriotic aprons for poll workers. They can purchase signs to direct people to where they need to go at the polls. They can buy a variety of machines: ballot printers to use before the election, voting machines for voters to cast their votes on Election Day, and tabulators for counting votes after the election. They can choose from several varieties of voting booths, so that voters can vote in secret. They can buy "I Voted" stickers and patriotic mints for voters to carry away with them. They can buy ballot boxes and bags and plastic seals to make sure no one tampers with ballots before they are counted. See examples at right and below.

Gowanus, New York
Voting Machines

New York City, New York
Voting Booths and Other Equipment

San Mateo County, California
Ballot Bags

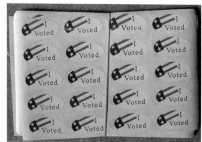

211

Voting Early and Absentee

Voting actually begins long before Election Day. Many Americans vote early or absentee because of special needs or personal preference. Some people vote early by going to a local facility, like a county courthouse, to cast their vote. Others vote absentee by mail because they will be away from home on Election Day. Many states allow absentee or early voting only under certain special circumstances, while these types of voting are more common in other states. In some states, voters must have someone serve as a witness or get a notary public to sign their absentee ballot and put his official seal on it. A notary public is someone whom the government has given authority to witness signatures and certify that a document is valid (not a fake). In the photo below, Grace Coolidge votes by mail on the White House lawn just three days after becoming First Lady. Notice the notary seal on the table.

Many Americans live and work overseas as missionaries, members of the U.S. military, and employees of international companies. Since they are American citizens who care about what happens in their home country, many choose to vote absentee. Absentee voting is also important for people who are elderly or

Washington, D.C.

Grace Coolidge, wife of President Calvin Coolidge, votes by mail on August 6, 1923, just three years after women gained the right to vote. President and Mrs. Coolidge were residents of the Commonwealth of Massachusetts.

Baumhaulder, Germany

U.S. postal worker Deborah Boetcher and Army Sergeant Gilber Valdez prepare absentee ballots from soldiers serving at Camp Arifjan in Kuwait for delivery to the U.S.

Camp As Sayliyah, Qatar

At left, U.S. Army Major Ashantas Cornelius from Macon, Georgia, fills out her absentee ballot. At right, Private First Class Crystal Miller from Auburn, New York, looks up her local election office's mailing address.

Elderly woman votes absentee.

who have disabilities that make it difficult for them to come to their local polling place. Notice the elderly woman at left and the soldiers on page 212 who are voting absentee. Also on page 212, a soldier and a U.S. postal employee work with absentee ballots sent by soldiers serving in Kuwait.

Each absentee voter must follow the absentee voter guidelines of his home state and of his local government. Each must request an absentee ballot from his local election official. The voter must then return the absentee ballot by the deadline set by local election laws. These deadlines vary from state to state. Some deadlines are before the election, some are on Election Day, and others are after the election. Mail was once the primary way that absentee ballots were sent to voters, but as of 2012, all U.S. citizens can request and receive a ballot electronically by e-mail, fax, or Internet download.

Since 1998 Oregon has conducted their elections by mail. Read about that in the box below. In 2011 Washington state passed a law to do the same.

Voting By Mail in Oregon

Election officials in the State of Oregon are especially busy before Election Day. They mail ballots to all registered voters, first to Oregonians who are in the military or living outside of the state for a long time, then to those living out of state for a short time, and then to the rest of Oregon voters. Voters can complete their ballots, sign them, and mail them. They may also place them in special boxes, like the ones pictured at right, on Election Day.

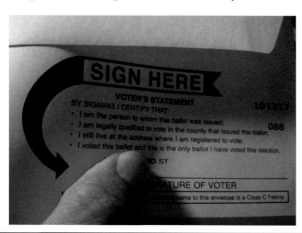

Voting in Languages Other Than English

In 1975 Congress passed a law which requires certain counties, cities, towns, townships, and census areas to prepare ballots and other election materials in languages other than English. These languages include Spanish, Native American languages, Alaskan Native languages, and Asian languages.

In addition to providing printed materials, local governments must also provide translators who can help voters at the polls. This law makes it possible for more citizens to take part in elections, but meeting these requirements is expensive for state and local governments.

The U.S. Census Bureau decides every five years which places must provide election materials in multiple languages. The chart below shows the deteriminations from 2015.

California Election Materials in Three Languages

Places Which Must Provide Voting Materials in Multiple Languages

State	Number of Places	Languages
Alaska	15 Boroughs & Census Areas	Alaskan Athabascan, Aleut, Filipino, Inupiat, Spanish, Yup'ik
Arizona	10 Counties	Apache, Navajo, Spanish
California	26 Counties	American Indian, Cambodian, Chinese, Filipino, Japanese, Korean, Spanish, Vietnamese
Colorado	6 Counties	Spanish, Ute
Connecticut	10 Towns	American Indian, Spanish
Florida	Statewide	Spanish
Georgia	1 County	Spanish
Hawaii	2 Counties	Chinese, Filipino
Idaho	1 County	Spanish
Illinois	3 Counties	Gujarati, Hindi, Chinese, Spanish, Urdu
Iowa	2 Counties	Algonquian, Fox, Spanish
Kansas	5 Counties	Spanish
Maryland	1 County	Spanish
Massachusetts	11 Cities & 1 Town	Cambodian, Chinese, Spanish
Michigan	2 Cities & 1 Township	Bangladeshi, Spanish
Mississippi	10 Counties	Choctaw
Nebraska	3 Counties	Spanish
Nevada	1 County	Filipino, Spanish
New Jersey	8 Counties	Gujarati, Hindi, Korean, Panjabi, Spanish
New Mexico	20 Counties	Apache, Navajo, Pueblo, Spanish, Ute
New York	7 Counties	Bengali, Chinese, Hindi, Korean, Panjabi, Spanish
Oklahoma	1 County	Spanish
Pennsylvania	3 Counties	Spanish
Rhode Island	3 Cities	Spanish
Texas	Statewide	Chinese, Kickapoo, Pueblo, Spanish, Vietnamese
Utah	2 Counties	Navajo, Ute
Virginia	1 County	Spanish, Vietnamese
Washington	4 Counties	Chinese, Spanish, Vietnamese
Wisconsin	2 Cities & 1 Town	Spanish

Each of the counties, cities, or other areas mentioned in the chart must provide voting materials in English and at least one other language. Some of them must provide materials in several languages. These places include Los Angeles and San Diego Counties in California; Cook County (Chicago), Illinois; Queens County (New York City), New York; and Harris County (Houston), Texas.

A volunteer puts up a sign in four languages.

People who make things ready for America's elections must work with diligence, a characteristic that God praised in Proverbs.

A lazy man does not roast his prey,

But the precious possession of a man is diligence.

Proverbs 12:27

Lesson Activities

Literature — Read "Reach Out to Potential Poll Workers" in *The Citizen's Handbook*, pages 38-39.

Creative Writing — In your notebook, write one paragraph telling your opinion about whether you think the Federal government should require state and local election officials to provide materials and assistance in languages other than English.

Find Out! — Have your parents ever voted absentee?

Picture This! — Design a poster or sign that encourages people to vote.

Student Workbook or Lesson Review — If you are using one of these optional books, complete the assignment for Lesson 41.

Going to the Polls on ELECTION DAY

In many rural precincts, small towns, and big city neighborhoods, Election Day can be a fun social event where people get to see people they know. Many of the officials working at the polls are their friends and neighbors. It's a fun day.

Going to the polls is exciting. Voters know they are part of something important. They are helping to make important decisions. They are taking action to help their city, state, and country. They are making history!

When citizens cast a vote to re-elect officials who are already in office, they are saying, "I want things to continue the way they have been." When they vote against an incumbent and for someone new, they are saying, "I want things to change. I want to try something new."

As mentioned on page 155, a voter votes at the assigned polling place for his precinct. There he can vote in the local, state, and/or Federal elections that are taking place that day. His polling place may be in a courthouse, a school, a National Guard armory, a community center, or another public building. See photos on this opening.

Ripton, Vermont
Community House, November 4, 2008

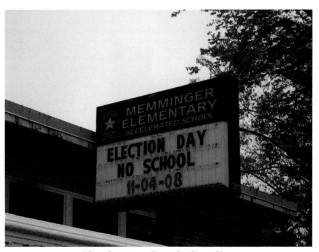

Charleston, South Carolina
November 4, 2008

Election Day Rules For Candidates

When voters approach the polls on Election Day, they see many signs advertising candidates; and they may also see and talk to campaign workers who are still trying to get people to vote for their candidates. However, in most states voters will not see these at a polling place. Most states prohibit electioneering and campaign signs, posters, and pamphlets within a certain number of feet (notice signs at right and below). In some states it is illegal to wear political hats, buttons, pins, or T-shirts, too. Voters must remove them or cover them (perhaps with a jacket).

Candidates may not enter polling places on Election Day, except to cast their own personal votes. They can, however, send poll watchers to the polls to observe the election and make sure that it is conducted fairly. A poll watcher is a person who

Manhattan, New York
Waiting in Line to Vote

Boxborough, Massachusetts
November 7, 2006

North Carolina
November 4, 2008

represents a candidate, political party, or civic organization. States may limit how many poll watchers any one candidate or organization may send to represent them at the polls.

A Voter's First Steps on Election Day

The first step in voting is to arrive at the polling place during the hours that have been posted by local election officials. The next step could be to stand in a line, perhaps for a long time. See photo 1 at left.

Once inside, voters check in with a poll worker who checks to see that he or she is a registered voter and is on the list of voters for that polling place. The worker also makes sure that the voter has not already voted early. The voter may have to show a picture ID (identification card) and sign his name. See photos 2 and 3.

The poll worker will then give the voter what he needs to cast his vote. What he needs depends on what voting method is used at that polling location. See photo number 4.

The Voter Casts His Vote

In the United States today, voters are guaranteed the opportunity to vote in private. A variety of voting booths are used to shield the voter from the eyes of fellow voters and election officials. At the top of page 219 is a corrugated plastic stand with three sides, which can be placed on a table; below it is a voting booth stand where three voters can vote at the same time. Depending on the voting method, the voter may also place his ballot in a secrecy folder.

As mentioned in Lesson 32, in the early years of America, voice voting was common. It was far from secret. George Caleb Bingham, who lived from 1811 to 1879, painted images of life on the American frontier. One in his series on American elections is called "The County Election." It illustrates an election in Saline County, Missouri, in 1850. Bingham himself was a candidate in that election. Bingham painted a crowded street. On the steps of a building is a judge. Before the judge is a voter with his hand on a Bible. The voter was swearing that he is entitled to vote and that he has not voted already. On the porch are election clerks. Each of these has a poll book in which he writes down the voter's vote. Having more than one person write down votes helped the count be more accurate. Methods used after voice voting included paper ballots, punch cards, and mechanical lever machines. Most voters today use the MarkSense technology or Direct Recording Electronic methods. An explanation of these methods follows.

Plastic Voting Booth

Paper Ballots. A paper ballot is a piece of paper on which voting choices have been printed. Examine the ballot below. Near the top left is the printed signature of the Secretary of the Commonwealth of Massachusetts. He is the elected official who is ultimately responsible for the election being held according to state and Federal laws. Included on this ballot in the left column are six President/Vice President choices from these parties: Constitution, Libertarian, Republican, Green-Rainbow, and Democratic, plus one Independent candidate. These voters are also voting for one U.S. Senator (listed as Senator in Congress) and one U.S. Congressman (listed as Representative in Congress). In the center column are choices for one state office with a choice of two candidates and one local office with a choice of only one candidate. In the right column is a question about lowering taxes.

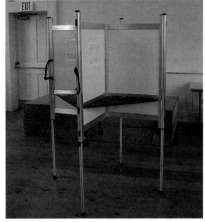

Three-Person Voting Booth

A voter using a paper ballot marks his choices on his ballot and drops it into a sealed ballot box. After the election, officials look at each ballot to count them. Paper ballots are often used by absentee voters.

People in a small town mark paper ballots on November 7, 2006, using wooden voting booths.

Mechanical Lever Voting Machines. Mechanical lever voting machines were first used in 1892. They were a common voting method during the 1900s. A voter cast his votes by moving a lever

Massachusetts
Official State Election Ballot for Federal, State, and Local Candidates

Ripton, Vermont
November 4, 2008

next to the name of each candidate of his choice. When he finished, mechanical counters inside the machine rotated to keep track of the votes for each candidate. These machines are no longer made. See example below.

Mechanical Lever Machine

Optical Scan Memory Pack

Direct Recording Electronic Machine

Punch Cards. In the punch card system, voters used a punching device provided at the polling place to mark their votes on punch cards. Special machines scan the cards to detect where voters have punched them. Punch card voting systems are no longer made.

Marksense. When polling places use a Marksense voting system, the voter makes marks on a printed ballot. Beside each candidate or issue is an empty rectangle, circle, oval, or a partially-drawn arrow. Voters fill in the empty spaces beside their choices or finish drawing the arrow. Voters place their ballot cards in a sealed box or into a computer tabulating machine. The tabulating machine recognizes the dark marks made by the voter by using an optical scan. See optical scan memory pack at left.

Direct Recording Electronic. Voters using Direct Recording Electronic (or DRE) voting machines touch a touch screen or push a button to record their votes. Votes are stored in the machine on some form of electronic memory (like in a computer). The machines often have a keyboard so voters can write in choices which are not on the official ballot if they wish to do so. See Direct Recording Electronic machine at left.

Many Americans believe that paper ballots are the safest way to get an accurate picture of what the American people want. They fear that computer hackers could tamper with any type of electronic voting machine. Many states require that in addition to an electronic record, voting machines produce some kind of paper record of votes which a voter can check before leaving the voting booth.

Voters Who Need Extra Help

Most American voters can walk into a polling place, read the ballot, and mark it with their choices. However, not everyone can do this. People with physical disabilities, people who cannot read or write, and people who are elderly may find voting a challenge. There are many ways that election officials provide help. Voters who have trouble seeing can request a magnifying sheet. Voting booths must be set up so that people in wheelchairs can use them.

When a person cannot come into their polling place, they may be able to vote at the curb. Voters can take an assistant into the voting booth with them, as long as the assistant is not their employer or a member of their labor union. These restrictions on who can go with them is to prevent a voter from being pressured to vote a certain way by a person involved in their employment.

Your First Vote

As you prepare for your first vote, be thankful for the ways God has blessed our country and be prayerful about its needs. Learn about the candidates and make wise voting decisions. A good way to prepare for your first vote is to read the second chapter of Proverbs.

> My son, if you will receive my words
> And treasure my commandments within you . . .
> Then you will discern righteousness and justice
> And equity and every good course.
> Proverbs 2:1, 9

Lesson Activities

Thinking Biblically — Read Proverbs 2:1-15.

Vocabulary — Copy these words in your notebook, each on a separate line: prohibit, corrugated, examine, signature, magnifying. Look up each word in the dictionary. Next to each word, write what part or parts of speech it is according to the way the word is used in the lesson.

Literature — Read "The High School Tax Election" in *The Citizen's Handbook*, pages 40-43.

Creative Writing — Sometimes a state legislature passes a bill and then asks voters to make the final decision. The vote by the voters on this bill is called a referendum. In your notebook, make a list of at least five issues you would like to see on a ballot so that voters could make the final decision.

Picture This! — Draw a picture or take a photograph of the voter registration card belonging to one of your parents.

Student Workbook or Lesson Review — If you are using one of these optional books, complete the assignment for Lesson 42.

Finding Out
ELECTION RESULTS

As people return home or go back to work after voting, they wonder if the candidates for whom they voted are winning. In a presidential election year, they are anxious to hear who has been elected as the next President. In each Federal election, they want to know how many U.S. Senators and Congressmen will be Republicans and how many will be Democrats. They look forward to hearing about state offices, too. A voter in a county or small town may wonder if his cousin was victorious in his bid for county commissioner or road supervisor. And, of course, the candidates themselves are anxious to hear the news. In the evening, many people gather for election night parties in homes and restaurants. Campaign workers gather at campaign headquarters around the country.

But how do people find out who is winning? When George Washington became the first President in 1789, newspapers reported the news. Since the fastest way to transport newspapers was by horse, it took weeks before some citizens were able to learn the news. As new technologies were invented, election news traveled faster. Today most citizens turn to some form of technology for election news.

Pasadena, California
Republicans await election results at an election night party after mid-term elections in 2006.

Arlington, Virginia
Democrats at an election night party mark votes from various precincts in a congressional race in the 2010 mid-term elections.

New York City, New York
Crowds gather to receive election results that have come in by telegraph, Frank Leslie's Newspaper, *November 1856.*

Lantern Slide of President William McKinley Projected onto a Building

New York City, New York
This searchlight from a tower in Madison Square Garden beams out the news that Grover Cleveland has been elected President, 1892.

Telegraphs, Pony Express, Searchlights, Lantern Slides, and Telephones

When Abraham Lincoln won the presidential election on November 7, 1860, telegraph lines ran from the East Coast to Fort Kearny, Nebraska, and from Fort Churchill in Nevada Territory to the West Coast. Election results were sent speeding to Fort Kearny by telegraph. A Pony Express rider took over then, taking it to the next Pony Express station. A series of Pony Express riders carried the news to Fort Churchill where the news was then telegraphed to the West Coast.

Today people living in small towns and big cities hear the news at the same time, but big cities once had an advantage. Notice the crowds gathered in New York City in the illustration above. They wait to hear election results from a nearby telegraph office.

At left is another scene from New York City. In 1892 the *New York Herald* newspaper rented this tower in Madison Square Garden. The crowd standing below knew that if the searchlight flashed to the west, voters had chosen Benjamin Harrison as President, but if it flashed east, New Yorker Grover Cleveland had won. Cleveland was victorious. He had voted that day himself at his local polling place, a little cigar store on Sixth Avenue.

The New York City crowd in the drawing above is looking at a photograph of William McKinley projected by lantern slide onto a building. This method of reporting election results was used in large cities in the late 1800s and early 1900s.

C. B. Slemp, secretary to President Coolidge, receives news by telephone.

In the photo above, C. B. Slemp, personal secretary to President Calvin Coolidge receives election results by telephone in 1924.

Radio, Television, and the Internet

Washington, D.C.
Fred C. Reed, Senior Scientific Aide at the Smithsonian, receives the donation of an historic microphone on October 28, 1938. This microphone was used to broadcast the victory of Warren G. Harding on November 2, 1920.

At right above is a photograph of a Smithsonian employee receiving the donation of an historic microphone. This "tomato-can-style" microphone was used to broadcast the victory of Warren G. Harding from station KDKA in Pittsburgh, Pennsylvania, on November 2, 1920.

When Herbert Hoover was elected President in 1928, then-President Calvin Coolidge heard the news while traveling by train to Washington, D.C. The RCA company had installed a special radio receiving set in his railroad car so that he could hear the news.

Regular television news shows began as fifteen-minute programs in the late 1940s. In the late 1950s, television networks began to send crews out to film news as it was happening. In the early 1960s, Americans began increasingly to rely on television to give them news about politics and elections. Television news programs expanded to thirty minutes in 1963. In the sixties, the NBC, ABC, and CBS television networks began to broadcast election news live to the American public on election night. During the evening, they reported election counts from one state after another. They displayed the results on a U.S. map.

In 1980 television entrepreneur Ted Turner began Cable News Network, America's first television network devoted solely to news. Other cable news channels followed. Americans could now get political and other news twenty-four hours a day.

Internet websites and social media outlets, like Twitter, YouTube, and Facebook are new sources of election news. However, a survey conducted early in 2012 by the Pew Research Center indicated that only a small percentage of Americans were using those sources for news. More than one third of Americans continued to use cable channels on television as their main source of election news, while 2% used Twitter, 3% used YouTube, and 6% used Facebook.

Exit Polls

Actually counting the votes across America takes time. In the 1960s television networks began asking people for whom they voted as they were leaving the polls. This questioning is called exit polling. Networks use this information to make guesses (called projections) about who the likely winners are.

Arlington, Virginia
Democratic campaign worker checks for election news after mid-term elections in 2010.

U.S. citizens living in the fifty states vote in six time zones on Election Day: Eastern, Central, Mountain, Pacific, Alaskan, and Hawaiian. Those in the Eastern Time Zone vote first and those in the Hawaiian Time Zone vote last. Voters in New York City have finished voting long before voters in Los Angeles, California.

In 1980 the NBC network announced that Republican candidate Ronald Reagan had won the presidency, defeating Democratic President Jimmy Carter. They made this announcement before the polls closed in the Pacific time zone, which includes California, Nevada, Oregon, Washington, and a portion of Idaho. The U.S. Congress held meetings to discuss the fear that people in western states may have decided not to vote since a winner had already been announced before they could even vote. The networks voluntarily decided to stop announcing their projections about winners in a given state until after the polls close in that state.

The photos below were taken in the newsroom of *The Washington Post* newspaper on election night in 2004. At left is an employee with a newspaper and a computer. The chart at right shows the projected winners for each state, as reported by ABC, CBS, NBC, CNN, FOX News, and the Associated Press. In the center is a map showing the states that have been projected for President George Bush in red and his opponent John Kerry in blue. You will learn why state vote counts are important in Lesson 44.

Washington, D.C.
Behind the Scenes on Election Night 2004
Center: Map with Red Republican and Blue Democrat States for President
Right: Chart Showing Projections of Major News Organization

Counting the Votes

What matters more than what the news media says about election winners is who the actual winners are. Votes from all precincts from a certain city or county are counted at a local counting facility. A local election official, often called an election judge, seals the ballot boxes at his precinct. See one type of seal on page 227. Law enforcement officers usually carry these boxes to the central counting location. If computerized voting was used, voting information may be sent electronically to the counting facility. If external computer memory devices are used, these are carried to the counting facility.

Paper ballots are removed from ballot boxes and counted by hand. If voters used punch cards, election officials count the cards and then run them through a punch card reader which counts both the cards and the votes. If the number of cards counted by the reader is different from the number counted manually, election officials sometimes order a recount. MarkSense (or optical scan) and Direct Recording Electronic voting results are counted electronically.

Candidates and observers from political parties are allowed to watch vote counters while they do their work. The photos on this page were taken by an election observer in San Mateo County, California.

These antennae help keep track of voting equipment and machines.

Counting Votes in San Mateo County

Locked Room with Scanned Ballots

Sorting Ballots

Recounting 1% of Electronic Votes by Hand

Many Election Workers

Television Coverage

Honest and Accurate Elections

Candidates, American voters, and local election officials must work together to make sure that American elections are honest and that vote counts are accurate. When election results are close or someone suspects illegal tampering with votes, candidates and certain government officials can demand that the votes be recounted. Vice President Al Gore asked for a recount of certain precincts in 2000.

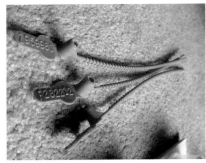
Ballot Box Seal

The best way to insure accuracy is for everyone involved to be honest. God cares about accuracy. In Proverbs Solomon taught this by telling how God feels about a seller's weights and measures. The same principle is true for elections.

Alameda County, California
Ballot Box

A just balance and scales belong to the Lord;

All the weights of the bag are His concern.

Proverbs 16:11

Lesson Activities

Marin County, California
Primary Election Tally Sheet

Thinking Biblically — Copy Proverbs 16:11 in your notebook, using the version of your choice.

Vocabulary — Write a paragraph using all of these words: supervisor, advantage, donation, external, accuracy. Consult a dictionary if you need help with their definitions.

Literature — Read "Business of the Greatest Moment" in *The Citizen's Handbook*, page 44.

Find Out! — Take a poll of your family. Decide on three questions to ask each person privately. Give each question three possible answers. Suggested questions are: What should we have for dinner? Where should we go on a family outing? What should be our next family read-aloud? Share the results with the whole family, keeping each person's votes private.

Picture This! — Draw a picture or take a photograph of two people in your family posed as if on the news discussing the outcome of an election.

Student Workbook or Lesson Review — If you are using one of these optional books, complete the assignment for Lesson 43.

The Electoral College and the
TRANSITION TEAM

When the Founding Fathers planned how the Federal government would be organized, they discussed two ideas about how to choose a President and Vice President. The people could vote for him directly or the U.S. Congress could elect him. They decided on a compromise. States would choose a group of electors who would vote for the President and Vice President. This method is described in Article II of the Constitution. Today these are the only two elected offices in America that are not chosen directly by the people.

The Origin of the Electoral College

The Founding Fathers got the idea of electors from the Holy Roman Empire, which existed in Europe from 962 to 1806. The princes of various states elected their emperor. The word college comes from the Latin *collegium*, which means a group of people who act as one. People began using the term Electoral College in the early 1800s, but the Constitution does not use the term. It only speaks of electors.

Choosing Electors

Arizona Electors	
Senators	2
Congressmen	9
Total Electors	11

The number of electors from each state is equal to the total number of Senators and Representatives that state has in Congress. The chart at right shows the number of electors for Arizona as an example. The total number of U.S. Senators is 100 and the total number of Congressmen is 435. Since 1961 the District of Columbia has also had three electors. When these are added, the total number of presidential electors is 538.

States decide how to choose their electors, but according to the Constitution: "No Senator or Representative or person holding an office of trust or profit under the United States may be appointed an elector." The common way that states choose electors is to allow each party that has a presidential candidate on the ballot in that state to choose a list of electors who will serve as the official electors if their party's presidential candidate wins on Election Day.

Since California has fifty-five electors, more than any other state, let's look at how its political parties choose electors. By October 1, the presidential candidate of each political party must file a list of his electors with the State of California. The state Democratic Party gives each U.S. Senator and each U.S. Congressman from California the responsibility of choosing one elector each. As seen in the chart below, the state Republican Party has a very detailed method. The Green, American Independent, and Libertarian parties nominate their electors at their state conventions.

On Election Day

Voters in each of the fifty states and the District of Columbia vote for a pair of candidates, a President and a Vice President. When they do so, they are also choosing the electors their party chose before the election. In some states, the names of the electors are actually on the ballot under the names of the candidates for President and Vice President.

In other states, the ballot may say something like: "Presidential Electors for:" followed by the names of a presidential candidate and a vice presidential candidate.

Look at the Ohio Democratic ticket from 1836 at top right. Notice that it lists Democratic candidates Martin Van Buren and Richard M. Johnson along with a list of electors from the Ohio Democratic Party.

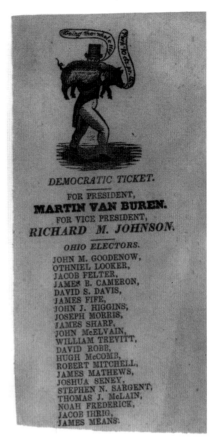

DEMOCRATIC TICKET.

FOR PRESIDENT,
MARTIN VAN BUREN.
FOR VICE PRESIDENT,
RICHARD M. JOHNSON.

OHIO ELECTORS.

JOHN M. GOODENOW,
OTHNIEL LOOKER,
JACOB FELTER,
JAMES B. CAMERON,
DAVID S. DAVIS,
JAMES FIFE,
JOHN J. HIGGINS,
JOSEPH MORRIS,
JAMES SHARP,
JOHN McELVAIN,
WILLIAM TREVITT,
DAVID ROBB,
HUGH McCOMB,
ROBERT MITCHELL,
JAMES MATHEWS,
JOSHUA SENEY,
STEPHEN N. SARGENT,
THOMAS J. McLAIN,
NOAH FREDERICK,
JACOB IHRIG,
JAMES MEANS.

Democratic Ticket from Ohio, 1836

Republican Electors from California

The Current Republican Candidates for:

Governor

Lieutenant Governor

Treasurer

Controller

Attorney General

Secretary of State

U.S. Senate Candidates in the Last Two Elections

The Republican Leaders of the California State Senate and California State Assembly

All Elected Officers of the Republican State Central Committee

All National Republican Committeemen and Women from California

President of Republican County Central Committee Chairmen's Association

Chairman or President of Each Republican Volunteer Organization Which is Officially Recognized by the Republican State Central Committee

Popular Votes and Electoral Votes

The number of votes that voters cast for candidates is called the popular vote. If the voters of Wyoming cast 500,000 votes for Sammy Samuel, 100,000 votes for Bobby Roberts, and 50,000 for Jimmy James, Samuel wins the popular vote.

Since Sammy Samuel received the most popular votes in Wyoming, he will receive all of its electoral votes. This practice of the candidate receiving all of the electoral votes is called "winner-take-all." All states give all of their electoral votes to the candidate who wins the popular vote except Maine and Nebraska. In those states electoral votes can be split between candidates in a formula based on their congressional districts. Maine changed to this method in 1972 and Nebraska in 1996.

A Washington Post employee studies map showing electoral vote counts on election night, 2004.

A state's electoral votes are the votes its electors will cast in December after the November election. Bobby and Jimmy will receive none from Wyoming. The photo above was taken earlier in the evening than the one on page 225. Notice that news of electoral votes is still coming in. Now you know why citizens want to know which candidate has the most votes in each state.

Because there is so much difference in the number of electoral votes from state to state, a President can win less than half of the fifty states and still win the presidency, if he wins in enough states to give him the majority of electoral votes. Some people believe the Electoral College system should be changed because a candidate may win the most total votes in the whole country but still not receive the most votes in the Electoral College. This happened when Rutherford B. Hayes defeated Samuel J. Tilden in 1876, when Benjamin Harrison defeated Grover Cleveland in 1888, and when George W. Bush defeated Al Gore in 2000.

The National Archives and Records Administration

As mentioned on page 32, the Archivist of the United States oversees the National Archives and Records Administration (NARA). A little-known responsibility of the Archivist and the NARA is overseeing the Electoral College process so that it is conducted according to the Constitution and Federal law. The NARA must be sure that

Washington, D.C.
Skaters on the National Mall in front of the National Archives

all 538 electoral votes are counted. The Federal Register plays an important role in this. The Federal Register is the official written record of the Federal government. It is operated by the National Archives and Record Administration and the U.S. Government Printing Office.

A Governor's Responsibility

After Election Day in November, the Governor of each state must prepare seven Certificates of Ascertainment, which list the names of the electors from the political party whose presidential candidate won in the state. These Certificates must say how many votes each of the candidates on the ballot received. The Governor must sign each Certificate. Each must be sealed with the State Seal.

Carson City, Nevada
*Governor-Elect Brian Sandoval
and Governor Bob List, 2010*

The Governor must send one original Certificate and two copies (or two additional originals) to the Archivist of the United States as soon as possible after Election Day. They must arrive no later than the day after the Electoral College meets on the first Monday after the second Wednesday in December. Look at the picture of the Archives on page 230 and imagine the Certificates arriving on a cold day like this in December.

Lawyers working for the Office of the Federal Register in Washington, D.C., examine the Certificates sent by each of the fifty states to be certain that they meet legal requirements. The two copies each Governor sent are then given to the U.S. Senate and House of Representatives.

The remaining original Certificates stay in the states so they can be used when the states' electors meet in the fifty states in mid-December.

Meetings of the Electoral College

The meeting of the Electoral College is not one meeting; it is actually fifty meetings. Each state's electors meet in their state on the first Monday after the second Wednesday in December. States may not change the date, but they may choose the location of the meeting. It is usually held in the state capitol.

Electors vote for a President and a Vice President at the meeting. There is no Federal law requiring electors to vote the way the voters in their state voted, but some state laws require this. It is rare for an elector to vote against the political party who chose them as electors. In all of American history, more than 99% of electors have voted the way they promised to vote when they were chosen as electors.

The electors make a record of their votes on six "Certificates of Vote." Each of the six remaining Certificates of Ascertainment is attached to one of the Certificates of Vote. The electors sign, seal, and certify these. They send one set to the President of the U.S. Senate and two to the Archivist of the United States.

Electoral Votes Given to Congress

The First Congress of the United States convened in 1789. The Congress that convened in 1801 was the 7th Congress, the one that convened in 1901 was the 57th, and the one that convened in 2001 was the 107th. A new Congress convenes around January 3 of each odd-numbered year. Its members include all members of the House of Representatives who were elected on the previous Election Day, plus all newly-elected Senators and Senators who are continuing their six-year term. On or before January 3, a ceremony is held in which the Archivist gives copies of the Certificates of Ascertainment to Congress.

Washington, D.C.
Counting the Votes of the Electoral College in the Chamber of the U.S. House of Representatives, February 9, 1921

A Joint Session of Congress

The electoral votes of the fifty states are officially counted in a joint session of Congress. A joint session is a meeting of the members of the Senate and the House of Representatives. The joint session is held on January 6, unless Congress passes a law to change the date (in 2008, they met on January 8). When Congress counts the vote, the President and Vice President must have a majority of all electoral votes to be elected. A majority of 538 is 270 votes. Pictured on page 232 is the joint session of Congress when its members counted the votes of the Electoral College which elected Warren G. Harding in 1920.

If no person receives a majority, the House of Representatives must choose the President. In that case, the Representatives from the various states vote as a group with one vote counted per state. Two Presidents have been elected this way: Thomas Jefferson in 1801 and John Quincy Adams in 1825.

The Transition Team

When a person goes through a big change in his or her life, like moving from one town to another, the person is said to be going through a time of transition. Countries go through transitions, too. Presidents have many responsibilities and many people working for them. The change from one President and his group of helpers to another is a transition.

The winner of the presidency on Election Day is called the President-elect. Though he is not officially elected until the Electoral College meets in December and Congress meets in January, he must begin making many decisions about his new job immediately after Election Day. In fact, the candidates in a presidential race actually start making plans between the time of their party's convention and Election Day. The top people who helped in the President-elect's campaign often continue to help as he prepares to move into the White House and take on his new responsibilities. The group of people who help make the transition from one President to another is called the transition team.

The General Services Administration (GSA) is an agency of the Federal government. When Congress passed the Presidential Transition Acts of 1963 and 2000, they gave the GSA responsibilities to help the President-elect and Vice President-elect take on their new duties. The Pre-Election Transition Act of 2010 gives the GSA authority to provide candidates with help before Election Day, too.

The GSA provides the incoming President with a staff and a budget of several million dollars to help with the transition. The GSA provides office space, furniture, telephones, vehicles, and parking spaces. It also gives the President-elect, Vice President-elect, and their team help with receiving and answering mail and with computer technology. They also help with plans for the upcoming Inauguration Day ceremonies when the President-elect and Vice President-elect will take the oath of office.

The GSA helps the outgoing President, Vice President, and their staffs make the transition out of office, as well. The outgoing President is sometimes called a lame duck. This term means that he really cannot make many important decisions. Another expression that is used is that "his hands are tied," because he knows that he will soon be out of office.

All people experience transitions in their lives. For Christians the most important transition was when they became a child of God.

> Therefore if anyone is in Christ, he is a new creature;
> the old things passed away; behold, new things have come.
> 2 Corinthians 5:17

Lesson Activities

Thinking Biblically — In your notebook, write a prayer for elected officials. Pray that they would speak and act kindly and honorably and that they would not fall into the temptations that are particularly hard for people who seek political office.

Vocabulary — In your notebook, write the vocabulary words and the letter of the definition that goes with each word: elector, profit, official, legal, convene.

    a. the difference of gain over loss
    b. according to law
    c. to come together officially in a group
    d. a member of the United States electoral college
    e. authorized and authoritative

Literature — Read "Lincoln's Farewell to the Citizens of Springfield" and "Sample Letter from the Archivist to the Governors" in *The Citizen's Handbook*, pages 45-46.

Creative Writing — In your notebook, write at least 2-3 paragraphs about a time in your life when you went through a transition, such as moving, going to a different church, or welcoming a new sibling into your home. Which aspects were difficult and which were exciting?

Find Out! — Ask your parents about a memorable election they remember hearing about in the news.

Student Workbook or Lesson Review — If you are using one of these optional books, complete the assignment for Lesson 44.

★ Remember to choose an American Holiday to study this week! ★

234

UNIT 10 – WASHINGTON, D.C., OUR NATION'S CAPITAL

BOOKS USED IN UNIT 10

- A Letter to Mrs. Roosevelt

- The Citizen's Handbook

- Student Workbook (optional)

- Lesson Review (optional)

The Lincoln Memorial

Introducing the People of
WASHINGTON, D.C.

When people think of Washington, D.C., they usually think about the gleaming granite government buildings and large monuments. However, for this lesson let's not think about the buildings and monuments. Instead, let's think about the people of Washington.

Elected Officials and Other People, Too!

Washington, D.C., is home to over 600,000 people. It is the nation's 24th largest city. Many more live in its Maryland and Virginia suburbs. About 5.8 million people live in what is called the greater Washington area. This total makes it the seventh largest metropolitan area in the country. Many in the suburbs come into Washington to work. On a typical work day, about one million people are living or working within the borders of our nation's Capital.

It might surprise you to know that, of all those hundreds of thousands of people in Washington, only 552 of them are elected by the American people. We elect the President and Vice President of the United States, 435 members of the House of Representatives, and 100 members of the U.S. Senate. Voters who live in the District of Columbia also elect a mayor, thirteen members of a city council, and one delegate to the House of Representatives who does not vote. This makes a total of 552 elected officials. The District also chooses three electors in the presidential election every four years. The rest of the people who work in government jobs in Washington are either appointed (many by the President) or are hired by the various departments of government.

Elected Officials

Senator Mark Warner, a Democrat, and Senator Bob Corker, a Republican, tape an interview on the balcony of the Russell Senate Office Building.

Appointed Officials

Under Secretary of Defense for Acquisition, Technology, and Logistics Frank Kendall; Secretary of Defense Leon Panetta; and Deputy Under Secretary of Defense for Installations and Environment Dorothy Robyn

Jobs in Washington

People who work in Washington have many kinds of jobs. Many are ones you would find in any city: store owners and employees, hotel and restaurant workers, people who fix things, attorneys, doctors, police officers, and so forth. At right are the Willard Hotel, known as the Hotel of Presidents, and Anthony's Italian Coffee House and Chocolate House.

Willard Hotel, Known as the Hotel of Presidents

But there are also many jobs that people fill in Washington because it is our nation's Capital. What do those people do? Employees of the Bureau of Engraving and Printing make paper money. National Park Service rangers work at the many national monuments and memorials. High ranking government officials advise the President. Top military leaders guide the troops. Judges, lawyers, and clerks work at the Supreme Court. Workers in the Federal Bureau of Investigation (FBI) investigate people who might have broken Federal law. Maintenance workers repair plumbing at the Capitol. Members of the Marine Band play concerts for the President and his guests. Custodians mop the floors of the Air and Space Museum. Guards protect the paintings at the National Gallery of Art. Zookeepers feed the animals at the National Zoo. People from every state work on the staffs of their Senators and Congressmen. The list goes on and on and the work of the Federal government spreads beyond Washington, D.C., to government offices now located nearby in Virginia and Maryland, too.

Anthony's Italian Coffee House and Chocolate House

Cleaning a Washington Escalator

Another kind of job in Washington is lobbyist. A lobbyist is someone who tries to influence Senators and Congressmen regarding bills that are being considered by Congress. The word lobbyist comes from the idea that these people stand in the lobbies outside of the actual chambers of the U.S. Senate and House of Representatives to talk to elected officials. More often today, lobbyists either go to the offices of elected representatives or send information to them. Many organizations in the United States pay lobbyists to give information to members of Congress in the hope that the Congressmen and Senators will support or oppose bills the way those organizations desire. For instance, the trucking industry has lobbyists in Washington, groups that want to preserve the environment have lobbyists there, farming organizations have lobbyists, home builders have lobbyists, homeschoolers have lobbyists, and on the list goes. People must think that lobbying is really important because over twelve thousand lobbyists work in Washington!

Many people work in one of the non-profit organizations that have their headquarters in Greater Washington, organizations like the American Red Cross, the American Association of Retired Persons (AARP), the United States Chamber of Commerce, the Corporation for Public Broadcasting, and Goodwill Industries International. Others work in one of the professional organizations or corporations that are headquartered or have offices in greater Washington.

Washington is an international city. Ambassadors come here from countries all over the world as do the staffs of its many embassies. Colleges, universities, and foreign companies with offices in Washington also attract people from other countries.

National Association of Realtors Washington, D.C., Office

Constitution Hall, Headquarters of the Daughters of the American Revolution

Washington Churches

The people of Washington are members of many churches. Two historic churches are St. John's Episcopal Church and the New York Avenue Presbyterian Church. St. John's Church is across from the White House. Many Presidents have visited St. John's at least once while in office, and several have attended regularly. Pew 54 is the President's Pew. President James Madison was a member. Its building was designed by Benjamin Henry Latrobe, one of several architects who worked on the U.S. Capitol. Latrobe wrote the hymn that was sung at the church's dedication and played the organ when the building was consecrated. The church bell was cast by Paul Revere's son Joseph. President James Monroe authorized $100 of government funds to help pay for the bell, which was used as an alarm bell for the neighborhood.

Abraham Lincoln and his family attended New York Avenue Presbyterian Church on the first Sunday after his inauguration. Its minister preached the funeral for Lincoln's son and the funeral of President Lincoln. Presidents John Quincy Adams, Andrew Jackson, William Henry Harrison, James K. Polk, Franklin Pierce, James Buchanan, Andrew Johnson, Benjamin Harrison, Dwight D. Eisenhower, and Richard Nixon have worshipped with this congregation, as have many members of Congress and justices of the Supreme Court.

Two other well-known churches are the Washington National Cathedral (an Episcopal Church) and the Basilica of the National Shrine of the Immaculate Conception, which is the largest Catholic church in North America and one of the ten largest churches in the world. It is also home to Franciscan Monastery of the Holy Land in America, a monastery begun in 1899.

Washington National Cathedral

The Boys Choir Practices Inside the Washington National Cathedral

Basilica of the National Shrine of the Immaculate Conception

St. John's Episcopal in Lafayette Square

New York Avenue Presbyterian Church

Colleges Around Town

Washington is the home of George Washington University, American University, the University of the District of Columbia, Catholic University of America, Georgetown University, and Howard University. It is also the location of Gallaudet University, the only university in the world in which all programs and services are designed especially for deaf and hearing impaired students.

Washington Transportation

Many people who live and work in greater Washington use the Washington Metropolitan Area Transit Authority rail, subway, and bus system. The Amtrak train system has service

Three Scenes from the Washington Metropolitan Area Transit Authority

Amtrak

Dulles International Airport

Two Scenes Inside Ronald Reagan National Airport

there and the area has two airports, Ronald Reagan National Airport and Dulles International Airport. See public transportation photos at left.

Hometown Sports

Washington is home to several professional sports teams. The Washington Redskins play in the National Football League. DC United is its professional soccer team. Professional basketball teams include the Wizards for men and the Mystics for women. Washington's major league baseball team is the Washington Nationals. Its pro hockey team is the Capitals.

Washington's Largest Group

Let's not forget the largest Washington group: the tourists. According to the National Park Service, more than twenty-five million people visit the nation's Capital every year. The attractions of Washington are well-known around the world, so over one and a half million visitors are from other countries. Someday we hope you can visit Washington. It is a great example of civics at work.

Washington Tourists

Though it is rarely reported in the news, here and there in Washington believers quietly gather with other believers to study the Bible. Many believers work in Washington for the purpose of serving God through what they do. These believers know:

All Scripture is inspired by God and profitable for teaching,

for reproof, for correction, for training in righteousness;

so that the man of God may be adequate, equipped for every good work.

2 Timothy 3:16-17

Lesson Activities

Thinking Biblically — In your notebook, make a list of at least five people who held a government position in the Bible.

Vocabulary — In your notebook, make a simple drawing for each of these words that illustrates what it means: gleaming, logistics, custodian, consecrated, impaired. Write the word under the drawing. Check in a dictionary if you need help with their definitions.

Literature — Read "Washington in 1845" in *The Citizen's Handbook*, pages 47-49, and chapters 1-3 in *A Letter to Mrs. Roosevelt*.

Creative Writing — If you have ever visited Washington, D.C., write 2-3 paragraphs in your notebook about your visit. If you have not been there, write 2-3 paragraphs about what you would like to see and do on a visit.

Find Out! — What is the history of the building where your church meets? When was it built?

Student Workbook or Lesson Review — If you are using one of these optional books, complete the assignment for Lesson 46.

Becoming the CAPITAL CITY

Washington, D.C.
United States Capitol

Brasilia, Brazil
National Congress

London, England
Houses of Parliament

The capital city of a nation is where the leader of the country lives and has his or her office, where the elected legislature meets, and where the highest court in the country hears cases. In the United States, our President lives and has his office in the White House; our legislature, called Congress, meets in the U.S. Capitol; and the Supreme Court meets in the Supreme Court Building.

The leaders of government want to meet and work where important activity takes place in the country. Throughout history in many countries of the world, a city has become a nation's capital because it was an important place for buying and selling, a center for the country's main religion, or a place where music, art, or education has been important. Sometimes a country has chosen a city to be its capital because it is near the center of the country. Some countries build a new city to serve as the capital. For instance, in 1956 Brazil started building the city of Brasilia in the central part of the country. Four years later Brasilia became the new capital of Brazil.

At left are the national legislative centers of the U.S., Brazil, and the United Kingdom.

242

Governments choose a capital at a particular point in history. A far away section of the country might later grow in population or have more business activity, but by then it is very difficult to move the seat of government to another place. When Washington was established as the Capital of the United States, it was near the geographic center of the country. As the nation expanded, the location of Washington became distant from the geographic center of the country, although it is still within a day's drive of about forty percent of the American population.

How Washington Became Our Nation's Capital

The way that Washington became the Capital of the United States and how it has functioned over the years is a good example of how Federal, state, and local governments work (and sometimes how they don't work very well). The story also shows the importance of civic pride and responsibility.

By the 1770s, Philadelphia was the largest city in the colonies. It had become an important trading city, and it was centrally located among the thirteen colonies. The First and Second Continental Congresses had met in the Pennsylvania State House in Philadelphia, now called Independence Hall. See photo at right. Here the colonies had declared the United States to be a separate nation from Great Britain. Congress continued to meet in Philadelphia under the Articles of Confederation as the Confederation Congress.

Philadelphia, Pennsylvania
Independence Hall
from Liberty Bell Center

In 1783, a mob of angry soldiers gathered in Philadelphia to demand that the Confederation Congress pay them for their service in the Revolutionary War. Congress asked the Governor of Pennsylvania, John Dickinson, to bring in the state militia to defend Congress. Dickinson, however, agreed with the soldiers' demands and refused to call up the militia. Congress then ran away from the city and began meeting in Princeton, New Jersey. Over the next few years, Congress met at times in Annapolis, Maryland, and in Trenton, New Jersey, before they finally settled in New York City.

When the Constitutional Convention met in Philadelphia in 1787, one issue that the delegates discussed was the location of a national Capital. The experience of the previous few years was on their minds. The delegates agreed that the nation's seat of government should not have to depend on a state if it needed to be defended by an army. Among the powers of Congress listed in Article I, Section 8 of the Constitution was:

To exercise exclusive Legislation in all Cases whatsoever, over such District (not exceeding ten Miles square) as may, by Cession of particular States, and the acceptance of Congress, become the Seat of the Government of the United States.

New York City, New York
President George W. Bush speaks at Federal Hall.

New York City, New York
President Barack Obama speaks at Federal Hall.

When the new government under the Constitution began, the decision about where to build the new Capital was still undecided. New York City served as the first national Capital. George Washington took the oath of office to become the first President in New York's Federal Hall. Congress also met in New York City. In the photos at left, President George W. Bush and President Barack Obama speak in Federal Hall.

The Federal government made plans to move to Philadelphia in 1790 and to stay there until a new Capital City was ready. Several states offered to donate land to the national government for a national Capital. Northern states wanted it to be in or near a large city in the North. Southern states wanted it to be closer to them.

James Madison, Thomas Jefferson, and Alexander Hamilton worked out a compromise. Hamilton believed that the Federal government should pay the debts that many states had after the Revolutionary War. Northern states owed more money than southern states, which had already paid most of their debts. It was decided that the Federal government would take over the debts states still owed from the Revolution and the Capital would be located toward the South.

Congress passed the Residence Act in 1790, which called for the district to be located along the Potomac River. The Potomac lay between Virginia and Maryland and was close to the middle of the country. It was agreed that some location along this river would be selected. Notice people enjoying recreation on the Potomac River at left.

Washington is about 137 miles from Philadelphia. Today we can drive that distance in about two hours, but in 1790 choosing a site

Kayaking and Boating on the Potomac River

along the Potomac made the location closer to southern representatives by several days' journey. Maryland and Virginia both agreed to give or cede land to the Federal government.

The Residence Act of 1790 authorized President Washington to determine the exact location. He chose an area a few miles north of his Mount Vernon home. Its location was a good one for the purposes of transportation. Ocean-going vessels could travel to the District of Columbia from Chesapeake Bay. The small port cities of Georgetown, Maryland, and Alexandria, Virginia, were already there. On this parcel of rural land that was mostly undeveloped, our forefathers began to build our national Capital City, Washington, D.C.

Planning the New Capital

Washington appointed three commissioners to oversee purchasing land and planning the district and the city. The commissioners decided to name it the District of Columbia, in honor of Christopher Columbus, and to give the name of Washington to the Federal City within the district. It is not unusual to see the name of a state capital spelled out completely, as in Bismarck, North Dakota, even though it can also be written, Bismarck, ND. Both of these mean, of course, that Bismarck is a city in the State of North Dakota. Our national Capital is different. If you spelled out the entire name of our nation's Capital, you would write, Washington, District of Columbia, which means Washington in the District of Columbia. However, you will almost always see it written simply Washington, D.C.

Surveyors Andrew Ellicott and free African American Benjamin Banneker laid out the ten-mile-square district. Some of the sandstone markers they put in place still stand. The President also appointed artist and engineer Peter L'Enfant to design the city. L'Enfant, who had been born in France, was familiar with the capital cities of Europe. He designed a beautiful city with wide streets, numerous parks, and inspiring monuments. However, L'Enfant did not get along with the commissioners. President Washington fired L'Enfant after a little more than a year's service. His plans were revised by others and then largely abandoned for several years.

Construction Begins

A design competition was held to choose designers for the Executive Mansion (now known as the White House) and the Capitol. Among those who submitted designs for the Mansion was future President Thomas Jefferson. James Hoban, an Irish immigrant, working in Charleston, South Carolina, was chosen as the winner. He moved to Washington, D.C., in 1792. The cornerstone of the Executive Mansion was laid on October 13 on a site President Washington had chosen. Construction continued for eight years at a cost of $232,372. When completed, the Executive Mansion was the largest house in the United States.

President Washington chose Dr. William Thornton as the winner of the design competition for the Capitol. The President laid its cornerstone in 1793. Construction began that year. James Hoban oversaw construction of both the Executive Mansion and the Capitol. Materials and labor were more expensive than planned, so the commissioners decided to build only the Senate wing.

The Federal Government Moves to Washington, D.C.

The Federal government moved to Washington, D.C., in November of 1800. Government facilities consisted of an unfinished White House, an unfinished Capitol, and a road between them. John Adams moved into the Executive Mansion on Saturday, November 1. On November 2, he wrote these words to his wife, Abigail.

> *My dearest friend,*
>
> *We arrived here last night, or rather yesterday, at one o Clock and here we dined and Slept. The Building is in a State to be habitable. And now we wish for your Company. . . .*
>
> *I shall say nothing of public affairs. I am very glad you consented to come on, for you would have been more anxious at Quincy than here. . . .*
>
> *Before I end my Letter I pray Heaven to bestow the best of Blessings on this House and all that shall hereafter inhabit it. May none but honest and wise Men ever rule under this roof.*
>
> *I shall not attempt a description of it. You will form the best Idea of it from Inspection. . . .*
>
> *I am with unabated Confidence and affection your*
>
> *John Adams*

A welcoming parade was planned for arriving Senators and Congressmen, but a snowstorm caused it to be canceled. These Federal legislators held their first sessions in the Capitol on November 17. On the following day President Adams traveled the short road from the Executive Mansion to the Capitol and gave an address to a joint session of the Senate and the House of Representatives.

The Supreme Court also moved to Washington in 1800. Since no plan had been made for a building for it, the Court moved into a space in the Capitol that had originally been planned for a committee of the House of Representatives.

In 1803 Jefferson hired Benjamin Henry Latrobe to continue work on the Capitol. In 1806 Latrobe drew the design drawing of the Capitol seen on page 247. In 1807 he drew a floor plan and landscaping plan for the President's House. It is also pictured on page 247.

With an unfinished Capitol and an unfinished White House, the President, the Congress, and the Supreme Court began to conduct our nation's business in its new Capital. The city was small and muddy, a far cry from the beautiful city of Philadelphia. One Senator from New

York commented that the city was not so bad. He said that to make it perfect, it only needed "houses, cellars, kitchens, well informed men, amiable women, and other little trifles of the kind."

Abigail Adams joined her husband and they lived in the Executive Mansion during the winter of 1800-1801. Abigail returned to their family home in Quincy, Massachusetts, in February 1801. President Adams left on the morning that President Jefferson was inaugurated in March.

President Adams prayed that wise men would occupy the Executive Mansion. This verse is one of many that can help a President be wise.

Listen to counsel and accept discipline,
That you may be wise the rest of your days.
Proverbs 19:20

Watercolor, Ink, and Wash Drawing on Paper of the United States Capitol by Architect Benjamin Henry Latrobe, 1806

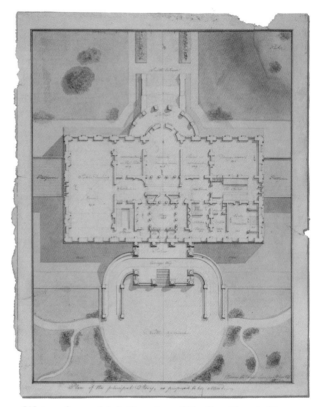

Watercolor and Ink Drawing of the President's House Site Plan and Principal Floor Plan by Architect Benjamin Henry Latrobe, 1807

Lesson Activities

Literature — Read "Brackets, Stairs, and Roofs & c." in *The Citizen's Handbook*, pages 50-53, and chapters 4-5 in *A Letter to Mrs. Roosevelt*.

Creative Writing — In your notebook, write a letter of at least one page to someone in another country describing Washington, D.C. You could describe some of the city's history that you just read about in this lesson. You could also write about some of the buildings in the city and what happens in them.

Find Out! — How far is Washington, D.C., from where you live?

Picture This! — Take a photograph or draw a picture of a construction site in your town.

Student Workbook or Lesson Review — If you are using one of these optional books, complete the assignment for Lesson 47.

From Mud Streets to GRAND AVENUES

The city of Washington, D.C., today is home to many beautiful and impressive buildings and inspiring monuments. However, this has not always been the case. During the 1800s, Washington suffered many difficulties. Keeping the Capital clean, keeping its streets and buildings in good repair, and helping it grow were not high priorities for Congress. Beginning in the early 1900s, however, Congress changed its attitude toward Washington, D.C. Many citizens thought about what the city could become and helped to make Washington the impressive city that it is today.

Early Trials

When Washington became the nation's Capital, the population was small and the city was incomplete. Congress did not move quickly. For instance, a canal system was planned to connect the Potomac River with the Ohio River. People thought this would help Washington become a major trading city as goods would be brought from inland states and sent to other countries. However, Congress was slow about appropriating funds for the canal system. By the time much progress was made on the canals, railroads had become an important means of trade and transportation. The canal system was outdated, so the project was abandoned.

In August 1814, during the War of 1812, the city of Washington was attacked by British troops. President James Madison and other government officials fled the city. The invaders used Supreme Court documents to set fire to the Capitol. They set fire to the Executive Mansion and to several other new government buildings as well. Rebuilding

Watercolor Painting of Buildings by the Chesapeake and Ohio Canal in Georgetown in Washington, D.C., by Susan Brown Chase, May 1916

took several years. President James Monroe was able to move into the restored Executive Mansion in 1817. Congress started meeting in the new Capitol two years after that.

Virginia's Part of the District Is Returned

The arrangements made for the part of the District of Columbia that had been given (or ceded) by Virginia were not popular among the people there. According to law, no Federal buildings could be built in that section of the District. Business developed much more rapidly in the Georgetown area, which had been given by Maryland. Most residents of the District lived on the Maryland side. When Virginia gave land for the District, the people of Alexandria and the area around it gave up the right to vote in Virginia elections. Because Congress made government decisions for the District of Columbia, the residents also had little voice in the District's government.

The people of the Virginia part of the District sent a petition to Congress asking that the area be returned to the State of Virginia. Congress agreed, as did the Virginia legislature, and the area was given back to Virginia as of 1847. This is why the District of Columbia no longer has a square or diamond shape. All of the current District lies on the Maryland side of the Potomac. Alexandria, Virginia and the area around it now have many government buildings and enjoy a bustling civic life that is closely connected to Washington, D.C.

The city of Arlington, Virginia, was also once in the District of Columbia. Scenes of Arlington are pictured at right.

The Effect of the Civil War

By the time of the Civil War, many government buildings had been built in Washington. Homes and businesses had also been built and the city population had grown to 75,000. The Civil War had a huge impact on life in Washington and the District of Columbia. A major part of Union war strategy was to defend the District from possible attack by Confederate armies, so many troops were stationed in and around the District. The

Scenes from Arlington, Virginia

Two Scenes from Arlington National Cemetery

Guarding the Tomb of the Unknowns at Arlington Cemetery

United States Marine Corps War Memorial

number of people who worked for the Federal government and lived in the District grew significantly as the war caused a large increase in government activity. In addition, Congress abolished slavery in the District in 1862, several months before President Lincoln issued the Emancipation Proclamation that freed slaves in the rest of the South. Many freed slaves moved to the District to obtain help from the Federal government in starting their lives over again. By 1870 the population had grown to 132,000. The photo at right was taken during Lincoln's inauguration in 1861, while the Capitol dome was under construction.

Inauguration of Abraham Lincoln, 1861

The Renewal of the City

Washington continued to grow. More government buildings and more homes and businesses were built, but when our Capital City reached its one hundredth birthday, it was in poor shape. Many houses and apartment buildings in the District were shabby. Congress had continued its pattern of not providing enough money to keep the city in good repair or to make improvements. Many other cities in America were also run down. A group of concerned Americans began thinking about how to improve them. Read about them below.

Helping Others Through the City Beautiful Movement

Around 1900 many citizens began to notice the poor condition of American cities. Some had grown quickly because large numbers of immigrants had moved into them. Many houses and apartments were unsafe and ugly. City residents were not taking pride in their communities.

In many places, groups began to encourage government and private businesses to provide money to build parks, monuments, and better houses and apartments, believing that this would improve the lives of poor people who lived in cities. These efforts were called the City Beautiful movement.

People in the City Beautiful movement believed that if the leaders of cities did not care how their cities looked, the poor had little encouragement to care. They thought that parks, monuments, and good housing would inspire citizens to work together for the betterment of everyone.

American citizens and visitors from around the world got to see ideas of the City Beautiful movement when they visited the World's Columbian Exposition in Chicago in 1893. The buildings at the fair were called the "White City." The planners of the San Francisco City Hall, completed in 1915 and pictured at right, used ideas from the City Beautiful movement.

The vision of a beautiful and noble national Capital was quite different from the city that Washington had become. Michigan Senator James McMillan led the effort to make Washington beautiful. Senators and Congressmen worked together, along with architects Charles F. McKim and Daniel Burnham, landscape architect Frederick Law Olmsted Jr., and sculptor Augustus St. Gaudens. They tried to fulfill much of what L'Enfant had originally planned and to improve on it with what was available in the twentieth century. The ideas they formed came to be called the McMillan Plan. Congress quickly began to carry out the plan. Pictured at right are two of the many projects proposed by the McMillan Plan that have now been completed.

Congress passed a law in 1910 that limited the height of buildings in Washington to no more than 130 feet (160 feet along certain parts of Pennsylvania Avenue). Buildings can be no wider than the width of the street by which they are located plus twenty feet. These limitations have meant that Washington does not have the skyscrapers found in other cities. The city's growth in population and activity has spread out instead of up. The lower building height and open spaces help visitors be able to enjoy the beautiful buildings and monuments.

Efforts to improve Washington have continued with the 1939 National Mall Plan, the 1976 National Park Service Plan, the 1999 Legacy Plan, and the 2010 Final National Mall Plan. Continued work to repair and improve the Capital is essential so that the twenty-five million visitors who come each year can enjoy

Two Views of the Arlington Memorial Bridge

Irises in West Potomac Park
This hand-colored lantern slide was photographed by Frances Benjamin Johnston. The park was completed in 1922. See page 223 for more about lantern slides.

its sights in a safe way and so that people from all over the world can come to this inspiring place to learn about America's history and ideals for generations to come. The tourists at right are pictured in front of the Lincoln Memorial with a reflection of the Washington Monument in the pool that lies between the Lincoln and Washington Memorials.

Reflecting Pool Between Washington Monument and Lincoln Memorial

Local Government in Washington, D.C.

Washington, D.C., has its own city government. However, as laid out in the Constitution, the United States Congress is ultimately responsible for governing the District of Columbia. It has the power to reject any law that the city government passes. At times in history, Congress has not even let the people who live in Washington elect a government of their own.

The way that Congress governed the District changed several times between 1800 and 1973. The first government that Congress created for the city consisted of a mayor appointed by the President and a twelve-member council elected by the people. Architect James Hoban was one of the first city councilmen, serving from 1802 until 1831.

In 1871 Congress changed the government of the District. It abolished the separate charters for the cities of Washington and Georgetown and put the entire District under a single government as a territory. This territorial government consisted of a Governor and council appointed by the President and a house of delegates elected by the people. From this point, Washington was no longer a city within the District of Columbia; Washington was the same as the District of Columbia.

D.C. Police in 1989 Inaugural Parade

D.C. Police Vehicle

The new government spent too much money, so in 1874 Congress abolished the territorial government and replaced it with a Board of Commissioners. The President appointed the three members of this board. This form of government remained in place until 1967. At that time Congress replaced the Board of Commissioners with an appointed mayor and council and an elected city commission. Finally, in 1973, Congress approved another change that went into effect the following year. The city would now be governed by an elected mayor and an elected city council. This is the form of government that Washington has today. However, Congress still has control over the city's budget; and Congress has the right to reject any laws passed by the city council.

Notice the pictures related to the local government of Washington, D.C., on page 252. The D.C. police force is pictured in the inaugural parade for George H. W. Bush in 1989. The truck is also used by the police force.

The District had no voice in the national government until 1961, when the Twenty-Third Amendment to the Constitution made voters in the District able to take part in presidential elections. The District has three electoral votes in the electoral college. The District also elects a delegate to the U.S. House of Representatives every two years. The delegate is allowed to take part in debates and all other activities, but he is not allowed to vote on bills.

Those who planned our nation's Capital wanted it to be a beacon of hope to the world, a place where people could learn about American ideals. Let us expand the prayer of President John Adams so that it can fulfill that dream and an even greater one. May all the leaders in Washington, D.C., be honest and wise men and remember that if they turn to Christ this can be said about them:

You are the light of the world. A city set on a hill cannot be hidden . . . .

Matthew 5:14

Lesson Activities

Thinking Biblically — Read Psalm 122, a psalm written by King David about Jerusalem, the capital city of Israel.

Vocabulary — Find each of these words in a dictionary: fled, strategy, fulfill, council, delegate. Copy each word into your notebook with the definition that corresponds to the way it is used in this lesson.

Literature — Read "The Crows at Washington" in *The Citizen's Handbook*, page 54, and chapters 6-8 in *A Letter to Mrs. Roosevelt*.

Creative Writing — Do you think it is important for the Capital of the United States to look fancy? Do you think it is worth the investment of time and money to make it so? Why or why not? In your notebook, write 1-2 paragraphs to tell your opinion.

Picture This! — Take a photograph or draw a picture of a location in your town that either used to be run-down and has been renewed or is currently run-down and needs some caring attention to make it beautiful again.

Student Workbook or Lesson Review — If you are using one of these optional books, complete the assignment for Lesson 48.

Timeline of D.C.
NATIONAL PARK SITES

In September of 1870 a group of men explored the Yellowstone region of the West. They had paid their own way to come and see for themselves the wonders that others had reported. As the group began to talk about how money could be made from this amazing place, Montana lawyer Cornelius Hedges shared a different idea. He suggested that the area be set aside for all time as a place that all people could use and enjoy. Hedges had hit upon an amazing idea. Land could be protected so that generations to come could experience for themselves the wonders of America. The idea grew and many citizens got involved. Land was set aside. Laws were passed.

The National Park Service

In 1916 President Woodrow Wilson signed a law creating the National Park Service. Over the years, the idea expanded to include not only God's creations like Yellowstone, but also the sites of important events in American history. Today the Park Service is responsible for sites across the country, including monuments and memorials in Washington, D.C.

National Park Service Law Enforcement Vehicles

National Park Sites in
Washington, D.C.

*National Park Service Director
Jonathan B. Jarvis with Representative
of Wounded Warriors, April 2011*

*Park rangers, U.S. Parks Police, volunteers,
and Wounded Warriors and their family members
cycle in Washington, D.C., April 2011.*

When we think of who takes care of America's National Park sites, we probably think first of park rangers. The park service employs almost 4,000 rangers, but it hires people in many other professions, too. See the list on page 254 for examples. Many American citizens volunteer each year in our national parks as well.

Americans have been building monuments since our nation began. In the last few years, many of our national monuments have been placed under the care of the National Park Service. The following is a timeline of many in our nation's Capital.

Washington Monument

1885 — The Washington Monument was dedicated on February 21, the day before Washington's birthday, which fell on Sunday that year. The monument weighs 81,120 tons. Its exterior is white marble from Maryland with a few stones from Massachusetts. Inside are 193 memorial stones from individuals, cities, organizations, states, and other nations.

1922 — The Lincoln Memorial was dedicated by Chief Justice of the Supreme Court William Howard Taft on May 30 before a crowd of approximately 50,000 people. The memorial is modeled after the ancient Greek Parthenon. Above each of its thirty-six columns is the name of one of the states that had been reunited after the Civil War. Sculptor Daniel Chester French created the statue of a seated Lincoln for the inside of the memorial. French studied Lincoln's life and photographs of the President for several years. One of Lincoln's hands is clenched in strength while the other is open in compassion.

Lincoln Memorial

Lincoln Statue by French

1931 — The District of Columbia War Memorial was dedicated on Veterans Day in 1931. President Herbert Hoover spoke and famed band conductor and composer John Philip Sousa conducted the Marine Band. Etched around the memorial's base are the names of 499 residents from the District of Columbia who died during World War I.

District of Columbia War Memorial

1943 — The Thomas Jefferson Memorial was dedicated on the two hundredth anniversary of his birth, April 13, 1943. Architect John Russell Pope, who designed the National Archives, designed the memorial. Pope honored Jefferson's life and work with a design similar to the ancient Pantheon in Rome and the Rotunda at the University of Virginia, which Jefferson himself designed. Pope died before the memorial was completed but his partners, Daniel Higgins and Otto Eggers, continued to oversee the planning.

Thomas Jefferson Memorial Along the Tidal Basin

Quotations from the Declaration of Independence and from other writings by Jefferson circle the interior walls of the Memorial. Sculptor Rudolph Evans created the bronze statue of Jefferson for the center of the open air memorial. However, the statue that was first erected was made of plaster painted to look like bronze because of a shortage of bronze during World War II. The finished bronze statue, nineteen feet tall, was put in place in 1947.

The stonework on the exterior is Vermont marble, and the interior walls are Georgia marble. These marbles represent New England and the Deep South. Tennessee marble in the floor and Indiana limestone in the inner dome represent the Union expanding westward. The statue of Jefferson stands on a block of Minnesota granite that has a ring of Missouri marble around the base. Parts of both of these states were in the Louisiana Purchase, which was one of Jefferson's most famous accomplishments as President.

Writer and geographer Eliza Scidmore returned from a trip to Japan in 1889 with the idea of planting Japanese cherry trees to beautify Washington, D.C. She discussed her idea with officials and private citizens for many years. Some individuals imported cherry trees to plant on their private property. First Lady Helen Taft became involved with the project. The government purchased ninety trees and the city of Tokyo donated 3,020 more. On March 27, 1912, First Lady Helen Taft and the wife of the Japanese Ambassador planted two trees on the north bank of the Tidal Basin. These trees still stand.

Jefferson Statue by Evans

In 1952 Japan asked for American help to restore a cherry grove near Tokyo that had suffered during World War II. This grove had been the source for the original trees planted around the Tidal Basin. The National Park Service sent budwood from the Washington cherry trees to Tokyo. In 1965 Japan donated 3,800 more trees that were planted in other

Springtime Along the Tidal Basin

parts of Washington. Then-First Lady Lady Bird Johnson was a strong advocate for beautifying America. She and the wife of the Japanese Ambassador re-enacted the original 1912 planting. In 1982 America again helped Japan when it lost cherry trees in a flood. The festival and the planting of cherry trees here and in many other parts of Washington are great examples of individual, civic, government, and international cooperation.

The President's Box in Ford's Theater

1960s — Ford's Theater was the site of President Abraham Lincoln's assassination in 1865. In 1933 the National Park Service purchased the theater and the William A. Peterson house across the street where the President died. In the 1960s, the NPS restored the interior of the theater to look as it did in 1865. In the Peterson house, they have recreated the setting where Lincoln died. Residents and tourists enjoy performances in Ford's Theater.

1965 — Pennsylvania Avenue National Historic Site celebrates one of the world's most famous addresses. It has been the setting for inaugural parades, protest marches, victory parades, and the funeral processions for Presidents and other leaders. A portion of the avenue was designated a national historic site in 1965.

Pennsylvania Avenue

Theodore Roosevelt Island National Memorial

1967 — The Theodore Roosevelt Island National Memorial is an 88.5-acre island in the Potomac River. It was dedicated on October 27, 1967. The park has a seventeen-foot-tall statue of Roosevelt. An outdoor plaza is engraved with Roosevelt quotes about preserving America's natural resources. See statue at left.

1974 — The Lyndon Baines Johnson Memorial Grove is on an island in the Potomac River. Lady Bird Johnson worked with landscape architect Meade Palmer to plan the memorial. She chose Columbia

Granite Monolith in Lyndon Baines Johnson Memorial Grove

Island as its setting, a place where she and her husband had stopped many times to enjoy its quiet beauty. The memorial grove has nine hundred white pines. A granite monolith, quarried in Johnson's home state of Texas, is inscribed with four Johnson quotations chosen by Mrs. Johnson. The quotes are about the environment, civil rights, the presidency, and education. The island has been renamed Lady Bird Johnson Park.

A View of the Washington Monument from Constitution Gardens

1976 — Constitution Gardens was dedicated in 1976. It is an oasis of green near the Vietnam Memorial. The Fifty-Six Signers of the Declaration of Independence Memorial, dedicated on July 2, 1984, is within Constitution Gardens. On an island in the middle of an artificial lake are fifty-six stones. On each is the name and signature of one of the signers of the Declaration of Independence.

1982 — The Vietnam Veterans Memorial was dedicated on November 13, 1982. The memorial features two walls of granite which seem to rise out of the earth. The names of those who died are carved on the walls in chronological order. In 1984 a statue of three servicemen was added. More than 275,000 individuals, civic organizations, corporations, foundations, unions, and veteran organizations donated to build the memorial. No Federal dollars were used. The competition for a design drew registrations from 2,573 people. Maya Ying Lin, a twenty-one year old senior at Yale University was the winning designer.

Left: Vietnam Memorial in the Snow; Center: Mementoes Left at the Wall; Right: "Three Soldiers" Statue by Frederick Hart

1983 —The Old Post Office Tower is the third tallest building in Washington, D.C. In 1983 the Bells of Congress were placed in the tower. The Ditchley Foundation, which was established to improve relations between America and Great Britain, gave the bells to the United States to celebrate the 200th anniversary of American independence. The volunteer Washington Ringing Society rings them

Old Post Office Tower

on Federal holidays, days of national mourning, on the opening and closing of Congress, and on every Thursday evening. The Old Post Office, built between 1892 and 1899, was scheduled to be demolished in the 1970s, but was saved by a group of concerned citizens. It was restored between 1977 and 1983.

1991 — The National Law Enforcement Officers Memorial honors Federal, state, and local law enforcement officers who have died while serving their fellow citizens. The memorial, dedicated on October 15, 1991, has two tree-lined pathways where the names of fallen officers are engraved. The names go back to 1791 and new names are added each spring. At the entrance to each pathway is an adult lion protecting its cubs. These symbolize how law enforcement officers protect citizens.

Two Scenes at the National Law Enforcement Officers Memorial

1995 — The Korean War Veterans Memorial was dedicated by President Bill Clinton and South Korean President Kim Young Sam on July 27, 1995. Each of the memorial's nineteen stainless steel statues are approximately seven feet three inches tall. They include one Navy, one Air Force, three Marine, and fourteen Army statues. Twelve are Caucasian, three are African American, two are Hispanic, one is Oriental, and one is a Native American. Each is wearing or carrying equipment that was used in the Korean War.

The memorial includes an Academy black granite wall etched with a mural of photographs from the National Archives. The photographs depict military equipment, rescue helicopters, surgeons, chaplains, pilots, nurses, ambulances, stretcher bearers, paratroopers, submarines, hospital ships, military police, Red Cross workers, and other people and

Korean War Veterans Memorial

equipment that the soldiers depended on to do their jobs. The wall reflects the statues so that it appears that there are thirty eight soldiers. This represents the thirty-eight months of the war and the 38th Parallel which divides North and South Korea.

African American Civil War Memorial

1997 — The African American Civil War Memorial honors the 209,145 "United States Colored Troops" who served in the Union army during the Civil War. The D.C. Commission on the Arts and

Humanities commissioned Ed Hamilton of Louisville, Kentucky to create the sculpture. "The Spirt of Freedom," was completed in 1997. Etched into it are the names of the 209,145 African American troops who served in the Union army during the War.

1997 — The Franklin Delano Roosevelt Memorial opened on May 2, 1997. It has four outdoor "rooms," one for each term Roosevelt served as President. It features the work of several American artists. Master stonecarver John Benson carved many of FDR's quotations seen throughout the memorial. The project cost $42 million in Federal funds and $10 million in private donations.

First Lady Eleanor Roosevelt

Franklin Roosevelt and His Dog Fala

Man-made Waterfalls at the Memorial

President Roosevelt's grandson David Roosevelt and Great Britain's Princess Margaret speak at the memorial's dedication ceremony.

Sculptures Depicting Scenes During Roosevelt's Terms in Office, Entitled "The Breadline," "Fireside Chat," "The Rural Couple"

Japanese American Memorial to Patriotism During World War II

2000 — The Japanese American Memorial to Patriotism During World War II was dedicated in 2000. It honors the 120,000 Japanese Americans who were interned in relocation camps during World War II and the 30,000 Japanese Americans who volunteered to serve in the U.S. military. The names of 800 Japanese American soldiers who died in the war are engraved on the memorial.

2002 — The George Mason Memorial was dedicated on April 9, 2002. Founding Father George Mason was the author of the Virginia Declaration of Rights and the Constitution of Virginia. Thomas Jefferson called Mason "one of our greatest men."

George Mason Memorial

2004 — The National World War II Memorial honors the sixteen million men and women who served in the U.S. military during World War II. It honors the 405,399 Americans who died and the millions of Americans who sacrificed on the home front to help the soldiers and help win the war. It was dedicated on May 29, 2004, as part of a four-day reunion of World War II veterans, held on the National Mall.

National World War II Memorial

Martin Luther King Memorial

2011 — The Martin Luther King Jr. Memorial was dedicated on August 28, 2011. It features a statue of Martin Luther King Jr. emerging from a "Stone of Hope." King was a minister who encouraged people to work for the civil rights of minorities through non-violent efforts. On a long stone wall are many quotes from his sermons and speeches. Learn more about this memorial in the holiday lesson for Martin Luther King Jr.'s Birthday.

The monuments and memorials in Washington, D.C. remind us of American ideals and our shared history. Remembering is important. When the Israelites were ready to enter Canaan, God gave them instructions about setting up stones to remember.

Now when all the nation had finished crossing the Jordan, the Lord spoke to Joshua saying, ". . . Take up for yourselves twelve stones from here . . . . Let this be a sign among you, so that when your children ask later, saying, 'What do these stones mean to you?' then you shall say to them, 'Because the waters of the Jordan were cut off before the ark of the covenant of the Lord; when it crossed the Jordan, the waters of the Jordan were cut off.' So these stones shall become a memorial to the sons of Israel forever."

Joshua 4:1, 3, 6, 7

Lesson Activities

Thinking Biblically — Copy Joshua 4:21-22 in your notebook, using the version of your choice.

Vocabulary — Write five sentences in your notebook, using one of these words in each: hydrologist, clenched, bronze, landscape, Hispanic. Check in a dictionary if you need help with their definitions.

Literature — Read chapters 9-12 in *A Letter to Mrs. Roosevelt*.

Find Out! — Ask your parents about a special monument they have visited and why it was meaningful for them to see it.

Picture This! — Draw a design for a new monument that you think would be a fitting addition to those that already stand in Washington, D.C. Design your monument to honor a particular American or group of Americans you admire. Look at the photographs in the lesson to get some inspiration.

Student Workbook or Lesson Review — If you are using one of these optional books, complete the assignment for Lesson 49.

★ Remember to choose an American Holiday to study this week! ★

UNIT 11 — THE PRESIDENCY I

BOOKS USED IN UNIT 11

- A Letter to Mrs. Roosevelt
- The Citizen's Handbook
- Student Workbook (optional)
- Lesson Review (optional)

President and Mrs. George W. Bush, President and Mrs. George H. W. Bush, and President and Mrs. Bill Clinton and their daughter Chelsea at Washington National Cathedral on the National Day of Prayer and Remembrance for the victims of the 9/11 terrorist attacks, September 14, 2001

Responsibilities of the PRESIDENT

The President of the United States is the highest ranking official in the U.S. government. He is the leader of the world's most powerful military and the world's biggest economy. He has the opportunity to be the world's best defender of freedom and human rights. Many people say that the President is the single most powerful person in the world. The Constitution lists several important jobs that the President carries out.

Head of the Executive Branch

The President is the head of the executive branch of the Federal government. This means that he is responsible for seeing that the laws passed by Congress are faithfully carried out or executed (this is the meaning of the term executive). This work is carried out by the many departments of the executive branch. The heads of these departments make up what is called the President's Cabinet. The President meets with his Cabinet regularly to discuss what the government is doing or should be doing.

Read about the painting of Lincoln and his Cabinet below.

Using Talents to Serve: Francis B. Carpenter

Artist Francis B. Carpenter painted "The First Reading of the Emancipation Proclamation Before the Cabinet" at the White House in 1864. From left to right are the Secretary of War, Secretary of the Treasury, President Lincoln, Secretary of the Navy, Secretary of the Interior, Secretary of State, Postmaster General, and Attorney General. Lincoln had signed the Emancipation Proclamation which freed slaves in the Confederate states on January 1, 1863.

President Wilson (front row center) with His Cabinet

President Truman (in center chair on right side of table) with His Cabinet

President Clinton (front row third from right) with His Cabinet and Senior Advisors

Pictured above are the Wilson, Truman, and Clinton Cabinets, plus President Clinton's Senior Advisors. In the photograph below, President George W. Bush and his Cabinet pray at a Cabinet meeting on September 14, 2001, just three days after terrorists attacked the World Trade Center in New York City and the Pentagon near Washington, D.C.

Independent agencies created by Congress do some of the work of the executive branch. They are not part of a department but report directly to the President. Examples include the Central Intelligence Agency (CIA), which gathers information important to our nation's safety, and the Social Security Administration which distributes benefits to retired and disabled persons. We will discuss many things that the executive branch does in later lessons.

Almost three million people work in the departments and independent agencies of the U.S. government. When you add in about one million people who serve in the military, the President is responsible for the work of about four million people!

By far most of these four million people are hired to do their jobs and are already serving when a new President takes office. They are called civil service employees and are hired because they have the needed qualifications and not because of a President's decision. However, the President chooses a few thousand of the highest ranking officials in the various departments and agencies. The President nominates them and the Senate has the power to confirm or reject the President's nominations. This is another example of checks and balances.

The President has a staff of almost five hundred people

President Bush and His Cabinet During a Cabinet Meeting, September 14, 2001

who are known as the White House staff. Each person has his own job title and set of responsibilities. Together they advise and assist the President, write speeches for him, plan his travel, answer his mail, counsel him on legal matters, talk to the news media, schedule his activities, and do a host of other things to make it possible for him to do his job. A few members of the White House staff assist his wife, the First Lady.

The President is responsible for them all, but the actual job of overseeing their work is carried out by the Chief of Staff. Even the Chief of Staff has a staff to help him oversee the White House staff!

In 2012 White House staff salaries ranged from $41,000 to $172,200. Three employees made $41,000, including the Associate Director for Scheduling Correspondence, the Associate Director of Online Engagement, and an Analyst. Twenty employees made $172,200. Read the boxes at right and below to learn about the salaries of the White House staff.

White House Staff Salaries in 2012

Salary Range	# of Employees
$40,000-$49,000	114
$50,000-$59,000	67
$60,000-$69,000	56
$70,000-$79,000	33
$80,000-$89,000	28
$90,000-$99,000	29
$100,000-$109,000	26
$110,000-$119,000	20
$120,000-$129,000	11
$130,000-$139,000	32
$140,000-$149,000	12
$150,000-$159,000	15
$160,000-$169,000	3
$170,000-$172,200	20

White House Staff Members Who Earned the Highest Salaries, 2012

Assistant to the President for Economic Policy and Director of the National Economic Council

Assistant to the President for Homeland Security and Counterterrorism

Cabinet Secretary*

Chief of Staff*

Chief of Staff to the First Lady*

Counsel to the President*

Counselor to the President

Deputy Chief of Staff for Operations*

Deputy Chief of Staff for Planning*

Deputy Chief of Staff for Policy*

Deputy National Security Advisor*

Deputy National Security Advisor for International Economics*

Director of Communications*

Director of Speechwriting*

Director, Office of Legislative Affairs*

Director of the Domestic Policy Council*

National Security Advisor*

Press Secretary*

Senior Advisor*

Senior Advisor and Assistant to the President for Intergovernmental Affairs and Public Engagement

*These staff members also serve as Assistants to the President.

Most of the White House staff has offices in the Eisenhower Executive Office Building which is located next to the West Wing of the White House. The building was originally called the

State, War, and Navy Building. It was completed in 1888 to house those executive departments. In 1949 the building was turned over to the Executive Office of the President and renamed the Executive Office Building. In 1999 it was named the Eisenhower Executive Office Building.

The massive building was constructed of granite, slate, and iron to make it fireproof. The interior is mainly cast iron or plaster. The building originally had 553 rooms and 1.73 miles of black and white tiled floors. Eighty-three of the 151 original fireplaces remain. It has four skylight domes. See one of these below. The Indian Treaty Room, pictured at right, has been used for many presidential news conferences. It is now used for conferences and receptions. The Eisenhower Executive Office Building has sixty-five staircases with a total of 1,784 stairs, just seventy-six less than the Empire State Building. Of these, eight are grand curved staircases, made of granite. See black and white photo. The staircases have 4,004 bronze balusters (handrail supports) which were each cast individually.

Indian Treaty Room

Eisenhower Executive Office Building

Skylight, Balusters, and Handrail

Curved Staircase with Black and White Floor Tiles

Head of State

The President is the head of state and the highest official representative of our country to other countries. He is ultimately responsible for our country's relations with other nations of the world. When the President makes an official visit to another country, or when the leader of another country comes to meet with the President, this is called a state visit. At right President Bush greets British Prime Minister Tony Blair at the White House.

President George W. Bush greets British Prime Minister Tony Blair on September 20, 2001.

A President wants to have good relations with other countries to avoid war and so that the countries can help one another. The President can make treaties or agreements with other countries, although these treaties have to be approved by the Senate before they take effect.

Commander in Chief

The President serves as Commander in Chief of all United States military forces. The President can order any part of the military into action when he believes the country or any of its citizens are in danger. When the United States becomes involved in a war, the President is responsible for overseeing the activities of the military. It is important to

President Obama visits the Pentagon in 2009.

understand that the President, the Secretary of Defense in the Cabinet, and the leaders of each branch of the military are civilians. Ultimate control of the military forces rests in the hands of civilians, not military leaders. In the photos above and at left, Presidents Obama and Bush encourage troops.

President Bush says thank you while visiting troops in Iraq and Afghanistan during the Christmas holidays in 2008.

Nominations of Ambassadors and Judges

In addition to the members of the Cabinet and other members of the executive branch, the President also nominates Ambassadors to represent the United States in foreign countries. He nominates people to serve as Federal judges, too. There are almost seven hundred Federal district judges and almost three hundred full-time and part-time justices on U.S. Circuit Courts of Appeal. The presidential nominations that receive the most attention are the people he selects to serve on the nine-member United States Supreme Court. See President Ronald Reagan with one of his Supreme Court nominees at left. All of the nominations described here must be confirmed, or approved, by the U.S. Senate.

Granting Reprieves and Pardons

The President is able to grant reprieves and pardons to persons who have been convicted of crimes against the United States. A reprieve is a change of a heavy sentence to a lighter

President Reagan with Supreme Court Justice Nominee Sandra Day O'Connor

sentence, while a pardon removes the person's penalty altogether. The President is not able to grant a pardon to someone who has been impeached and removed from office by Congress.

The State of the Union

The Constitution says that the President must inform Congress from time to time of the condition of the country or the state of the Union. The President does this each year in his State of the Union address. He also may recommend to Congress any laws that he thinks would be good for the country. When the President gives his State of the Union address each year, he talks about what he has accomplished, his ideas about laws he wants Congress to enact, and his hopes and dreams for the country.

President Reagan gives the State of the Union address, January 25, 1984.

The President has a great deal of authority and many government workers answer to him. However, the President is still under authority, as well. He is under the authority of God and under the authority of the American people. A centurion with great responsibility and authority once came to Jesus to ask for His help. The centurion told Jesus:

For I also am a man under authority, with soldiers under me;

and I say to this one, "Go!" and he goes, and to another, "Come!" and he comes . . . .

Matthew 8:9

Lesson Activities

Thinking Biblically — In your notebook, write a comparison between the pardons a President is able to give and the pardon Christians receive through the death and forgiveness of Jesus.

Literature — Read "Proclamation of Pardon" in *The Citizen's Handbook*, pages 55-56, and chapters 13-14 in *A Letter to Mrs. Roosevelt*.

Creative Writing — Look at the positions held by members of the White House staff listed in the box on page 266. If you could pick one of these positions for yourself, which would it be? Write a paragraph in your notebook about why you think you would enjoy it.

Find Out! — How many more stairs are in the Eisenhower Executive Office Building than are inside and outside your house?

Student Workbook or Lesson Review — If you are using one of these optional books, complete the assignment for Lesson 51.

The Leadership Role of the PRESIDENT

The President of the United States must fulfill the roles described for him in the Constitution. He must also fulfill many leadership responsibilities in the United States and around the world.

Personal Appearances Around the Country

The President travels around the country to meet and speak to American citizens. In the early years of our nation, traveling long distances was difficult. A President might make a few long trips called goodwill tours. A presidential visit was a major event for a town or city; and each one would have a parade, a large banquet, or other special events. Today, when the President can fly to any part of the country and return to Washington the same day, the chief executive might pay a quick visit to any number of places. See photos below.

Clockwise from Left: President George W. Bush (center) and Defense Department officials break ground for new Walter Reed National Military Medical Center, July 3, 2008. President Clinton waves to the crowd after giving a speech in Charleston, West Virginia. President George H. W. Bush speaks to a crowd at the Norristown Area High School in Pennsylvania, September 9, 1992. President Obama visits a new factory which makes solar cells, May 26, 2010.

Traveling Around the World

Modern Presidents travel overseas many times during their terms in office. They visit other heads of state. They visit American troops. They attend international meetings and events. The first President to leave the United States while in office was Theodore Roosevelt, who traveled to Panama in 1906. In the photos at right, President Reagan visits in Europe and President Obama visits in Africa.

President Reagan speaks to the British Parliament, June 8, 1982.

President Obama shakes hands with members of a crowd in Ghana after making a speech to that country's Parliament, July 11, 2009.

Hosting and Attending Special Events

Back in Washington, the President hosts many events. It is considered a great honor for anyone to be invited to the White House to meet him. When the head of state from another country visits the United States, the President often hosts a state dinner with hundreds of guests. The President

President Reagan, Entertainer Michael Jackson, and Mrs. Reagan launch an anti-drunk driving campaign, 1984.

also hosts events where people are awarded for outstanding accomplishments. He hosts sports champions, like Olympic athletes, the football team that won the Super Bowl, and the baseball team that won the World Series. From time to time the President will conduct a press conference, during which he will answer questions from reporters who cover the White House. The President also attends many special functions in Washington, D.C., and its suburbs.

Getting There

As technology changes, so does the way Presidents travel. Before he was President, William Howard Taft got interested in motor vehicles. He especially liked the White Steamer, a steam-powered automobile built by the White Sewing Company. When Taft became President, he convinced

Taft's Pierce Arrow

Congress that cars were neither too expensive nor too dangerous for use by the President. With the $12,000 Congress appropriated, Taft purchased a Steamer, two Pierce-Arrow limousines, and two other vehicles. The White House stables were converted to a garage, and chauffeurs were hired. See one of the Pierce Arrows above.

Limousine Used by President George H. W. Bush

President Truman and his wife Bess travel to an Army-Navy football game on the Ferdinand Magellan, *1950.*

Every President since Taft has traveled in limousines. Today the President's limousine is a heavily-armored vehicle. He travels in a motorcade that includes police cars; a vehicle that detects chemical or biological dangers; vans carrying members of the press; an ambulance; and SUVs carrying Secret Service agents, a military aide, a physician, an assault team to protect the President in case of attack, and communication equipment.

Presidents Franklin Roosevelt and Harry Truman traveled on a specially-designed armored railroad car, the *Ferdinand Magellan*, pictured at left. The *Ferdinand Magellan* was a regular Pullman sleeping car that was altered for the President. Nickel-steel armor was riveted to its roof, floor, sides, and ends. The window glass was replaced with glass three inches thick, and two escape hatches were installed. The car had four bedrooms, a dining/conference room, and an observation lounge to be used by the President and his guests, plus a kitchen and a steward's bedroom. Presidents Roosevelt and Truman entertained guests on the car. Eisenhower used the car only a few times before it was taken out of government service. The Gold Coast Railroad Museum in Miami, Florida, acquired the car in 1959.

As mentioned on page 198, modern Presidents travel often by air. Many times they leave the White House grounds on a Marine One helicopter, travel to Joint Base Andrews (formerly Andrews Air Force Base), and there board Air Force One. President Franklin Roosevelt was the first President to travel by plane on official business. He flew to Casablanca, Morocco, in North Africa in 1943 to meet with British Prime Minister Winston Churchill. Travel by ship was too dangerous because of German U-boats in the Atlantic. Roosevelt rode on the *Ferdinand Magellan* to Miami and then flew from Florida to the Caribbean to Brazil to the African country of Gambia and on to Casablanca. The stops were necessary for refueling. After returning home the same way, he had traveled 17,000 miles. After Roosevelt's first flight, Presidents flew on various airplanes that used propellers. The first President to use a jet was President Kennedy.

Marine One arrives at the White House and President Obama boards.

Air Force One is actually the call sign for any plane carrying the President, just as Marine One is the call sign for any helicopter carrying the President. However, the U.S. government actually owns two Boeing 747-200B presidential planes. A number of helicopters can be used as Marine One. When a President flies on a helicopter, the presidential seal is attached to it. The first time a President rode on a Marine helicopter was in 1957 when President Eisenhower needed to get back to the White House quickly while he was on vacation. His two-hour motorcade travel time was reduced to seven minutes.

President Bush talks with his Chief of Staff Andy Card, September 11, 2001.

Air Force One can refuel in the air, so it can take the President anywhere in the world. It is often accompanied by several cargo planes which arrive before the President, carrying items needed when he and his companions land.

President Bush talks on phone aboard Air Force One while his senior advisors discuss plans, September 11, 2001.

The interior of the plane has three levels, with the same amount of living and office space as a very large home—4,000 square feet. The plane has a stateroom, office space, and a conference room for the President, plus space for senior advisors, Secret Service officers, members of the press, and other guests. The two kitchens can serve one hundred people. A doctor is always on board and the plane's medical suite can serve as an operating room. See interior of Air Force One at right.

President Bush talks with his Chief of Staff Andy Card, September 11, 2001

Serving as Leader of His Party

The President is seen as the leader of his political party. Political parties did not exist when the Constitution was written, but they became part of American political life a few years later. A political party is made up of people who support particular individuals or ideas. A political party wants to have one of its members as President and other members as Representatives and Senators in Congress. When the President and a majority of Congress are members of the same political party, Congress is more likely to enact laws that the party likes. The President has a great deal of influence in determining official party policies. When he campaigns for his own re-election, he hopes to help his political party. He will often campaign for members of his party when they are running for the Senate or House of Representatives, in the hope that his influence with voters will help those candidates get elected. See photos at left.

President Obama speaks at a fundraiser for his campaign in Michigan on April 18, 2012.

President Obama campaigns for Washington Senator Patty Murray during the 2010 mid-term elections.

President George H. W. Bush speaks at the Yale University commencement, 1991.

President Clinton gives radio address.

The formal and informal roles that the President fills keeps him almost constantly in the news. He is the most visible person in government.

Using the Bully Pulpit

Often the President will travel to make a speech that will emphasize a program he wants to highlight, such as job creation or preserving the environment. In May and June the President will deliver a few commencement addresses at university graduations. See photo at left. The President receives hundreds of invitations to make speeches. He is only able to accept a small number of them, so he chooses carefully.

Like all Presidents, Theodore Roosevelt used his role as President to speak about issues that were important to him. He once said, "I suppose my critics will call that preaching, but I have got such a bully pulpit." President Roosevelt was fond of the using the word "bully." At the time it was a sort of slang word meaning really good. Roosevelt was saying that the President has a great opportunity to promote ideas with the American people.

The President might deliver a speech on television from the White House when he wants to address the nation on an important subject. Many Presidents have delivered addresses on the radio or Internet. See photo at lower left.

President Ronald Reagan was called the "Great Communicator." Many Presidents have been excellent communicators. Let's end this lesson with some of the words of our Presidents, words that reveal their character.

President Grover Cleveland — "What is the use of being elected or re-elected unless you stand for something?"

President Woodrow Wilson — "No one but the President seems to be expected . . . to look out for the general interests of the country."

Future President Herbert Hoover (when he was criticized in 1921 for feeding starving people in Russia) — "Twenty million people are starving. Whatever their politics, they shall be fed!"

President Harry Truman (upon becoming President) — "I felt like the moon, the stars, and all the planets had fallen on me."

President Jimmy Carter (speaking of his political opponent President Gerald Ford, who came into the presidency after President Nixon resigned) — "For myself and for our Nation, I want to thank my predecessor for all he has done to heal our land."

President Ronald Reagan — "If we ever forget that we're one nation under God, then we will be a nation gone under."

Let your speech always be with grace, as though seasoned with salt,

so that you will know how you should respond to each person.

Colossians 4:6

Lesson Activities

Literature — Read "General Instructions for the Western Trip" in *The Citizen's Handbook*, pages 57-58, and chapters 15-16 in *A Letter to Mrs. Roosevelt*.

Vocabulary — Copy these words in your notebook, each on a separate line: goodwill, press, interior, emphasize, predecessor. Look up each word in the dictionary. Next to each word, write what part or parts of speech it is according to the way the word is used in the lesson.

Creative Writing — If you or anyone in your family has even seen a President of the United States, write about that experience in your notebook. If no one in your family has, write a one page fictional story in which someone gets to see the President.

Find Out! — How many methods of transportation have members of your family used to get from one place to another? Count automobiles, boats, animals, skateboards, bicycles, etc.

Picture This! — Take a photograph or draw a picture of someone in your family pretending to be President. The person could be making a speech, waving to an imaginary crowd, or working at a desk.

Student Workbook or Lesson Review — If you are using one of these optional books, complete the assignment for Lesson 52.

The President's DAY

College Station, Texas
*George Bush Presidential Library and Museum
on the Texas A & M University Campus*

The President probably feels as if his day is not his own, but belongs to all the people of America, and, on some days, to the people of the whole world. A President's day is packed with activity.

Records of what a President does each day are kept by the Office of Appointments and Scheduling. The information in this lesson was found in its "Daily Diary of President George Bush" (President George H. W. Bush, who served from 1989 to 1993). After a President leaves office, he and his supporters raise money to build a presidential library which becomes part of the National Archives. The daily diaries of President George H. W. Bush are stored at his presidential library. See photos of the George Bush Presidential Library on this page.

The following is what President George H. W. Bush did on one day of his presidency, November 30, 1989. The world was in a time of transition. The Berlin Wall had just been torn down on November 9. The U.S.S.R. was starting to fall apart. Countries it had once controlled were pulling away and becoming independent. President Bush's day began at 5:45 a.m. in the White House in Washington, D.C., and ended on Air Force One over the Atlantic Ocean. We found no photographs for that day, so we have illustrated this lesson with President

"Meet Ben Franklin!" Storytelling Event; Barbara Bush Literacy Corps; Christmas 2010—Programs at the Bush Library

276

George H. W. Bush doing similar activities on different days and photographs of Presidents Kennedy, Clinton, George W. Bush, and Obama doing similar activities.

Schedule of George Herbert Walker Bush November 30, 1989

Family Living Quarters

5:45 a.m. Eastern Time— President Bush had breakfast with First Lady Barbara Bush.

Oval Office

7:08 a.m. — President Bush went to the Oval Office.

7:25 a.m. — President Bush talked with the First Lady.

7:29 a.m. — President Bush talked with his Assistant for Communications.

7:53 a.m. — President Bush talked with a Democratic Senator from Oklahoma.

8:00 a.m. — President Bush had an intelligence briefing where he was given secret information important to the security of the United States. Briefing the President were the Director of the Central Intelligence Agency, two people who worked with National Security Affairs, and the President's Chief of Staff.

8:28 a.m. — Vice President Dan Quayle joined the meeting, as did Bush's Assistant for Communications.

9:00 a.m. — President Bush had a conference call with the Prime Minister of Italy, Bush's Director of European and Soviet Affairs in the National Security Council, and an interpreter provided by the U.S. Department of State. A conference call is one in which people from more than two places talk over the telephone at the same time.

9:17 a.m. — The President met with the Vice President, the Secretary of State, his Chief of Staff, and other members of his staff.

Cabinet Room

9:40 a.m. — The President went into the Cabinet Room.

President George H. W. Bush talks on the telephone in the Oval Office.

President George H. W. Bush meets with Press Secretary Marlin Fitzwater.

President George H. W. Bush meets with Secretary of State James Baker.

President George W. Bush works in the Oval Office, October 29, 2001.

French President Francois Mitterrand greets President George H. W. Bush at Elysee Palace in Paris, France.

President George H. W. Bush meets with his National Security Council, August 2, 1990.

Replica of Cabinet Room in the William J. Clinton Presidential Library

President George W. Bush meets with his National Security Council.

President Kennedy meets with the Shah of Iran Mohammed Reza Shah Pahlavi and Secretary of Defense Robert McNamara in the Cabinet Room, April 13, 1962.

Oval Office

9:41 a.m. — The President returned to the Oval Office. He had a conference call with the President of France. They used an interpreter provided by the Department of State.

Cabinet Room

9:57 a.m. — The President returned to the Cabinet Room. There he met with the National Security Council.

Oval Office

10:44 a.m. — The President returned to the Oval Office, where he met with the Director of the CIA.

10:52 a.m. — The President met with the Chief White House Usher (who is the head of the Residence staff), the Director of White House Operations (who also takes care of matters related to the Residence), and with a decorator from New York City.

10:56 a.m. — The President met with an assistant who also served as Secretary to President Bush's Cabinet.

10:58 a.m. — The President talked with his son Jeb Bush.

Cabinet Room

11:02 a.m. — The President returned to the Cabinet Room where he participated in a Cabinet meeting.

Oval Office

11:58 a.m. — The President returned to the Oval Office where he met with the Secretary of the Treasury, and then with the Secretary of State and the President's Chief of Staff.

12:05 p.m. — The President had lunch with Vice President Quayle.

1:01 p.m. The President met with the First Lady, the chairman of the Republican National Committee, a city councilwoman from New York City, his Director of Political Affairs, his Chief of Staff, and his Deputy Chief of Staff.

Rose Garden

1:16 p.m. — The President and the First Lady went to the Rose Garden. The President made a statement to the press about his upcoming trip to Malta to meet with Mikhail Gorbachev, the President of the Union of Soviet Socialist Republics (U.S.S.R.).

Oval Office

1:23 p.m. — The President returned to the Oval Office with the chairman of the Republican National Committee, his Chief of Staff and two of his assistants.

1:40 p.m. — The President met with his Chief of Staff, two assistants for National Security Affairs, and with one of his lawyers (called his Counsel).

2:02 p.m. — The President telephoned the Director of the CIA. The call was not completed.

2:14 p.m. — The President telephoned the Ambassador of the Kingdom of Saudi Arabia to the United States. The call was not completed.

2:35 p.m. — The President talked to the Director of the CIA.

2:46 p.m. — The President talked with his son Jeb Bush.

2:51 p.m. — The President talked with the Administrator of the Environmental Protection Agency.

2:57 p.m. — The President talked with his son Jeb Bush.

Swimming Pool Cabana

3:15 p.m. — The President went to the swimming pool cabana on the White House grounds.

3:17 p.m. — The President talked with his Chief of Staff.

3:47 p.m. — The President received a telephone call from the Ambassador of the Kingdom of Saudi Arabia to the United States. The member of the National Security Council who served as the Senior Director of Near East and South Asia Affairs took the call for the President.

3:48 p.m. — The President spoke with an assistant.

President George W. Bush speaks to the press in the Rose Garden.

President Clinton works in the Oval Office, April 20, 1994.

President George H. W. Bush meets with Boyden Gray, Counsel to the President.

President George W. Bush meets with Advisor Karen Hughes in the Oval Office. Mrs. Hughes was a homeschooling mother.

Oval Office

4:15 p.m. — The President returned to the Oval Office. He met with the Director of White House Operations.

4:23 p.m. — The President met with his Press Secretary.

4:27 p.m. — The President met with Vice President Quayle.

4:34 p.m. — The President met with the Chief of Staff and one of his assistants, two assistants to the National Security Council, and his Press Secretary.

4:49 p.m. — The President talked with the Secretary of State.

5:08 p.m. — The President met with an assistant to the National Security Council.

5:11 p.m. — The President met with the Director of White House Operations.

Family Living Quarters

5:16 p.m. — The President returned to the Family Residence Quarters. There he met with his Chief of Staff and two of his assistants, and the Director of White House Operations.

5:56 p.m. — The President talked with his mother.

South Grounds of the White House

6:32 p.m. — The President and the First Lady went to the South Grounds.

6:35 p.m. — The President flew on Marine One to Andrews Air Force Base. Seven people accompanied him — his Chief of Staff, his Press Secretary, his physician, a White House photographer, an Air Force aide, and two others.

6:54 p.m. — The President flew on Air Force One to Valletta, Malta, an island in the Mediterranean Sea. Eighteen people accompanied the President, including his Chief of Staff, his Press Secretary, the Secretary of State, the Senior Director for European and Soviet Affairs for the National Security Council, and others.

President George H. W. Bush boards Marine One.

President Obama with his Director for Afghanistan, Chief of Staff, a Senior Advisor, and a Deputy National Security Advisor Aboard Marine One

President Obama boards Air Force One.

President George H. W. Bush deplanes from Air Force One.

Midnight — The President was over the Atlantic Ocean traveling toward the Luga Airport at Valletta, Malta. The President arrived at 9:41 a.m. Malta time, which was 3:41 a.m. Eastern time on December 1, 1989.

The President of the United States has twenty-four hours in his day, just like every other citizen. Each morning begins a new day for him, just as it does for us.

George H. W. Bush with His Mother at the Family Vacation Home in Kennebunkport, Maine, while Bush Served as Vice President Under President Reagan

The Lord's lovingkindnesses indeed never cease,

For His compassions never fail.

They are new every morning;

Great is Your faithfulness.

Lamentations 3:22-23

Lesson Activities

Thinking Biblically — Discuss with a parent: What are ways in which you can use your time each day to serve God even more than you already do?

Literature — Read chapters 17-19 in *A Letter to Mrs. Roosevelt*.

Creative Writing — In your notebook, write a detailed account of one day in your life. Write the time and what you do from when you get up until you go to bed.

Picture This! — Take five photographs or draw five pictures of five routine activities that happen at your house every day.

Student Workbook or Lesson Review — If you are using one of these optional books, complete the assignment for Lesson 53.

The President's CABINET

As we learned in Lesson 51, the President of the United States is head of the executive branch of the Federal government. This means that he is responsible for executing or carrying out the laws that Congress passes. These laws are carried out by the millions of people who work for the Federal government.

Federal workers are organized into departments, which work in different areas of the Federal government. The title that is used for the head of each department in the executive branch is Secretary. The Secretary of State is over the State Department, the Secretary of the Treasury runs the Treasury Department, the Secretary of Agriculture is responsible for the Department of Agriculture, and so forth. The only exception to these titles is the Department of Justice, which is led by the Attorney General.

The heads of the executive departments are part of the President's Cabinet. The word Cabinet comes from French, where it is used as the name for a small, private room. The term began to be used in English in the late 1500s and early 1600s to describe a small group of people who gave their advice to the king privately. Since the heads of the executive departments in the U.S. government meet with the President and give their advice to him, this group came to be called the President's Cabinet. However, the term Cabinet is not used in the U.S. Constitution.

All of the executive departments have been created by Congress. President Washington's Cabinet had four members (see art at left). Since 2003, the Cabinet has had twenty-three members, including the Vice President.

George Washington and His Cabinet
as Drawn by Currier and Ives, c. 1876
Pictured from left to right: President Washington, Secretary
of War General Henry Knox, Secretary of the Treasury
Alexander Hamilton, Secretary of State Thomas Jefferson,
and Attorney General Edmund Randolph

Department of State

The Department of State was the first executive department to be organized. It began under President George Washington in 1789. The Secretary of State is the highest-ranking member of the Cabinet. See photos at right and at lower left. The State Department oversees America's relations with other countries.

President Barack Obama chose Senator Hillary Clinton as his Secretary of State. Here she conducts a conference on global business, February 2012.

Department of the Treasury

The Department of the Treasury also began in 1789. It oversees printing our nation's paper money and making its coins. The department also collects taxes through the Internal Revenue Service (IRS), makes sure that the nation's banks obey laws passed by Congress, and develops ideas to help keep our economy strong. See a former Secretary of the Treasury below.

Department of Defense

The Department of Defense was the third executive department created in 1789. It was called the Department of War until after World War II. The Defense Department protects our country from attack by terrorists and the armies of other countries. It coordinates the activities of the branches of the military: Army, Navy, Air Force, and Marines. Counting all those who are on active duty in the military, the Defense Department is the nation's largest employer. See photo of a Secretary of Defense below. The headquarters of the Department of Defense is the Pentagon, located in Arlington, Virginia. The Secretary of Defense oversees the Joint Chiefs of Staff, who are the highest-ranking members of each of the four branches of the military.

Former Secretaries of State James Baker and Warren Christopher chair a commission at the University of Virginia's Miller Center. Baker served President George H. W. Bush and Christopher served President Clinton.

Former Secretary of the Treasury Paul O'Neill speaks at a conference on military health services in 2011. O'Neill served President George W. Bush.

Leon Panetta, Secretary of Defense under President Obama, eats with military personnel aboard the USS Enterprise, January 21, 2012.

Department of Justice

The position of Attorney General was created in 1789. The Attorney General heads the Justice Department. He or she is responsible for giving the President and the members of his Cabinet advice on legal matters. See an Attorney General seated in top photo at left. The Department of Justice was created in 1870. The Attorney General was given the responsibility of heading the Justice Department at that time. The Department of Justice enforces Federal law, prosecutes cases in Federal courts, and oversees the Federal prison system. The Federal Bureau of Investigation (FBI) is part of the Justice Department.

Secretary of Housing and Urban Development Mel Martinez speaks at a National Fair Housing Month Event, April 11, 2001. Also on the program is Attorney General John Ashcroft. The event is being interpreted for the deaf.

Secretaries of Agriculture celebrate 150 years of the Department of Agriculture, February 12, 2012.

President George W. Bush's Secretary of Commerce Don Evans holds new Iraqi paper money at a warehouse in Baghdad, Iraq. Behind him are millions of new Iraqi dinars. FOX News is filming him in October 2003.

Department of the Interior

The executive branch had only four departments until 1849, when the Department of the Interior was created. At first the department handled many different areas of responsibility. Today the Interior Department is responsible for, among other things, protecting the natural environment, overseeing the National Park System, and managing the mining of minerals on land owned by the Federal government. See top photo on page 285.

Department of Agriculture

The Department of Agriculture was established in 1862 during the presidency of Abraham Lincoln. It became a Cabinet-level department in 1889. This department helps farmers, inspects food that is sold in the U.S., and helps educate Americans about nutrition. At left, seven men and one woman who have served as Secretaries of Agriculture celebrate 150 years of the Department of Agriculture.

Department of Commerce

The Department of Commerce became a separate department in 1913. It encourages business in the U.S. to grow and trade with other countries to increase. The Commerce Department gathers and publishes statistics about the economy. The Census Bureau, which takes a census of the U.S. every ten years, is part of the Department of Commerce. See photo at left.

Department of Labor

The Department of Labor was also created in 1913. A Department of Commerce and Labor had been formed in 1903, but the two areas were divided into separate departments ten years later. The Labor Department protects the rights and safety of American workers. It also collects and publishes information about the labor that American workers perform, including average pay and how many Americans are unemployed. See photo at right.

Secretary of the Interior Gale Norton and Secretary of Labor Elaine Chao, who served under President George W. Bush, speak at the National Press Club, December 12, 2005.

Department of Health and Human Services

The Department of Health and Human Services was formed in 1979. The Department of Health, Education, and Welfare was organized in 1953; but a separate Department of Education was formed in 1979, and the rest of the programs were reorganized in a new department the same year. The Department of Health and Human Services spends about one-fourth of the Federal budget. Its programs include Medicare, which provides health care for the elderly; Medicaid, which provides health care for the poor; and the Food and Drug Administration, which decides which prescription drugs can be sold in America. See center photo at right.

President Obama's Secretary of Health and Human Services Kathleen Sebelius at a health meeting in Geneva, Switzerland, May 2011.

President Obama's Secretary of Transportation Ray LaHood speaks at the International Paris-Le Bourget Air Show, June 20, 2011.

Department of Housing and Urban Development

The Department of Housing and Urban Development was created in 1965. This department works to help families own their own homes and provides houses and apartments for families who do not earn much money. It also helps businesses improve downtown areas of large cities. They do this to encourage more business activity to take place in these areas. See top photo on page 284.

Department of Transportation

The Department of Transportation was begun in 1966. This department oversees traveling and shipping goods on rivers, highways, railroads, and airplanes; and bus, rail, and subway mass transit systems in cities. A safe and well-kept transportation system helps the American economy and also helps individual Americans and families travel safely. See photo above.

President Obama's Secretary of Energy Steven Chu speaks at the Idaho National Laboratory, September 13, 2010.

President Obama's Secretary of Education Arne Duncan speaks at a Conference of Mayors, 2011.

President Obama's Secretary of Veterans Affairs Eric Shinseki speaks to a Leadership Conference for the National Guard, 2009.

President Obama's Secretary of Homeland Security Janet Napolitano speaks to the 131st National Guard Association National Conference, September 13, 2009.

Department of Energy

The Department of Energy began in 1977. The President makes plans for America to have the energy it needs for homes and businesses, including oil, coal, atomic, solar, and wind energy. The Department of Energy tries to carry out his plans while protecting the environment. See photo at left.

Department of Education

The Department of Education, begun in 1979, makes sure public schools obey Federal laws about education. It loans money to college students and provides them grants for their education. The department studies how well public schools are educating the nation's children. See photo at left.

Department of Veterans' Affairs

The Department of Veterans' Affairs was created in 1989, but the Federal government had provided programs for veterans of military service for many years before the separate department was formed. This department provides help for veterans who have served in America's military. Two of the many ways they help veterans are health care and education. See photo at left.

Department of Homeland Security

The Department of Homeland Security was formed in 2003. It combined several agencies in the Federal government so they could work together to protect our country and to provide help in emergencies. These agencies include the Coast Guard, the Federal Emergency Management Agency, and the agencies that oversee people and goods from foreign nations coming into this country (usually called immigration and customs). See photo at left.

Other Cabinet-Level Officials

A few government officials who are not heads of executive departments also meet with the President's Cabinet. The

President considers the work of these people to be important enough that they need to hear and discuss the issues in Cabinet meetings. These officials are not department heads, but they still have the status of Cabinet-rank. They are listed at right.

Cabinet Meetings

The heads of the executive departments make sure that the laws and regulations of the U.S. government are carried out. In addition, the Constitution says that the President can ask for the written opinions of the heads of the executive departments.

An important part of the work of the President and the heads of the executive departments are their regular meetings. There is no rule about how often the President meets with the Cabinet, but generally a President and his Cabinet meet once per week. See Reagan and Bush Cabinet meetings below. The department heads and other Cabinet-level officials serve two important roles for the President. First, they give the President and the other Cabinet officials any important information about their particular departments and any advice they have about their area of work. Second, they hear what the President says; and then they try to help the President accomplish what he believes he was elected to do.

Cabinet meetings help the leaders of the different parts of the Federal government communicate with each other. An accomplishment or a problem in one area will probably affect the work of several other areas. For instance, if the U.S. trade representative makes a trade agreement with another country

Cabinet Meetings in the Cabinet Room
Left: Reagan, September 11, 1986; Right George H. W. Bush, September 5, 1989

Members of the President's Cabinet

**Vice President
of the United States**

Secretaries of Departments

Secretary of State
Secretary of the Treasury
Secretary of Defense
Attorney General
Secretary of the Interior
Secretary of Agriculture
Secretary of Commerce
Secretary of Labor
**Secretary of Health
and Human Services**
**Secretary of Housing
and Urban Development**
Secretary of Transportation
Secretary of Energy
Secretary of Education
Secretary of Veterans Affairs
Secretary of Homeland Security

Government Officials with the Status of Cabinet Rank

White House Chief of Staff
**Administrator of the
Environmental Protection Agency**
**Director of the Office of
Management and Budget**
**Ambassador Serving as the
U.S. Trade Representative**
**U.S. Ambassador
to the United Nations**
**Chairman of the Council
of Economic Advisors**
**Administrator of the Small
Business Administration**

to send American products there, it will probably affect the Agriculture, Commerce, and Labor Departments. An idea to produce more oil in the United States will directly affect the Energy, Interior, and Commerce Departments. If the Secretary of Education wants to change the program that provides lunches for low-income students at public schools, it will likely involve the Departments of Agriculture and Health and Human Services.

The wise person knows that he needs advice. The wise President chooses wise people to serve in his Cabinet and then he listens to their wise counsel.

Without consultation, plans are frustrated,
But with many counselors they succeed.
Proverbs 15:22

Lesson Activities

Thinking Biblically — Copy Proverbs 15:22 in your notebook, using the version of your choice.

Vocabulary — Look up each of these words in a dictionary and read their definitions: coordinate, prosecute, transit, solar, consultation.

Literature — Read "Debt of Gratitude" in *The Citizen's Handbook*, page 59, and chapters 20-21 and Author's Note in *A Letter to Mrs. Roosevelt*.

Find Out! — Who are some people who have given your parents wise advice through the years? What is some of the advice those people gave them?

Picture This! — Draw a collage of pictures or create a photo collage that includes one item related to each of the executive departments described in this lesson. Here are some ideas with the related department in parentheses: world map (State), money (Treasury), military uniform (Defense), gavel (Justice), nature (Interior), produce (Agriculture), sign for a business (Commerce), tool (Labor), bottle of vitamins (Health and Human Services), house (Housing and Urban Development), vehicle (Transportation), light fixture (Energy), school supplies (Education), military medal (Veterans' Affairs), bag of sand used to control flooding (Homeland Security).

Student Workbook or Lesson Review — If you are using one of these optional books, complete the assignment for Lesson 54.

★ Remember to choose an American Holiday to study this week! ★

UNIT 12 – THE PRESIDENCY II

BOOKS USED IN UNIT 12

- Brighty of the Grand Canyon

- The Citizen's Handbook

- Student Workbook (optional)

- Lesson Review (optional)

The White House

The Role of the
FIRST LADY

Simi Valley, California
First Lady Barbara Bush (center back) stands beside former First Lady Nancy Reagan at the Ronald Reagan Presidential Library on the day of its dedication, November 4, 1991. In the front row are former First Ladies Lady Bird Johnson, Pat Nixon, Rosalynn Carter, and Betty Ford.

She is not elected to any office, nor is she appointed to any official position; but she holds great influence in government and in the nation. She receives no salary; but the government provides her with housing, personal protection, travel expenses, and a staff of assistants. In some ways she is simply an American citizen, while in other ways she holds a position far more important than almost any other citizen. She is the First Lady.

Who is the First Lady?

The First Lady is the hostess of the White House. She organizes and attends official White House functions. She welcomes and entertains large numbers of guests; and these guests include prominent American politicians, scholars, and entertainers as well as leaders of other countries of the world.

Most of the time in American history, the First Lady has been the wife of the President. However, other women have occasionally served in this role. The wives of four Presidents died before their husbands took office; in these cases a relative filled the role. Martha Jefferson died long before Thomas Jefferson became President. Their daughter Martha Jefferson Randolph served as hostess. Andrew Jackson's wife Rachel died shortly before he was inaugurated.

The social planning during his presidency was carried out at different times by his niece Emily Donelson and his daughter-in-law Sarah Jackson. Martin Van Buren was also a widower. His daughter-in-law Angelica Van Buren was in charge of White House social events. Widower President Chester Arthur's First Lady was his sister, Mary Arthur McElroy.

Two Presidents were bachelors. James Buchanan's First Lady was his niece Harriet Lane. When Grover Cleveland became President, the role of First Lady was filled by his sister, Rose Elizabeth Cleveland. When President Cleveland married Frances Folsom just over a year after taking office, his new wife began serving as First Lady.

Four First Ladies were in poor health during their husbands' terms. They were able to give only limited attention to their responsibilities. In each case, a daughter stepped in to help. These First Ladies and their daughters were: Elizabeth Monroe, wife of James Monroe, and daughter Eliza Monroe Hay; Abigail Fillmore, wife of Millard Fillmore, and daughter Abby Fillmore; Peggy Taylor, wife of Zachary Taylor, and daughter Betty Taylor Bliss; and Eliza Johnson, wife of Andrew Johnson, and daughter Martha Johnson Patterson.

Three First Ladies have died while their husbands were President. Letitia Tyler died in 1842 while her husband John Tyler was President. For a time, their daughter-in-law Priscilla Tyler and daughter Letty Tyler Semple filled the role of First Lady. In 1844 President Tyler married Julia Gardiner, who was First Lady for the rest of his term. Caroline Harrison, wife of President Benjamin Harrison, died in October 1892 during her husband's re-election campaign, which he lost to Grover Cleveland. The Harrisons' daughter Mary Harrison McKee served as hostess of the White House for the remaining months of Harrison's term. Ellen Wilson, wife of Woodrow Wilson, died in August of 1914. The responsibilities of First Lady were filled by Wilson's daughter, Margaret Wilson, until the President married Edith Bolling Galt in December of 1915.

First Ladies

Jacqueline Kennedy
Hillary Clinton
Barbara Bush
Betty Ford
Rosalynn Carter
Nancy Reagan

Welcome to the White House

President and Mrs. Obama welcome President and Mrs. Bush for a ceremony presenting the official portraits of President and Mrs. Bush which will hang in the White House, May 2012.

First Lady Bess Truman welcomes Girl Scouts who give her a glass paperweight to thank her for being their honorary president, December 1952.

First Lady Nancy Reagan hosts King Fahd of Saudi Arabia (sitting to her right) at a state dinner, February 1985.

President and Mrs. Reagan welcome Mother Teresa, June 1985.

Why Do We Call Her First Lady?

In the early years of our country, the wife of the President was usually called "Lady": Lady Washington, Lady Adams, and Lady Madison. It was Dolley Madison, wife of President James Madison, who helped change the title to First Lady.

Mrs. Madison was an especially good hostess with many social graces. She enjoyed people and made them feel welcome. In many ways Dolley Madison set the standard for what future First Ladies should do. Her husband served as Thomas Jefferson's Secretary of State and she was already a popular Washington hostess long before her husband was elected President. In fact, she had already served occasionally as the White House hostess for Thomas Jefferson.

Dolley Madison died in 1849. During his eulogy at her funeral, President Zachary Taylor called her "first lady of our land." Ten years later, the phrase was first used in print in *Frank Leslie's Illustrated Newspaper* to describe Harriet Lane, niece of President Buchanan. Since Miss Lane was not the President's wife but filled the role of White House hostess, what was she to be called? The newspaper described her as "first lady of the White House." The term has been used ever since, even though it is not an official title.

When someone speaks to the President, he is called "Mr. President." When someone speaks to his wife, she is called "Mrs. _____ (her last name)." However, she is often referred to as "First Lady of the United States" in a news story or when she is introduced. So the term is used to describe her but not as a term of address. By the way, the wife of the Vice President is sometimes called "Second Lady of the United States."

What Does the First Lady Do?

The main roles of the First Lady are to give her husband and children love, comfort, and support while he serves in one of the most difficult jobs a person can have and to help her family live as normal a life as possible.

However, the First Lady has many other responsibilities as well. Some First Ladies have also been unofficial advisors to their husbands, while others have not taken this role. Eleanor Roosevelt was the first wife of a President to have an assistant who was paid by the government. The First Lady now has a staff of sixteen to twenty persons provided by the Federal government. Her staff includes a chief of staff, a personal secretary, a social secretary, an appointments secretary, a speechwriter, and a press secretary.

The First Lady attends many events, sometimes with her husband and sometimes as his representative. She might visit a school that is trying out a new idea. She might take part in the ribbon-cutting ceremony for a new Federal building, or represent the administration at the funeral for a former leader of another country.

The First Lady will often accompany the President when he travels to other countries. She might visit a university or the city's marketplace while the President is meeting with that nation's leader. Since Franklin Roosevelt was paralyzed as a result of polio, Eleanor Roosevelt traveled extensively to represent her husband.

In recent years each First Lady has adopted a cause to which she gives special attention with the goal of helping it become a high priority for the country. Jackie Kennedy emphasized historic preservation, primarily through the remodeling of the White House. Lady Bird Johnson made beautification of the American landscape her priority. Rosalynn Carter encouraged the compassionate treatment of people with mental illnesses. Laura Bush encouraged the development of libraries. Hillary Clinton worked to reform the American healthcare system. See special projects of Michelle Obama, Nancy Reagan, and Barbara Bush at right.

The First Lady is a leader and an example for American women. Sometimes she becomes a trendsetter in things like fashion and hair styles.

First Families

President and Mrs. George H. W. Bush board Marine One.

President and Mrs. Bill Clinton sit with their daughter Chelsea and dog Buddy inside Marine One.

President Jimmy Carter returns with daughter Amy and First Lady Rosalynn Carter after a Trip to Europe, January 2, 1980.

President and Mrs. Obama sits with their daughters Sasha and Malia at the White House Easter Egg Roll, April 9, 2012.

First Lady Michelle Obama greets chefs who have gathered for a "Let's Move" event on the White House lawn. She is encouraging them to adopt a school and help the children there to eat healthier.

First Lady Nancy Reagan speaks at a "Just Say No" rally in Los Angeles on May 11, 1987. She worked to get people to "Just Say No" to illegal drug use.

First Lady Barbara Bush works to increase literacy.

First Lady Nancy Reagan reads mail received during the Pennies for Pandas campaign she began to help save Giant Pandas in China, 1984.

Many First Ladies remain popular long after their husbands leave office. They continue to do important work to help others. Rosalynn Carter has worked with her husband in projects like Habitat for Humanity, helping people in poor countries have clean drinking water, and helping people be healthier. She also encourages people who are taking care of ill family members. Barbara Bush has continued to encourage literacy. Eleanor Roosevelt and Hillary Clinton stayed active in politics. Mrs. Roosevelt served as a U.S. delegate to the United Nations. Hillary Clinton was elected as a U.S. Senator, was later appointed Secretary of State by President Obama, and was the Democratic nominee for President in 2016.

First Ladies help to raise funds for their husbands' presidential libraries and stay involved in the many activities held there. They often support other Presidents and their wives in causes important to them.

Only two First Ladies have been born outside the United States. Louisa Adams, wife of John Quincy Adams, was born in England in 1775. Her father was an American, and her mother was English. Melania Trump, wife of Donald Trump, was born in 1970 in the European country of Slovenia, then part of Yugoslavia.

What If...?

Of course, many traditions that surround a President's spouse will likely change if and when a female is elected President. What will her husband be called — First Gentleman? Will he be expected to be the social host of the White House? Will he pursue his own career?

The First Ladies National Historic Site

The First Ladies National Historic Site, which includes the National First Ladies Library, is located in two buildings in Canton, Ohio, the family home of First Lady Ida Saxton McKinley as well as a former bank building.

After Leaving the White House

Former First Lady Jacqueline Kennedy Onassis (center), stands with Senator Edward Kennedy, President and Mrs. Reagan, Ethel Kennedy (Jacqueline's sister-in-law), Caroline and John F. Kennedy, Jr. (President and Mrs. Kennedy's children) at a fundraising reception for the John F. Kennedy Library Foundation at the home of Senator Kennedy, 1985.

Former First Ladies Barbara and Laura Bush participate in a panel discussion at the "America's First Ladies: An Enduring Legacy" conference at Texas A & M University, November 2011.

Secretary of State and former First Lady Hillary Clinton meets with Foreign Minister of India S. M. Krishna, May 2012.

Former First Lady Bess Truman Outside Her Church, 1965

Senator and former First Lady Hillary Clinton campaigns for President, 2008.

Historic Marker at Former First Lady Rosalynn Carter's Childhood Home in Plains, Georgia

President and Mrs. George H. W. Bush welcome former President and Mrs. Reagan to the White House to present Reagan the Medal of Freedom, 1993.

Former First Lady Barbara Bush reads Horton Hatches the Egg to elementary school children at the Bush Library, 2004.

Former First Lady Rosalynn Carter meets with National Guard leaders about helping the caregivers of wounded soldiers, August 2011.

President Johnson visits with former President and Mrs. Truman, 1966.

First Lady Barbara Bush shares a laugh with former First Lady Lady Bird Johnson at the opening of the Gerald R. Ford Presidential Library, 1981.

Former First Lady Barbara Bush (left) speaks with two historians and with Lynda Johnson Robb, daughter of President and Mrs. Lyndon Johnson (third from left), November 2011.

The Library collects documents and information about our nation's First Ladies and provides teaching materials and seminars about First Ladies and their times. The site is managed by the National Park Service and operated by the National First Ladies Library.

The First Lady welcomes thousands of people into her home every year. She treats them with respect and makes them feel honored. She practices hospitality. With America's fast-paced lifestyle, the art of hospitality is often forgotten and people are lonelier because this is true. It is good that our First Family continues to be an example of the welcoming grace of hospitality.

Do not neglect to show hospitality to strangers,

for by this some have entertained angels without knowing it.

Hebrews 13:2

Lesson Activities

Thinking Biblically — Read Proverbs 31:10-31. In your notebook, write five attributes listed in the passage that you think should also be attributes of a First Lady.

Vocabulary — Write five sentences in your notebook, using one of these words in each. Check in a dictionary if you need help with their definitions: salary, prominent, scholar, widower, term.

Literature — Read "Letter to Mrs. Abraham Lincoln" in *The Citizen's Handbook,* page 60, and the chapters titled "Brighty's World," "A Stranger in the Canyon," and "Blue-Flecked Rocks" in *Brighty of the Grand Canyon.*

Creative Writing — In your notebook, write 2-3 paragraphs about a cause you think would be worthwhile for a First Lady to choose to emphasize during her husband's presidency.

Picture This! — Draw a picture or take a photograph of your mom doing something for other people, such as cooking a meal or doing laundry.

Student Workbook or Lesson Review — If you are using one of these optional books, complete the assignment for Lesson 56.

The WHITE HOUSE

It is the home of a family very much in the public eye.

It is a meeting place for kings and queens, presidents and prime ministers, Senators and Congressmen, and citizens who want to influence government policy.

It is a national and world landmark visited each year by over a million citizens and tourists from around the world.

It is the White House at 1600 Pennsylvania Avenue.

In the 1800s, this beautiful building was called the President's Palace, the President's House, and the Executive Mansion. It was also called the White House, and President Theodore Roosevelt made this the official name in 1901. The White House and the U.S. Capitol are probably the buildings that are the most recognized symbols of American government to the country and the world.

Building the White House

On October 13, 1792, a brass plate was placed on top of foundation stones on one corner of what would become the White House. Inscribed on the plate were these words:

> THIS FIRST STONE OF THE PRESIDENT'S HOUSE WAS LAID ON THE 13TH DAY OF OCTOBER 1792, AND IN THE SEVENTEENTH YEAR OF THE INDEPENDENCE OF THE UNITED STATES OF AMERICA.
>
> GEORGE WASHINGTON, PRESIDENT
> THOMAS JOHNSON, DOCTOR STEWARD,
> DANIEL CARROLL, COMMISSIONERS
> JAMES HOBAN, ARCHITECT
> COLLEN WILLIAMSON, MASTER MASON
>
> VIVAT REPUBLICA

Welcome to the White House

The cornerstone of the White House was placed on top of the brass plate. Workers, who included many slaves, free African Americans, and immigrants, began to build the grand white-gray limestone structure designed by architect James Hoban. It would be eight years before the house was ready for its first occupants. President George Washington is the only President who has not lived in the house. He chose the site. Construction was under way, but far from completed, when he retired from the presidency. It was second President John Adams and his wife Abigail who became the first White House residents late in 1800.

President Thomas Jefferson replaced Adams in the White House just four months later and remained there for his eight years as President. President James Madison and his wife Dolley became the third set of residents in the house. The War of 1812 began during Madison's third year in office. In 1814 the British burned the White House. The fire destroyed the rooms inside, but the exterior walls remained. See an engraving of the burned White House and read about the artists below.

Using Talents to Serve:
George Munger and William Strickland

In 1814 artist George Munger drew this picture of the burned White House. It is entitled: A view of the President's house in the city of Washington after the conflagration of the 24th August 1814. William Strickland created an engraving so that Munger's art could be reproduced.

The print was hand-colored. It is in the collection of the Library of Congress.

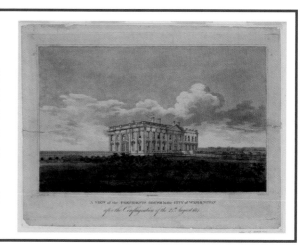

Modern Photo Showing South Portico

Historic Photo Showing North Portico

Original White House architect James Hoban was chosen to rebuild and enlarge the burned mansion. The Madisons were not able to return to the White House, but our fifth President James Monore and his wife moved into it a few months after he became President in 1817.

Many construction projects have been completed since:

1824 — The South Portico was added during the presidency of President Monroe. The portico is a porch, topped with a pediment held up by columns.

1829 — The North Portico was added during Andrew Jackson's presidency. It is the Pennsylvania Avenue entrance of the White House. The South and North Porticoes can be seen in the photos at left.

1902 — During the presidency of Theodore Roosevelt, architect Charles McKim began a major renovation of the White House. East and West Wings were added. The West Wing was called the White House Executive Office Building until 1949. The East Wing was built on the foundations of one built during the Jefferson presidency.

1909 — President Taft had the West Wing made larger and added an Oval Office.

1913 — First Lady Ellen Wilson planted the Rose Garden by the West Wing.

1927 — President Coolidge had the attic remodeled into a third floor and added a rooftop sunroom.

1929 — A fire broke out in the West Wing during the Hoover presidency and it had to be reconstructed.

1933 — President Franklin Roosevelt added a second story and a larger basement to the West Wing. He moved the Oval Office to another location within it. Notice photos at right. President Clinton sits behind the Resolute Desk, given to President Hayes by British Queen Victoria. Clinton's daughter Chelsea plays with Socks, the family cat. Bush meets with Saudi Foreign Minister. Notice that each President redecorates according to his taste. Bush meets with the National Security Council in the Cabinet Room and with religious leaders in the Roosevelt room. It is named for Presidents Theodore Roosevelt and Franklin Roosevelt. A painting of Theodore Roosevelt hangs above the mantle.

In the West Wing

President Clinton's Oval Office, Christmas Eve 1994

President Bush's Oval Office, September 20, 2001

The Cabinet Room, September 12, 2001

The Roosevelt Room, September 20, 2001

In the Residence

President and Mrs. Obama host family, friends, and staff at a Passover Seder, Family Dining Room, First Floor, 2012

First Lady Barbara Bush with Puppeteer Shari Lewis in the China Room, Ground Floor, 1990

The Dave Brubeck Quartet entertains Uruguay President Julio Maria Sanguinetti in the East Room, First Floor, 1986

The Vermeil Room, Ground Floor

1942 — A new East Wing was constructed. It included a formal entrance, offices, and an underground air raid shelter. The Presidential Emergency Operations Center and certain military offices are in the modern East Wing.

1949 — While the Trumans lived in the White House, a leg of their daughter's piano went through the ceiling of the first floor State Dining Room. A committee working under Truman found that the additions of 1927 were too heavy for the home's timber frame. Much of the interior had to be disassembled and rebuilt. The Trumans moved across the street to Blair House from 1949 to March of 1952 during the reconstruction. Two underground floors were added and a balcony, named the Truman Balcony, was installed within the South Portico. The capital of one of its columns is pictured above.

1961 — First Lady Jacqueline Kennedy oversaw an extensive restoration of the White House to preserve and restore its history. Mrs. Kennedy began a garden by the East Wing. Completed by First Lady Lady Bird Johnson, it was named the Jacqueline Kennedy Garden. See photo above.

1968 — President and Mrs. Johnson donated a Children's Garden. It has a goldfish pond and an apple tree to climb.

2009 — First Lady Michelle Obama revived the practice of growing a kitchen garden on the White House grounds.

Capital of a Column on the Truman Balcony

Jacqueline Kennedy Garden

The White House Today

The White House today is much larger than the one that President Adams moved into in 1800. Look at the photo below. In the center is the original White House residence (R) with its many changes, improvements, and expansions. At far left is the East Wing (E); at far right, the West Wing (W). The glass-enclosed East Colonnade (EC) and the open-air West Colonnade (WC) connect the wings to the residence.

The White House residence alone has 55,000 square feet on six levels. It has 132 rooms, 35 bathrooms, 412 doors, 147 windows, 28 fireplaces, eight staircases, and three elevators. See some of its rooms on pages 299 through 302. The President and his family live on the second floor. Though it is private, they often welcome guests into their living quarters.

The White House complex includes a tennis court, jogging track, swimming pool, movie theater, and bowling lane. Its fenced-in grounds cover about eighteen acres.

In the Residence

President George W. Bush and Secretary of State Colin Powell in the Blue Room, First Floor, 2001

The Red Room, Ground Floor

The White House Complex

A Bird's Eye View of the White House Complex
E: East Wing; EC: East Colonnade; R: White House Residence; WC: West Colonnade; W: West Wing

In the Residence

Kennedy (right) with the President of the Republic of Congo (left) in the State Dining Room, First Floor, 1961

First Lady Nancy Reagan in the Red Room, First Floor

First Lady Betty Ford in the Dressing Room, Second Floor, 1976

The Green Room, First Floor
The walls are covered with green silk.

In Lesson 47 we learned about John Adams' prayer for future residents of the White House: "I pray Heaven to bestow the best of blessings on this House, and all that shall hereafter inhabit it. May none but honest and wise men ever rule under this roof." In the last year of World War II, President Franklin Roosevelt had these words carved into the fireplace in the State Dining Room. The photo at left shows how the fireplace looked when President Kennedy entertained the President of the Republic of Congo there in 1961.

When you think about our country's grand mansion, remember these words of comfort from Jesus.

> In my Father's house are many mansions:
> If it were not so, I would have told you.
> I go to prepare a place for you.
> John 14:2 KJV

Lesson Activities

Thinking Biblically — Read 1 Kings 7:1-12, which describes the palace that King Solomon built.

Vocabulary — In your notebook, write which of the following words belongs in each sentence: landmark, committee, complex, republic, restoration
   a. My parents are serving on the church playground ___.
   b. Representative government is a key characteristic of a ___.
   c. The historic gates were sent to a Pennsylvania blacksmith for ___.
   d. The Civil War memorial is our town's best-known ___.
   e. The entire ___ has five buildings and is surrounded by a chain-link fence.

Literature — Read "Remembering Mr. and Mrs. Madison" in *The Citizen's Handbook*, pages 61-62, and the chapters titled "Good-Bye Old Timer!" "The Sheriff Learns a Lesson," and "A Free Spirit" in *Brighty of the Grand Canyon*.

Find Out! — How many rooms, bathrooms, doors, windows, fireplaces, staircases, (and elevators!) are in your house?

Picture This! — Draw a picture or take a photograph of your house.

Student Workbook or Lesson Review — If you are using one of these optional books, complete the assignment for Lesson 57.

The White House
RESIDENCE STAFF

In the photo at right, Hillary Clinton is the guest of First Lady Barbara Bush on November 19, 1992. Since Mrs. Clinton's husband Bill had just won the presidential election sixteen days before, Mrs. Bush invited her to the White House. She wanted to make Mrs. Clinton feel welcome and help her know what to expect when she moved into the White House. Think about how exciting this must have been for Mrs. Clinton. She sat in this beautiful room with a view of the West Wing and the Eisenhower Executive Office Building out the window behind her, realizing that this would soon be her home. In just two months, the Clintons moved in. Imagine that it was you!

Welcome to the White House

Hillary Clinton and First Lady Barbara Bush visit in the private residence at the White House.

Okay, so you've just moved into your new house. Well, it's actually an old house. It's been around for over two hundred years. You've got 132 rooms, 35 bathrooms, and eighteen acres of lawn and gardens to keep clean and well repaired. Some weeks you are going to have a few thousand people over for dinners, concerts, receptions, and other events. In addition, thousands of tourists are going to walk through parts of your house every week. Your house will be seen on television by people all over the world. You want to be a good host, and you want to make sure that everything runs smoothly. But you're going to be really busy. What are you going to do? GET HELP! That's no problem because the help was there before you arrived, and they have been running the White House well for years.

The President has hundreds of people to help him get the job of chief executive done: advisors, counselors, experts, secretaries, and so forth. This lesson looks at the staff of the White House residence, the people who rarely get attention but who help the busy and important operations of the Executive Mansion get accomplished. These are everyday citizens serving the most famous family in the world in the best known house in the country.

Who's in Charge Here?

The person in charge of the residence staff has a long title: the Director of the President's Executive Residence and Chief Usher. He or she is responsible for hiring people to work in the residence and for making sure they do their jobs. He oversees repairs and construction projects. He makes sure that the money budgeted for the residence is spent wisely.

The Chief Usher has a museum of antiques and art to protect; a busy schedule of ceremonies, parties, and meals to plan and carry out; and the First Family to serve. To accomplish all of these jobs, he has a staff of about ninety-five persons who work full time, plus about two hundred workers hired for specific jobs. Notice the photo of a former Chief Usher above.

Meet a Chief Usher

President George W. Bush greets the new Chief Usher, Admiral Stephen W. Rochon. Rochon served from 2007 to 2011, when he left for a new post in the Department of Homeland Security.

Decorating for Christmas

When the Christmas tree arrives, the First Lady (see First Lady Nancy Reagan above) may receive it, but it is the staff who must bring it inside and set it up and keep it watered. It is the staff who hangs garland, waters poinsettias, and performs countless other tasks.

Can Someone Take Care of This?

The same jobs that need to be done at your house need to be done at the White House. Housekeepers dust, vacuum, and make the beds. Launderers take care of the First Family's clothes and the linens used at official functions (into the 1920s, laundry was hung out to dry on the South Lawn of the White House!). Seamstresses take care of alterations and repairs. Gardeners and groundskeepers work carefully, knowing that thousands of people will see their work. Then there are the people who fill roles that the First Family especially needs: maids, butlers, ushers, and valets or personal assistants.

The White House staff includes carpenters, painters, and plumbers. After all, with 35 bathrooms, you can count on problems somewhere fairly often. Electricians are also on staff. Wiring needs to be safe and up-to-date, especially at Christmas time. Can you imagine putting up all those lights?

Much of the work of the residence staff is performed on the ground floor of the White House. Here is the giant kitchen. Nearby is the chocolate shop (beside the bowling alley) and the carpenters' shop. Also on the ground level is the flower shop.

What Do We Need to Do Today?

The work of the White House residence staff is as varied as you might expect it to be, serving a busy family whose dad is the leader of the free world. Eleanor Roosevelt frequently hosted two tea parties in the same afternoon, which meant almost continuous food preparation and dishwashing besides the daily washing and folding of two hundred to three hundred tea napkins.

For special events, White House calligraphers use their talents to produce beautiful invitations, menus, place cards, and programs. Workers set up tables (and sometimes build tables), arrange chairs, and set out linens and tableware. Pantrymen make sure that the food supplies are sufficient and that the specific items needed are on hand. The five full-time chefs with their kitchen crew can serve dinner to 140 or hors d'oeuvres to over one thousand. The floral designers add their special touch. The doormen receive the guests, the cloakroom staff cares for coats and hats, and servers bring the meal to the guests.

Help! The Australian Prime Minister is Coming for a State Dinner!

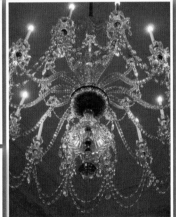

Can you clean out the fountain and water the flowers and mow the grass and trim the shrubs and blow the cuttings off the sidewalk and vacuum the East Room and dust the painting of Mrs. Ford and get the cobwebs off the North Portico and polish the side tables and hem the tablecloths and fold the napkins and choose the china and set the table and purchase the flowers and create floral arrangements and polish the silver and straighten the candles on the mantle and wash the windows and mop the kitchen and order the lobster and clean the spot on the carpet and hire extra waiters and make sure the microphones are working and set up the music stands for the orchestra and choose the entertainment and clean the crystals on the chandelier and find the Australian flag and cut the fresh basil for the salads and steam the asparagus and roll out the red carpet?

How Can I Help?

The residence staff helps the First Family with celebrations of birthdays, anniversaries, and weddings. At times staff members have been called upon to perform such chores as helping wash the First Family's pet dog. They help during the time of transition when one family leaves and another moves in. All too often, the residence staff has helped and comforted grieving families when the President has died. After President Kennedy's death, Mrs. Kennedy gave doorman Preston Bruce the tie that the President changed out of just before starting the fatal motorcade, saying, "The President would have wanted you to have this." The President's brother, Robert Kennedy, gave Bruce the gloves that he had worn to the funeral, with the comment, "Keep these gloves and remember always that I wore them to my brother's funeral."

Do We Need to Check With Anybody About This?

When a large remodeling or redecorating project is being considered, the Chief Usher must consult with the White House Office of the Curator, the Committee for the Preservation of the White House, and the White House Historical Association. You can't just decide to rearrange the furniture or hang a picture in a new location if you are living in the White House.

When you plan an event for your family, you probably want to check everyone's schedule to make sure there are no conflicts. When the First Family hosts an event, it's much more complicated.

The Chief Usher must coordinate plans with the Executive Office of the President. He has to check with the White House Social Secretary to be sure of what else is happening. The National Park Service is involved since the White House and grounds are part of the NPS. The Chief Usher must make arrangements with the military so they can provide a band or color guard. If the function involves officials from other countries, the Chief Usher must talk with the Chief of Protocol of the United States, who is an official in the State Department. After all, you wouldn't want to give someone the wrong place at the dinner table or seat together officials of countries that are enemies.

The Chief Usher must also check with the Secret Service, who work to keep the President safe. Read about the Secret Service at right.

The Secret Service

Another group of people work at the White House, but are not part of the residence staff. The Secret Service is a law enforcement agency that protects the President, other national leaders, and visiting foreign officials. They protect certain sites and help make certain events safer. Most wear business attire and not uniforms like the officer at left.

An executive chef, pastry chefs, a nutritionist, and others make White House food delicious and beautiful.

We Won't Be Needing You Any Longer

As times have changed, certain roles on the residence staff have disappeared. Some Presidents before the Civil War owned slaves whom they brought with them to serve in the White House. Presidents once commonly used messengers to carry important information or documents to other officials in Washington, but telephones and computers do most of that work now. At one time the White House needed the work of lamplighters when evening came, but no more. And coachmen and stable hands will find little work in the modern White House, although they once were essential.

Two Special Servants

Many people on the White House residence staff work there for decades, serving and developing special relationships with the families of several Presidents. In addition, many families have worked at the White House: brothers and sisters, parents and children. The stories of two staff members illustrate these truths.

Lillian Rogers Parks' mother joined the White House staff during the Taft administration in the early 1900s. Mrs. Rogers sometimes took Lillian with her to the White House. Lillian herself joined the White House staff in 1929. She served as a maid and seamstress until her retirement in 1960. Mrs. Parks had a special friendship with Franklin Roosevelt since they both had polio. In 1961 she published her memoir, *My Thirty Years Backstairs at the White House*. The book became the basis for an NBC-TV miniseries in 1979. Lillian Rogers Parks died in 1997 at the age of 100.

Eugene Allen served as a butler at the White House for eight Presidents, Truman through Reagan, from 1952 to 1986. He eventually was promoted to the position of maitre d', the chief butler. Allen was at the White House when President Kennedy died, during the Vietnam War (his son served in the military in Vietnam), when President Nixon resigned, and during many other historic events. He was able to meet and serve entertainers such as jazz legend Duke Ellington and singer Elvis Presley. Once he met civil rights leader Martin Luther King Jr.

Allen was invited to attend the funeral for President Kennedy, but he did not accept the invitation because he wanted to be at the White House to serve people when they returned from the funeral. Allen was still serving as butler when the Reagans were in the White House. One day Nancy Reagan told him that his services would not be needed at the upcoming state dinner for German Chancellor Helmut Kohl. Allen was concerned about what he might have done wrong, but Mrs. Reagan informed him that he and his wife were to attend the dinner as guests of the President and Mrs. Reagan. At the dinner, Mr. and Mrs. Allen were served what he had earlier helped prepare in the White House kitchen. Allen, who was African American, received a VIP invitation to attend the inauguration of Barack Obama. The retired White House butler was escorted to his seat by a Marine guard. Allen died the next year at age ninety.

As a staff member once told a First Lady, "Presidents come and go. Butlers stay."

As each one has received a special gift, employ it in serving one another as good stewards of the manifold grace of God. Whoever speaks, is to do so as one who is speaking the utterances of God; whoever serves is to do so as one who is serving by the strength which God supplies; so that in all things God may be glorified through Jesus Christ, to whom belongs the glory and dominion forever and ever. Amen.

1 Peter 4:10-11

Lesson Activities

Literature — Read "White House Menus" in *The Citizen's Handbook*, page 63, and the chapters titled "Over the Rimtop," "The Fight in the Cave," and "Curious First Aid" in *Brighty of the Grand Canyon*.

Creative Writing — Imagine that you are in charge of preparing a meal for some special guests at the White House. What will be on the menu? How will the table be set? Will there be flowers or other decorations on the table? What kind? What color will the tablecloth be? Who will be at the dinner? Write a description of the dinner in your notebook.

Find Out! — What are some tasks your parents have done in their lifetimes that also have to be done at the White House?

Picture This! — Draw a picture of a room in the White House. You can use one of the images in this lesson as a guide, or you can find a picture in another resource.

Student Workbook or Lesson Review — If you are using one of these optional books, complete the assignment for Lesson 58.

Going Home to
MONTICELLO

President and Mrs. George H. W. Bush (at right) with former Presidents and First Ladies from Left to Right: Lady Bird Johnson, Jimmy and Rosalynn Carter, Gerald and Betty Ford, Richard and Pat Nixon, and Ronald and Nancy Reagan at the Dedication of the Ronald Reagan Presidential Library, November 4, 1991

After four years in the White House, or eight years if he is re-elected, the President and the First Lady leave the White House and another couple or family takes their place. We have already learned about some of the things that First Ladies have done afterwards. What do Presidents do? Most modern Presidents write a book about their presidency or about their lives. Some write several books. Jimmy Carter has written more than twenty-five.

Each President works to build his presidential library. Former Presidents attend ceremonies and give speeches. Presidents who come after them look to them for advice, and the former Presidents are glad to help. Many stay actively involved in politics. Bill Clinton helped his wife campaign for President. George H. W. Bush saw his son elected to the presidency.

Though many remain active in their political parties, most enjoy the company of other former Presidents without regard to their party. Presidents George H. W. Bush, a Republican,

Independence, Missouri
*Top: Truman Home
Lower: President Harry Truman
in His Office in His Presidential
Library, July 1961*

Austin, Texas
*Top: President Jimmy Carter speaks
at the LBJ Presidential Library,
February 2011
Lower: President Lyndon
Johnson's Office in the
J. J. Pickle Federal Building*

and Bill Clinton, a Democrat, became close friends. After an earthquake devastated the Caribbean country of Haiti, Clinton and George W. Bush joined together to help rebuild it.

Many Presidents continue to do what they did when they were in office. They serve the American people and try to help the people of the world. Jimmy Carter is an excellent example. He began the Carter Presidential Center in Atlanta, Georgia, in 1982. Through the center, he works for democracy around the world and, as mentioned in Lesson 56, helps people in poor countries have clean drinking water and be healthier. His and Rosalynn's work for Habitat for Humanity have inspired many people around the world to get involved in building homes for the poor. See President Johnson's post-presidential office and Carter speaking at the LBJ Library at lower left.

Going Home

Harry and Bess Truman returned to the only home they had ever owned in Independence, Missouri; and Jimmy and Rosalynn Carter returned to their home in Plains, Georgia; but many Presidents purchased a new home. Since President Eisenhower had been a career military officer, he and Mamie had never owned their own home. While he was President,

Gettysburg, Pennsylvania
The Home of President and Mrs. Eisenhower

they purchased a house overlooking the Gettysburg Battlefield in Pennsylvania. They moved there after leaving the White House. See Truman and Eisenhower homes on page 310.

Bill Clinton was born in Arkansas and served as its Governor before becoming President, but he and Hillary bought a home in Chappaqua, New York, just before leaving the White House. Two presidential couples, the Reagans and the Nixons, returned to California. The Nixons later moved to New Jersey. Though Ford had served as a Congressman from Michigan for many years before becoming President, he and Betty also moved to California. Our three Presidents and First Ladies who came from Texas all returned to Texas, including the Lyndon Johnsons and both of the Bushes (in the family they are sometimes called "Forty-one" and "Forty-three," since they served as the Forty-first and Forty-third Presidents).

The homes of some Presidents have been preserved for tourists to visit. Two such houses are Mt. Vernon in Virginia, home of George Washington, and the Hermitage in Tennessee, home of Andrew Jackson. Another famous presidential home is Monticello, near Charlottesville, Virginia, the home of Thomas Jefferson. Jefferson was interested in many areas of life and learning. The home is not only beautiful, but it also helps visitors learn about the brilliant man who wrote the Declaration of Independence and who served as our third President. Monticello is visited by over a half-million tourists each year.

Building Monticello

As a young man, Thomas Jefferson decided to build a home on the top of an 850-foot peak on land he inherited from his father. The word Monticello is Italian for "little mountain." Jefferson drew up plans for the home, and construction began in 1769. Jefferson moved in when one room was finished in 1770. He married Martha Wayles Skelton in 1772. When they got married, the home had two completed rooms. The home was largely finished by 1779. Sadly, Jefferson's wife died just three years later.

In 1784 Jefferson became the Minister (Ambassador) to France from the new United States of America. While living in France, Jefferson became fascinated with French architecture. When he returned home in 1789, he began planning to enlarge and remodel Monticello, using ideas he had seen in Paris.

However, Jefferson spent most of the next twenty years as Secretary of State under Washington, Vice President under John Adams, and then as President for eight years. The remodeling work on Monticello was begun in 1796 but was not completed until 1809, the year that Jefferson left the presidency. The structure grew to about 11,000 square feet of floor space in its three main levels and the cellar. Even after it was completed, Jefferson continued to make

Charlottesville, Virginia
Clockwise from Top Left: Monticello, Home of Thomas Jefferson;
The Study as Seen over Jefferson's Bed in the Alcove in His Bedroom; The Exterior Face of the Seven-Day Clock;
Books in Jefferson's Library; Native Artifact Hanging from the Second Floor Balcony in the Entrance Hall

improvements in his home almost until his death in 1826. As Jefferson reportedly once told a visitor, "Architecture is my delight, and putting up and pulling down, one of my favorite amusements."

The Entrance Hall

When visitors walk into Monticello between the columns of the East Front portico, they enter the Entrance Hall, which Jefferson called Indian Hall. This large square room was Jefferson's museum of artifacts. On display are antlers from the Lewis and Clark expedition, other natural objects, numerous Indian artifacts, pieces of art and sculpture, maps, a model of the Great Pyramid of Egypt, and many other items. At times Jefferson had twenty-eight chairs for visitors in this room. Overhead is a balcony with doors leading from second floor rooms.

One of the most prominent items in the room is the seven-day clock that hangs above the entrance doors. The clock is believed to have been designed by Jefferson. The clock and chimes are powered by round weights that are attached to chains leading from the clock. The weights hang in the two front corners of the room. As time passes and the chimes sound, the weights move down the wall. The top weight on the right indicates the days of the week, which are written on the wall. Since the room was not tall enough for the clock to run for the entire week or for the entire week to be shown, Jefferson had holes cut in the floor. Friday afternoon and

Saturday are marked on the wall of the cellar below. The clock is wound with a twenty-two-inch long wrought-iron key on Sunday morning. This makes the weights return to the top of the wall. As seen in one of the photos on page 312, the face of the clock is on the outside of the house above the entrance to the Entrance Hall.

Jefferson's Bedroom, Study, and Library

Skylight

To the right of Indian Hall is Jefferson's bedroom with its high ceiling and the skylight at right. The bed is in an alcove that is open on both sides to save space and for warmth. A clothes closet is above the bed and is reached by a ladder stored in a smaller closet at the head of the bed. The room has large mirrors to increase light and to give the look of more space.

Jefferson could roll out of bed one way into his bedroom and another way into his study or Cabinet. Here he wrote letters, often using a revolving chair and a revolving-top table. Also in the room is one of the polygraph machines that he used (but did not invent). As Jefferson used the polygraph machine, he wrote with a pen. A bar attached to the pen connected to another pen. The second pen reproduced his writing on another piece of paper. This action created copies of his letters for his personal files. Also in the room were a telescope, a surveying instrument called a theodolite, and a globe. Adjoining the study is Jefferson's library. This room once held 6,487 books; but Jefferson sold these to the government in 1815 to re-start the Library of Congress. After the sale, Jefferson began buying more books. In the room is an octagonal filing table, which has drawers labeled with the letters of the alphabet.

Parlor and Dining Room

To the left of the Indian (or Entrance) Hall is a set of double doors into the parlor. Jefferson designed them with a figure-eight chain which is attached to both doors and runs below the floor. When one door is opened or closed, the chain causes the other door to open or close. The parlor is in the shape of a half-octagon and was the scene of family musical performances and marriage ceremonies. This room contained the finest of Jefferson's collection of paintings.

The family gathered in the dining room at 3:30 p.m. for the evening meal. A serving door with shelves that revolved on a central axis is situated in a wall between the dining room and the passage leading to the kitchen. Dishes of food were brought from the kitchen, placed on the shelves, and the door was turned. Dining room servants then picked up the dishes and served the food to those seated at the table. The dining room has tall windows that reach to the floor. The windows can be raised both for ventilation and to serve as doors to the outside.

Monticello Gardens

Other Features

Also on the main floor is the North Octagonal Room, an eight-sided bedroom. The second and third story bedrooms and other rooms were reached by two narrow staircases only twenty-four inches wide.

The home has matching L-shaped porches on each side of the house. Beneath them are the kitchen, smokehouse, dairy, servants' quarters, horse stalls, and an icehouse.

Jefferson died at Monticello on July 4, 1826, and here he is buried.

Jefferson loved plants and kept detailed records of the flowers, trees, shrubs, vegetables, fruit orchards, and numerous crops he had planted on his plantation.

Then God said, "Let the earth sprout vegetation, plants yielding seed, and fruit trees on the earth bearing fruit after their kind with seed in them"; and it was so.

Genesis 1:11

Lesson Activities

Thinking Biblically — Read Psalm 127:1. Think about the home you hope to have some day. In your notebook, write a list of five God-honoring things you want to take place there.

Vocabulary — Find each of these words in a dictionary, then find the definition that corresponds to the way the word is used in this lesson. Copy the words and definitions into your notebook: democracy, artifact, prominent, alcove, shrub.

Literature — Read the chapters titled "On the Mend," "The Lion Hunt," and "Brighty Goes to Work" in *Brighty of the Grand Canyon*.

Creative Writing — Imagine that you have just served eight years as President of the United States. Write 2-3 paragraphs about what you would like to do with your life after leaving the presidency.

Find Out! — Choose a President who was not mentioned in this lesson and find out what he did after leaving the presidency.

Student Workbook or Lesson Review — If you are using one of these optional books, complete the assignment for Lesson 59.

★ Remember to choose an American Holiday to study this week! ★

UNIT 13 — THE U.S. CONGRESS I

BOOKS USED IN UNIT 13

- Brighty of the Grand Canyon

- The Citizen's Handbook

- Student Workbook (optional)

- Lesson Review (optional)

The United States Capitol

The United States
CAPITOL

The United States Capitol

The United States Capitol in Washington, D.C., is a powerful symbol of civics. It represents American citizenship, national unity, representative government, the rule of law, strength and security, truth and liberty. It is a reminder that our nation is a cause greater than any single individual but a cause in which the loyalty and service of every individual are needed. The Capitol has been the setting for celebrations of triumph, memorable speeches, presidential inaugurations, and days of national mourning. Its majestic appearance reminds us of what our country stands for and what we have accomplished. It is a demonstration of American artistic, architectural, and engineering skill. In one picture, one scene, the Capitol says America.

The Capitol is the center of the Federal legislative branch of government. Here the two houses of the United States Congress meet: the Senate with its one hundred Senators and the House of Representatives with its 435 Congressmen. These legislators gather in the Capitol from every state to write America's laws.

The Story of America

Like our country, the Capitol began as part of a grand vision. When Pierre Charles L'Enfant laid out his plan for the new Capital City, he planned for the Capitol to be located on Jenkins Hill at the east end of the National Mall. In L'Enfant's words, the location was "a pedestal waiting for a monument."

The original design for the Capitol was the brainchild of an immigrant. Dr. William Thornton, a Scottish-trained physician and amateur architect from the British West Indies, became an

American citizen in 1787. Just five years after Thornton became a citizen, his design for the U.S. Capitol was chosen by the commissioners overseeing the building of Washington, D.C., and approved by President George Washington. Thornton planned a dome for the center and two matching rectangular wings, a south wing for the House of Representatives and a north wing for the Senate. As payment he received $500 and a building lot in Washington, D.C.

Like our country, George Washington helped with the beginning of the Capitol. President Washington laid the cornerstone on September 18, 1793. Sandstone for the building was quarried in Aquia, Virginia and ferried by boats on the Potomac River to the construction site. Work was slow; the north wing was the part most finished when Congress, the Supreme Court, the Library of Congress, and the District of Columbia courts moved into the building in late 1800 (all of these would eventually get their own buildings). Benjamin Latrobe, the country's first professional architect and engineer, was appointed to take over as Architect of the Capitol in 1803. He oversaw the work until 1813.

Like our country, the Capitol saw war. On August 24, 1814, during the War of 1812, invading British troops set fire to the building. It was saved from complete destruction by a heavy rainstorm. After the burning, Congress met first in a hotel and then for four years in a building near the Capitol. Latrobe returned to the work in 1815 and continued until 1817. Charles Bulfinch took his place and served until 1829. The first Capitol dome was constructed under Bulfinch's leadership. Like our country, the Capitol was built in part by the work of slaves.

Our Capitol is a beautiful building filled with art. Like the Capitol itself, the art tells the story of America. On blue boxes on many pages in Units 13 and 14 is a U.S. Capitol art gallery for you to enjoy. The portraits below are the first three Architects of the Capitol.

A CAPITOL ART GALLERY

Dr. William Thornton
by George B. Matthews, 1931,
after Gilbert Stuart

Benjamin Henry Latrobe
by George B. Matthews, 1931,
after C. W. Peale

Charles Bulfinch,
by George B. Matthews, 1931,
after Alvan Clark Drawing

Like our country, the Capitol changed and grew. As new states were added to the Union, the number of Congressmen and Senators increased. By the mid-1800s, the Capitol was too small. Larger north and south wings were planned. On July 4, 1851, President Millard Fillmore laid the

cornerstone for the first part of the expansion and Philadelphia architect Thomas Walter oversaw the work. By this time, the sandstone exterior of the Capitol was deteriorating so it was replaced with marble.

The Capitol Dome and the Rotunda

The creation of the Capitol dome that we know so well is symbolic of our country's willingness to go full speed ahead on a new idea. The expansion of the Capitol building made the original Bulfinch dome too small. That dome was made of wood and covered with copper. It required considerable upkeep and was a fire hazard. Walter hung a drawing in his office of what the Capitol would look like when the expansion was finished. Instead of the Bulfinch dome, the drawing showed a taller dome with windows, columns, and a statue on top. Senators and Congressmen who saw the drawing were thrilled with the idea. Ten weeks after Walter first displayed the drawing, and without any committee hearings, Congress authorized the first funds for the new cast-iron, fireproof dome. The old dome was removed in 1856, and a steam-powered derrick was installed to lift the pieces of the new dome into place. Wood from the old dome was burned

Views of the Capitol Dome

A CAPITOL ART GALLERY

TOP OF DOME
*"The Statue of Freedom"
by Thomas Crawford, 1857*

ROTUNDA CEILING
*"The Apotheosis of Washington"
by Constantino Brumidi, 1865*

ROTUNDA RELIEF
"William Penn's Treaty with the Indians, 1682" by Nicholas Gevelot, 1827

to create steam. Work continued on the dome even during the Civil War, although for a brief period construction was halted and the building was used as a military barracks, hospital, and bakery.

The Statue of Freedom for the top of the dome was designed by Thomas Crawford, an American sculptor who lived and worked in Rome. It is pictured on page 318. The original plan was for the statue to be 16 feet 9 inches tall; but Crawford made it 19 feet 6 inches tall. This made it too heavy, so the dome had to be changed to provide the correct base for the statue. The top of the almost-15,000 pound statue was put in place on the 8.9 million-pound dome in December of 1863. The dome was completed in 1866.

Beneath the dome is the rotunda. It features paintings and sculptures that honor people and events in our past. At the top, 180 feet above the floor, is a fresco painting by Constantino Brumidi called "The Apotheosis of Washington." Windows encircle the dome letting in natural light. At right is the frescoed "Frieze of American History," which was painted to look like relief sculptures. In the center of the rotunda floor is a bronze statue of George Washington. On its lower walls are paintings from American history and relief sculptures. The room also has statues and busts of people who have made major contributions to America, including several Presidents. See art from the dome and rotunda below.

Views Inside the Rotunda

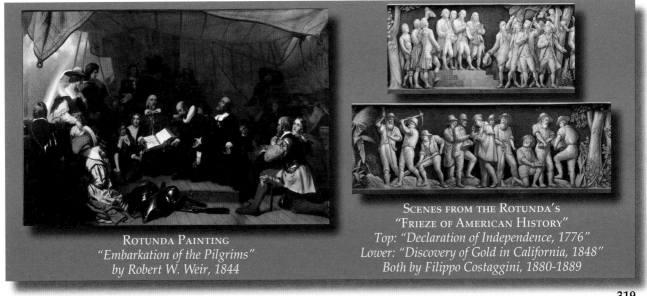

ROTUNDA PAINTING
"Embarkation of the Pilgrims"
by Robert W. Weir, 1844

SCENES FROM THE ROTUNDA'S
"FRIEZE OF AMERICAN HISTORY"
Top: "Declaration of Independence, 1776"
Lower: "Discovery of Gold in California, 1848"
Both by Filippo Costaggini, 1880-1889

National Statuary Hall

Until 1857 the meeting place of the U.S. House of Representatives was in a room now called the Old Hall of the House, or more commonly, National Statuary Hall. Corinthian columns surround the two-story, semi-circular room. The columns are made of Breccia marble which was quarried along the Potomac River. Their capitals are of white marble carved in Carrara, Italy. The hall is lighted with natural light which comes through a lantern in the ceiling. The floor is marble. The black tiles were purchased specifically for the room, but the white marble is scrap left over from another construction project in the Capitol. See photo at right.

National Statuary Hall

Congressmen found it difficult to hear in the room because its ceiling caused echoes. When attempts to solve the problem failed, it was decided that a new chamber for the House of Representatives would be built in space created by the 1851 expansion project. Seven men who later became President served in the House of Representatives while it met in the Old Hall: Millard Fillmore, John Tyler, Franklin Pierce, Abraham Lincoln, James Buchanan, James K. Polk, and Andrew Johnson. John Quincy Adams served in the House after he was President. The locations of their desks are marked with plaques on the floor of the room.

In 1864 Congress invited each state to contribute two statues to be displayed in the room and renamed it National Statuary Hall. Rhode Island donated the first statue, one of Revolutionary War hero Nathanael Greene in 1870. Eventually the collection outgrew the hall and became too heavy for the floor. In 1933 Congress decided to display the statues throughout the

NATIONAL STATUARY HALL COLLECTION

MISSIONARIES

Arizona
Eusebio F. Kino by Suzanne Silvercruys, 1965

California
Junipero Serra by Ettore Cadorin, 1931

Oregon
Jason Lee by Gifford Proctor, 1953

Washington
Marcus Whitman by Avard Fairbanks, 1953

Capitol. The 100th statue, of Gerald R. Ford Jr. of Michigan, was placed in the Capitol in 2011. The statues on page 320 honor missionaries. At right and below are others who cared for people's souls. Damien was a priest who cared for lepers on the island of Molokai. Marquette was a missionary and an explorer. Mother Joseph was a nun and a missionary to the Northwest where she served as architect and fundraiser for eleven hospitals, twelve schools, and two orphanages. States have also donated statues of six Presidents, also pictured below. The captions tell what state donated the statue, plus the name of the honoree, the artist, and the year of the donation.

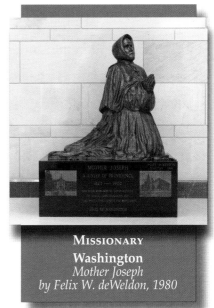

MISSIONARY
Washington
*Mother Joseph
by Felix W. deWeldon, 1980*

MISSIONARIES
Wisconsin
*Jacques Marquette
by Gaetano
Trentanove, 1896*
Hawaii
*Father Damien
by Marisol Escobar,
1969*
PRESIDENTS
Virginia
*George Washington
by Jean Antoine
Houdon, 1934*
Tennessee
*Andrew Jackson
by Belle Kinney &
Leopold F. Scholz,
1928*

PRESIDENTS
Ohio
*James Garfield
by Charles H.
Niehaus, 1886*
Kansas
*Dwight
Eisenhower
by Jim Brothers,
2003*
Michigan
*Gerald R. Ford
by J. Brett Grill,
2011*
California
*Ronald Reagan
by Chas Fagan,
2009*

Modernization and Respect for the Past

The United States Capitol now covers about four acres of ground. The interior is measured in acres instead of square feet. The five floors of the Capitol total about sixteen and a half acres in floor area. The building contains 540 rooms, 850 doorways, and 658 windows, including 108 in the dome.

Like our country, the Capitol has been restored and improved many times. Numerous interior projects through the years have kept the building modernized. However, in addition to the modernizing changes we experience, our country also has respect for the past. When America celebrated its 200th birthday in 1976, the Old Supreme Court Chamber, the Old Senate Chamber, and the National Statuary Hall were restored to the way they looked in the mid-1800s. The U.S. Capitol Visitor Center, which opened in 2008, covers almost 580,000 square feet and is the largest single project in the history of the Capitol. It was built underground so that it does not detract from the building's appearance. Approximately three to five million visitors come to the Capitol each year from around the world.

When people build a magnificent structure like the Capitol, they use materials that God created. It was God who created the metals to make bronze and also the beautiful marble in the earth. Man's creative abilities come from God who made man in His image.

For every house is built by someone, but the builder of all things is God.

Hebrews 3:4

Lesson Activities

Thinking Biblically — Copy Hebrews 3:4 in your notebook, using the version of your choice.

Vocabulary — In your notebook, write your own definition for each of these words: demonstration, brainchild, ferried, gallery, deteriorate. Look in the lesson for clues for the meaning of the words. When you are finished writing your definitions, look in a dictionary for comparison.

Literature — Read "Field Trip to the Capitol" in *The Citizen's Handbook,* pages 64-65, and the chapters titled "Within the Black Tunnel," "Caged Over the Colorado," and "The Battle Scars o' Freedom" in *Brighty of the Grand Canyon.*

Find Out! — How is marble quarried?

Picture This! — If you were chosen to design another statue from your state for National Statuary Hall, who would you choose to be represented? Draw a statue of the honorable person you choose.

Student Workbook or Lesson Review — If you are using one of these optional books, complete the assignment for Lesson 61.

Organization of the U.S. CONGRESS

About two months after Federal elections are held in each even-numbered year, the people who were elected as Congressmen travel to Washington, D.C. Since congressional terms last for only two years, every Congressman who goes to Washington to serve has just been elected or re-elected. Those serving for their first term are called freshmen. The percentage of Congressmen who are freshmen is usually fairly small, because most Congressmen are re-elected many times. As we have mentioned before, Congressmen are called by various titles, including Representative and member of the House of Representatives, or simply member of the House. Honored in the National Statuary Hall Collection are three of the thousands of Americans who have served as Congressmen since the first Congress began in 1789. Their statues are pictured below.

Senators who have just been elected (also called freshmen), Senators who have just been re-elected, and Senators who are in the midst of their six-year terms also come to Washington at this time. The term member of the Senate can be used instead of Senator. Both Senators and Representatives are called members of Congress.

CONGRESSMEN IN THE COLLECTION

Alabama
*Joseph Wheeler
by Berthold Nebel,
1925*

Georgia
*Alexander Hamilton
Stephens
by Gutzon Borglum,
1927*

Montana
*Jeanette Rankin
by Terry Mimnaugh,
1985*

Senate Classes

A Senator is elected to serve a term of six years. One-third of the Senate seats are up for election every two years. When the Senate met in the 1st Congress, the Senators divided themselves into three classes. One class served for two years before they had to be re-elected, one for four years, and one for the full six years. As new states came into the Union, their Senators were also assigned to one of these three classes. Unlike the House of Representatives where it is possible for every person to be a freshman Congressman, the Senate is more stable. It is only possible for one-third of the Senators to change at any one time. Since most Congressmen do get re-elected, the House actually is stable, but the Senate was organized so that it has to be stable.

*The Six Female Members
of the House of Representatives, 1940:
(left to right) Frances Bolton of Ohio
Clara McMillan of South Carolina
Mary Norton of New Jersey
Caroline O'Day of New York
Edith Rogers of Massachusetts
Jessie Sumner of Illinois*

*The U.S. Senate convenes
in the 107th Congress, 2003.*

*The U.S. House of Representatives convenes
in the 60th Congress, 1907.*

Congress Convenes

On January 3rd (or sometimes the 4th, 5th, 6th, or 7th), Senators gather in the Senate chamber at the U.S. Capitol and Congressmen gather in the House chamber (people often use the word House as an abbreviation for House of Representatives). In their separate chambers, Senators and Congressmen begin a new Congress. You can learn about the special ceremonies that take place in the Convening of Congress holiday lesson. As mentioned in Lesson 44, Congresses are numbered. The photos at left were taken on the days that Congress convened in 1907 and 2003.

After Congress begins meeting in January of an odd-numbered year, it continues meeting well into the fall, sometimes even into December, though it takes several breaks or recesses throughout the session. This is called its first session. In January of the following year, Congress begins its second session. Then in November of that year, elections are held again and, in January of the following odd-numbered year, a new Congress convenes. The chart at right gives the schedule of Congress from the November election of 2006 through the November election of 2024.

Congressmen

The House of Representatives is made up of Democrats, Republicans, and a few Independents. Most are men, but many are women. Some represent big cities; others represent rural areas. However, because of the requirements set forth in the U.S. Constitution, all have three traits in common. Each is at least twenty-five years old, has been a U.S. citizen for at least seven years, and lives in the state from which he was elected. Their average age is about fifty-five years old. Six female Representatives who were serving in 1940 are pictured on page 324.

The Constitution states that "the number of Representatives shall not exceed one for every thirty thousand" population. The first House of Representatives began with sixty-five members. It grew in number as the population of the country grew. By 1912, the number had reached 435. In 1929 Congress decided to limit permanently the number of seats in the House to 435. From then on, these 435 seats would be apportioned or divided up among the states after each U.S. census. When each state learns how many seats it will have, its state legislature must divide that state into congressional districts.

Schedule of the 110th to 118th Congresses and the Elections of Those Serving in Them

November 2006 — Election of Class I Senators and All Congressmen

January 2007 — 110th Congress convenes; first session begins.

January 2008 — Second session of the 110th Congress begins.

November 2008 — Election of Class II Senators and All Congressmen

January 2009 — 111th Congress convenes; first session begins.

January 2010 — Second session of the 111th Congress begins.

November 2010 — Election of Class III Senators and All Congressmen

January 2011 — 112th Congress convenes; first session begins.

January 2012 — Second session of the 112th Congress begins.

November 2012 — Election of Class I Senators and All Congressmen

January 2013 — 113th Congress convenes; first session begins.

January 2014 — Second session of the 113th Congress begins.

November 2014 — Election of Class II Senators and All Congressmen

January 2015 — 114th Congress convenes; first session begins.

January 2016 — Second session of the 114th Congress begins.

November 2016 — Election of Class III Senators and All Congressmen

January 2017 — 115th Congress convenes; first session begins.

January 2018 — Second session of the 115th Congress begins.

November 2018 — Election of Class I Senators and All Congressmen

January 2019 — 116th Congress convenes; first session begins.

January 2020 — Second session of the 116th Congress begins.

November 2020 — Election of Class II Senators and All Congressmen

January 2021 — 117th Congress convenes; first session begins.

January 2022 — Second session of the 117th Congress begins.

November 2022 — Election of Class III Senators and All Congressmen

January 2023 — 118th Congress convenes; first session begins.

January 2024 — Second session of the 118th Congress begins.

November 2024 — Election of Class I Senators and All Congressmen

Senators

The Senate is called the upper house of the United States Congress; the House of Representatives is called the lower house. The Senate has more prestige than the House. There are only 100 Senators in the Senate, two from each state. Senators serve longer terms. The requirements for being a Senator are more strict. As we learned in Lesson 21, a

Senator Robert Bennett (third from left), Congressman Rob Bishop (fourth from right), and others officially open a test facility at Hill Air Force Base in Utah, 2010.

Senator must have been a U.S. citizen for at least nine years, must be at least 30 years old, and must be a resident of the state he represents. When the first Congresses met in New York and Philadelphia, the House met on the first floor of the building being used and the Senate on the second. Historians believe that may be the reason the Senate is called the "upper house."

Senators were originally chosen by state legislatures, but this practice was changed in 1913 by the Seventeenth Amendment to the U.S. Constitution. Senators are now elected by popular vote. As with House incumbents, most incumbent Senators who run for another term are re-elected. The average age of a Senator is about sixty years old. Of the 100 statues in the National Statuary Hall Collection, more than one-fourth are former Senators. Statues of Senators are pictured on pages 326-328 and page 68.

Replacing a Congressman or Senator

When a member of the House dies or resigns, a special election is held within a few weeks to fill the vacancy. When a Senator dies or resigns, in almost all states the Governor of the state appoints someone to serve as Senator until the next Federal election. In that election, candidates run to serve out the rest of that Senator's class (either two years or four years), until

SENATORS IN THE COLLECTION

Alaska
Ernest Gruening by George Anthonisen, 1977
Arkansas
James Paul Clarke by Pompeo Coppini, 1921
Delaware
John Middleton Clayton by Bryant Baker, 1934
Idaho
William Edgar Borah by Bryant Baker, 1947

the time for the election to a full six-year term comes around. However, a few states fill vacant Senate seats the same way they fill vacant House seats.

Majority and Minority Parties

The Constitution does not talk about political parties, but parties are very important in the way both the House and the Senate are organized. The political party with the most members in the House or the Senate is, of course, in the majority. The majority party in each house of Congress chooses one of its members to be Majority Leader. His assistant is the Majority Whip. These two people in each house try to get Congressmen in their party to support the proposed laws that they think are best for the country. Meanwhile, the party with the minority of members chooses a Minority Leader and Minority Whip. The minority leaders encourage their members to vote together. The minority often opposes what the majority supports.

Members of the same political parties even sit together in the House and Senate chambers. When someone is standing on the rostrum at the front of each chamber, he sees Democrats to his right and Republicans to his left.

House and Senate Chairmen

The chairman of the House of Representatives is called the Speaker of the House. The Speaker of the House decides what bills the House considers and which ones are voted on. He or she also has the most influence in deciding who serves on the various House committees. Between the November elections and the convening of Congress, congressional leaders from the party that has won a majority of the House seats choose the Speaker for the next two-year session. A formal vote is taken on the day that Congress convenes, but the decision has really already been made. When the House meets in a session on a given day, often the Speaker of the House does not preside over the meeting. Usually another member of the House is given the

Idaho
George Laird Shoup
by Frederick E. Triebel,
1910
Illinois
James Shields
by Leonard W. Volk,
1893
Iowa
Samuel Jordan
Kirkwood
by Vinnie Ream, 1913
Kansas
John James Ingalls
by Charles H. Niehaus,
1905

honor of serving as temporary Speaker. During that day, he is called the Speaker *pro tempore* which means "for a time" in Latin.

The chairman of the Senate is the Vice President of the United States. However, the Vice President rarely presides over meetings of the Senate. He is usually busy carrying out other responsibilities that are given to him by the President. As is the custom in the House, the Senate elects a president *pro tempore*. The president *pro tempore* can in turn appoint others to preside, and he often names younger Senators to fill this role.

Once in the book of Acts, the apostles were brought before a Senate.

Now when the high priest and his associates came, they called the Council together,

even all the Senate of the sons of Israel . . .

Acts 5:21

Lesson Activities

Literature — Read "The Highest Good of the Country" in *The Citizen's Handbook,* pages 66-69.

Creative Writing — Think of someone you know personally who would be a good Senator or Representative. In your notebook, write 1-2 paragraphs about the qualities this person has and why you think he or she would be a good choice.

Find Out! — Has there ever been a Majority or Minority Leader of the Senate or House of Representatives from your state?

Picture This! — Draw a picture or take a photograph of someone in your family posing like one of the statues in National Statuary Hall that is pictured in this lesson.

Student Workbook or Lesson Review — If you are using one of these optional books, complete the assignment for Lesson 62.

SENATORS IN THE COLLECTION

Kentucky
*Henry Clay
by Charles H.
Niehaus, 1929*
Louisiana
*Huey Pierce Long
by Charles Keck, 1941*
Maryland
*Charles Carroll
by Richard E. Brooks,
1903*
Michigan
*Lewis Cass
by Daniel Chester
French, 1889*

How the U.S. CONGRESS WORKS

Doorway into the House Chamber

Senators gather in the Senate chamber in the Capitol to have formal meetings to discuss laws that have been proposed. Four quotations decorate the walls of that chamber. Over the west doorway is *Novus ordo seclorum*, meaning "A new order of the ages." Over the east doorway is *Annuit coeptis*, meaning "God has favored our undertakings."

The Senate has met at three different locations in the Capitol. Since 1859 it has met in the current Senate chamber. Before that it met in what is now called the Old Senate Chamber, pictured below. In the photo on page 324, notice that the 100 Senators sit at 100 desks. Among the matching desks are forty-eight made for the Senate in 1819. As new states were added, more matching desks were built.

Special desks include those used by Daniel Webster, Henry Clay, and Jefferson Davis. The senior Senator from Webster's birth state of New Hampshire sits at his desk. The Henry Clay desk is occupied by the senior Senator from Kentucky. The senior Senator from Mississippi uses the Jefferson Davis desk. The Senate has many traditions. All Senators carve their names on the inside of their desk drawers. A fun tradition is the candy desk. One Republican Senator always keeps candy in his desk drawer and any Senator is free to enjoy it.

Congressmen gather in the House chamber. Pictured above are the hall outside and a doorway into the chamber. At one time, members of the House had desks, but in 1913 the

Old Senate Chamber

Left: President George W. Bush addresses a joint session of Congress; Center: British Prime Minister Tony Blair (second from left) is applauded as he watches and listens in the visitors gallery. Both photos are from September 2001. Right: Vice President Dan Quayle and House Speaker Tom Foley stand beneath the words "In God We Trust" and in front of the American flag, while President George H. W. Bush prepares to address a joint session.

desks were replaced with rows of theater-style seats, none of which are assigned to a particular Congressman. The House chamber is pictured above.

Reminders of American ideals and history adorn the House chamber. On the rostrum are the words: "Union, Justice, Tolerance, Liberty, Peace." To the left of the flag is a portrait of George Washington; to its right a portrait of Lafayette, the French general who helped the American colonies win the American Revolution. In 1950 twenty-three marble relief portraits were installed in the House chamber. They depict lawmakers whose work laid a foundation for American law. Three of these portraits are pictured below.

As we have seen before, our government vocabulary can be confusing. Each Congress has two year-long sessions, but when the House or the Senate meet in their separate chambers in the Capitol for a formal meeting on a given day, that meeting is also called a session. In formal sessions of the Houses of Congress, the words a Senator speaks are said to be coming from the "floor of the Senate" and what a Congressman says comes from the "floor of the House."

Visitors can watch daily sessions of the House and Senate from visitors galleries located in balconies in both chambers. The House and Senate chambers are on the second floor of the Capitol. Visitors enter the visitor galleries on the third floor. They can also watch on C-SPAN.

A CAPITOL ART GALLERY

JEFFERSON   MOSES   MASON

RELIEF PORTRAITS OF LAWGIVERS IN THE HOUSE CHAMBER

Thomas Jefferson by C. Paul Jennewein, 1950

Moses by Jean de Marco, 1950

George Mason by Gaetano Cecere, 1950

Joint Session of Congress in the House Chamber, 1921

American Flag

Vice President Calvin Coolidge

Speaker of the House Frederick H. Gillett

President Warren G. Harding

Visitors Gallery

Portrait of Lafayette

Senators and Congressmen on the Floor of the House

When the House and Senate meet together, it is called a joint session of Congress. Joint sessions are rare, but at least one is held each year when the President gives his State of the Union address to Congress. Joint sessions are held in the House chamber because it is larger than the Senate chamber. Notice photos of joint sessions on page 330 and above.

Meetings and More Meetings

Senators and Congressmen do not spend all of their time meeting in formal sessions in their chambers. Both the Senate and the House are organized into several committees, each of which works in one area. Examples are the Senate Committee on the Budget and the House Committee on Science, Space, and Technology. The Senate and the House have a few joint committees. Therefore, both Senators and Congressmen spend time a great deal of time "in committee," looking into proposed laws with fellow committee members. Lesson 64 explains the purpose of congressional committees.

Senators also meet informally with other Senators and Congressmen. Sometimes they meet with the President or with members of his Cabinet. In the photo at right, Senator Richard Russell meets with President Johnson. Senators and Representatives also meet with lobbyists, with people from their home states or districts, and also with members of their political party. They meet with individuals and groups, including ones that contribute to their re-election campaigns.

Senator Richard Russell (right) meets with President Lyndon Johnson, 1963.

Senators and Congressmen work in their offices. They send out e-mail messages and articles to newspapers. They travel to and from their home states and districts, attending special events, giving speeches, and keeping in touch with the people who elected them. Each Congressman and Senator has a staff of several people who help with the many responsibilities he carries.

Russell Senate Office Building,
First Occupied in 1909

Dirkson Senate Office Building,
First Occupied in 1958

Hart Senate Office Building,
First Occupied in 1982

Where Senators and Congressmen Work

Senators and Congressmen have many rooms in the Capitol that they can use for their various meetings. They have also constructed three Senate and three House office buildings, pictured at left and on page 333. They and their staffs have offices there and some committees meet there as well.

Each Senate office building is named for a Senator: Senator Richard Brevard Russell from Georgia, who served from 1933 to 1971; Senator Everett Dirksen from Illinois, who served from 1951 to 1969; and Senator Philip A. Hart from Michigan, who served from 1959 to 1976. Senator Russell is pictured on page 331.

Each House office building is named for a Speaker of the House. Joseph Cannon of Illinois was Speaker from 1903 to 1911. Cannon is standing in front of the American flag in the photo on page 324. Nicholas Longworth of Ohio served from 1925 to 1931; and Sam Rayburn of Texas served from 1940 to 1945, 1949 to 1951, and 1955 to 1961. In the lower photo on page 333, a committee meets in the Rayburn building.

Responsibilities Shared by the House and the Senate

The House and the Senate must both approve (or pass) bills before they can become law. We learn more about this in the next lesson. The Constitution authorizes the House and Senate to keep a journal of their proceedings so that everyone can know what the two Houses of Congress are doing. This journal is called *The Congressional Record. The Congressional Record* includes speeches given on the floor of the House and Senate, votes that are taken, activities of the various committees, and other information. Senators and Congressmen can also insert into the *Record* information that they do not speak from the floor of their chambers but want to be made part of the official record of Congress. Recognition of special service or heroism by someone from their home state or district is an example of something that might be inserted into the *Record*.

The salary for Senators and Congressmen is the same. In 2011, it was $174,000 per year. The salaries of the Speaker of the House and the Majority and Minority Leaders are somewhat higher. Congress has given itself an annual cost of living adjustment that takes effect automatically unless Congress votes not to accept it. Each Senator and Representative receives about one million dollars per year to pay staff and to have offices in Washington and in their home states or districts.

Cannon House Office Building, First Occupied in 1908

One difficult role that the House and Senate share is the impeachment of Federal officials. To impeach someone means to accuse him of doing wrong. If a President, Vice President, Cabinet member, Federal judge, or someone in another high position in the United States government is suspected of "high crimes and misdemeanors," the House of Representatives has the authority to investigate and vote on the accusations. If a majority of Representatives votes to impeach an official, the Senate holds a trial and acts as the jury. The Chief Justice of the U.S. Supreme Court presides at an impeachment trial. Two-thirds of the Senate must vote to convict the official in order for him to be removed from office.

Longworth House Office Building, First Occupied in 1933

Rayburn House Office Building, First Occupied in 1965

A few Federal judges have been removed from office through impeachment trials. Two Presidents, Andrew Johnson and Bill Clinton, have faced impeachment trials; but neither was removed from office. A House committee voted to impeach President Richard Nixon, but Nixon resigned before the entire House could vote on impeachment.

General John R. Allen and the acting Under Secretary of Defense for Policy testify before the House Armed Services Committee. The meeting was held in the Rayburn House Office Building, March 2012.

Senators and Congressmen cannot be arrested when they are going to or from a meeting of Congress or during a meeting of Congress. They cannot be questioned about or arrested for anything they say during a speech or debate in Congress. The writers of the Constitution wanted to give the members of Congress freedom in their work. They also wanted to prevent a President from arresting members to keep them from voting or participating in the activities of Congress.

Advice and Consent

One special responsibility that the Constitution gives to the Senate alone is called the advice and consent role. The Senate is responsible for giving the President advice. It must also give its consent to certain decisions the President suggests. When the President makes a treaty with another country, two-thirds of the Senators must vote to approve or ratify the treaty before it can take effect. The House does not vote on treaties. In addition, when the President nominates people to serve as ambassadors, Federal judges, and other high-ranking officials, the Senate must approve the nominations before those people can take office. The House does not vote on these nominations.

Two American ideals decorate the walls of both the House and Senate chambers: *E Pluribus Unum* and our national motto, "In God We Trust."

Identical Plaques were placed in the Longworth and Dirksen House Office Buildings in 1961.

> Trust in Him at all times, O people; Pour out your heart before Him; God is a refuge for us.
>
> Psalm 62:8

Lesson Activities

Thinking Biblically — Read these passages about trusting God: Psalm 31:14, Psalm 25:2, Psalm 52:8, Psalm 56:4, Psalm 62:8.

Vocabulary — In your notebook, write these vocabulary words and the letter of the definition that goes with each word: undertaking, tolerance, contribute, journal, convict

    a. to find guilty
    b. a record of transactions or events
    c. to give or supply
    d. a project or enterprise
    e. respect for beliefs or practices that are different from one's own

This plaque in the Capitol was unveiled in 1944.

Literature — Read "A Loyal Kansan" in *The Citizen's Handbook,* page 70, and the chapters titled "The Carrot Cure," "Spider Web of Steel," "Brighty B.A." and "A Gift for Uncle Jim" in *Brighty of the Grand Canyon.*

Creative Writing — In your notebook, list five ways your family can show other American citizens that you trust in God.

Picture This! — Draw a picture or take a photograph of the workplace of your dad or someone else you know.

Student Workbook or Lesson Review — If you are using one of these optional books, complete the assignment for Lesson 63.

How a BILL BECOMES LAW

Every law of the government of the United States must be passed, or enacted, by Congress. The Constitution sets out some steps in how this is to be done, and Congress itself has added other steps that it follows in making laws.

Introducing a Bill

A bill is a suggestion or proposal for a new law. A bill is also sometimes called a piece of legislation or a measure. Any member of Congress, whether in the House of Representatives or the Senate, can introduce a bill. However, any bill that is intended to raise taxes must be introduced first in the House.

The way that a bill becomes law is largely the same whether it is introduced in the House or the Senate first. Let's suppose that Congressman Foghorn Throckmorton wants to introduce a bill that would increase the Federal tax on gasoline by five cents per gallon the first year it becomes law, ten cents more the second year, and twenty cents more the third year. Congressman Throckmorton has proposed this tax increase because he wants the government to have more money to build and repair roads. He also hopes that the higher taxes will cause

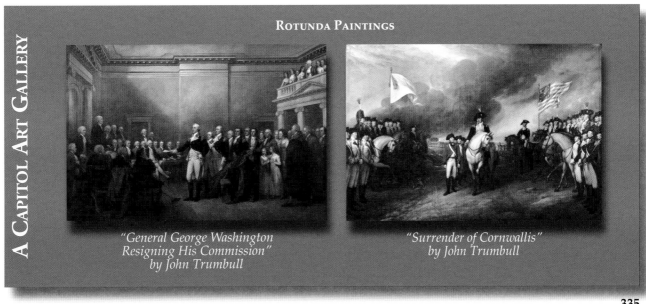

A CAPITOL ART GALLERY

ROTUNDA PAINTINGS

"General George Washington Resigning His Commission" by John Trumbull

"Surrender of Cornwallis" by John Trumbull

Representative Louis Ludlow of Indiana puts a bill into the hopper in 1936.

people to drive less, which would mean that the United States would be less dependent on oil from other countries.

The Congressman or one of his assistants writes the bill. Then Rep. Throckmorton gives his bill to the House Clerk or places it in a box called a hopper at the front of the House. See photo at left. The Clerk is a paid position in the House of Representatives. He is recommended by the majority party and voted on by the House. The Clerk assigns each bill a number (in this case H101; H stands for House) and sends it to the Government Printing Office for copies to be printed and sent to all of the members of the House. When a Senator wants to introduce a bill in the Senate, he must be recognized by the presiding officer of the Senate when the Senate is meeting; and then it is numbered (such as S352; S stands for Senate) and sent to the printing office. During the two-year period in which a Congress meets, thousands of bills are proposed by Senators and Congressmen.

Assigned to a Committee

The Speaker of the House assigns H101 to a committee of Congressmen. Committees study and discuss bills to decide which ones they think the full House should take the time to consider out of the thousands that are introduced. Rep. Throckmorton's proposed gasoline tax bill, H101, is assigned to the House committee that considers new taxes. It is called the House Ways and Means Committee.

When a committee studies a bill, it will often invite people to talk to the committee about it. This is called testifying before a committee. A committee might want to hear from the head of the Cabinet department that would enforce the new law, a scientist who is an expert on the subject of the bill, businessmen who would have to follow the new law, and private citizens who might be affected if the bill becomes law.

In the case of H101, the Ways and Means Committee hears from the Secretary of Energy, who tells the committee how much his department experts say the new tax will probably affect gasoline sales and our use of oil. The President of the American Automobile Association tells the committee how he

A Bill Proposed in the House, 2009

thinks the new tax will affect how much people travel. A representative of the trucking industry testifies about how much the cost of sending goods by truck will increase, which will cause the price of those goods to increase for people who buy them. The head of the national highway construction association talks about how many road construction projects could be paid for by the new taxes, which would help their business. The leader of an association of convenience store owners tells the committee that he expects gasoline sales to go down, which would hurt their business. Representatives of mass transit departments in big cities tell how they expect the number of riders to increase because people will drive their cars less. The committee also hears from individual citizens who tell how the new tax will be hard for them to afford. If the bill is of interest to a large number of Americans, Senators and Representatives sometimes hold

press conferences to talk publicly to citizens through radio, television, Internet, and other news sources. See photo at right.

Republican Congressmen hold a press conference concerning a bill proposed in 2009.

The committee then votes on whether it wants to recommend the bill to the full House (all the members) for a vote. If a majority of the committee votes in favor of sending the bill to the full House, the Speaker schedules a time to discuss the bill on the House floor. Most bills that are assigned to a committee never get considered. Of those that are considered by committees, relatively few are considered by the entire House. In the case of H101, the Ways and Means Committee votes to send it to the full House.

Consideration by the House and Senate

The Speaker of the House of Representatives schedules H101 for debate. In this case, debate means that the full House will meet in a formal session and talk about the bill. Each Congressman who wishes to do so can take a few minutes to tell the rest of the members why he or she supports or opposes the bill. Sometimes amendments or changes are suggested, and the members have to vote on whether to accept or reject these changes. Then a vote on the bill is taken. If the bill is defeated, that is the end of it for that session of Congress. If it passes, it goes to the Senate for consideration. If a bill begins in the Senate and is approved there, it goes to the House. H101 passes the House by a close vote and will now be considered by the Senate.

In the Senate, the same process is followed. The bill is assigned to a committee, which can hold hearings on it. In the photo on page 339, Rose Wilder Lane testifies before a Senate

Minnesota
Henry Mower Rice by Frederick E. Triebel, 1916

Mississippi
Jefferson Davis by Augustus Lukeman, 1931

Missouri
Thomas Hart Benton by Alexander Doyle, 1899

Missouri
Francis Preston Blair by Alexander Doyle, 1899

Nevada
Patrick Anthony McCarran by Yolande Jacobson, 1960

New Hampshire
Daniel Webster by Carl Conrads, 1894

New Mexico
Dennis Chavez by Felix W. de Weldon, 1966

North Carolina
Zebulon Baird Vance by Gutzon Borglum, 1916

Ohio
William Allen by Charles H. Niehaus, 1887

South Carolina
Wade Hampton by Frederic W. Ruckstull, 1929

Texas
Sam Houston by Elisabet Ney, 1905

West Virginia
John E. Kenna by Alexander Doyle, 1901

Wisconsin
Robert M. La Follette by Jo Davidson, 1929

Writer Rose Wilder Lane, daughter of Almanzo and Laura Ingalls Wilder, urges support of a bill before the Senate Judiciary Subcommittee, 1939.

subcommittee (a subcommittee is a smaller group of the committee members). After the hearings, the committee must vote on the bill. If it passes the committee, it is sent to the entire Senate for consideration. Since the Senate has fewer members, Senate rules allow for longer debate by the Senators on bills they are considering. Senators can also propose amendments to a bill. If the Senate passes the bill in exactly the same form as it passed in the House, the bill goes to the President. If the Senate defeats a bill that is the end of the bill for this session. If any changes are made in the Senate, the bill is sent to a conference committee. A conference committee is a specially-chosen group from the House and the Senate that meets to determine a form that they think would be passed by both houses. In the Senate's consideration of H101, an amendment is adopted to make the third-year increase in the gasoline tax only twelve cents per gallon instead of twenty; so the bill goes to a conference committee. The committee decides to compromise on the third-year tax increase and make it sixteen cents per gallon, which is halfway between twelve and twenty. This version passes both houses of Congress and is sent to the President.

The President's Choices

When the President receives a bill that has passed both houses of Congress in exactly the same form, he has three choices of what to do.

★ He can sign the bill. If he does, the bill becomes law.

★ He can veto the bill, which means that he refuses to sign it. When the President vetoes a bill, he sends it back to Congress stating his objections to it. If the House and the Senate each vote again and pass the bill with two-thirds of the members of each body voting in favor of it, Congress is said to override the veto and the bill becomes law without the President's signature. A two-thirds majority is difficult to achieve, so a President's veto is often the end of a bill.

★ The President can also choose to do nothing. If Congress remains in session for ten more days (not counting Sundays), the bill becomes law anyway. This is called a pocket veto (as if the President put it in his pocket and did not sign it or return it to Congress). A pocket veto is a President's way of saying that he does not approve of the bill but he knows that Congress is likely to override a veto. If Congress adjourns before the ten days have passed, the bill dies without becoming law. This provision is intended to keep Congress from passing last-minute, unwise bills.

Of the thousands of bills introduced in each two-year session of Congress, only a few hundred are voted on. Of those, even fewer are passed by Congress and signed into law by the President. What do you think the President does when he receives H101? Does he sign it, veto it, or use his pocket veto?

American citizens have a responsibility to honor the laws that Congress passes. Christians are blessed with the opportunity to abide by God's perfect law of liberty.

> But one who looks intently at the perfect law, the law of liberty, and abides by it,
>
> not having become a forgetful hearer but an effectual doer,
>
> this man will be blessed in what he does.
>
> James 1:25

Lesson Activities

Thinking Biblically — Discuss with a parent: What does it mean to abide by the perfect law of liberty (see James 1:25)?

Vocabulary — Write a paragraph using all of these words. Consult a dictionary if you need help with their definitions: enact, proposal, preside, testify, amendment.

Literature — Read the chapters titled "Well Done!" "Battle on the Mesa," "A New World for Brighty," and "A Voice from the Past" in *Brighty of the Grand Canyon*.

Creative Writing — In your notebook, write the details of a bill you think would be a good law for Congress to consider.

Find Out! — Have either of your parents ever been on a committee for any organization?

Student Workbook or Lesson Review — If you are using one of these optional books, complete the assignment for Lesson 64.

★ Remember to choose an American Holiday to study this week! ★

UNIT 14 — THE U.S. CONGRESS II

BOOKS USED IN UNIT 14

- Brighty of the Grand Canyon

- The Citizen's Handbook

- Student Workbook (optional)

- Lesson Review (optional)

The Capitol as Seen Through a Window in the Thomas Jefferson Building of the Library of Congress

The Congressional STAFF

WANTED: A group of people who can: answer the phone, open mail, welcome visitors, write letters, do research, help people who are having problems, make travel plans, become knowledgeable in one or a few subjects, write proposed laws, write speeches, talk to lobbyists and experts, advise Senators and Congressmen, talk to reporters, work well with other people, make a difference, and work long hours—without generating much publicity about yourself. Interested? Apply on Capitol Hill.

The work that a Senator or Congressman is expected to do—writing and considering new laws, handling requests for help from the people they represent, investigating the need for government action, meeting people, and making speeches—is more than any one person can do. So Senators and Congressmen hire staff to help them in their work.

People of many talents can work as a congressional staffer, as you can tell from reading the job description above. One way that congressional staffers help their member of Congress

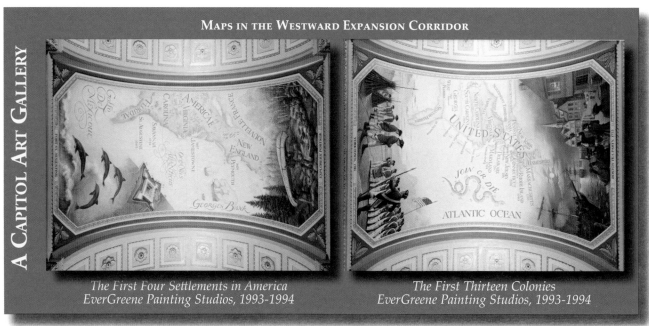

A CAPITOL ART GALLERY

MAPS IN THE WESTWARD EXPANSION CORRIDOR

The First Four Settlements in America
EverGreene Painting Studios, 1993-1994

The First Thirteen Colonies
EverGreene Painting Studios, 1993-1994

is by being their eyes and ears. To do this, they have to do what Senators and Congressmen do—go to many meetings. See photos at right.

Members of the House and Senate have not always had a staff. It was not until the late 1800s that Congress voted to provide the salaries for two or three assistants for each member. As the work of the Federal government has increased, the number of staff personnel has increased also. Today, the total number of people who help members of Congress and who carry out other work in the Capitol and on behalf of Congress as a whole is over 24,000!

Each member of the House can have up to eighteen full-time and four part-time workers. A Senator can hire as many workers as he has the money for; the average Senator has about thirty-five staff members. In addition, those who are in leadership positions (such as Speaker of the House, House Majority and Minority Leaders, and Senate Majority and Minority Leaders) are given money to hire even more staff. Every committee in the House and Senate also has a staff.

As a staff member you would have a beautiful place to work. Though most of their offices are in one of the Senate or House office buildings, many have responsibilities in the Capitol, too. Going between the office buildings and the

Secretary of the Army Pete Geren and Chief of Staff of the Army General George W. Casey Jr. answer questions posed by congressional staffers at a breakfast meeting, October 2008.

Congressional staffers learn about a bill being considered by Congress.

Military leaders meet with congressional staffers who work for Congressmen from Maryland, 2012.

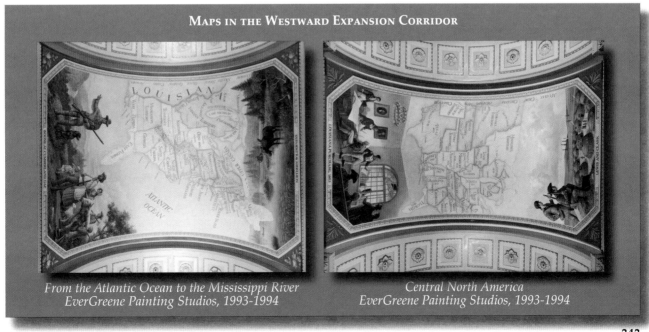

MAPS IN THE WESTWARD EXPANSION CORRIDOR

From the Atlantic Ocean to the Mississippi River
EverGreene Painting Studios, 1993-1994

Central North America
EverGreene Painting Studios, 1993-1994

Subway Scenes
Lower: Senator Joe Lieberman
and His Wife

Capitol is easy on the subway that connects them. See photos at left.

In this lesson are photos of the walls, floors, and ceilings of the United States Capitol. Imagine walking on these floors, past these walls, and looking up at these ceilings while you are at work. In the blue boxes we have featured art from the Westward Expansion Corridor in the House wing of the Capitol. This corridor and two others in the House wing are decorated with murals designed by artist Allyn Cox, who lived from 1896 to 1982. It took the work of many talented people to design them, to paint them on canvas, to prepare the ceilings, and to put the artwork in place.

The Westward Expansion Corridor was dedicated on Constitution Day, September 17, 1993. The murals were completed in 1993 and 1994, using Cox's designs plus designs that were similar to his. The Westward Expansion corridor has two types of vaulted ceilings, barrel vaults and cross vaults. A barrel vault is a simple curved ceiling. This is the kind of ceiling in a tunnel. A cross vault is constructed when two barrel vaults come together. See drawing below. The map

murals pictured in this lesson are on the barrel vaults. It looks like parts of the paintings are upside down, but they were painted so that they can be viewed from two angles, facing the left wall and looking up or facing the right wall

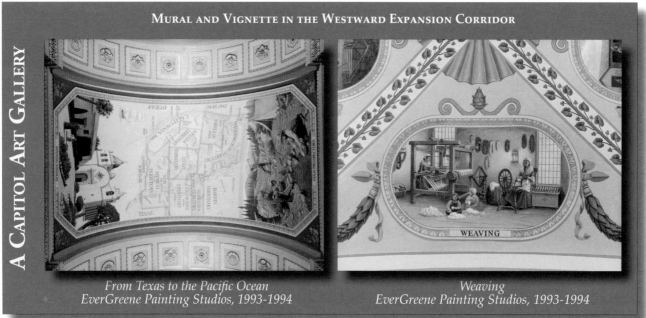

A CAPITOL ART GALLERY

MURAL AND VIGNETTE IN THE WESTWARD EXPANSION CORRIDOR

From Texas to the Pacific Ocean
EverGreene Painting Studios, 1993-1994

Weaving
EverGreene Painting Studios, 1993-1994

and looking up. Each of the oval vignettes pictured in this lesson are in one of the four sections of one of the cross vaults in the Westward Expansion Corridor.

Chief of Staff

The head of a Congressman's or Senator's staff is called the chief of staff. He or she reports directly to the Congressman or Senator. The chief of staff assigns jobs to staff members and makes sure that the work gets done. However, the chief of staff is more than an office manager; he is usually the closest advisor to the member of Congress for whom he works. Together they think about everything the member says and does and how it will impact both the citizens the member represents and the reputation of the member of Congress.

Senator Mark Warner of Virginia with his Director of Communications Kevin Hall and Chief of Staff Luke Albee

Director of Communications

Pictured above are Senator Mark Warner of Virginia along with his Chief of Staff and Director of Communications. Each member of Congress must have good communication with the people he represents, the media, and the general public. Therefore he hires a communications director, also called a press secretary. The communications director helps the Congressman or Senator communicate well to reporters and to citizens in newspapers, on radio and television, and on the Internet. Communication directors write press releases or oversee others who write them. Press releases are written statements or short articles that tell what the Congressman

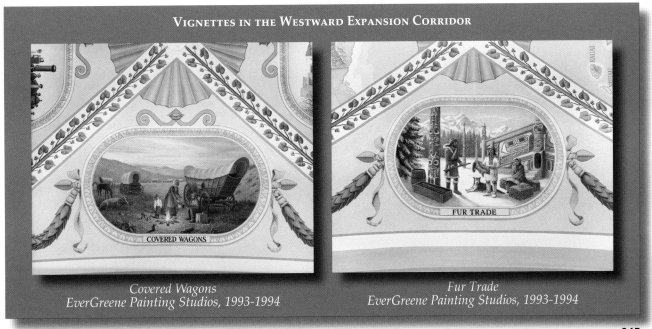

VIGNETTES IN THE WESTWARD EXPANSION CORRIDOR

COVERED WAGONS

FUR TRADE

Covered Wagons
EverGreene Painting Studios, 1993-1994

Fur Trade
EverGreene Painting Studios, 1993-1994

or Senator believes and is doing about issues that people care about. The communications director also makes arrangements for his boss to give press conferences. He finds a place to have them and lets reporters know when and where they will be. Some members of Congress hire speechwriters and researchers who help them communicate well when they gives speeches.

Legislative Staff

Each Senator and Representative has several people on his legislative staff. These staffers help him in his work of considering and voting on bills that are before Congress.

★ The legislative director keeps up with the bills that Congress is considering and gives the Congressman or Senator advice about them.

★ The legislative counsel is an attorney who is an expert in specific areas of law or government.

★ The legislative assistant researches information and writes bills for the member of Congress to introduce, finds out how bills are moving through committees, and meets with lobbyists and voters.

★ A legislative correspondent reads mail that the member of Congress receives on particular bills and writes first drafts of letters that the member might send in reply. A legislative correspondent might also do some writing for the legislative assistant.

Caseworker

A caseworker (also called a staff assistant or a research assistant) will help people in the member's home state or district with problems they are having with Federal agencies. They help citizens who are having trouble collecting Social Security benefits or veteran's benefits or having

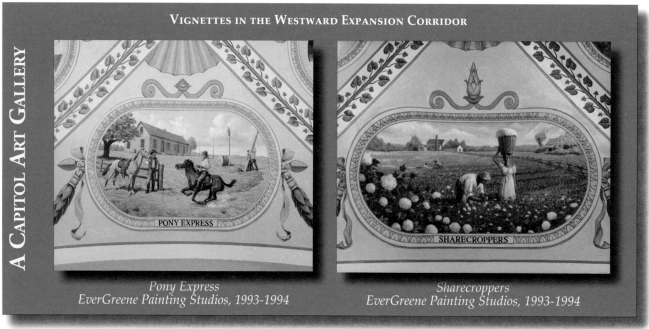

A Capitol Art Gallery

VIGNETTES IN THE WESTWARD EXPANSION CORRIDOR

Pony Express
EverGreene Painting Studios, 1993-1994

Sharecroppers
EverGreene Painting Studios, 1993-1994

PONY EXPRESS

SHARECROPPERS

some other problem related to the Federal government. Some caseworkers are in Washington, D.C., but most caseworkers are in an office in the home state or district.

Office Staff

Other members of a Senator's or Congressman's staff are more like the workers who would be found in a typical business office. The receptionist answers the phone, welcomes visitors, and arranges tours or passes to the House or Senate gallery for people from back home who are visiting Washington. The office manager makes sure that things run smoothly in the office. Some offices might have a systems administrator to take care of the computer network. The scheduler (or appointments secretary) makes appointments for the member, determining who gets to see and who doesn't get to see him or her, usually with the advice of the chief of staff or other staff members. The scheduler also makes the arrangements for trips that the member takes.

Congressmen and Senators can give college students opportunities to work in their offices for a few months as interns. College students can also work as interns for congressional committees.

Committee Staffs

Each Senate and House committee has two staffs that are responsible for work related to that committee, one staff for the majority party and one for the minority party. Members of the committee staff become experts on their committee's subject. They advise committee members on the meaning and possible consequences of proposed bills, such as how much it will likely cost to put a plan into action and what impact it might have in each member's home state or district. These two staffs will often be working at cross purposes. One staff might be working to help a bill get passed while the other could be working to try to get a bill defeated.

Imagine being a congressional staffer. You would have a chance to make a real difference. A speech you wrote could be given by one of the most powerful leaders in Washington. A bill that you wrote could change people's lives for the better. Travel arrangements you made for your Senator could enable him to encourage American troops overseas.

Many congressional staffers are in their twenties and thirties. When the Israelites were in captivity in Babylon, the Babylonian king chose young men to serve in his court. He told one of his chief officials to choose:

Youths in whom was no defect, who were good-looking, showing intelligence in every branch of wisdom, endowed with understanding and discerning knowledge, and who had ability for serving in the king's court.

Daniel 1:4

Lesson Activities

Thinking Biblically — In your notebook, write a paragraph about why it was important for the young men serving in the king's court to have the attributes listed in Daniel 1:4.

Vocabulary — In your notebook, make a simple drawing for each of these words that illustrates what it means: publicity, mural, vignette, corridor, defect. Write the word under the drawing. Check in a dictionary if you need help with their definitions.

Literature — Read "Senate Firsts" in *The Citizen's Handbook*, pages 71-72, and the chapters titled "On to Utah!" "The Deserted Cabin," "Thief's Plunder," and "In the Kaibab Forest" in *Brighty of the Grand Canyon*.

Creative Writing — In your notebook, write an imaginary conversation between a Senator or Representative and that person's chief of staff. The conversation can be a serious one about a bill or an upcoming meeting, or it can be a humorous one about something funny that happened on the subway between the Capitol and the office building.

Picture This! — Copy one of the vignettes pictured in this lesson that decorate the Westward Expansion Corridor.

Student Workbook or Lesson Review — If you are using one of these optional books, complete the assignment for Lesson 66.

Working on CAPITOL HILL

How does the United States Capitol work? Do the Congressmen take turns giving tours to visitors and running the gift shop? Does the United States Army protect the Capitol? Do you have to be a Democrat or Republican to hold an important job there? Do you have to be a politician and be elected to office to do anything that matters in Washington?

The answer to all of these questions is no. This lesson talks about some of the agencies that work at the Capitol or with Congress to serve the American people. Those who are a part of these agencies are not politicians or in the military, but what they do helps the work of government take place every day.

Capitol Police and Capitol Guides

In 1828, President John Quincy Adams sent his twenty-five year old son, also named John, with some papers to the U.S. Senate chamber. In those days newspapers often printed vicious stories about politicians that were not true. John had expressed his displeasure with a particular newspaper writer in a conversation with someone a few days earlier. As the President's son walked through the Rotunda of the Capitol, that newspaper writer came up behind him and struck him. The attack was witnessed by several people, and the incident went no further. President Adams wrote about it in his diary that evening. As a result of this attack on the son of the President, Congress created the Capitol Police force.

Capitol Police

349

The original purpose of the Capitol Police was to provide security for the Capitol building. Over the years, its duties and the area it protects have greatly expanded. Today the 1,800 Capitol policemen guard the Capitol, the Congressional Office Buildings, the parks and streets in a large area around the Capitol, and the members of Congress and their families not only at the Capitol but in the District of Columbia and in the fifty states and the five U.S. territories.

Capitol Guide

The Capitol Police force is overseen by a three-member board. The members of the board are the Architect of the Capitol, the Sergeant at Arms of the House of Representatives, and the Sergeant at Arms of the Senate. This same board oversees the Capitol Guide Service. In honor of the centennial of the United States, Congress established the Guide Service in 1876. It provides tours of the Capitol free of charge.

Office of the Architect of the Capitol

The Architect of the Capitol is responsible for taking care of the Capitol Complex, which is also called the Capitol Campus. The Complex includes the Capitol, the Capitol Visitor Center, the congressional office buildings, the Library of Congress, the Supreme Court Building, the Thurgood Marshall Federal Judiciary Building, the U.S. Botanic Garden, the Capitol Power Plant, and the Capitol Police Headquarters. The Architect is responsible for maintenance of the buildings and for remodeling, restoration, and preservation projects, as well as caring for the grounds. He is responsible for about 17.4 million square feet of floor space in buildings and about 620 acres of land.

The first three Architects of the Capitol are pictured on page 317. In the past, the Architect might serve for many years. Edward Clark served from August 1865 to January 1902 and David Lynn from August 1923 to September 1954. In 1989 Congress decided that Architects of the Capitol would serve for ten-year terms and would be chosen by the President from three candidates that a congressional nominating commission recommends. The Senate gives official consent.

Capitol Visitor Center

Stephen T. Ayers became the eleventh Architect of the Capitol in 2010. He is pictured at right. Ayers oversees a multi-talented staff that cares for a wide variety of tasks needed to keep the Capitol in good repair and operating smoothly. The remaining pictures in this lesson showcase their skills and show the results of their excellent work.

Stephen T. Ayers

Capitol Flag Program

One special project of the Architect's office that touches the lives of many Americans is the Capitol Flag Program. This is the program by which flags that have flown over the Capitol are presented to schools, Scout troops, civic organizations, and other groups. The program began in 1937 when a member of Congress asked for a flag that had flown over the Capitol. The idea quickly became popular, and members of Congress now request more than 100,000 flags each year. Flags that fly over the Capitol on national holidays and during special events are especially in demand. Accompanying each flag is a Certificate of Authenticity issued by the Architect of the Capitol. The first astronauts that landed on the moon in July of 1969 carried with them two flags that had flown over the Capitol.

Obviously the Capitol has more than one flagpole. Special flagpoles have been erected on the roof of the Capitol for the flying of these commemorative flags, so several flags are flown over the Capitol each day. On July 4, 1976, 10,471 flags flew over the Capitol in honor of the bicentennial of our country. Eighteen temporary flagpoles were installed, a hoist raised and lowered large pallets with boxes of flags to and from the roof of the Capitol, and beginning at 12:01 a.m., a crew of workers raised and lowered the flags on the poles. They finished the job in nine hours. Almost 70,000 flags were flown over the Capitol that summer.

Plasterer in Cannon House Office Building

The grounds crew plants 120,000 to 140,000 annuals, tulips, and spring bulbs each year.

Conservator in Brumidi Corridor

Inspecting Equipment in the Capitol Power Plant

351

Government Accountability Office

The Government Accountability Office (GAO) is an independent agency that investigates how the Federal government spends taxpayer dollars. The GAO works for Congress and is not influenced by political parties. It is led by a Comptroller General, who is appointed for a fifteen-year term by the President, who chooses from nominees recommended by Congress. The President's selection must be confirmed by the Senate.

The mission of the GAO is "to support the Congress in meeting its constitutional responsibilities and to help improve the performance and ensure the accountability of the Federal government for the benefit of the American people." The GAO prepares reports on what government agencies spend. They point out ways that money is spent unwisely or against the law. Committees in Congress can request the GAO to write reports. Over three thousand workers are part of the GAO in Washington and eleven other major cities. GAO employees include economists, accountants, social scientists, computer experts, and attorneys.

Congressional Budget Office

The Congressional Budget Office (CBO) was established in 1974 to help with each year's Federal budget. The CBO produces cost estimates for bills that are before Congress, such as estimating how much revenue a new tax will probably generate or how much a new regulation might cost businesses and the general public. The CBO tries to predict what will

Setting Up and Decorating the Capitol Christmas Tree

Snow Removal

happen in the economy and what might be the cost of various policy options. It also produces reports on such segments of the economy as health care, education, national security, the environment, and the impact of roads and railroads.

Government Printing Office

In 1813 Congress announced that it wanted to make information readily available to the American people. The Government Printing Office (GPO) was created in 1860. The GPO prints official government publications and provides them to Congress, Federal agencies, universities, certain libraries, and the American people. The GPO prints, among other things, *The Congressional Record*, printed copies of Federal regulations, and the passports that are issued to Americans. In general, if it is a government document, the GPO produced it. As computer documents have become more common, the need for documents printed on paper has decreased.

Metal Worker

Electrician

The Clerk of the House

Members of the House of Representatives are elected for two-year terms. When those two years are over, the members' terms are over and that Congress goes out of existence. How does the House of Representatives get started again in the next numbered Congress? Who produces the roll of the 435 people elected to make up the new House of Representatives? Who keeps the official records of what the House does?

The answer to these questions is the Clerk of the House. Every new Congress elects a Clerk. The Democrats nominate someone, the Republicans nominate someone else, and the party that has the most members wins. The Clerk keeps a record of what the House does. He or she keeps a record of the

Groundskeeper

votes of members and certifies a bill when it passes. At the end of a session, the Clerk sends a copy of the House Journal to each member and to the Governors and legislatures of each state. The Office of the Clerk is responsible for keeping the records of previous Congresses and for overseeing the office staff of a Congressman who dies, resigns, or is removed from office until a new Congressman is elected and takes the oath of office.

Find: 1) dome keepers; 2) people working with the Statue of Freedom when it was removed from the Capitol dome by helicopter for restoration work; 3) a man caring for orchids in the U.S. Botanic Gardens; 4) a welder; 5) someone repairing historic brick; 6) someone attaching lights to the Statue of Freedom; 7) decorative painters; 8) stone masons; 9) pipefitters; and 10) a building engineer wearing yellow gloves.

The Architect of the Capitol has a loyal staff. At the end of 2011, 176 of his employees had taken care of the Capitol for thirty years or more.

> . . . make it your ambition to lead a quiet life and attend to your own business
>
> and work with your hands, just as we commanded you.
>
> 1 Thessalonians 4:11

Lesson Activities

Literature — Read "Pages of the House" in *The Citizen's Handbook,* page 73, and the chapters titled "The Voice inside the Snowman," "Trapped by the Snow," and "Alone with the Night" in *Brighty of the Grand Canyon.*

Creative Writing — If you could choose a job working for the Architect of the Capitol, what would it be? Look at the pictures in this lesson to get an idea of different jobs that are available. In your notebook, write a short story of at least one page telling about one day's work. Perhaps you could write about famous politicians who walked by you or about an interesting group of tourists you saw.

Find Out! — Find out what 450 acres of land looks like (the amount of land for which the Architect of the Capitol is responsible). Visit a large farm in your area and have the owner show you, or look at a map or online to see an area of your town that matches that size.

Picture This! — Draw a picture or take a photograph of your dad doing one of the tasks described or pictured in this lesson.

Student Workbook or Lesson Review — If you are using one of these optional books, complete the assignment for Lesson 67.

The Office of
VICE PRESIDENT

The Constitution gives the Vice President only three responsibilities. One job he rarely does, one he does only once every four years, and the other he does only if the President cannot do so himself.

President of the Senate

This lesson about the Vice President is included in this unit about Congress because the Constitution says that the Vice President is the president of the Senate. However, the Vice President does not take part in the debates in the Senate; and he cannot vote in the Senate unless Senators are voting on a bill and the vote is tied. Because of the way that the Senate operates today, presiding over meetings of the Senate is a largely ceremonial role. As a result, the Vice President does so rarely. In the photos at right, President Franklin Roosevelt's Vice President prepares to open the 75th Congress and administers the oath of office to two Senators.

Every four years the Vice President has the responsibility of making a formal announcement of the votes cast for President

Vice President John Garner is ready to call to order the 75th Congress, 1936.

Vice President Garner (right) administers the oath of office to Florida Senators Claude Pepper and Charles Andrews, 1936.

and Vice President in the Electoral College. This announcement takes place at a joint session of Congress. Four Vice Presidents have announced their own victory: John Adams, Thomas Jefferson, Martin Van Buren, and George H. W. Bush. Two Vice Presidents, Richard Nixon in 1961 and Al Gore in 2001, had been candidates for the presidency but lost and had to announce the victory of their opponents. Vice President Hubert Humphrey lost to Richard Nixon in 1968; but when the joint session took place, Humphrey was out of the country attending the funeral of a former secretary general of the United Nations.

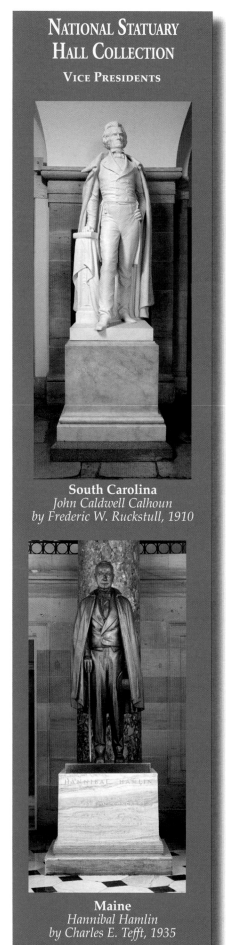

South Carolina
*John Caldwell Calhoun
by Frederic W. Ruckstull, 1910*

Maine
*Hannibal Hamlin
by Charles E. Tefft, 1935*

Vice Presidents Who Became President

The third duty of the Vice President is to take over the duties of the President if the President dies, resigns, or is removed from office. Since the Vice President is next in line to become President, it is sometimes said that he is one heartbeat away from the presidency. Eight times in our history the Vice President has had to step into the presidency because a President died, and once because a President resigned.

Some Presidents have had serious health problems while in office. When President Woodrow Wilson had a stroke, some people believed his wife made too many important decisions. The Twenty-fifth Amendment outlines the official way that the Vice President is to take responsibility temporarily should the President become unable to fulfill his duties (for example, while a President is under anesthesia during surgery).

Several Vice Presidents have run for President during the last months of their term as Vice President. Vice Presidents John Adams, Martin Van Buren, and George H. W. Bush were victorious. Vice Presidents Richard Nixon, Hubert Humphrey and Al Gore were not. Richard Nixon ran again in 1968 and was elected.

Top Secret Information

Each morning the Vice President goes to the Oval Office in the White House to hear the President's Daily Brief (PDB). The PDB is prepared every morning to tell the President information that the government collected the day before. The President's Daily Brief tells the President and the Vice President about matters from around the world that have to do with the safety of American citizens both in the U.S. and in other parts of the world. It also tells about American troops around the world. The Secretary of State, the Secretary of Defense, and the President's National Security Advisor usually attend this meeting as well.

The office of Vice President has not always been considered very important. The first man to hold the office, John Adams, thought that it was largely powerless and meaningless. This changed when Harry Truman had to become President during World War II. Since then, top secret information has been given to the Vice President.

New Roles for the Vice President

Harry Truman was Vice President for three months before he became President in April of 1945, near the end of World War II. During those months, Truman never met with President Franklin Roosevelt. Truman did not know the President's war plans, and he did not know about the secret program to develop an atomic bomb. Truman had to make a decision about using the bomb against Japan less than four months later. In 1949 the Vice President was made a member of the National Security Council so that he could stay informed on important issues. The Vice President also takes part in Cabinet meetings.

In recent years the Vice President has become an important advisor to the President. The Vice President talks with Senators and Congressmen. He makes speeches around the country promoting the President's ideas. The Vice President sometimes accompanies the President when he fulfills various responsibilities. He may show his support symbolically by physically standing by the

Vice President George H. W. Bush speaks on the aircraft carrier USS Enterprise *during the Peace in the Pacific program that celebrated forty years of peace after World War II. To his left are Secretary of Defense Caspar Weinberger and Mrs. Bush, 1985.*

Vice President Dan Quayle meets with the governor of Okinawa (to his left), 1989.

Vice President Dan Quayle and his wife Marilyn are greeted by an Air Force honor guard, 1989.

President while he gives a press conference or signs a bill that has been passed by Congress. The Vice President sometimes makes trips to meet with foreign leaders and attends state dinners at

357

the White House when foreign leaders visit the United States. He also visits American troops around the country and overseas. Examine the photos on pages 357 through 359 to see Vice Presidents performing some of their many responsibilities.

Politics is why someone gets to be Vice President. No one runs for the office of Vice President the way people run for the presidency. A person is chosen as a party's vice presidential nominee by the presidential nominee of the party. This choice is confirmed by the party's national convention. The presidential nominee tries to select someone who will be a help to him in the election and later in office if they win.

Vice President Dan Quayle meets a George Washington actor during a fund raising race.

Vice President Al Gore greets Crown Prince His Royal Highness Abdullah bin Ad Al-Aziz Al-Saud of Saudi Arabia at Andrews Air Force Base, 1998.

Soldiers welcome Vice President Al Gore and his wife Tipper to the U.S. Army Garrison Yongsan in South Korea, 1997.

The Vice President's Offices

The Vice President works in an office in the West Wing of the White House. He also has two ceremonial offices, one in the Eisenhower Executive Office Building (EEOB) and one in the U.S. Capitol. The office in the EEOB, called the Vice President's Ceremonial Office, is used mostly for meetings and interviews with the press. This office once belonged to the Secretary of the Navy. One President used it. President Hoover moved into it after the Christmas Eve fire in the West Wing in 1929.

The office is decorated in a Victorian style. It has symbols of the Navy and a bust of Christopher Columbus. It has a beautiful floor made of mahogany, white maple, and cherry. The two fireplaces are Belgian black marble. Since 1960 every Vice President except Hubert Humphrey has used this office.

The desk in the Vice President's office in the EEOB was used first by President Theodore Roosevelt. It was also used by Presidents Taft, Wilson, Harding, Coolidge, Hoover, Truman, and Eisenhower. The first Vice President to use the desk was Lyndon Johnson. Every Vice President since then has used it. Since the 1940s, each President and Vice President who has used the desk has signed his name on the inside of the top drawer.

The Vice President's Room in the Capitol is just outside the Senate chamber. It was the only office of these Vice Presidents: Hannibal Hamlin, who served under President Lincoln; Chester A. Arthur, who served under James Garfield; and Theodore Roosevelt, who served under William McKinley. After James Garfield was assassinated, Arthur took the presidential oath in this room. Here Vice President Thomas R. Marshall signed the Nineteenth Amendment giving women the right to vote.

Harry Truman was in the House wing of the Capitol on April 12, 1945, when he got a call telling him about the death of President Roosevelt. He ran through the Crypt below the Rotunda, passed the Senate barber shop, bounded up a flight of stairs, and ran into the Vice President's Room to get his hat. In a few minutes, he took the oath and became the new President of the United States.

Vice President Dick Cheney and his wife Lynne disembark from Air Force Two (the Vice President's airplane) at Elmendorf Air Force Base in Alaska, 2004.

Vice President Joe Biden at an Everglades Restoration Project in Florida, April 2012

The Crypt Beneath the Capitol Rotunda

Vice President Joe Biden speaks to a crowd of military personnel and civilians at Camp Victory, a former palace of Iraqi dictator Saddam Hussein, 2011.

In the left photo, President-elect Donald Trump (left) and Vice President-elect Mike Pence (right) meet with Speaker of the House Paul Ryan. In the right photo, Pence takes the oath of office to become Vice President.

The Vice President's Home

The Vice President's Home is located on the grounds of the United States Naval Observatory. His address is Number One Observatory Circle, Washington, D.C. Vice Presidents and their families had to provide their own housing in Washington until 1974, when Congress voted to remodel the home at the observatory for the nation's second highest official. The first Vice President to live in the home was Walter Mondale, beginning in 1977.

The Vice President's main job today is to support the President. In public he is careful to honor the President and his goals and not to call attention to himself.

Do nothing from selfishness or empty conceit, but with humility of mind regard one another as more important than yourselves; do not merely look out for you own personal interests, but also for the interests of others.

Philippians 2:3-4

Lesson Activities

Thinking Biblically — In your notebook, copy Philippians 2:3-5, using the version of your choice.

Vocabulary — In your notebook, write your own definition for each of these words: resign, anesthesia, meaningless, bounded, bust. Look in the lesson for clues for the meaning of the words. When you are finished writing your definitions, look in a dictionary for comparison.

Literature — Read the chapters titled "Strange Thanksgiving," "Moon-Lily Tea," and "No Escape?" in *Brighty of the Grand Canyon*.

Find Out! — Has there ever been a Vice President from your state?

Picture This! — Draw a picture or take a photograph of the person you would choose as your vice presidential running mate if you were running for President.

Student Workbook or Lesson Review — If you are using one of these optional books, complete the assignment for Lesson 68.

The LIBRARY OF CONGRESS

The Library of Congress is an agency of the Federal government that is overseen by Congress. It is the largest library in the world with almost 150 million items. The original purpose of the Library was to assist members of Congress in research and gathering information, but today it serves the entire nation.

The Librarian of Congress oversees its operations. Dr. James Billington, at right, became its thirteenth librarian in 1987. Before becoming the Librarian, he taught history at Harvard and Princeton Universities and served as the director of the Woodrow Wilson International Center for Scholars.

Librarian of Congress Dr. James Billington with One of the Library's Rare Books

In 1800 Congress set aside $5,000 "for the purpose of such books as may be necessary for the use of Congress . . . , and for fitting up a suitable apartment for containing them." The original Library of Congress was in the Capitol. It contained three maps and 740 books, mainly law books.

When the British burned the Capitol in 1814, the library was destroyed. President Thomas Jefferson offered to sell his personal library to Congress as a replacement. Congress agreed to buy Jefferson's library of 6,487 books which he had collected over fifty years. He received $23,950. Jefferson's collection contained books on many subjects. This opened the door for the

Thomas Jefferson Building

John Adams Building

James Madison Memorial Building

Library of Congress to collect a wide variety of publications and not just law books.

In the early years of the Smithsonian Institution, its librarian wanted to make the Smithsonian the nation's library instead of the Library of Congress. However, in 1854 the head of the Smithsonian ended the competition by dismissing the librarian. The Smithsonian Institution later gave its 40,000 books to the Library of Congress.

In 1851 the Library suffered another devastating loss with a fire which destroyed about 35,000 of the library's 55,000 books, including about two-thirds of the books that had once belonged to Jefferson. The next year Congress voted to provide the money needed to replace the books. After the Civil War, the Library grew in size and importance.

The Thomas Jefferson, John Adams, and James Madison Memorial Buildings

In 1897 the first building devoted entirely to the Library of Congress opened near the Capitol. It is called the Thomas Jefferson Building. At left are three photos of its Great Hall, including a bust of Jefferson, plus a view of the Main Reading Room at lower left. A second building was completed in 1939. It is now called the John Adams Building to honor the President who signed the law establishing the Library of Congress in 1800. On page 363 are examples of its art and architecture.

Artwork of the James Madison Memorial Building: "Falling Books," a Four-Story Relief (above) and Bronze Reliefs (right)

The top mural has musicians from three generations. The lower mural is a scene from Chaucer's Canterbury Tales. The other photos show details of the building's architecture. The James Madison Memorial Building opened in 1980. Artworks decorating this building are at the bottom of page 362. The Library also has a large storage facility in Culpeper, Virginia.

Tours of the Library of Congress buildings are offered several times every day. The Library welcomed about 1.7 million visitors in 2010.

The Library of Congress in the Twentieth Century

When the Library of Congress moved into the Thomas Jefferson Building in 1897, it contained over 840,000 volumes. The Library continued to increase its collection. It also began to serve the entire nation. In 1903 President Theodore Roosevelt ordered the papers of the Founding Fathers to be transferred from the Department of State to the Library of Congress. The Library purchased materials from libraries in other countries and also acquired a wide variety of items of historic value, including one of only three known complete copies of the Gutenberg Bible which were printed on vellum (animal skins) in Germany around 1439. The Bible was the first book Johann Gutenberg printed with the new system of printing he had just invented. The Library also purchased violins made by Italian instrument craftsman Antonio Stradivarius, who lived from 1644 to 1737.

John Adams Building

The Library of Congress Today

The Library of Congress has thirty-three million books and other print materials in 470 languages. It has the largest law library in the world. The Library's smallest printed book is a copy of "Old King Cole," published in 1985 and measuring 1/25" by 1/25". One must use a needle to turn its pages. The largest book measures five feet by seven feet. It is a collection of color pictures from Bhutan in southeast Asia. Read about other items in the Library's collection in the chart below. The Library collections fill about 838 miles of shelves. It has offices in some foreign countries to help in purchasing materials from international sources.

Library of Congress Conservators

The Library of Congress Classification System catalogs books and other resources so that they can be found easily. This system is used in most American research and university libraries. Many public libraries use the Dewey Decimal Classification System instead.

Every working day the Library receives over 22,000 items and adds about 10,000 items to its collection. What it does not keep it exchanges with libraries in other countries or donates to Federal agencies, educational institutions, and tax-exempt organizations. The U.S. Copyright Office is part of the Library of Congress. This office registers the copyright of original creative works. An original work is considered to be copyrighted when it is completed. However, sending copies of original works to the U.S. Copyright Office for registration provides proof of authorship and date of copyright if any legal question arises. Notice Library conservators at work above. One is sitting among thousands of items deposited for copyright. The other is repairing a poster.

In recent years the Library of Congress has made available millions of items in digital format on the Internet. Many pictures in Notgrass Company publications are from the Library of Congress collection. We only use ones that are no longer under copyright or ones that have been donated to the Library of Congress and made available for such use.

At the Library of Congress

Copy of the Gutenberg Bible

Draft of the Declaration of Independence

Copy of the Bay Psalm Book of 1640, The First Book Printed in America

One Million Issues of Newspapers from Around the World Covering Three Centuries

Over Five Million Maps

Six Million Works of Sheet Music

Three Million Sound Recordings

Early Movies, Including Ones Donated by Inventor Thomas Edison

Almost Fifteen Million Prints and Photographs

About Six Thousand Comic Books

One photographer who has made her photos available to the public through the Library of Congress is Carol Highsmith. In the box below, read about how she uses her talents to serve.

Using Talents to Serve: Carol M. Highsmith, America's Photographer

A girl born in 1946 grew up to give generously to the America she loves. In the photo at left, she enjoys her sister's company on their grandparents' farm in North Carolina. In her twenties, she studied photography. Today Carol M. Highsmith photographs America. She has been called "America's Photographer" and has published more than fifty coffee-table books about places in America. Along the way she has met famous people, like President Ford, pictured at left

Carol has photographed museum artifacts for the National Park Service, including items that once belonged to General Robert E. Lee, former slave and abolitionist Frederick Douglass, poet Carl Sandburg, American Red Cross founder Clara Barton, and Presidents Lincoln, Truman, Eisenhower, and Theodore Roosevelt. For many years, she has photographed Federal buildings around the country for the General Services Administration. The GSA is an independent agency in the executive branch that takes care of Federal buildings and vehicles.

An image Highsmith took of the Jefferson Memorial was chosen for the Priority Mail stamp for the U.S. Postal Service, which printed one hundred million of them.

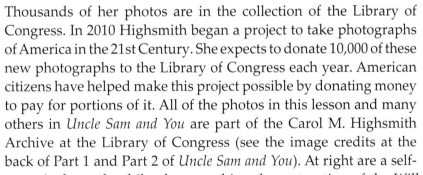

Thousands of her photos are in the collection of the Library of Congress. In 2010 Highsmith began a project to take photographs of America in the 21st Century. She expects to donate 10,000 of these new photographs to the Library of Congress each year. American citizens have helped make this project possible by donating money to pay for portions of it. All of the photos in this lesson and many others in *Uncle Sam and You* are part of the Carol M. Highsmith Archive at the Library of Congress (see the image credits at the back of Part 1 and Part 2 of *Uncle Sam and You*). At right are a self-portrait she took while photographing the restoration of the Willard Hotel in Washington, D.C., and a picture of Carol while she was taking photographs in Monument Valley, a Navajo Tribal Park in northern Arizona and southern Utah. The center photo on page 20 is her family's reunion, held at the log cabins where her grandfather and great-grandfather were born in North Carolina.

The original purpose of the Library of Congress was to conduct research for members of Congress. The Congressional Research Service continues to do this. The Library keeps the records of Congress through its THOMAS archive system (named for Thomas Jefferson). These archives include a record of the bills that are introduced in Congress, the proceedings of congressional committees, and *The Congressional Record*. Senators and Representatives use the Members of Congress Room, pictured on page 366.

People who have a Research Identification Card can use the materials in the Library of Congress. This card is available to anyone sixteen and over with proper identification. Only members of Congress, justices of the Supreme Court, congressional and court staff, Library of Congress staff, and a few other government officials can actually check out materials. Everyone else must use them in the

The Members of Congress Room

Library itself. The Library does loan books to other libraries in the United States, but loaned materials can only be used inside the library that borrowed the materials. The Library of Congress also provides a National Library Service for the Blind and Physically Handicapped. It makes audio and Braille materials available for over 800,000 patrons.

The Library of Congress plays an important role in the civic life of the United States. It fulfills its mission "to support the Congress in fulfilling its constitutional duties and to further the progress of knowledge and creativity for the benefit of the American people." Although it has never officially been declared to be the nation's library, the Library of Congress in fact serves this role for America.

The fear of the Lord is the beginning of knowledge;

Fools despise wisdom and instruction.

Proverbs 1:7

Lesson Activities

Thinking Biblically — Discuss with a parent: Why is the fear of the Lord the most important thing we should learn as we homeschool?

Vocabulary — Look up each of these words in a dictionary and read their definitions: publication, dismiss, conservator, authorship, proceeding.

Literature — Read "Moving the Books" in *The Citizen's Handbook,* page 74, and the chapters titled "Blazing Guns," "A Score to Settle," and "The Way Home" in *Brighty of the Grand Canyon.*

Creative Writing — Choose an interior or exterior photograph of one of the Library of Congress buildings pictured in this lesson and write a description of it in your notebook.

Find Out! — The Library of Congress maintains about 4,424,640 feet of shelf space. Measure how many feet of bookshelf space are in your house. Divide 4,424,640 by that number. The answer is how many times you would have to multiply your bookshelves to equal the Library of Congress shelves!

Student Workbook or Lesson Review — If you are using one of these optional books, complete the assignment for Lesson 69.

★ Remember to choose an American Holiday to study this week! ★

UNIT 15 – AMERICA RELATES TO THE WORLD

BOOKS USED IN UNIT 15

- The Citizen's Handbook

- Student Workbook (optional)

- Lesson Review (optional)

U.S. Embassy in Brussels, Belgium, celebrates America's Independence Day in 2010.

America and the
WORLD

In August of 2012, boys aged eleven to thirteen from across the U.S. and around the world gathered in Williamsport, Pennsylvania, for the Little League World Series. In the stands were friends and family members, who were also from across America and around the world. For eleven days, the boys enjoyed filming clips to be shown on ESPN, riding amusement rides, visiting the Little League museum—and playing baseball.

Each team had played many other teams before winning the opportunity to come to Williamsport. Eight American teams represented the Great Lakes, Mid-Atlantic, Midwest, New England, Northwest, Southeast, Southwest, and West regions. World teams represented Asia-Pacific, Canada, Caribbean, Europe, Japan, Latin America, Middle East-Africa, and Mexico.

In 2012, 2.5 million children participated in the worldwide Little League program. Little League is one of the many programs that average American citizens started that now benefit people in many parts of the world. Through Little League, the boys in Williamsport got to spend time with children who did not speak their language, who did not share their history, and whose governments were different from theirs. Programs like these help people from different countries understand one another and care about people who are different from themselves.

Of all the words in the Bible, two verses from the gospels are among the most remembered. These words give comfort and instruction that we need every day.

> *For God so loved the world, that He gave His only begotten Son, that whoever believes in Him shall not perish, but have eternal life. John 3:16*

> *In everything, therefore, treat people the same way you want them to treat you, for this is the Law and the Prophets. Matthew 7:12*

The United States and most other countries of the world want to be at peace with other countries, just as most people want to be at peace with one another. Keys to peace are recognizing that God loves all people of the world, not just people like you and people from your own country, and treating others the way you want to be treated.

The ways that people live with, work with, and relate to other people are sometimes called interpersonal relationships. The way governments of the world relate to one another is called international relations. Because countries are made up of people, the United States and every other nation must decide how it will behave toward other countries.

Princess Elizabeth of the United Kingdom and President Harry Truman, 1951

Having good relations between the U.S. and other countries is important for many reasons. American citizens want to be able to travel freely to other parts of the world. Our businesses and farmers want to be able to sell their goods to people in other countries, and we want to be able to purchase goods that other countries have to sell. Throughout history, when countries have had problems relating to one another, wars have been fought. Perhaps the most important reason that American citizens want good relationships with other countries is to avoid war and enjoy peace.

Russian President Boris Yeltsin and President Bill Clinton, 1995

Look at the photos at right. In each photo, a U.S. President is enjoying the company of a foreign dignitary. Both countries have been friends of the U.S. and both have been enemies. America has enjoyed a close relationship with Great Britain and the rest of the United Kingdom for many years, but the two countries fought against each other in two wars in America's early history. Russia was an ally of the U.S. during World War II, then they became enemies after the war, and now relations are better. Relations between two countries can change for the worse—and for the better.

Official Recognition

Though it may seem that the world has a certain number of countries and that those countries have had the same borders for many years, this is not true. Countries change. Remember the history of the United States that we discussed at the beginning of *Uncle Sam and You*. The thirteen colonies were part of Great Britain until our Founding Fathers declared that they were independent. That same sort of event continues to happen in our world today.

The first step in official relationships between two countries is for one country to announce diplomatic recognition of another. When a national government gives diplomatic recognition, that government is saying that it believes the other government is real and that it is in control of that country. France, for example, gave diplomatic recognition to the United States after the U.S. declared its independence from Great Britain. When a revolution takes place in a country today, the United States government watches what happens and announces formal recognition

Juba, Bahr al Jabal, South Sudan
South Sudan Independence Day Celebration, July 9, 2011

Washington, D.C.
Embassy of Greece

Wolfsburg, Germany
U.S. Ambassador to Germany (center) and Staff Members of U.S. Consulate Office at the Consulate Booth at the FIFA Women's World Cup, 2011

of a new government when the U.S. government believes that the new government is real and in control. Sometimes two governments that do not recognize each other can contact each other through a third country's government that both nations do recognize, although this is often hard to accomplish.

The government of the United States has relations with almost all of the other governments of the world. The African nation of South Sudan received recognition from the United States on July 9, 2011. The photo at top left was taken that day while the country was celebrating its Independence Day.

Ambassadors

When diplomatic recognition is announced, the governments exchange Ambassadors between the two countries. An Ambassador is the official representative of a head of state to the government of another country. An Ambassador's office in the capital of another country is called an embassy. Notice the Embassy of Greece at left.

Consuls

Another important official in international relations is a consul. A consul helps people from his home country when they are in the country where the consul is located. A consul is not an official representative from one government to another, but they must be given permission to live and work in the host country. One country might have several consulates (a consulate is a consul's office) in another country. For instance, a foreign country might have consulates in New York, Houston, and Los Angeles. Diplomatic recognition is not necessary for countries to exchange consuls. See Ambassador with consulate staff members above.

What Is Helped by Diplomatic Relations

Governments of two countries might agree to encourage trade between them. The government of Bangladesh, for instance, might agree to allow an American company to build a factory there to make clothes that will be sold in the United States. This provides income for workers in Bangladesh and helps the American company to hold down its costs of making clothes. At the same time, Bangladesh might agree to buy a certain amount of American farm products. This helps the people of Bangladesh as well as American farmers.

One government might agree to provide assistance to another country in many different ways. The United States government might arrange with the government of South Sudan for American companies to build schools and hospitals there. The U.S. might send agriculture experts to Korea to help Korean farms grow more food or health experts to Honduras to help Hondurans have better health care. In the photos at right, the U.S. is providing supplies for refugees in Tunisia and health care for cholera victims in Haiti. Such programs of assistance are examples of American generosity to those in need. These programs also help the people and governments of other countries to be friendly toward the United States and to be less likely to become friends with America's enemies.

USAID arrives for Libyan refugees who have fled to Tunisia.

Two nations might agree to allow some of their university students to attend each other's colleges. In this way, the students and the nations will benefit from the training the students receive in medicine, engineering, and other fields.

Port-au-Prince, Haiti
Secretary of State Hillary Clinton speaks with the staff of a USAID cholera treatment center.

Countries might make exchanges in art and education. Country A might arrange for museum displays to go to country B, while symphonies or ballet companies from country B might visit country A. Sports help people from different countries to interact. In August of 2012, the U.S. State Department brought athletes and coaches from Ecuador, Panama, and Mexico to the U.S. so that they could attend baseball clinics and learn about nutrition, settling conflicts, and sports for people with disabilities. While they were here, they attended the Little League World Series. See two examples of ways the U.S. cooperates with other countries in scientific research at right.

Star City, Russia
An American astronaut (left) and two Russian cosmonauts in training for a mission to the International Space Station.

A treaty is a formal, written agreement between two or more countries in which the countries agree to act in certain ways. Treaties can be used for several purposes. Sometimes two countries make a treaty agreeing to buy from and sell to each other. When two nations have been at war, the conflict is ended by a peace treaty. The United States and the Soviet Union were never at war, but they signed treaties to limit or reduce the number of nuclear weapons that each had.

A U.S. Coast Guard cutter and a Canadian Coast Guard ship map the continental shelf in the Arctic Ocean, 2011.

From time to time, the United States has used its influence to improve the human rights of people living in other places. Human rights are those essential protections and liberties that most people have seen as basic to humans. These rights include the right to vote, freedom of religion, freedom from slavery and torture, and freedom to move from place to place. American representatives will sometimes express concern over these issues with the leaders of countries where these rights are not protected. At times the U.S. has refused to trade with such countries or has used other pressures to help people have basic human rights. The U.S. Department of State gives awards to people who work to defend human rights. See photo of 2011 recipients at right.

Kampala, Uganda
U.S. Secretary of State Hillary Clinton with Recipients of the U.S. State Department's 2011 Human Rights Defender Award

When Relations Become Complicated

Sadly, relations between nations are not always positive. Government leaders at times do not do what they should. Diplomatic relations are important in these times also.

Sometimes an individual has a difficulty when visiting another country. An American in another country might do something he shouldn't or get arrested by mistake. When this happens, diplomats work to resolve the dispute and the uneasy feelings between the two countries. A diplomat is a person who works in a foreign country on behalf of the country that sent him. We learn more about diplomats in Lesson 73.

A nation that has been on friendly terms with the United States might get a new leader who wants better relations with a country that has been unfriendly toward the U.S. Our government wants to keep good relations with the country that has the new leader, and it does not want more nations to be unfriendly toward it. Or, two nations, both of whom have been on good terms with the United States, have an unresolved difficulty that develops into war. The U.S. might try to end the fighting by diplomacy (talking to both nations together, to each one separately, and to nations that are friendly with each one) without taking one side or the other.

Keeping peace in troubling situations is difficult. This is why diplomats have to be careful about what they say. They must learn a great deal about other countries and how their leaders think. When conflict develops between two nations that have diplomatic relations, one or both of the nations might tell its Ambassador to come home. One or both host countries might tell the other country's Ambassador to go home. The next step is to sever diplomatic relations. In the worst case, one country declares war on the other.

The United Nations

At the end of World War II, the countries that had been fighting Germany and Japan formed a world organization called the United Nations (UN). The purpose of the UN is to give nations a place to talk over their differences before starting to fight each other and to bring about better lives for all of the world's citizens. The United Nations has sent dozens of peacekeeping missions into tense situations and has provided medical and food assistance to many countries. Almost all the countries of the world are members of the United Nations.

The most powerful part of the UN is the Security Council. The five permanent members of the Security Council are the United States, the Russian Federation, the People's Republic of China, Great Britain, and France. The Council has ten other seats that rotate among the other member nations of the UN. Each permanent member can veto any policy statement or resolution decided in the Security Council.

The United Nations has done good, but it has also been a place where nations that are unfriendly toward the United States can unfairly blame the U.S. for problems in the world. The U.S. provides a significant part of the UN budget each year, but some countries complain that the U.S. does not do enough. The United States participates in the United Nations in an effort to keep peace and to encourage freedom and a high standard of living in the countries of the world; however, the UN is very controversial and many Americans would like to see the United States withdraw from being a member.

The Bible mentions peace more than three hundred times. God teaches us:

> If possible, so far as it depends on you, be at peace with all men.
>
> Romans 12:18

Lesson Activities

Thinking Biblically — In your notebook, write three paragraphs that tell what you, your family, and the United States can do to be at peace with all men.

Vocabulary — In your notebook, write which of the following words belongs in each sentence: amusement, interpersonal, consul, symphony, treaty.

    a. Deborah and I have been arguing so much, Dad said he's going to make us sign a peace _____.

    b. _____ skills are essential to being a good leader of a group.

    c. The U.S. _____ in Morocco was very helpful when our cousin lost her passport on her vacation.

    d. After we do our chores, we can play some games for _____.

    e. One day I would like to hear a _____ orchestra play in person.

Literature — Read "The Dimensions of a Kind Deed" in *The Citizen's Handbook*, pages 75-76.

Picture This! — Create a collage using the art medium of your choice that incorporates the U.S. flag and at least ten flags of other countries around the world.

Find Out! — When was the United Nations building in New York City built?

Student Workbook or Lesson Review — If you are using one of these optional books, complete the assignment for Lesson 71.

Presidential Visits
AROUND THE WORLD

When Solomon became king after the death of his father David, God told him to ask for what he wanted God to do for him. Solomon prayed: "You have made Your servant king in place of my father David, yet I am but a little child; I do not know how to go out or come in . . . . So give Your servant an understanding heart to judge Your people to discern between good and evil" (1 Kings 3: 7, 9). God was pleased with Solomon's prayer. He gave Solomon a wise and understanding heart and also blessed him with honor and with great riches.

Solomon, his kingdom, and the wisdom God gave him became well known. After the queen of Ethiopia, then called Sheba, heard about the wisdom God have given to Solomon, she came to Jerusalem to visit him. She traveled in a camel caravan, bringing spices, very much gold, and precious stones. She spoke with Solomon all that was in her heart and he shared with her the wisdom God gave him.

The queen was amazed at his wisdom, his palace, and the way his servants served him and his guests. She said: "Blessed be the Lord your God who delighted in you to set you on the throne of Israel; because the Lord loved Israel forever therefore He made you king, to do justice and righteousness" (1 Kings 10:9). The queen gave gifts to Solomon and he gave gifts to her. Then she and her servants went back home.

One way that modern Presidents promote good relations with other countries is by visiting them. In many ways the visits are similar to the one described in 1 Kings. The President arrives with a retinue of people. He admires the beautiful buildings in the host country, exchanges gifts with its leaders, and talks face to face with them about important issues.

A visit from a head of state is considered to be one of the highest honors one country can give another. Until President Theodore Roosevelt visited the work site of the Panama Canal in Panama in 1906, no President had ever left the country while in office. Since then, every President except Herbert Hoover has traveled abroad while in office. Though President Hoover stayed in the U.S. while he was President, he went on a goodwill tour of several South American countries between his election as President and his inauguration.

The first visit that a U.S. President makes to another country is an historic event both for the U.S. and for the other country. In the remainder of this lesson, let's learn about first presidential visits to other countries. Remember that these are not the only times that a U.S. President has visited these countries; they are just the first visits.

The Panama Canal in Panama, 2012

First Presidential Visits to Countries in the Western Hemisphere

Our nearest neighbors are Canada and Mexico, the islands of the Caribbean, and the countries of Central and South America. At right is a chart showing the first visits our Presidents have made to the countries of the Western Hemisphere. As we have already mentioned, President Theodore Roosevelt went to Panama in 1906. See Panama Canal above. Three years later President William Howard Taft went to Texas. While there, he and the President of Mexico exchanged visits across the border. Warren Harding became the first President to visit Canada in 1923.

Throughout the world, countries that are close geographically or that have other things in common form organizations to help one another. Today's Presidents often attend meetings of these organizations. President Calvin Coolidge addressed the Sixth International Conference of American States in the island nation of Cuba in 1928.

The first presidential visits to South America occurred a few years before the U.S. got involved in World War II. President Franklin Roosevelt visited Argentina in 1936, where he attended an Inter-American Conference for the Maintenance of Peace. He also went to Brazil and Uruguay. President Dwight Eisenhower attended a meeting of the Presidents of the American Republics in Panama City, Panama, in 1956. In 1960 Eisenhower traveled to Chile and met with its president.

First Presidential Visits to Countries in the Western Hemisphere

President Theodore Roosevelt
Panama 1906

President Taft
Mexico 1909

President Warren Harding
Canada 1923

President Calvin Coolidge
Cuba 1928

President Franklin Roosevelt
Brazil 1936
Argentina 1936
Uruguay 1936

President Dwight Eisenhower
Chile 1960

President John Kennedy
Venezuela 1961
Colombia 1961
Costa Rica 1963

President Lyndon Johnson
El Salvador 1968
Nicaragua 1968
Honduras 1968
Guatemala 1968

President Ronald Reagan
Jamaica 1982
Barbados 1982
Grenada 1986

President Bill Clinton
Haiti 1995

President George W. Bush
Peru 2008

President Barack Obama
Trinidad and Tobago 2009

Both Presidents John Kennedy and Lyndon Johnson attended the Conference of Presidents of the Central American Republics during the 1960s. When President Ronald Reagan went to the Caribbean in 1982, he met with the prime ministers of several island nations in Bridgetown, Barbados. President Clinton attended a ceremony for a United Nations mission in Port-au-Prince, Haiti, in 1995. President Obama attended the Summit of the Americas in Port-of-Spain in Trinidad and Tobago in 2009.

First Presidential Visits to Europe and Eurasia

The nation was shocked when President Woodrow Wilson announced that he would go to Europe in December of 1918 to attend the Paris Peace Conference that began in January. No President had ever left the western hemisphere while in office. In Paris Wilson worked with other world leaders to try to bring peace after World War I. While in Europe, he traveled to Belgium, Italy, and the United Kingdom. He also became the first President to visit Vatican City, where he had an audience with Pope Benedict XV. See photo below.

The next President to travel to Europe was President Franklin Roosevelt, who traveled to Yalta, Russia, in February of 1945 to meet with Soviet Premier Stalin and British Prime Minister Churchill. Russia was then part of the Union of Soviet Socialist Republics or U.S.S.R. The three leaders worked together to plan for the end of World War II. This meeting is called the Yalta Conference. President Harry Truman traveled to Potsdam, Germany, later that year as the war was ending. He met with Allied leaders: outgoing British Prime Minister Churchill, incoming British Prime Minister Attlee, and Soviet Premier Stalin. On page 377 is a chart showing the first visits our Presidents have made to Europe and Eurasia.

When Presidents visit foreign countries, they sometimes give speeches to that country's legislature. When President Dwight Eisenhower visited Greece in 1959, he met with its king and its prime minister and also addressed the Greek Parliament. In 1963 President John Kennedy traveled to Ireland,

Vatican City

Czech Republic

First Presidential Visits to Europe and Eurasia

President Woodrow Wilson
France 1919
Belgium 1919
Italy 1919
United Kingdom 1919
Vatican City 1919

President Franklin Roosevelt
Russia 1945

President Harry Truman
Germany 1945

President Dwight Eisenhower
Switzerland 1955
Greece 1959
Spain 1959
Portugal 1960

President John Kennedy
France 1961
Austria 1961
Ireland 1963

President Richard Nixon
Romania 1969
Yugoslavia 1970
Poland 1972
Iceland 1973

President Gerald Ford
Finland 1975

President George H. W. Bush
Hungary 1989
Netherlands 1989
Malta 1989

President Bill Clinton
Czech Republic 1994
Ukraine 1994
Belarus 1994
Latvia 1994
Poland 1994
Bosnia & Herzegovina 1996
Croatia 1996
Denmark 1997
Slovenia 1999
Macedonia 1999
Norway 1999
Bulgaria 1999
Serbia-Montenegro 1999

President George W. Bush
Sweden 2001
Lithuania 2002
Slovakia 2005
Georgia 2005
Albania 2007
Estonia 2007

the land from which his ancestors had immigrated to America. While there, he addressed the Irish Parliament. Notice that President George H. W. Bush was the first U.S. President to travel to Malta. You learned about that trip on page 281.

All of the countries that Presidents Bill Clinton and George W. Bush visited first are in Eastern Europe, except Denmark, Norway, and Sweden. Eastern Europe was once dominated by the U.S.S.R. The U.S.S.R. gradually lost power over the countries in Eastern Europe during the presidencies of Ronald Reagan and George H. W. Bush, two Presidents who did much to help them gain freedom. Notice the photo from the Czech Republic on page 376.

First Presidential Visits to East Asia and the Pacific

The first U.S. President to travel to East Asia was President Dwight Eisenhower. He met with Prime Minister Chung in Seoul, South Korea in 1960. He was also the first President to travel to the Philippines while in office. He met with President Garcia in Manila in 1960. President Eisenhower visited a country that the United States no longer recognizes when he visited President Chiang Kai-shek in Taipei, Taiwan, in 1960.

President Lyndon Johnson was the first President to travel to Australia. He met with Prime Minister Holt in 1966. The two had met during World War II, long before either became their country's

Seoul, South Korea

Philippines

377

Beijing, China

First Presidential Visits to East Asia and the Pacific

President Dwight Eisenhower
South Korea 1960
Philippines 1960
Taiwan 1960

President Lyndon Johnson
New Zealand 1966
Australia 1966
Vietnam 1966
Thailand 1966
Malaysia 1966

President Richard Nixon
Indonesia 1969
China 1972

President Gerald Ford
Japan 1974

President George H. W. Bush
Singapore 1992

President Bill Clinton
Brunei Darussalem 2000

President George W. Bush
Mongolia 2005

Accra, Ghana
U.S. Army General William E. Ward (center front) and U.S. Ambassador to Ghana Pamela Bridgewater (rear) inspect Ghana military in 2007.

head of state. Johnson also traveled to Vietnam to encourage U.S. soldiers at Cam Ranh Bay during the Vietnam War.

U.S. stores are filled with goods that were made in China. U.S. universities have Chinese students. Americans travel to China on vacations and many American businesses have factories there. This is a major change from forty years ago. For many years, China stayed isolated from the rest of the world. A huge step in encouraging better relations between China and the U.S. was President Richard Nixon's visit there in 1972. While in China, Nixon met with Chairman Mao Zedong and Premier Chou En-lai. See young people in Beijing, China, at top left. See chart of first presidential visits to East Asia and the Pacific at left.

First Presidential Visits to Sub-Saharan Africa

The Sahara Desert spreads across most of northern Africa. Sub-Saharan means south of the Sahara Desert. The Sahara Desert separates the African countries along the Mediterranean Sea from those to the south. We will talk about presidential visits to countries in North Africa when we discuss the Near East, because the people in those countries live more like the people of the Middle East than like the people who live in the rest of Africa. The first President to visit Sub-Saharan Africa was President Franklin Roosevelt, who met with President Barclay in Monrovia, Liberia, in 1943. The country of Liberia was founded as a refuge for people who had once been slaves in

First Presidential Visits to Sub-Saharan Africa

President Franklin Roosevelt
Liberia 1943

President Jimmy Carter
Nigeria 1978

President George H. W. Bush
Somalia 1992

President Bill Clinton
Ghana 1998
Uganda 1998
Rwanda 1998
South Africa 1998
Botswana 1998
Senegal 1998
Tanzania 2000

President George W. Bush
Benin 2008

America. Its capital city is named for President James Monroe. President Jimmy Carter traveled to Nigeria in 1978 and met with its president in Lagos. President George H. W. Bush visited international relief workers in Somalia in 1993.

President Bill Clinton traveled to several Sub-Saharan countries in 1998 and met with their heads of state. He also visited Chobe National Park in Botswana and a Peace Corps project in Accra, Ghana. The photo at lower left on page 378 was taken in Accra. Especially important was Clinton's visit to South Africa, where he met with President Nelson Mandela, who had previously been jailed for many years because of his work to bring equality to all the people of South Africa.

First Presidential Visits to South and Central Asia

Two Presidents have made initial visits to countries in this region. President Dwight Eisenhower traveled to India in 1959 where he met with President Prasad and Prime Minister Nehru. He also went to Pakistan and met with President Ayub Khan. President Bill Clinton met with the president and prime minister of Bangladesh in 2000. At right see chart of first presidential visits to this region and a photo from India.

First Presidential Visits to South and Central Asia

President Dwight Eisenhower
Pakistan 1959
India 1959

President Bill Clinton
Bangladesh 2000

Alleppy, India
Houseboats for Rent

First Presidential Visits to the Near East

The first place that people lived on earth was in the Garden of Eden. The oldest countries in the world are in the region around it. For thousands of years, this region has struggled with international relations. The region includes northern Africa and the Middle East. The first U.S. President to visit the area did so during World War II. President Roosevelt traveled to Morocco in 1943 to meet with British Prime Minister Winston Churchill. This was called the Casablanca Conference. Later that year he stopped in Tunisia, where he spoke with one of his generals, future President Dwight Eisenhower. From Tunisia he went to Egypt to meet with Churchill and Chinese Generalissimo Chiang Kai-shek. From Egypt, he traveled to Tehran, Iran. President Dwight Eisenhower made visits to Afghanistan and Turkey and met with the presidents of both countries.

In 1974 President Richard Nixon became the first U.S. President to travel to Israel. He met with President Katair and Prime Minister Rabin. While in the region, he traveled to Jordan and met with King Hussein; to Saudi Arabia where he met with King Faisal; and to Syria where he met with President Assad.

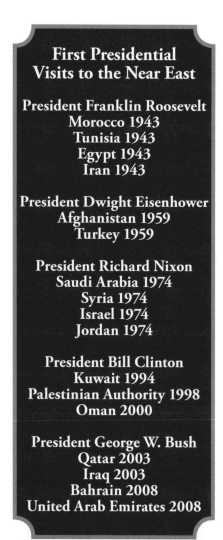

First Presidential Visits to the Near East

President Franklin Roosevelt
Morocco 1943
Tunisia 1943
Egypt 1943
Iran 1943

President Dwight Eisenhower
Afghanistan 1959
Turkey 1959

President Richard Nixon
Saudi Arabia 1974
Syria 1974
Israel 1974
Jordan 1974

President Bill Clinton
Kuwait 1994
Palestinian Authority 1998
Oman 2000

President George W. Bush
Qatar 2003
Iraq 2003
Bahrain 2008
United Arab Emirates 2008

Former President and Mrs. George W. Bush greet National Guardsmen returning from Afghanistan at the Dallas/Fort Worth International Airport, 2010.

One of the most difficult problems in international relations is the conflict between the nation of Israel and the Palestinian people, in which both claim the same land. President Clinton visited Israel in 1998 and met with Prime Minister Netanyahu. While there, he visited the government of the Palestinian people. He gave a speech to the Palestine National Council and met with Palestinian Authority Chairman Arafat.

While President George W. Bush was in office, Muslim terrorists attacked the World Trade Center in New York City and the Pentagon near Washington, D.C. Afterwards, the U.S. military fought against terrorism in Iraq and Afghanistan. President Bush visited each country while he was President both to encourage American troops and to support the new governments the U.S. helped to establish in those countries. Since leaving the presidency, he has continued to encourage American troops. See photo at lower right.

We hear a great deal about the leaders of the nations of the world, but we should always remember who is the true Ruler of all the earth.

For the Lord Most High is to be feared,

A great King over all the earth.

Psalm 47:2

Lesson Activities

Thinking Biblically — Read 1 Kings 10:1-13.

Vocabulary — Write five sentences in your notebook, using one of these words in each: retinue, geographically, recognize, region, conference. Check in a dictionary if you need help with their definitions.

Creative Writing — Imagine that you are a child living in one of the countries mentioned in this lesson. In your notebook, write a letter to your pen pal in the U.S. about the day you got to see the President of the United States when he came to your country on a visit.

Find Out! — Choose five of the countries mentioned in this lesson and find out how far the capital of each one is from Washington, D.C.

Student Workbook or Lesson Review — If you are using one of these optional books, complete the assignment for Lesson 72.

The Work of an AMBASSADOR

As our country's head of state, the President is responsible for making sure that the United States relates well with every other nation. Obviously, he cannot do this alone. The executive department that helps the President with diplomatic relations is the Department of State, usually called the State Department. The head of the State Department is the Secretary of State. Recent Secretaries of State have traveled widely to visit with leaders of other nations. Working under the Secretary of State are thousands of employees, some of whom work in the U.S. while others live and work around the world. At right is Secretary of State Hillary Clinton, who was appointed by President Barack Obama.

Buenos Aires, Argentina
Argentine President Cristina Fernandez de Kirchner and U.S. Secretary of State Hillary Clinton

An Ambassador is the highest-ranking representative of one nation to another nation. He serves as the personal representative of his government to the country where he is sent.

The Origin of Ambassadors

In the ancient world, a king who wanted to have contact with another king sent his personal representative on a specific mission that needed to be carried out. For instance, King David sent servants to Hanun, king of Ammon, to express David's condolences following the death of Hanun's father (2 Samuel 10:2). Sennacherib, king of Assyria, sent messengers to Hezekiah and the people of Judah to try to convince Judah to surrender to him (2 Kings 18:17). In these situations, representatives were sent to fulfill a specific mission and then returned home.

In Europe during the 15th and 16th centuries, kings began to send permanent representatives to live in the capital cities of other countries. These representatives worked to avoid conflicts between the two countries and to make agreements when they were needed. These Ambassadors shared information about the goals of their home governments and gathered information about the country in which they served that they could send home. National leaders hoped that this direct, personal contact and sharing of information would help avoid wars and result in trade agreements that would help both countries involved.

Over the years, Ambassadors were given rights and privileges in the countries where they worked. These developed into accepted ways of doing things that is often called protocol. These accepted ways of doing things are still largely followed today. For instance, a new Ambassador to the United States formally meets with and presents his credentials (official documents declaring him to be an Ambassador) to the President, Vice President, or Secretary of State. See photos at left.

Damascus, Syria
U.S. Ambassador to Syria Robert Ford presents his credentials to Bashar Assad, 2011.

During the Renaissance and for centuries afterward, travel and communication were slow, so Ambassadors had a fair degree of leeway to make agreements and conclude treaties on behalf of the kings who sent them. The role of an Ambassador has changed somewhat in modern times. Today leaders of countries can talk to each other on phones or communicate electronically. The U.S. Secretary of State and an official of a foreign country can talk face to face on fairly short notice since air travel can bring them together in a matter of hours.

The Role of Ambassadors Today

Jerusalem, Israel
U.S. Ambassador to Israel Daniel Shapiro meets with the President of Israel after presenting his credentials at the President's residence, 2011.

A modern Ambassador has less authority than those of earlier times. He can no longer make agreements on behalf of the country who sent him without getting permission from his government. However, Ambassadors are still an important part of diplomatic relations among nations. A personal representative from another nation can bring assurance to the host country in times of conflict, confusion, or disaster. The President does not have time to pick up the phone and talk to every other head of state, so a personal message from the President delivered by an Ambassador is an important diplomatic event. An Ambassador can offer assurance of continued American friendship if the government of the host country changes unexpectedly, as with a revolution. In times of change and uneasiness, the work of an Ambassador is especially important.

An Ambassador can have talks with high government officials about matters that are important to his home country and the country where he is working. Sometimes an Ambassador will present a speech to a group about his or her home country, or about the importance of the two countries continuing to have a good relationship. He may explain changes taking place in the Ambassador's home country that people where he is serving might not understand. The Ambassador will represent his home country at official activities. For instance, if a company from the Ambassador's home country builds a factory in the country where he is serving, the Ambassador will probably represent his country when the factory is opened. And an Ambassador will attend many dinners and receptions that are held by the host country's government leaders. When a new leader takes office or if the leader celebrates a birthday, Ambassadors will likely attend the festivities.

An Ambassador-at-large is someone who is appointed by the President to represent our country in several countries in a region. If there is tension among several countries in a region of the world, an Ambassador-at-large can make the United States' relationship better with them all. Heads of state also use special representatives called envoys, who carry out specific missions for a given length of time. Envoys do jobs that are similar to those we discussed from the books of 2 Samuel and 2 Kings.

The United States sends an Ambassador to almost every country in the world and almost every country sends an Ambassador to the U.S. The U.S. also has Ambassadors who represent the United States in many international organizations, such as the United Nations, the European Union, and the North Atlantic Treaty Organization (NATO).

How Someone Becomes an Ambassador

In the photo at right, an Ambassador is taking the oath of office. Someone becomes an Ambassador primarily in one of two ways. One way is to work in the State Department for many years, gaining knowledge and experience and taking increasingly important roles. Such a person can apply to be an Ambassador, and if he or she passes the examination he or she might be appointed as an Ambassador when a vacancy occurs. About two-thirds of Ambassadors have worked their way up through the ranks of the State Department.

Sometimes Presidents appoint someone to serve as an Ambassador as a way to reward him or her for supporting his presidential election campaign or for being a valuable member of his political party. These Ambassadors are not expected to have experience in foreign service. It is important

Secretary of State Hillary Clinton administers the oath of office to Daniel Rooney to be Ambassador to Ireland, 2009.

Bangkok, Thailand
U.S. Ambassador to Thailand Eric John presents a gift to the Queen's Lady-in-Waiting, 2009.

India
U.S. Ambassador to India Timothy Roemer visits Jammu and Kashmir to interact with the people, 2011.

Wolfsburg, Germany
U.S. Ambassador to Germany Philip Murphy and His Family with Second Lady Jill Biden (to the Ambassador's left) and Chelsea Clinton (daughter of President Bill Clinton and Secretary of State Hillary Clinton) at the FIFA Women's World Cup, 2011

Potsdam, Germany
U.S. Ambassador to Germany Philip Murphy gives a speech on the twentieth anniversary of German unity, 2010.

Swat, Pakistan
U.S. Ambassador to Pakistan Cameron Munter and his wife observe areas affected by a flood, 2010.

Ambassador Murphy with Thanksgiving Turkey

that an Ambassador fit well in the country in which he or she serves, so someone who is appointed as a favor might not be the best choice in a country that is troubled, especially if that person has little or no knowledge about that country. But many nations are at peace within and with the United States, so a political appointment works out fine in those situations.

American Ambassadors are appointed by the President and confirmed by the Senate. They serve "at the pleasure of the President," so the President can decide to recall or dismiss an Ambassador at any time. Ambassadors routinely offer their resignations after a presidential election, so that the President-elect (even if the President is re-elected) can choose who he wants to serve as Ambassadors.

The photos on this page show Ambassadors at work. They also show them enjoying their lives overseas. Read the captions to learn about some of their many responsibilities.

Dublin, Ireland
Residence of the U.S. Ambassador to Ireland

Canberra, Australia
The residence of the U.S. Ambassador to Australia, is decorated for a "California Dreamin'"-themed U.S. Independence Day Celebration, 2010.

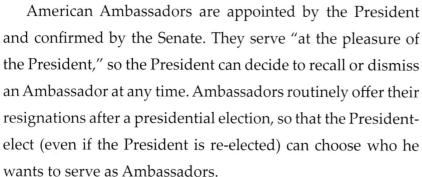

Ambassadors are the highest ranking officials working for the State Department, but thousands of other American citizens work to help international relations between the U.S. and other countries.

Foreign Service Officers

The State Department hires foreign service officers. Like Ambassadors, they are diplomats. Foreign service officers and their families live and work overseas. They work with foreign governments on technology, science, economic, trade, energy, and environmental concerns. They manage the facilities where they and their fellow foreign service officers work. They meet with foreign officials to discuss matters of concern to the United States. They share American ideals with officials in foreign governments and with other leaders in the country where America has sent them. They help Americans get out of a country if they are in danger. They help protect America's borders. The photos at right were taken at Cairo International Airport in Egypt during unrest in 2011. U.S. Foreign service officers from the U.S. Embassy helped Americans get out of the country safely.

Civil Service Officers

The State Department hires people with many skills as civil service officers. Some are experts in international relations and some are lawyers. Some are secretaries; others are bookkeepers. Some manage computer systems and some work with financial matters. Some design embassies; others keep them in good working order. Some do the tasks necessary to issue passports for Americans so they can visit overseas, and some work on visas for foreign travelers wanting to visit the U.S. A passport is a form of identification issued by a citizen's home country, while a visa is permission to visit a foreign country. A visa is issued by the country being visited.

Diplomatic Security Personnel

The State Department hires a variety of diplomatic security personnel. Special agents are federal law enforcement officers who serve around the world. They advise Ambassadors about how to keep a foreign mission safe. They protect the Secretary of State when he or she is traveling outside the U.S.

Cairo, Egypt
Top: Foreign service officers call for Americans while holding a flag at Cairo International Airport.
Center: Foreign service officers pose with an American couple.
Lower: Foreign service officers check documents and handle paperwork to help American citizens leave Cairo on a U.S. government-chartered flight.

and foreign dignitaries who visit the U.S. They investigate illegal use of passports and visas. Security engineering officers work to keep computer systems secure at U.S. diplomatic and consular posts around the world. Diplomatic couriers make sure that classified U.S. government material is carried safely across the borders between countries.

A Citizen Serving His Country Overseas

The job of an Ambassador involves a great deal of time outside of one's home country. It offers excitement and fascinating experiences, although sometimes in some situations it can be dangerous. An Ambassador represents his home country in the cause of keeping peace and good relations with other countries. An American Ambassador has the opportunity to help people in other countries know more about the United States and to have a positive impression of what Americans are like.

Paul talks about Christians being Ambassadors:

Therefore, we are ambassadors for Christ,

as though God were making an appeal through us;

we beg you on behalf of Christ, be reconciled to God.

2 Corinthians 5:20

Lesson Activities

Thinking Biblically — In your notebook, copy 2 Corinthians 5:20, using the version of your choice.

Vocabulary — Find each of these words in a dictionary: condolences, degree, uneasiness, recall, facility. Copy each word into your notebook with the definition that corresponds to the way it is used in this lesson.

Literature — Read "Whatever May Be Our Wishes" in *The Citizen's Handbook*, pages 77-79.

Find Out! — Find out how to say "Hello" in at least five languages that you don't already know.

Student Workbook or Lesson Review — If you are using one of these optional books, complete the assignment for Lesson 73.

A Drive Down
EMBASSY ROW

The permanent diplomatic mission from one country to another is called an embassy. The head of such a mission is an Ambassador. The building or complex of buildings in the capital city which houses this mission is also called an embassy, although sometimes it is called a chancery. In some cases the Ambassador's dwelling is at the embassy, while in other cases his home is elsewhere in the capital.

By agreement among the nations of the world, the embassy building is given certain privileges. For instance, an embassy cannot be entered by representatives of the host country except by permission of the represented country. This arrangement shows respect for the people and property of the represented country. A diplomatic mission is also exempt from having to obey most local laws.

In addition, the Ambassador and other high-ranking diplomats are given diplomatic immunity. This prevents a host country from arresting the Ambassador of another country if the two countries are involved in a conflict. However, if this privilege is misused, a diplomat can be prosecuted or told to leave the country.

Embassy Row in the Georgetown Area of Washington, D.C.

Embassy Row

In many cities of the world, a number of foreign embassies are located in one area. Such an area is often called Embassy Row. In Washington, D.C., Embassy Row is in the section of the city that was once Georgetown, Maryland. See photo at left. The area is still called Georgetown. Embassy Row is primarily along a section of Massachusetts Avenue and the streets that cross that section of Massachusetts Avenue. Over 170 nations have

President George H. W. Bush (left)
Attends the Opening of the New
Canadian Embassy in 1989

The table is set for a
formal dinner in the
Canadian Embassy.
Notice the view of
the U.S. Capitol
through the window.

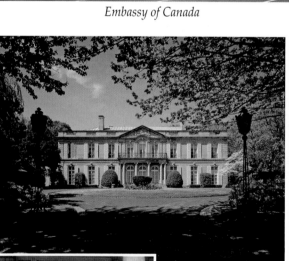

Embassy of Canada

embassies in Washington, and about half of these have their embassies in this area of Georgetown.

In the late nineteenth and early twentieth centuries, wealthy families built many large mansions in this part of Georgetown. During the Great Depression and after, many of these homes were sold; and wealthy families moved to another area. Following World War II, many nations remodeled these old mansions or built new buildings in the area. The first embassy on Embassy Row was the Embassy of the United Kingdom, also called the British Embassy. The British Embassy is beside the

Embassy of Belgium

Interior of the
Embassy of Belgium

Right Above: Pipe Organ in the Embassy of Mexico
Right: Statue of Ghandi on the Grounds
of the Embassy of India
Left: Children of the Counselor
of the Embassy of Chile,
Ages Two Months to Fourteen, 1919

United States Naval Observatory where the Vice President lives. The British Embassy has one of the largest diplomatic staffs of any embassy in Washington, with over four hundred diplomats and additional workers.

As you can see from the pictures of some of the embassies along Embassy Row, there is a wide variety of structures in the area. It is fun to drive down Massachusetts Avenue and see how many embassies from other nations you can identify. We have also included photos of rooms inside some embassies, photos of homes of Ambassadors to the United States, and photos of people who have been part of the diplomatic life in Washington, D.C. in the past.

Churchill Statue at British Embassy

Garden and Path at the British Embassy

Ambassador's Library at the British Embassy

Apostolic Nunciature (Mission) of the Vatican

Embassy of South Africa

Residence of the Ambassador of Italy

Residence of the Ambassador of Spain

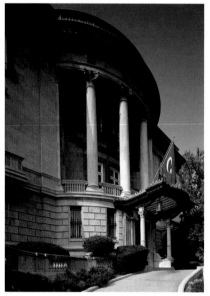

Embassy of Turkey

Embassy of Japan

Residence of the Ambassador of Egypt

Embassy of Haiti

Bust of Benjamin Franklin
in the Embassy of France

Embassy of Estonia

*Interior of Residence of the
Ambassador of South Africa*

Interior of Embassy of Turkey

Interior of Embassy of Indonesia

*Interior of Embassy
of Russia*

Embassy of Norway

*Left: Chinese theater star is
married in the garden of the
Embassy of China, 1938.
Center: Children of the
First Secretary of the
German Embassy
Right: Two American
children and children
of diplomats send
Christmas greetings
over NBC radio in
Washington, D.C., 1938.*

American Embassies in Other Countries

Courtyard of the U.S. Embassy in Berlin, Germany, during an Independence Day Reception, July 4, 2010

The first nation to recognize the new United States of America was Morocco in December of 1777. France was the second nation to do so. Benjamin Franklin established the first diplomatic mission from the United States when he settled in Paris as the American Ambassador in 1779. The Netherlands was the third country to extend diplomatic relations to the United States. John Adams served as the first Ambassador to the Netherlands. This was during the American Revolutionary War and, of course, before he was elected President. He bought a home in The Hague. This was the first American embassy building in the world.

Today the United States has embassies in foreign capitals around the world. It also has consulate offices in many other cities around the world. The American citizens who serve in these missions in other countries represent us to the governments and the citizens of those nations.

> A wicked messenger falls into adversity,
> But a faithful envoy brings healing.
> Proverbs 13:17

Lesson Activities

Literature — Read "Diplomat's Wife" in *The Citizen's Handbook*, pages 80-81.

Creative Writing — In your notebook, write at least two paragraphs telling why you think it is important for the United States to have good relations with other countries.

Picture This! — Draw a picture copying one of the photographs in this lesson.

Find Out! — Ask each of your family members: If you could be an Ambassador to the country of your choice, what would it be?

Student Workbook or Lesson Review — If you are using one of these optional books, complete the assignment for Lesson 74.

★ Remember to choose an American Holiday to study this week! ★

AMERICAN HOLIDAYS

Independence Day - July 4

National Aviation Day - August 19

Labor Day - First Monday in September

Patriot Day - September 11

Constitution Day and Citizenship Day - September 17

Leif Erikson Day - October 9

Columbus Day - October 12

Veterans Day - November 11

Thanksgiving Day - Fourth Thursday in November

Pearl Harbor Remembrance Day - December 7

Bill of Rights Day - December 15

Christmas Day - December 25

New Year's Day - January 1

The Convening of Congress - January 3

Inauguration Day - January 20

Independence Day Fireworks in New York City, 2011

Americans love to celebrate! We all have our own special memories of gathering with family and friends to have a cookout, watch a parade, listen to a speech, eat a delicious meal, see the fireworks, and remember events of the past. Have fun learning about the history behind America's holidays and what it is about each one that makes it a special day.

Top Left: National Christmas Tree in Washington, D.C.;
Top Right: Independence Day Patriotic Outfit Contest in Dallas, Texas;
Center: Tunnel to Tower Run on Patriot Day in New York City, New York;
Lower Left: Attendees at George H. W. Bush's 1989 Inauguration in Washington, D.C.;
Lower Right: Labor Day Parade in Minneapolis-St. Paul, Minnesota

INDEPENDENCE DAY

July 4

Oh who would not join with the throng,
Who welcome our nation's birthday,
Rejoice and lift up the glad song,
Shout Freedom forever and aye.

Then rally o'er mountain and plain,
Our bright starry flag waves on high,
While millions awaken the strain,
Huzza! 'Tis the 4th of July.

Huntington Beach, California
Independence Day Parade Beside the Pacific Ocean, 2004

The song lyrics above were written in 1874 by T. Waldron Shear. They reflect the patriotism and pride that have been a part of our country since we declared our independence in 1776. On July 4, 1776, there were approximately 2.5 million people living in America. By July 4, 2011, the population of our country had grown to approximately 313.9 million people. That's a lot of voices to cry, "Huzza! 'Tis the 4th of July!"

Celebrating Independence Day was not common until after the War of 1812. Congress did not declare the Fourth an official holiday until 1941, though some individual state governments made it official before that time. Massachusetts was the first state to do so in 1791. During the 1800s, some Independence Day celebrations were especially loud as people shot off leftover cannon balls and ammunition from recent wars. People enjoyed getting together to celebrate our nation's birth. In some places where farms were spread far apart, the Fourth of July was the only area-wide celebration in the whole year.

Fireworks and the Fourth

On July 4, 1777, one year after the Declaration of Independence was adopted, cities such as Philadelphia and Boston had fireworks displays for their citizens to enjoy. These displays started a Fourth of July tradition that has continued through the years. Cities and towns and private citizens across the country love to celebrate our country's birthday with fireworks.

It is estimated that around 14,000 fireworks shows take place each year across the country. Fireworks sales for private displays in 2007 reached $930 million! That was more than twice what was spent in the year 2000.

There are many spectacular fireworks displays in cities across the country. Here is a list of some that are considered the best (in alphabetical order):

Addison, Texas
Atlantic City, New Jersey
Boston, Massachusetts
Chicago, Illinois
Lake Tahoe, California

Nashville, Tennessee
New Orleans, Louisiana
New York City, New York
San Diego, California
Washington, D.C.

Lake Tahoe, California
Fourth of July Fireworks, 2011

The show in Lake Tahoe, California, is pictured at left. Big city fireworks shows cost big money. Boston, Massachusetts, spent an astonishing $2.5 million in 2010!

The fireworks display in New York City is put on by Macy's, the same department store that holds a famous Thanksgiving parade each year. Macy's Fourth of July Fireworks Spectacular is the biggest display in the country. An estimated two million people watch as approximately 75,000 pounds of explosives light up the sky.

It takes many government agencies to pull off an Independence Day celebration in Washington, D.C. With all those explosives and all those people, the planners work extra hard to make sure everything is safe and runs smoothly. The FBI; the Bureau of Alcohol,

Tobacco, Firearms and Explosives; the Federal Aviation Administration; the Secret Service; local fire and police departments; the National Park Service and its police department; and the Public Broadcasting Service all work together for up to a year in advance to pull off the annual event. That's a lot of people working a lot of hours for a twenty-minute show!

America's First Family of Fireworks

Angelo Lanzetta was an Italian pyrotechnician who immigrated to the United States through Ellis Island in 1870. A pyrotechnician is a person who specializes in explosives. After Angelo died in 1899, his son Anthony carried on the family fireworks business. Anthony's nephew Felix Grucci Sr. began working for him in 1923.

It was hard to make a living with fireworks, especially during the Great Depression, but Anthony and Felix kept going. Felix got married in 1940. He and his wife had three children, all of whom grew up to join the family business. The photos below show members of the Grucci family making fireworks at their first factory.

Over the next several years, Felix Grucci Sr. became a master fireworks artist. In addition to advances in fireworks technology, Grucci developed an atomic device simulator that the Defense Department used in training the military.

Grucci's company, now called Fireworks by Grucci, got a big break when they were hired to create a fireworks show for America's bicentennial celebration in 1976. Three years later the Gruccis won a gold medal at the annual Monte Carlo International Fireworks Competition in Europe. They were the first Americans to win the prize. This medal earned the Gruccis the title of "America's First Family of Fireworks." Today the business is operated by the fourth and fifth generations of the Grucci family.

Cities and other organizations hire Fireworks by Grucci to operate their local Fourth of July fireworks displays. In 2012 the company operated sixteen shows across the country on July 4 from Florida to Massachusetts to Hawaii. An average half-hour fireworks show costs about $30,000.

Bellport, New York
Members of the Grucci Family Making Fireworks at the First Factory, 1940 (Photos courtesy of Fireworks by Grucci)

In addition to Independence Day celebrations, Fireworks by Grucci has operated fireworks shows at events such as the Statue of Liberty centennial celebration in 1986 and the 2008 Olympic Games in Beijing. The company has also operated the fireworks display at every presidential inauguration since Ronald Reagan became President in 1981.

Nathan's Famous Contest

For many years, Coney Island in New York has been a popular destination for tourists and for New Yorkers who want to get out of the city and enjoy the beach and other amusements. One thing Coney Island is known for is hot dogs. A hot dog company called Nathan's Famous,

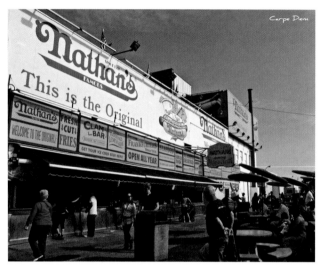

New York City, New York
Nathan's Famous Hot Dogs

pictured at left, opened on the boardwalk at Coney Island in 1916. The company was started by a Polish immigrant named Nathan Handwerker. It started out as a simple hot dog stand, but it turned into a huge success. By 1920 Nathan's business was selling around 75,000 hot dogs every weekend!

The legend goes that on July 4, 1916 (the year Nathan's Famous opened), four immigrants were arguing about which of them was the most patriotic. They decided to display their patriotism by eating hot dogs—a lot of hot dogs! They had a contest to see who could eat the most. An immigrant from Ireland named James Mullen won the contest when he downed thirteen hot dogs in twelve minutes. Whether or not that legend is true, Nathan's Famous has held a July 4 hot dog eating contest every year except two since then. An advertisement for the contest is pictured below. It has an electronic countdown to the next contest, 361 days from the time the photo was taken.

Nathan's Famous July 4 International Hot Dog Eating Contest is now the largest eating competition in the world. Tens of thousands of people watch the annual event. A separate contest for women was started in 2011. The 2012 women's champion was Sonya Thomas from Alexandria, Virginia. Ms. Thomas, who is five feet, five inches tall and weighs only

Advertisement for
Nathan's Famous Hot Dog Eating Contest

100 pounds, ate 45 hot dogs and buns in ten minutes! Forty-five was her goal since that was also her age. The winner of the 2012 men's competition was 28-year-old Joey Chestnut from San Jose, California. He ate a whopping 68 hot dogs and buns in ten minutes! Each of the winners won $10,000 in prize money.

New Citizens

Each year on July 4 in Seattle, Washington, the city holds a naturalization ceremony where hundreds of people become new citizens of the United States. Seattle is just one of many places in the U.S. that holds such a ceremony on Independence Day. The photos below were taken at the ceremony in Seattle on July 4, 2011. The top image shows a Native American performing at the start of the ceremony. Look at the immigrants in the center photo proudly waving their American flags. Notice the necktie worn by the man in a turban. In the bottom photo, Mark McGinn, mayor of Seattle, hugs a group of children at the ceremony. Mr. McGinn was the Master of Ceremonies at the event.

Independence Day Festivities

In addition to fireworks displays, some communities host a parade on Independence Day. Some churches, clubs, and other groups hold a cookout or a picnic. Many cities have races. People come up with all sorts of ways to celebrate America's birthday. At Fort Bragg, a U.S. Army installation in North Carolina, men can compete in a wife-carrying competition! Citizens of Tewksbury, Massachusetts, have a tradition of holding pie and watermelon eating contests.

In Matamoras, Pennsylvania, the community holds a plastic duck race each Independence Day. Local firefighters release the numbered ducks on the Delaware River,

Seattle, Washington
Independence Day Naturalization Ceremony, 2011

Matamoras, Pennsylvania
Painting of the Bridge over the Delaware River

pictured at left. Another group of firefighters catches the first six ducks who pass under a bridge that serves as the finish line. In 2012 it cost $5 to buy a plastic duck to compete in the race (or you could spend $20 and buy six). The owners of the six winning ducks each received a cash prize of $100, $75, $50, or $25. Proceeds from the event were used to fund the planting of trees in Matamoras.

Freedom

Americans have a lot of freedoms that many people around the world do not have. We should be thankful for these freedoms. We should be thankful for the men and women in history who worked and fought and died to help us have the freedoms we enjoy. Independence Day is a time to celebrate our freedoms. With a lot of freedom comes a lot of opportunity. With a lot of opportunity, we have a lot of responsibility. We should look at our freedom not just as something to make our own lives better; we should look at it as an opportunity to make things better for other people.

We who are Christians have freedom in Christ. We don't have to be slaves to sin because Jesus sets us free! With that freedom, however, comes a lot of responsibility. We have a responsibility to love and serve and give like Jesus did.

It was for freedom that Christ set us free;
therefore keep standing firm and do not be subject again to a yoke of slavery.
Galatians 5:1

Family Activity

Make a "Happy Birthday, America!" poster. Instructions are on page 486.

National Aviation Day

August 19

In 1939 President Franklin Roosevelt decided it was time to commemorate the advances in human flight that had taken place up until that time. He also wanted to honor aviation pioneers. August 19, the birthday of Orville Wright, was chosen as the date for National Aviation Day. Today this holiday is observed at some historic sites and schools with special crafts and programs related to aviation.

Dayton, Ohio
*Wilbur and Orville Wright
at Home, 1909*

The Wright Brothers

In the late 1800s, Wilbur and Orville Wright spent many years studying aviation. The brothers are pictured at right. Wilbur and Orville studied experiments that other people had made and conducted many experiments themselves. Finally, in 1903, they had a smashing success! The six hundred pound flying machine that they had created actually flew for twelve seconds. This was the first time a powered machine had taken off from level ground, flown through the air, and made a controlled landing.

Kill Devil Hills, North Carolina
Wright Brothers National Memorial

When this first successful flight occurred, Orville was piloting the machine. The brothers had agreed to take turns, and it was Orville's turn to try. That is why Orville is credited with the first flight and why his birthday was chosen as the date for National Aviation Day.

Pictured at left is the Wright Brothers National Memorial in Kill Devil Hills, North Carolina, the site of the historic 1903 flight. The granite monument was erected in 1932.

Airmail Service

Advances in aviation technology continued after the Wright brothers' 1903 flight. These advances brought many changes to American society. People could travel farther and faster. Mail could travel farther and faster, too. Letters were first transported by plane in the United States in 1911. Airplanes proved to be a much better method of transporting mail than what another country had tried about forty years before. The first country to transport mail by air was France in 1870. They used hot air balloons, but this turned out to be rather disastrous. The balloons could not be controlled, and some were carried by the wind many miles away from their destinations! Some went up loaded with mail and were never seen again.

Washington, D.C.
Airmail Service Airplane, 1918

Aviation technology advanced quickly during World War I. After the fighting was over, the War Department supplied planes and pilots to transport mail. The Post Office took over airmail operations in 1918 and hired forty pilots. At left is a photo of one of their first planes.

During its first year of operation, the airmail service brought in $162,000. The cost of operation was just $143,000. This was the first and only time in its history that the airmail service made a profit. The stamp pictured below is from 1924 and shows the kind of plane that was used to transport mail at that time.

By 1920 Post Office pilots had delivered 49 million letters. Sadly, between 1918 and 1920, at least half of the airmail pilots died in plane crashes. Despite its troubles, the Post Office Department continued to improve aviation in the United States. They established air traffic routes, tested aircraft, and trained pilots. The work of the Post Office Department helped lead the way for the development of passenger traffic across the country.

Postage Stamp, 1924

Charles Lindbergh

Charles Lindbergh was an airmail pilot who flew the route from Chicago, Illinois, to St. Louis, Missouri, beginning in 1926. Lindbergh had a long career in aviation. He is most remembered for his 1927 flight in his plane *The Spirit of St. Louis* when he became the first person to fly nonstop by himself across the Atlantic. The flight lasted thirty-three and one half hours. Imagine flying that long without being able to take a nap! Lindbergh became an international hero overnight. Countries around the world awarded him with high honors. The United States government presented him with a Congressional Medal of Honor and the first-ever Distinguished Flying Cross. Lindbergh is pictured at right beside *The Spirit of St. Louis*.

Charles Lindbergh with
The Spirit of St. Louis, *1927*

Air Commerce Act

Congress passed the Air Commerce Act in 1926. This legislation made flying safer. It called for issuing and enforcing air traffic rules and deciding on air travel routes that pilots could take. It also required pilots to be licensed and aircraft to be certified. The law required the use of devices that would make air travel safer and easier. President Calvin Coolidge signed the Air Commerce Act. Interestingly, Calvin Coolidge was the last President who never flew in an airplane.

Amelia Earhart

Amelia Earhart, pictured below, began her flying career in 1921 when she was twenty-three years old. In 1928 she became the first woman to fly across the Atlantic. Earhart continued to break aviation records and sought to prove to the world that women could fly as well as men. In 1932 she became the first woman to receive the Distinguished Flying Cross.

Amelia Earhart, c. 1928

In 1937 Earhart set out to break a new record as she embarked on a trip around the world. She and her navigator, Fred Noonan, left Miami on June 1. Sadly, the two never made it to their final destination. They were last heard from by radio as they flew over the Pacific, but their plane was lost and they were never seen again. The U.S. government spent $4 million on a search and rescue mission, but no sign of the plane or the aviators was ever found. It was the most costly and intensive land and sea search that had ever been made up to that time.

Streets, schools, and airports across the country have been named in honor of Amelia Earhart as a way to commemorate the courage and determination of this brave aviation pioneer.

Tuskegee Airmen

Tuskegee Airmen in Italy During World War II, 1945

One important part of the history of aviation in America is centered in Tuskegee, Alabama. Before World War II, African Americans were not allowed to fly for the U.S. military. Many people thought that African Americans weren't smart enough or patriotic enough to be military pilots. They didn't think these men had enough courage. Finally, after feeling pressure from civil rights groups, the Army Air Corps began operating an experimental training facility for African Americans in Tuskegee. The men trained there became known as the Tuskegee Airmen. The Tuskegee Airmen worked at a variety of jobs related to air combat from pilots and navigators to maintenance crews and instructors.

The Tuskegee Airmen became one of the most respected groups of aviators during World War II. They proved to the world that African Americans were indeed capable of flying and maintaining complex aircraft.

The airfield at Tuskegee continued to train airmen and women until 1946. The military began to integrate its units in 1947. Integration was a long process, but today people of all races are trained and serve in the military side by side. During the administration of President Bill Clinton, the Tuskegee Airmen National Historic Site was established and is now maintained by the National Park Service.

President George W. Bush awarded the Tuskegee Airmen the Congressional Gold Medal in 2007. This is the highest honor Congress gives to private citizens of the United States. Three hundred of the surviving airmen attended a ceremony to receive the medals at the U.S. Capitol in Washington, D.C.

The transportation authority in New York City renamed one of their bus depots the Tuskegee Airmen Bus Depot in 2012 to honor this brave group of American citizens. The photo at right shows two of the airmen who attended the ceremony standing with a New York City council member and three men who work for the city's transportation system.

New York City, New York
Honoring the Tuskegee Airmen, 2012

Blue Angels

After the fighting of World War II, the Chief of Naval Operations wanted to form a team of airmen who could show civilians the skill of Navy pilots. This group of pilots was named the Blue Angels. The team's first performance was in Florida in June of 1946. Over 240 men and women have flown as Blue Angel demonstration pilots since 1946. They have performed for millions of people all over the world. At right is a picture of a Blue Angels air show in Georgia.

The Air Force operates another aviation demonstration team called the Thunderbirds. The Thunderbirds and the Blue Angels never perform together, but sometimes they do perform with an Army or Navy parachute team.

Warner Robins, Georgia
Blue Angels Air Show, 2012

Private Space Travel

Throughout the twentieth century, space travel only took place in connection with a governmental agency. In 1996 a group called the X PRIZE Foundation announced that they would award a prize of $10 million to the first team of private citizens who could build and launch a spacecraft able to carry three people into outer space twice within the time frame of two weeks.

Eight years later, in 2004, a team called Scaled Composites won the prize. SpaceShipOne, pictured below, was designed and built by a team of about twenty people, led by Burt Rutan. Paul Allen, one of the co-founders of Microsoft, donated $20 million for the team to complete the project. On its winning flight, SpaceShipOne reached an altitude of nearly seventy miles above the earth's surface. By comparison, a typical airplane flying over the ocean is only about seven miles above the earth's surface.

Oshkosh, Wisconsin
SpaceShipOne on Display at an Air Show, 2005

Washington, D.C.
Mural at the National Air and Space Museum

SpaceShipOne is now on display at the National Air and Space Museum in Washington, D.C., in the Milestones of Flight gallery. Also on display in the gallery are the Wright brothers' flyer from 1903, Charles Lindbergh's plane *The Spirit of St. Louis* that took him across the Atlantic Ocean, a plane flown by Amelia Earhart, the first spacecraft that operated on Mars, and many other examples of historic aircraft and spacecraft. A mural at the museum is shown at left.

The achievement of private citizens reaching outer space opens up a whole new world of possibilities. Maybe one day private citizens will be able to take a weekend trip to the moon, or maybe even beyond. Maybe you will be the one to design the spacecraft that will take us there.

The Love of God

When we look up at the nighttime sky and see the stars, we are only seeing a tiny portion of what God has placed in the universe. If we take a trip into the clouds and go up into outer space, we are still only seeing a fraction of what God made. His creation is bigger and more grand and glorious than anything we can comprehend. Isn't it amazing that a God who could create such a universe loves each one of us? Isn't it amazing that His love for us is even bigger than the universe He created?

For as high as the heavens are above the earth,
So great is His lovingkindness toward those who fear Him.
Psalm 103:11

Family Activity

Make a model of your very own private spacecraft. Instructions are on page 487.

LABOR DAY

First Monday in September

On the first Monday in September of 1882, the sidewalks of lower Manhattan in New York City were lined with spectators young and old who were ready to watch what would come to be known as the first Labor Day parade. The parade that took place on that day began a long-standing tradition in America of celebrating our country's workers and giving them a day of rest and relaxation. In the picture at right, spectators line the streets of New York City for a Labor Day parade in 1908.

New York City, New York
Spectators Line the Streets for a Labor Day Parade, 1908

The First Labor Day

There is debate about who had the idea for the first Labor Day celebration. Some believe it was Peter J. McGuire, who was general secretary of the Brotherhood of Carpenters and Joiners. Mr. McGuire was also the co-founder of the American Federation of Labor. Others believe the holiday was begun by a machinist named Matthew Maguire, secretary of the Central Labor Union in New York. Whoever the originator was, the celebration happened. It was planned as a way to honor working men and women and to recognize their labor.

When the day for the celebration came, flags were flying and excitement was in the air. The New York City Police Department was concerned that a riot might start, so policemen were positioned around city hall with clubs in hand, ready to take action in case force was needed to maintain order. The time came for the parade to begin, but there were few marchers present and something was missing. There was no music! There was no band to accompany the parade. People wondered how a parade could start without tubas and trumpets and drums.

Some thought the parade should be canceled, but the grand marshal of the parade wouldn't hear of that. He wanted the celebration to go on no matter what. Just in time, around two hundred members of a jewelers union from nearby Newark, New Jersey, arrived on a ferry to join the parade—and they had a band! The parade started with the band playing "When I First Put This Uniform On," a song from an opera by Gilbert and Sullivan. Spectators watched from windows and rooftops. Some climbed up lampposts and sat on awnings to get a better view. Some of the spectators joined in the march themselves. By the time the parade reached its destination of Reservoir Park, between 10,000 and 20,000 men and women were marching along. More people joined the gathering after the parade was over and enjoyed speeches and a picnic. By the end of the day, an estimated 25,000 working men and women and their families had participated. The first Labor Day celebration had been a big success.

New York City, New York
Members of the Russian Labor Association Marching in a Labor Day Parade, 1909

New York City, New York
Bakers Carrying a Large Loaf of Bread in a Labor Day Parade, 1929

Labor Day Becomes Official

News of the celebration in New York spread across the country, and other cities decided to have their own festivities. In 1887 the state of Oregon became the first state to pass a law making Labor Day an official holiday. Colorado, Massachusetts, New Jersey, and New York passed similar resolutions later that year. Other states soon followed. Look at the photos above showing two groups of people marching in parades in New York City in 1909 and 1929.

In May of 1894, while President Grover Cleveland was in office, workers for the Pullman Palace Car Company went on strike in Chicago. At right is a picture of Pullman employees making upholstered chairs for the railroad cars that the company manufactured. In the strike of 1894, Pullman employees were striking against wage cuts and the firing of

Chicago, Illinois
Employees of the Pullman Palace Car Company Making Chairs, date unknown

union representatives. The next month, the American Railroad Union began a boycott of all Pullman cars, which caused major upsets in railroad traffic across the country.

Federal troops were sent to Chicago in an attempt to maintain order. This triggered rioting across the city. Historical accounts vary, but between twelve and thirty-four people were killed in the riots. After this disaster, the United States government wanted to make peace with American workers. Congress passed and President Cleveland signed into law legislation that established the first Monday in September as the official Federal holiday of Labor Day. In 1909 the American Federation of Labor declared the Sunday preceding Labor Day as Labor Sunday, a day to recognize the spiritual and educational aspects of labor.

Labor Day Proclamations

President Cleveland began a tradition that continues to this day of Presidents issuing Labor Day proclamations. Governors and other government leaders also issue Labor Day proclamations and give Labor Day speeches. Look at the pictures below of working Americans and read the portion of the Labor Day speech given by Massachusetts Governor Calvin Coolidge on September 1, 1919.

> *I cannot think of anything characteristically American that was not produced by toil. I cannot think of any American man or woman preeminent in the history of our Nation who did not reach their place through toil. I cannot think of anything that represents the American people as a whole so adequately as honest work. We perform different tasks, but the spirit is the same. We are proud of work and ashamed of idleness. With us there is no task which is menial, no service which is degrading. All work is ennobling and all workers are ennobled.*

Seattle, Washington
Cooks Working in a Restaurant, 1952

Houston, Texas
Construction Workers, 2006

Chicago, Illinois
Streets and Sanitation Worker, 2012

Ridgway, Colorado
Boys in a Labor Day Potato Sack Race, 1940

Labor Day and School

Until fairly recently, most American schools began their fall semester after Labor Day. Many years ago, families needed their children to help work on the farm during the summer, so schools did not start until September after most crops had been harvested. Another reason for starting in September was that there was no air conditioning. It was better to wait to start classes until the weather was cooler. Look at the school boys pictured above in a Labor Day potato sack race.

Today most schools start before Labor Day, but many people want to go back to waiting until after the September holiday. Schools in some places can save hundreds of thousands of dollars on utility costs by waiting until cooler weather comes so they don't have to run their air conditioners during the hot weeks of August. The tourism industry also likes schools to wait to open until after Labor Day so that families will have more time to take vacations and spend money at hotels and resorts and other recreational places.

Labor Day Traditions

Today many establishments such as post offices, government offices, private offices, factories, and schools close in observance of Labor Day. Many retail shops remain open. Shop owners like to benefit from people having more time to shop since they are off work or out of school for the day.

Labor Day parades are not as common as they used to be, but many cities still have them, as pictured below. Many Americans choose to spend Labor Day relaxing with family or friends, perhaps at someone's home or at a park. Some take the opportunity of time off from work to go on one more getaway before the summer ends.

Kansas City, Missouri
Labor Day Parade Float, 2008

Pittsburgh, Pennsylvania
A Labor Union Leader and U.S. Senator Walk with Others in a Labor Day Parade, 2008

Many communities across the United States have special Labor Day traditions. An annual Sonoita Labor Day Rodeo has been held in Santa Cruz County, Arizona, since 1916. Participants entertain their audiences with a ladies' barrel race, bareback riding, steer wrestling, wild cow milking, and much more.

Colorado Springs, Colorado
Colorado Balloon Classic, 2009

Each year since 1938, residents of Nauvoo, Illinois, have held their Grape Festival over Labor Day weekend, celebrating the grape harvest in their part of the country.

Independence, Missouri, hosts an annual Labor Day festival that honors that city's role as the starting point for many Americans who headed west in the 1800s along the Santa Fe, California, and Oregon Trails. People who attend can participate in a watermelon seed spitting contest, an ice cream eating contest, and a root beer chugging contest.

In 1958 a Labor Day tradition began in Michigan that continues to this day. Each year tens of thousands of walkers participate in the Mackinac Bridge Walk. Mackinac Bridge is five miles long and spans the water where Lake Huron and Lake Michigan come together. The bridge connects Michigan's Upper and Lower Peninsulas. Labor Day is the only day each year when the bridge is open to pedestrians.

San Diego, California
Festival of Sail, 2011

Look at the pictures at right that show Labor Day festivals in Colorado and California. The image below shows U.S. soldiers playing a game of tug of war during Labor Day festivities on their base in Afghanistan.

Labor in the Bible

God's plan from the beginning was for mankind to work. When He made Adam, God intended for him to cultivate the ground (Genesis 2:5-7). God made Eve to be Adam's helper (Genesis 2:18). God wants us to work diligently and honestly. He wants us to be fair and trustworthy in all we do.

U.S. Army Soldiers Playing Tug of War in Afghanistan, 2010

When workers do their jobs well, they deserve to be paid or compensated in some way. When Jesus sent out his twelve apostles with a special work to do, He told them not to take anything with them. He knew the people with whom the apostles stayed while they were away would take care of the apostles' needs because "the worker is worthy of his support" (Matthew 10:10).

People who are lazy and do not want to work should not expect to have what they need. Paul wrote that "if anyone is not willing to work, then he is not to eat, either" (2 Thessalonians 3:10). Paul went on to tell the Thessalonians that he had heard there were people in their midst who were "leading an undisciplined life, doing no work at all, but acting like busybodies" (3:11). To these people, Paul commanded and exhorted in the Lord Jesus Christ to work in a quiet way so they could earn their own bread (see 3:12).

Just as God created people to work, He also created them to rest. God doesn't want people to work all the time. When God created the world, He worked for six days and then rested on the seventh day. When God gave laws to the Israelite people, He told them about the special days and special years in which they were not supposed to work. He wanted them to have time to rest. God wants us to have time to rest, too. It is good and healthy for us to take time off from our routine, everyday work.

Whatever work we do, whether it is washing dishes, performing a medical operation, doing laundry, or building a house, we should do our work with a good attitude. Paul wrote to the Christians in Colossae about how slaves should view their work. We should all follow this principle in whatever work we have to do:

Whatever you do, do your work heartily, as for the Lord rather than for men,
knowing that from the Lord you will receive the reward of the inheritance.
It is the Lord Christ whom you serve.
Colossians 3:23-24

Family Activity

Play Labor Charades. Instructions are on page 488.

PATRIOT DAY

September 11

Some special days are reminders of happy things, like Mother's Day and the Fourth of July. Some special days, however, remind us of sad things.

September 11 has been designated as Patriot Day to help Americans remember the horrible acts of terrorism that happened on that day in 2001. Many people died on 9/11, when planes crashed into the two World Trade Center towers in New York City. More people died in Washington, D.C., when a plane hit the Pentagon, and in Pennsylvania when a plane crashed in a field. Terrorists took control of these planes because they wanted to do something that would hurt the United States. Even though they were successful in hurting our country and killing many, the people of the United States showed themselves strong. They united together and overcame the heartache and fear brought on by these acts of terrorism.

The pictures on this page show some of the first responders who were at the scene in New York City soon after the terrorist attacks happened.

New York City, New York
First Responders at the World Trade Center
Soon After the 9/11 Attacks

A Sad Remembrance

Three months after the terrorist attacks, the U.S. Senate and House of Representatives passed a law designating September 11 as Patriot Day. Congress wanted to honor the Americans who died as a result of 9/11. They also wanted to recognize that "in the aftermath of the attacks the people of the United States stood united in providing support for those in need." The law requests each President to issue a Patriot Day proclamation every year to ask the American people to observe the day with appropriate programs and activities, to fly flags at half-staff, and to observe a moment of silence in honor of the people who died

A Proclamation

The first presidential proclamation for Patriot Day was issued by George W. Bush in September of 2002. It began:

> On this first observance of Patriot Day, we remember and honor those who perished in the terrorist attacks of September 11, 2001. We will not forget the events of that terrible morning nor will we forget how Americans responded in New York City, at the Pentagon, and in the skies over Pennsylvania—with heroism and selflessness; with compassion and courage; and with prayer and hope. We will always remember our collective obligation to ensure that justice is done, that freedom prevails, and that the principles upon which our Nation was founded endure.

Members of the U.S. Air Force Observing Patriot Day at Kunsan Air Base in South Korea, 2009

Observing Patriot Day

Patriot Day has been observed every year since 2002. Some cities and towns have held special ceremonies to honor the victims of the attacks. The photo at right was taken during a memorial service in Sacramento, California. Some cities have memorial concerts. Since many of the 9/11 victims were firemen and other emergency responders, some communities take the opportunity on Patriot Day to honor their own emergency response workers.

Sacramento, California
Member of the U.S. Military Reads the Names of the 9/11 Victims at a Tenth Anniversary Memorial Ceremony at the California State Capitol, 2011

In September of 2011, more than 200 bicyclers commemorated 9/11 by riding over 500 miles on an eight-day trip from New York City to the District of Columbia. On their way they passed through the scene of the 9/11 crash in Pennsylvania. The riders included people in the military, veterans, first responders who were in New York City during 9/11, and family members of people who lost their lives that day.

The picture on the previous page shows members of the U.S. Air Force stationed at Kunsan Air Base in South Korea observing Patriot Day in 2009. They held a ceremony to honor the firefighters, police officers, and emergency responders who risked their lives to serve their fellow Americans on 9/11. The ceremony also honored members of the U.S. Armed Forces who have served since September 11, 2001.

Washington, D.C.
Freedom Walk Participants, 2008

Freedom Walks

In September of 2005, some Department of Defense employees who worked at the Pentagon in Washington, D.C., decided to do something that would honor the memory of their coworkers who died when the plane crashed into the Pentagon on 9/11. They did something simple and took a walk. The idea of a memorial walk quickly spread across the country, and now there are hundreds of Freedom Walks held each September. The walk in Washington, D.C., has thousands of participants every year. Some of the participants from the 2008 walk are pictured at left.

Like other memorials that take place on or around September 11, Freedom Walks are a way to remember the lives that were lost on 9/11, to remember the first responders who were at the scenes of the crashes, and to honor military veterans past and present.

Freedom Walks have taken place in all fifty states and in several foreign countries. When American citizens participate in one of these walks, it shows men and women in the military that we support them and appreciate what they are doing for each of us by defending our country.

The first Freedom Walk in Sebring, Ohio, was organized by a nine-year-old boy in 2006. Colton Lockner had an uncle serving in Iraq at the time. Colton talked to the mayor of his town who supported his idea. Colton's mom helped him plan the event. They expected around 75 people to show up, but they ended up with over 2,000 participants!

A Human Flag

The 2006 Freedom Walk in Hampton Roads, Virginia, started in a special way. Around 1,200 servicemen and women, civic leaders, and civilians from the area gathered on a hillside to create a human flag. Each participant held a piece of painted cardboard over his or her head, as pictured below.

Hampton Roads, Virginia
Freedom Walk Participants Create a Human Flag on September 11, 2006

Tunnel to Tower Run

One Patriot Day tradition in New York City is the Tunnel to Tower Run, which honors Stephen Siller and the 342 other New York City firefighters who gave their lives to save others in the attack on the World Trade Center. The pictures below are from the run that took place in 2010. The runners shown are cadets from the United States Military Academy at West Point.

The Tunnel to Tower Run begins in a tunnel in Brooklyn and follows the route that Stephen Siller took on the morning of 9/11. Just after the attacks occurred, Siller was in the tunnel in his truck on his way home from a night on duty. He heard on his radio what was happening at the World Trade Center. As soon as he heard the news, he got out of his truck, put on his firefighter gear, and headed to the scene to help. The annual Tunnel to Tower Run ends where Siller was last seen that morning. In 2011, the run had nearly 30,000 participants. The course is just over three miles long.

New York City, New York
Participants in the Tunnel to Tower Run, 2010

National Day of Service and Remembrance

In 2009 the name of the 9/11 commemoration was officially changed to Patriot Day and National Day of Service and Remembrance. Families of 9/11 victims had been working to establish the day of service for seven years. The act that made it official was signed into law by President Barack Obama in April of 2009. American citizens are encouraged to commemorate 9/11 by serving others as they take part in projects such as painting houses, collecting food for needy families, renovating schools, and honoring veterans and first responders.

Special projects were organized in all fifty states in 2009 in honor of the new official observance. Citizens of Anchorage, Alaska, gathered in a parking lot to collect non-perishable food for hungry men, women, and children. A group in Hattiesburg, Mississippi, renovated an old boarding house that was being transformed into a housing center for volunteer groups. Hispanic students at a high school in Oklahoma City worked together to pull weeds, plant

Phoenix, Arizona
Wesley Bolin Plaza 9/11 Memorial

Wellington, Florida
Patriot Memorial

flowers, and paint benches at their school. They also planted a tree in remembrance of 9/11. Hundreds of people gathered at the Wesley Bolin Plaza 9/11 Memorial in downtown Phoenix, Arizona, and held an Interfaith Prayer Circle. The Phoenix memorial is pictured at left.

Another 9/11 memorial is pictured at left below. It was erected in 2011 in Wellington, Florida, in honor of the tenth anniversary of the attacks. A section of steel from the World Trade Center was used in creating the memorial.

Remembering Our History

It is good to remember important things that have happened in our own lives, in our families and churches, in our communities, and in our country. These things have shaped us into who we are today. We can learn from them. When we learn about how situations were handled well, or how they were handled poorly, we can learn how to handle situations that we will face in our own lives.

When Moses spoke to the Israelites in Deuteronomy, he reminded them of things that had happened to them in their past. He wanted them to know their history and pass on their memories to their children. Moses told them:

Only give heed to yourself and keep your soul diligently,

so that you do not forget the things which your eyes have seen

and they do not depart from your heart all the days of your life;

but make them known to your sons and your grandsons.

Deuteronomy 4:9

Family Activity

Give a special thanks to first responders in your community. Instructions are on page 490.

CONSTITUTION DAY AND CITIZENSHIP DAY

September 17

William Randolph Hearst operated several newspapers across the country during the first part of the twentieth century. During the 1930s, Hearst began to use his newspapers to promote his idea for a new national holiday. He wanted Americans to celebrate their citizenship. As a result of his efforts, Congress passed a resolution in 1940 to designate the third Sunday in May as I Am An American Day.

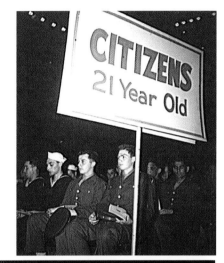

Look at the photos on this page. They show scenes from an I Am An American Day rally in Buffalo, New York, in 1943. The top image shows twenty-one-year-old soldiers and sailors sitting in a special section at the rally. In the center image, attendees are singing "The Star-Spangled Banner." The children in the lower image are watching a performance by a Scottish Highlander Band.

Cities across the country held I Am An American Day parades. People watched parades go by as they waved their American flags. Some people wore big buttons on their clothes that said "I Am An American Day." It was a time when Americans felt especially proud of being citizens of this country.

Buffalo, New York
Scenes from an I Am An American Day Rally, 1943

A Baltimore Tradition

The city of Baltimore began celebrating I Am An American Day even before it became

419

Baltimore, Maryland
Street Scene, 1939

a nation-wide observance. William Randolph Hearst's company sponsored a parade in Baltimore in 1938 to honor the Constitution. The photo at left shows how a street in Baltimore looked during this time. General Douglas MacArthur served as the grand marshal of the first parade. MacArthur had just retired from serving in the United States Army. A few years later he was called on to serve again during World War II. The 1938 parade began a tradition that continued in Baltimore for decades. The parades don't take place there any more, but Baltimore celebrated this holiday longer than any other city in the country. The parades drew many thousands of spectators and sometimes lasted as long as three and a half hours.

During the 1930s and 1940s, the Baltimore parades were attended by hundreds of thousands of people. This was right before and during the time of World War II, so military recruiters used to set up booths along the parade route. People arrived as early as 6:00 a.m. with lawn chairs and blankets to claim a good spot for watching the parade.

The Baltimore parades experienced some dramatic moments through the years. One year the temperature was over 100 degrees, and some band members dressed in heavy uniforms started fainting one after the other! Another year a group of majorettes was nearly trampled by some runaway horses. The girls were saved from the horses when a man threw himself on the animals to keep them from hurting the performers.

A Special Stamp

In 1937, many years before the official observance of Constitution Day began, the United States government issued a special stamp to commemorate the sesquicentennial of the signing of the Constitution. The word sesquicentennial means the 150th anniversary. The photo at right shows the first of these stamps coming off the press at the Bureau of Printing and Engraving in Washington, D.C., on September 10, 1937. The stamps went on

Washington, D.C.
Printing Sesquicentennial Constitution Day Stamps, 1937

sale on Constitution Day, seven days after the photo was taken. They were sold first in Philadelphia, where the Constitution had been signed one hundred fifty years earlier. The image at right shows the design of the stamp. It was based on a famous painting of the signing of the Constitution.

Sesquicentennial Constitution Day Stamp, 1937

Citizenship Day

In 1952, during the presidency of Harry Truman, the observance of I Am An American Day was moved to September 17, the date the Constitution was signed in 1787. The official name was changed to Citizenship Day. Congress wanted to promote "the complete instruction of citizens in their responsibilities and opportunities as citizens of the United States and of the State and locality in which they reside." The advertisement pictured at right is for a Citizenship Day celebration in New York City in 1954.

New York City, New York
Advertisement for a Citizenship Day Celebration, 1954

Constitution Town

Louisville, Ohio, is a small town with about 8,300 citizens. In 1951 a homemaker from Louisville named Olga T. Weber decided that something needed to be done to make sure Americans weren't taking their freedoms for granted.

Mrs. Weber handed out copies of the Constitution and the Bill of Rights all around her town. She passed out booklets about the American flag. She gave this literature to Louisville citizens at schools, libraries, and churches. She wanted her fellow Americans to be proud of their country. She wanted them to know the history of their country and to be familiar with the documents that had made America strong. As a result of her efforts, the mayor of Louisville proclaimed September 17, 1952, as Constitution Day. Mrs. Weber formed a committee for the "preservation of the Constitution."

Mrs. Weber kept working, and her work kept paying off. Her efforts convinced the Ohio General Assembly to proclaim Constitution Day across the state in 1953. Two years later, thanks to Mrs. Weber, the United States Senate and House of Representatives passed a bill that designated September 17-23 as Constitution Week throughout the United States. President Dwight D. Eisenhower signed the bill into law.

At a meeting in 1957, the Louisville City Council decided on the nickname "Constitution Town." Today an historical marker stands at each of the four main entrances into Louisville, commemorating the work of Olga Weber and explaining the town's role in the national observance of Constitution Day.

National Archives

The photo at left below was taken on Constitution Day in 1970 at the National Archives in Washington, D.C. This was the first time the entire Constitution was put on display at once. Today the Declaration of Independence, the Constitution, and the Bill of Rights are all on display in the Rotunda of the National Archives. The photo at right below shows a group of high school students participating in Constitution Day festivities on the steps of the National Archives building in 1974.

Washington, D.C.
Left: The Constitution on Display at the National Archives on Constitution Day, 1970
Right: High School Students Performing on the Steps of the National Archives on Constitution Day, 1974

National Constitution Center

The National Constitution Center, pictured on the next page, is a museum devoted to the Constitution that opened in Philadelphia in 2003. It promotes the ideals of the Constitution and encourages Americans to participate in acts of citizenship. The Center holds a special celebration each year on Constitution Day. Admission is free on that day and visitors can enjoy a variety of programs and activities. Everyone gets a piece of birthday cake and joins together to sing "Happy Birthday" and "The Star-Spangled Banner." In 2010 when the Constitution was 223 years old, 223 local high school students stood together on the Center's rooftop terrace and recited the preamble to the Constitution.

Philadelphia, Pennsylvania
National Constitution Center

Modern Observances

A law was passed in 2004 which requires schools and government offices to observe the holiday that is now called Constitution Day and Citizenship Day. On September 17, Federal agencies must provide their employees with materials that teach about the Constitution.

Each school that receives Federal funds is required to hold a program that relates to the Constitution on that day as well. Some of the ways schools observe this holiday is by holding essay contests, having patriotic concerts and art displays, and showing films related to the Constitution. Some schools host a fundraiser for military families or invite someone to make a special presentation to their students.

The photos at right show a group of people observing Citizenship Day in New York City in 2011. The group painted murals and built benches and bookshelves for public schools and other organizations in the city that work to give a better education to poor children.

New York City, New York
Observing Citizenship Day by Helping Others, 2011

423

Becoming a Citizen

Each year during Constitution Week, thousands of United States residents become citizens of this country at special ceremonies held by the U.S. Citizenship and Immigration Services (USCIS). In 2011 there were 27,000 people who became American citizens at USCIS naturalization ceremonies held during Constitution Week. These ceremonies have been held at a variety of places, including the Washington Monument, Yosemite National Park, Ellis Island, the St. Louis Arch, the Clinton Presidential Library, and Valley Forge National Historic Park. Some ceremonies have taken place at military bases and onboard military ships. The photos at right were taken at the naturalization ceremony held at the Grand Canyon on September 23, 2011.

Arizona
Taking the Oath of Allegiance at a Naturalization Ceremony at the Grand Canyon, 2011

A New U.S. Citizen Poses with an Air Force ROTC Honor Guard at the Grand Canyon, 2011

Citizens of Heaven

We who are Christians are to be good citizens of the countries in which we live. We should follow the laws and respect our leaders and try to make life better for our fellow citizens. Our American citizenship is important, but we should always keep in mind that this citizenship is only temporary. Our eternal citizenship is in heaven.

> For our citizenship is in heaven,
> from which also we eagerly wait for a Savior, the Lord Jesus Christ.
> Philippians 3:20

Family Activity

Have an immigrant dinner. Instructions are on page 491.

LEIF ERIKSON DAY

October 9

Leif Erikson (which is also spelled Eriksson, Ericson, or Erickson) was a Viking explorer from Iceland. The painting at right shows Erikson and his crew onboard their ship. On one of Erikson's explorations around the year 1000 A.D., he came upon an unknown land abundant with wheat and grapes. Erikson called it Vinland. Many believe the land he discovered is the eastern coast of what is now Canada.

Painting of Leif Erikson and His Crew by Christian Krohg, 1893

In honor of this early explorer, President Lyndon B. Johnson issued the following proclamation in 1964:

By the President of the United States of America

A Proclamation

Whereas Leif Erikson, Norseman, son of Erik the Red and great seafarer, in the year 1000 valiantly explored the shores of the American Continent; and

Whereas the intrepid exploits of the Vikings of Erikson's time strike a responsive chord in the hearts of all the American people, who as a nation are today embarked upon an adventurous exploration of the unfathomed realms of space; and

Whereas many of our citizens of Scandinavian descent take inspiration from and annually celebrate Leif Erikson's momentous voyage; and

Whereas the Congress of the United States by a joint resolution approved September 2, 1964, has authorized the President of the United States to proclaim October 9 in each year as Leif Erikson Day:

Now, Therefore, I, Lyndon B. Johnson, President of the United States of America, do hereby designate Friday, October 9, 1964, as Leif Erikson Day and direct Government officials to display the flag on all Government buildings on that day. Further, I invite the people of the United States to honor on that day the memory of Leif Erikson by holding appropriate exercises and ceremonies in schools and churches, or other suitable places.

In Witness Whereof, I have hereunto set my hand and caused the seal of the United States to be affixed.

DONE at the City of Washington this second day of September in the year of our Lord nineteen hundred and sixty-four, and of the Independence of the United States of America the one hundred and eighty-ninth.

LYNDON B. JOHNSON

Leif Erikson in Boston

In the late 1800s, a college professor in New England believed that he had discovered the remains of an ancient Norse settlement in Massachusetts. Several archaeological digs were made and many people became excited at the thought that Vikings may have once been in New England.

Boston, Massachusetts
Leif Erikson Statue on Commonwealth Avenue

One of the people excited about the possibility of Viking explorers having once been in New England was a Norwegian violinist named Ole Bull. Bull was a popular performer among the upper class citizens of Boston. One of his friends was Henry Wadsworth Longfellow, a well-known poet. One evening in 1870, Bull, Longfellow, and Longfellow's brother-in-law Thomas Appleton were having dinner together. The three began to discuss the idea of erecting a Leif Erikson statue in Boston. Mr. Appleton organized a committee of fifty-two prominent citizens of Boston to work toward getting the statue erected.

For a while it seemed that the project was going to fade away and come to nothing, but then Eben Horsford, one of the members of Appleton's committee, revived the idea. Horsford became convinced that he had discovered Viking remains in the area, and this spurred him to push for the statue in Boston. Apparently Horsford's discoveries were not true Viking artifacts, but they caused quite a stir at the time. A Boston sculptor named Anne Whitney was hired to create the statue. It was completed in 1877 and is pictured on the previous page.

The festivities on the day the statue was dedicated included a parade and speeches. Whitney pulled a cord to unveil the statue that had been placed on Commonwealth Avenue.

Leif Erikson in St. Paul

A statue of Christopher Columbus was erected near the Minnesota state capitol building in St. Paul in 1931. That same year, a group of area citizens formed the Minnesota Leif Erikson Monument Association. Apparently members of the association were not satisfied with a statue of Columbus because they were supporters of the legacy of Leif Erikson as the discoverer of North America as opposed to Columbus.

During the next eighteen years, the association sponsored radio broadcasts, printed pamphlets, and wrote newspaper articles and other material in an effort to educate the public about the explorations of Columbus and Erikson. Finally in 1949 the association's goal was reached and a statue of Leif Erikson was dedicated on Leif Erikson Lawn near the state capitol building. The statue, pictured at right, took sculptor John Karl Daniels fourteen years to complete. Dignitaries from Norway, Iceland, and Alaska attended the ceremony, as well as between three and five thousand citizens.

St. Paul, Minnesota
Leif Erikson Statue Near the Minnesota State Capitol

Leif Erikson in Seattle

Seattle, Washington, hosted a World's Fair in 1962. On Norway Day during the fair, the Leif Erikson League presented the city of Seattle with the gift of a statue of Leif Erikson. The Scandinavian-American community had been trying for three years to convince the city of Seattle to erect an Erikson statue. The Parks Department didn't want to agree to the statue

Seattle, Washington
*Leif Erikson Statue at
Shilshole Marina*

because they didn't want other ethnic groups to start asking for their own statues to be on display in the city. In the end the League was successful in their efforts, and the statue was erected at Shilshole Marina.

The statue was moved 200 feet in 2007 when the marina was renovated. The photos on this page show Leif in his new location. The statue weighs around 11,000 pounds, so moving it proved to be quite difficult. It took five days of hard work before the crew could get Leif to budge! They finally got him loose and the statue was restored and placed in its new location. The project of renovating and moving cost $76,000. A rededication ceremony took place the Saturday before Leif Erikson Day. The ceremony featured speeches and Scandinavian music performances.

At the base of the statue and on stones surrounding it are plaques with the names of over 1,700 Scandinavian immigrants. With each name is engraved the year that the person immigrated to America, from 1884 to 2004, as well as their home town in Norway, Sweden, Iceland, Denmark, or Finland. Seattle's Leif Erikson statue stands as a lasting tribute to the community's Nordic heritage.

Leif Erikson Statue at Shilshole Marina

Nordic American Heritage

In the late 1800s, immigrants from Norway, Sweden, Denmark, Iceland, and Finland immigrated to the United States in large numbers. As a group, these countries are called Norse countries and their people are called Nordic. Many of these Nordic immigrants chose to settle in the Pacific Northwest because the land was similar to what they had left behind in Europe, as illustrated in the images at right.

Many of the immigrants were fishermen, farmers, or loggers. Some built boats or worked in canneries, mills, or mines. Some settled in the countryside and built log homes like they had back home. Others moved to cities like Seattle and Tacoma where there were Nordic communities with Swedish and Norwegian newspapers available to them.

A Road in Rural Norway, c. 1895

Hurricane Ridge, Washington
A Road in Rural Washington State, 2009

Many Nordic immigrants settled in the Ballard neighborhood near Seattle's downtown. Ballard became its own city in 1890. In 1907 it became a part of the city of Seattle. Today the Ballard neighborhood is still home to a few Scandinavian bakeries and gift shops.

The Nordic heritage continues to thrive in Seattle with festivals, exhibits, and performances for the public. People can take classes to learn Nordic languages, songs, dances, and traditional folk art. Some churches still hold services in Nordic languages. The University of Washington has had a Scandinavian Studies Department for over one hundred years.

Seattle's Nordic Heritage Museum opened in 1980 to share Nordic culture with people of all backgrounds through art, historic artifacts, and special displays and programs. Visitors can see traditional folk costumes, textiles, tools, and furniture; displays about Nordic logging and fishing industries; a gallery for each of the five Nordic countries; and much more.

Kensington Runestone

In addition to Washington State, many Nordic immigrants settled in Minnesota and the Dakotas. Some of the land in these states is also similar to what the immigrants left behind in Europe. In 1898 a Swedish immigrant by the name of Olof Ohman made a significant discovery on his Minnesota farm near the town of Kensington. Among the roots of an aspen tree he and his son were cutting down, Mr. Ohman found an ancient stone believed to have been carved by Vikings in the 1300s. The carving on the stone indicates that Vikings once came to this part of North America.

The discovery of the Kensington Runestone has been the cause of much study and debate over the years. Some believe strongly that the stone is a true Viking artifact; others say it is a hoax. Mr. Ohman's farm is now a park where visitors can see the spot where he discovered the Runestone. The Runestone is on display at a museum in the nearby town of Alexandria. Whatever the source of this carved stone, the stone and the Viking symbol have been used extensively throughout the region as identifying symbols. Even Minnesota's professional football team was named the Vikings as a result of Mr. Ohman's discovery. The Viking statue pictured at right stands twenty-eight feet tall in a park in Alexandra.

Alexandria, Minnesota
Viking Statue

U-Haul International, Inc., a moving truck and trailer rental company, features images on the sides of its vehicles that represent different regions of the United States. The image they chose to decorate the sides of 2,300 new moving vans that were put into use in 2011 was the Kensington Runestone.

Seeking and Searching

One of Leif Erikson's early voyages took him to Norway. While in that country, Erikson and his men were introduced to Christianity. They all became believers and were baptized. Erikson shared his new faith with his people back home and some, including his mother, chose to become Christians as well.

Leif Erikson was not only a seeker of adventure and new lands; he was a seeker of the way of God and of Jesus Christ. We should also be continuously seeking after God's way so that we will gain wisdom, discernment, and understanding in how God wants us to live.

> For if you cry for discernment, lift your voice for understanding;
> If you seek her as silver and search for her as for hidden treasures;
> Then you will discern the fear of the Lord and discover the knowledge of God.
>
> Proverbs 2:3-5

Family Activity

Make a Nordic centerpiece. Instructions are on page 492.

COLUMBUS DAY

October 12

Christopher Columbus sighted land in the Bahamas on October 12, 1492. The first known celebration held in honor of this event was in New York City in 1792, three hundred years after Columbus' arrival. One hundred years later, in 1892, President Benjamin Harrison issued this proclamation:

> . . . I, Benjamin Harrison, President of the United States of America, in pursuance of the aforesaid joint resolution, do hereby appoint Friday, October 21, 1892, the four hundredth anniversary of the discovery of America by Columbus, as a general holiday for the people of the United States. On that day let the people, so far as possible, cease from toil and devote themselves to such exercises as may best express honor to the discoverer and their appreciation of the great achievements of the four completed centuries of American life.

New York City, New York
Columbus Day
School Assembly, 1942

> . . . Let the national flag float over every schoolhouse in the country and the exercises be such as shall impress upon our youth the patriotic duties of American citizenship. . . .

The photograph at right shows a Columbus Day school assembly fifty years after President Harrison's proclamation.

The World's Columbian Exposition

As the 400th anniversary of Columbus' arrival drew near, Congress wanted to have an elaborate public exposition in honor of the celebration. New York City, Washington, D.C., St. Louis, and Chicago all wanted to host the event. Congress finally decided on Chicago as the location. Dedication ceremonies were held in October of 1892, but the World's Columbian

Chicago, Illinois
View of the Grounds and Buildings of the World's Columbian Exposition, 1893

Exposition didn't actually open until May of 1893. Sometimes getting ready for a big event takes longer than expected! The exposition was open until October. Look at the illustration of the grounds at left. Twenty million people from across America and around the world visited the exhibition. Guests enjoyed grand displays of art, technology, architecture, electricity, and more.

One of the main attractions at the exposition was a grand theatrical production called "America." It was a show that told about four hundred years of American history. It was one of the greatest money-making ventures of the entire exposition. The production was written by Imre Kiralfy, a Hungarian man who was popular in show business in Europe and America. Kiralfy is pictured at right. Another of Kiralfy's productions that ran at the same time as "America" was "Columbus and the Discovery of America: A Grand Dramatic, Operatic, and Ballet Spectacle." That show was eventually produced in connection with Barnum and Bailey's Greatest Show On Earth, a famous circus. Kiralfy called Columbus "the greatest genius of the centuries." Kiralfy thought himself fortunate to be alive to see the fourth centennial of Columbus' famous voyage. "I have striven earnestly," Kiralfy wrote, "to make this historical production the greatest of all my works."

Imre Kiralfy, c. 1913

Columbus Day Becomes Official

In the years after 1892, the Knights of Columbus, a group that includes many Italian Roman Catholics, began to urge Federal and state legislatures to adopt October 12 as a legal holiday to honor Columbus. In 1907 Colorado became the first state to make the holiday official. New York did so two years later. President Franklin Roosevelt declared Columbus Day a national holiday in 1934, to be celebrated each year on October 12. In 1971 the observance of the holiday was changed to the second Monday in October.

Christopher Columbus Memorial in Washington, D.C.

In the early 1900s, the Knights of Columbus decided they wanted a grand Columbus memorial to be built in Washington, D.C. A member of the organization wrote a bill and it was presented to Congress. President Theodore Roosevelt signed the bill into law in 1907 and

Congress set aside $100,000 for the project. The memorial, pictured below, was built in front of Union Station in Washington, D.C. The Knights of Columbus spent $10,000 on a celebration when the memorial was completed in 1912. The Knights of Columbus organize a ceremony at the memorial every year on Columbus Day. The image at right shows a Knights of Columbus honor guard in front of the memorial on Columbus Day in 2011.

Knights of Columbus Honor Guard at a Columbus Day Ceremony, 2011

Washington, D.C.
Christopher Columbus Memorial Fountain

Columbus Day in Cleveland

Since Columbus was an Italian explorer, Columbus Day has become an important holiday for many Italian-Americans. Some cities, such as Cleveland, Ohio, hold parades and festivals that don't just focus on Columbus but also honor Italian-American heritage. Cleveland has hosted an annual Columbus Day parade since the early 1950s. Thousands of spectators line the streets to watch the parade pass through Little Italy, a section of the city where many

Cleveland, Ohio
Street Sign in Little Italy

Italian-Americans live and where many Italian businesses are located. A street sign from Little Italy is pictured at left. Notice the sign above the street sign with the colors of the Italian flag and the words "Historic Little Italy." The spectators at the parade wave Italian flags as they watch floats go by, listen to the music of marching bands, and scramble for candy that is tossed onto the street. Some politicians use the event to try to win votes, either by being in the parade itself or by mingling with the crowd on the sidewalks.

For the last several years, Cleveland's parade has ended the same way—with the Orlando Bread Company tossing out hundreds of rolls from a truck! Some spectators are serious about wanting to catch some of the free Italian bread. They try to intercept tosses or even grab the bread out of someone else's hands! The rolls are bagged so that they won't get dirty if they land on the street. The Orlando Bread Company has been baking Italian bread in Cleveland since 1904. Before that, the family had a bakery in Italy. Five generations of the Orlando family have worked in the company.

Attendees at the Cleveland Columbus Day festivities have other opportunities to enjoy Italian-American heritage in addition to the parade. One year, a shop owner had a competition outside his shop. He filled two wooden planters with fifteen pounds of grapes each. Competitors took their shoes off, stepped into the planters, and had four minutes to see how much grape juice they could stomp out of the grapes! Stomping grapes is an Italian tradition that goes back hundreds of years.

Columbus Day in San Francisco

San Francisco, California, began holding an Italian Heritage Parade even before Columbus Day became an official holiday. The city's first parade to honor Columbus and Italian-American heritage was held in 1868. Today spectators can see floats made by local businesses and community groups. They can

San Francisco, California
Italian Heritage Parade, 2011

watch people dressed up like Columbus, Queen Isabella, and her court parade down the street. They can also enjoy music by Italian musicians. Look at the images from San Francisco's 2011 Italian Heritage Parade at right above and on the next page.

CITY ATTORNEY
Dennis
Herrera

KELLY'S HAIR SALON
MEN·WOMEN·CHILDREN
TEL. 415-834-0519

Italian Heritage Parade, 2011

435

Courage

Some people do not like to celebrate Columbus Day because Columbus and his men did not treat the North American native peoples well. It is true that Columbus and his men should have behaved differently toward the people who were already living in America when they discovered it, but we cannot change the past. We can only learn from it. We can learn how to treat others and how not to treat them. We can be inspired by the bravery and courage of Columbus and his men. It took a lot of gumption to get on a ship and sail across an unknown ocean! We can have that kind of gumption to do hard things, too. Even if we never go exploring into an unknown part of the world, we are all going to face hard things. How we handle those hard things is up to us. We can give up and not even try, or we can be brave and have courage to face each challenge that comes our way. With God on our side, no challenge is too big. He will give us everything we need for everything that happens in our lives.

Be strong and courageous,

do not be afraid or tremble at them,

for the Lord your God is the one who goes with you.

He will not fail you or forsake you.

Deuteronomy 31:6

Family Activity

Enjoy an Italian heritage meal. Instructions are on page 493.

VETERANS DAY

November 11

World War I began in Europe in 1914. The United States stayed out of the war by remaining a neutral country until 1917. That year, however, a German submarine sank a British passenger ship called the *Lusitania*. There were 128 Americans who died when the *Lusitania* sank. This prompted the United States to join the fighting. The U.S. joined forces with Great Britain, France, Russia, and other countries to fight against Germany, Italy, Austria-Hungary, and the nations allied with them. American citizens across the country joined the war effort. They joined the military, worked in factories, grew gardens, and found many other ways to help the cause. The poster at right shows Uncle Sam calling on Americans to buy government bonds. Government bonds were a way that Americans could loan money to the government to help pay for the war.

*World War I
Government Bond Poster, 1917*

At the time it was being fought, World War I was called the Great War. Between 9 million and 13 million people died as a result of the Great War. Over one hundred thousand of them were Americans.

Germany finally asked for the fighting to end in November of 1918, and the other nations involved in the war agreed. This agreement was called an armistice, which is a temporary end to fighting. The armistice went into effect on November 11, 1918, at 11:00 a.m.—the eleventh hour of the eleventh day of the eleventh month. World War I officially ended on June 28, 1919, when the Treaty of Versailles was signed in France. Because of the armistice, however, the end of World War I is commonly recognized as November 11 instead of June 28.

Armistice Day

Woodrow Wilson was President of the United States during World War I. The image at right was taken at Camp Sherman in Chillicothe, Ohio. It is a portrait of President Wilson created by 21,000 officers and men standing in a special formation. Camp Chillicothe was the third largest U.S. military training facility during World War I.

After World War I was over, President Wilson decided that our country needed to honor the veterans of World War I in a special way. He proclaimed November 11, 1919, as Armistice Day and said, "To us in America, the reflections of Armistice Day will be filled with solemn pride in the heroism of those who died in the country's service and with

Chillicothe, Ohio
Formation Photograph of Woodrow Wilson, 1918

gratitude for the victory . . . ." The day was observed with parades and special gatherings across the United States. Businesses were encouraged to stop all transactions for two minutes beginning at 11:00 a.m., the time the armistice went into effect the year before.

Congress passed a resolution in 1926 declaring November 11 as a legal holiday. The resolution included these words:

> Whereas it is fitting that the recurring anniversary of this date should be commemorated with thanksgiving and prayer and exercises designed to perpetuate peace through good will and mutual understanding between nations;
>
> . . . Therefore be it Resolved by the Senate (the House of Representatives concurring), that the President of the United States is requested to issue a proclamation calling upon the officials to display the flag of the United States on all Government buildings on November 11 and inviting the people of the United States to observe the day in schools and churches, or other suitable places, with appropriate ceremonies of friendly relations with all other peoples.

Look at the photos on the next page from Armistice Day parades in Omaha, Nebraska, and Colchester, Connecticut. Notice the people watching the Omaha parade from the roof!

Omaha, Nebraska
Armistice Day Parade, 1938

Colchester, Connecticut
Armistice Day Parade, 1940

Armistice Day Sunday

In 1920 various church organizations wanted President Wilson to name the Sunday nearest November 11 as Armistice Day Sunday. President Wilson agreed and churches across the country were encouraged to hold services that focused on the subject of international peace.

Tomb of the Unknowns

After World War I, an unidentified American soldier who had died during the war was buried in a special tomb in Arlington National Cemetery in Washington, D.C., pictured at right. The burial place is called the Tomb of the Unknowns. It was a way to honor all of the soldiers who had died and could not be identified.

The Tomb of the Unknowns (also called the Tomb of the Unknown Soldier) has three

Washington, D.C.
Arlington National Cemetery

Guard at the Tomb of the Unknowns, 2008

sculptures on it that represent peace, victory, and valor. Inscribed on the back of the tomb are these words: *Here rests in honored glory an American soldier known but to God.*

Three other unidentified soldiers are buried near this tomb from World War II, the Korean War, and the Vietnam War.

To honor these and other unidentified soldiers who have died, a military guard is posted at the tomb twenty-four hours a day, 365 days per year. Look at the picture at left of a guard on duty at the tomb. A soldier must meet several requirements in order to become a tomb guard, including having a perfect military record and being between 5 feet 10 inches and 6 feet 4 inches tall.

The guards change at regular intervals, either on the hour or on the half hour, depending on the time of day and the season. They go through an elaborate ritual as one man or woman goes off walking duty and another goes on. Each guard has been trained to know exactly what to do. While on duty, the guard marches twenty-one steps, then turns and faces east for twenty-one seconds. After turning north for twenty-one more seconds, the guard marches twenty-one steps back. The guard repeats this process over and over until it is time for another guard to come on duty.

National Veterans Day Ceremony

A special Veterans Day ceremony is held each year at Arlington National Cemetery. The ceremony always begins at 11:00 a.m. when a wreath is laid at the Tomb of the Unknowns. Look at the pictures on the next page that show the wreath-laying ceremonies of 1924 and 2010. After the wreath is placed, the ceremony continues in the Memorial Amphitheater. Various veterans organizations participate in a parade of colors (or flags), as pictured at right. Attendees then listen to speeches made by dignitaries. The President is often one of the speakers at this event. The ceremony is a time to honor and thank the veterans of all wars for their service to our country.

Veterans Participate in the Parade of Colors at the National Veterans Day Ceremony at Arlington, 2011

Wreath-Laying Ceremonies at the Tomb of the Unknowns on Veterans Day
Left: President Calvin Coolidge, 1924; Right: Vice President Joe Biden, 2010

Observing Veterans Day

Communities across America observe Veterans Day with parades and special ceremonies. Some of these observances are pictured below. The blue sign in the photo from Portland is from a Quaker organization that lobbies Congress for peace and justice. The white flag next to the sign is from an organization called Veterans for Peace.

Beckley, West Virginia
Veterans Day Parade, 2010

Portland, Maine
Veterans Day Parade, 2011

Sebastian Inlet State Park, Florida
Veterans Day Potluck Gathering at a Campground, 2009

Crownsville, Maryland
Veterans Day Ceremony at a Veterans Cemetery, 2011

November 11 Around the World

America is not the only nation that commemorates the end of World War I. As illustrated in the photos on the next page, countries around the world honor veterans on November 11.

It is important that we remember the past and honor the people who lived before us who have helped make our lives what they are today. When God gave the Israelites the laws He wanted them to follow, He told them that He wanted them to remember the time when they were slaves in Egypt. Remembering their past would help them understand why He gave them certain laws and would help them appreciate where God had brought them. Remembering our past will help us understand why things in America are the way they are and will help us appreciate all that God has done for us.

Australia, 2011

You shall remember that you were a slave in the land of Egypt; therefore I am commanding you to do this thing.
Deuteronomy 24:22

England, 2008

Family Activity

Preserve the memories of a veteran you know by creating a Veteran Memory Book. Instructions are on page 494.

Poland, 2008

Scotland, 2010

South Korea, 2008

THANKSGIVING DAY

Fourth Thursday in November

The Pilgrims who settled in America in the 1600s had a tradition of holding special days of Thanksgiving when they felt they had received special blessings from God. We know that the Pilgrims held a special Thanksgiving during the summer of 1623 to thank God for sending rain that saved their crops. The Pilgrims' days of thanksgiving were typically held on Thursdays because that was the day of their regular mid-week gathering. The illustration at right was published in an American magazine at Thanksgiving time in the late 1800s or early 1900s.

Magazine Illustration Showing Early American Settlers with a Thanksgiving Turkey, date unknown

Over the years, settlements in New England began holding an annual Thanksgiving during the autumn months. During the Revolutionary War, the Continental Congress declared a day of Thanksgiving after American forces were victorious over the British at the Battle of Saratoga. The Continental Congress declared a Thanksgiving holiday every year until the war was over.

After the Revolutionary War, President George Washington issued the first presidential Thanksgiving proclamation. Washington's proclamation said in part:

> Now therefore I do recommend and assign Thursday the 26th day of November next to be devoted by the People of these States to the service of that great and glorious Being, who is the beneficent Author of all the good that was, that is, or that will be—That we may then all unite in rendering unto him our sincere and humble thanks . . . for all the great and various favors which he hath been pleased to confer upon us.

Thanksgiving Becomes Official

The tradition of an annual Thanksgiving was a special part of life in New England. As New Englanders moved west, they carried their Thanksgiving traditions with them and the holiday began to be celebrated in more and more places. Many states declared an annual Thanksgiving, but the day was not an official nationwide holiday until 1863. That year Abraham Lincoln declared the last Thursday in November as an official holiday for the entire country. From 1863 until 1938, each President declared a national Thanksgiving on the last Thursday in November every year except for two. President Theodore Roosevelt is pictured at right signing a Thanksgiving Proclamation in 1902.

Washington, D.C.
President Theodore Roosevelt Signs a Thanksgiving Proclamation, 1902

Franksgiving

When Franklin Roosevelt was President, he decided to do something different. In 1939 Roosevelt declared Thanksgiving to be the next to last Thursday in November instead of the last. This decision caused a nationwide uproar. Some people followed the President's proclamation, but some people waited until the last Thursday to carve their Thanksgiving turkey because they felt that was just when Thanksgiving was supposed to be! Some people called the altered holiday "Franksgiving."

San Antonio, Texas
Shoppers Look at a Shoe Display in a Department Store Window, 1939

Roosevelt made his decision because some merchants wanted the Christmas shopping season to be longer. This was during the Great Depression, and people weren't shopping as much as they used to because they didn't have as much money. Store owners wanted people to have as much time as possible to spend their money to buy presents during the Christmas shopping season. The photo at left shows people shopping in San Antonio,

Texas, in 1939. The sign in the window is encouraging people to buy merchandise so that other people can have jobs making goods and working in stores.

When Roosevelt made the decision to change the holiday, thousands of people sent letters and telegrams of protest to the White House. A man who worked for a company that printed calendars wrote that Roosevelt's change meant the calendars they had printed for 1939 were now wrong. The company had already printed their calendars for 1940, so now those were wrong, too. The man wrote, "If very many customers demand 1940 calendars to correspond with your proclamation, hundreds of thousands of dollars will be lost by the calendar companies, and in many instances it will result in bankruptcy."

A large clothing manufacturing company sent a telegram of "emphatic protest." The company believed the change would "hurt more merchants than it would help. It would shorten the season and curtail the fall business of clothes and all seasonable goods for the benefit of novelty and small gift items."

Schools had already planned their vacation schedules and their Thanksgiving Day football games, and now they didn't know what to do. In the end, some places celebrated their 1939 Thanksgiving on November 23, and some on November 30. For some families this meant they couldn't celebrate together because some relatives had to be at work while other relatives were having a holiday. It was a mess!

Roosevelt tried for two more years to have the country celebrate Thanksgiving on the second to last Thursday, but the general public was so upset that in December of 1941, Congress passed a law saying that Thanksgiving would be celebrated each year on the fourth Thursday in November. The photo at right shows a family giving thanks on Thanksgiving in 1942.

Neffsville, Pennsylvania
A Family Gives Thanks on Thanksgiving, 1942

Pardoning a Turkey

Americans have been sending gifts of Thanksgiving turkeys to the White House for many years. A Rhode Island citizen named Horace Vose sent a turkey to Washington, D.C., for President Grant's Thanksgiving dinner in 1873. Mr. Vose said the bird was the "noblest gobbler" in the whole state of Rhode Island. Mr. Vose continued to send a turkey to the White House every Thanksgiving for more than twenty-five years.

The tradition of a National Thanksgiving Turkey Presentation began in 1947 when Harry Truman was President. The tradition was that a special bird was selected for the White House Thanksgiving, it was presented to the President, and then he ate it. President George H. W. Bush began the annual tradition of pardoning the special Thanksgiving turkey. When a President pardons a turkey it means that instead of being cooked for dinner, the bird will be allowed to live. Other Presidents before Bush pardoned turkeys given to them as gifts, but President

St. Paul, Minnesota
Governor Mark Dayton with Ted, a Turkey Who Was a Part of the National Thanksgiving Turkey Presentation at the White House, 2011

Bush was the first to make the pardon official. The tradition has continued each year since 1989. Presidents actually pardon two turkeys. The second turkey is an alternate in case something happens to the first one before the ceremony.

In the picture at right, Governor Mark Dayton of Minnesota poses with Ted, a Minnesota turkey who was chosen to take part in the National Thanksgiving Turkey Presentation at the White House. Also pictured with the Governor are a senator, an agriculture commissioner, the president of the Minnesota Turkey Growers Association, and four high school students who are part of the Future Farmers of America organization.

For several years the pardoned turkeys were sent to Frying Pan Park in Herndon, Virginia, where they lived out the rest of their days in peace. From 2005 until 2009 the birds were sent

Anaheim, California
Courage, a Pardoned Turkey, 2010

to Disneyland in California. At left is a photo of Courage, a turkey who was pardoned by President Obama in 2009. After Courage was pardoned at the White House, he (along with the alternate turkey named Carolina) were flown first class to California. Courage served as the grand marshal of a Thanksgiving Day parade in Disneyland. In more recent years the pardoned turkeys have been sent to Mt. Vernon, the estate of President George Washington near Washington, D.C.

Thanksgiving In the Military

Sometimes men and women who are serving in the military have to celebrate Thanksgiving far away from home. Holidays such as Thanksgiving are often especially hard for people who are not able to celebrate it with their families. As a soldier remembers holiday gatherings and traditions of the past and thinks about his family celebrating at home when he can't be there, it can be a very sad time. The military tries to brighten the days of lonely soldiers with traditional Thanksgiving meals and some fun and silly activities to distract them. The photo at right above shows soldiers lining up for their Thanksgiving meal in Afghanistan. The other photos at right show soldiers enjoying a Thanksgiving football game and participating in an onion eating contest. Maybe the soldiers watching the contest had more fun than the competitors!

U.S. Soldiers in Afghanistan
Line Up for a Thanksgiving Meal, 2010

Soldiers in Iraq Play a Game of
Thanksgiving Football, 2008

Macy's Thanksgiving Day Parade

Several large cities in America host an annual Thanksgiving parade. The most famous is the Macy's Thanksgiving Day parade in New York City. Macy's is a company that has department stores across the country. This Thanksgiving tradition began in 1924. It actually began as a Christmas parade, but it

Members of the U.S. Marine Corps Participate in a
Thanksgiving Onion Eating Contest in Japan, 2010

soon switched to a Thanksgiving celebration. The parade has taken place every year except three years during World War II. The parade was canceled at that time so that the rubber and helium that would have been needed for the parade could be used for the war effort.

One special part of the Macy's parade is enormous balloons in the shapes of characters such as Felix the Cat, Mickey Mouse, Snoopy, and Uncle Sam. The public is invited to watch

New York City, New York
Macy's Thanksgiving Day Parades, 2009 and 2011

the balloons being inflated the evening before the parade. Inflating the balloons takes about seven hours.

Approximately 8,000 people take part in the Macy's parade each year by marching, dancing, riding, walking, and cheerleading down the streets of New York. Each parade is attended by an estimated 3.5 million people. Around 50 million more people watch it on television. Look at the photos at left from the 2009 and 2011 parades.

Being Thankful

The Bible has a lot to say about being thankful. God wants us to recognize that all the good things we have in our lives are gifts from Him (James 1:17). He wants us to be thankful for those good gifts. We should show our thankfulness to God on Thanksgiving and every day of the year.

Therefore I will give thanks to You among the nations, O Lord,

And I will sing praises to Your name.

Psalm 18:49

Family Activity

Make a model of a Thanksgiving parade float. Instructions are on page 496.

Pearl Harbor Remembrance Day

December 7

December 7, 1941, began as a quiet, peaceful Sunday on the islands of Hawaii. Half of the ships that the United States Navy had stationed in the Pacific were anchored near or docked along the piers at Pearl Harbor on the island of Oahu. Just before 8:00 a.m., the peaceful morning was shattered when the Japanese launched a surprise attack on the American fleet. Over the next two hours the Japanese rained down heavy fire. More than 2,300 Americans lost their lives. Most of the people who died were in the military, but forty-nine of the casualties were civilians. Several of the civilians who died were children.

The battleship USS *Arizona* was one of the ships that was totally destroyed. It is pictured at right as it looked earlier in 1941, as it burned during the attack, and after it was destroyed. The ship was hit by a bomb about fifteen minutes after the attack began. It sunk in less than nine minutes and 1,177 of the crew members died.

The United States responded to the attack on Pearl Harbor by declaring war on Japan. Since Germany and Italy were allies

Puget Sound, Washington
The USS Arizona, 1941

Pearl Harbor, Hawaii
The USS Arizona *after the Japanese Attack, 1941*

449

with Japan, those countries soon declared war on the United States. American life changed overnight. The country was now at war and every man, woman, and child was called upon to do all they could for the war effort. The photos below show newsboys in Redding, California, selling papers on the evening of December 7 that told of the Pearl Harbor attack.

Redding, California
Newsboys Selling Papers that Tell of the Pearl Harbor Attack, December 7, 1941

"A Date Which Will Live In Infamy"

The day after Pearl Harbor was attacked, President Franklin Roosevelt spoke to a joint session of Congress. He called December 7 "a date which will live in infamy." That line has become one of the most recognized of any that a President has ever given in a speech. Infamy means that which is shocking, brutal, or evil. December 7 was to the people of the World War II era like September 11 is for people of modern times. People remembered what they were doing when they heard the news. They remembered being scared of what was going to happen next. It was a frightening time. But Americans overcame their fear and joined together to fight with our allies against the enemy. In the end, we were victorious.

Kaneohe Naval Air Station, Hawaii
Members of the U.S. Navy Decorate the Graves of their Fallen Comrades, 1941

The photo at right shows members of the U.S. Navy decorating the graves of their comrades who died at Pearl Harbor.

Making Remembrance Day Official

Through the years following World War II, Congress approved resolutions for having an official Pearl Harbor Remembrance Day five different times. Each of these resolutions, however, was just for that specific year.

A World War II Marine veteran from Illinois named Richard Foltynewicz had a great deal to do with Pearl Harbor Remembrance Day becoming a day that is officially observed every year. Foltynewicz believed that God gave him the mission of working toward having the special day established.

Foltynewicz began working toward his goal in 1990. He contacted veterans groups and members of Congress. If a person wants an official observance of a special day to be established, a member of the House of Representatives has to agree to sponsor the request. The sponsor has to find 218 co-sponsors in the House to join with him before the Census and Population Subcommittee will even consider the request.

Foltynewicz tried to gain support for his idea by writing letters—thousands of them—and making phone calls. He even traveled across the country to make requests for support in person.

Thanks in large part to Foltynewicz's efforts, a resolution for a national observance to remember Pearl Harbor was passed in Congress in 1991. Foltynewicz was disheartened when he found out that the observance was just for that year. He didn't give up, though, and with the help of U.S. Representative George Sangmeister from Illinois, a resolution was passed in 1994 and signed by President Bill Clinton that made Pearl Harbor Remembrance Day an official annual observance.

USS *Arizona* Memorial

The WWII Valor in the Pacific National Monument is located on the Hawaiian island of Oahu, pictured at right. The arrow in the image is pointing to Pearl Harbor. The World War II monument is made up of several different sites, including the USS *Arizona* Memorial.

After World War II, the remains of the USS *Arizona* were left largely untouched. A tradition began in 1950 of flying a flag over

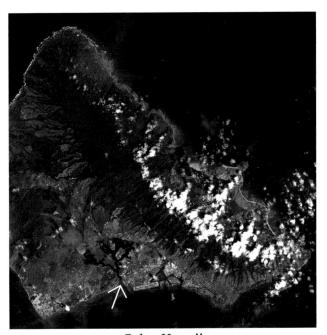

Oahu, Hawaii
Pearl Harbor is Marked with an Arrow in this NASA Satellite Image, 2001

the ship every day. Over time, people became more and more interested in seeing some sort of memorial put up to honor the ship and the lives that were lost when it sank.

Legislation was passed in 1958 which authorized the Navy to construct a memorial. Members of Hawaii's state legislature were among the people who contributed money for the project. Elvis Presley held a fundraising concert for it in 1961. Construction began the next year directly over the site where the remains of the *Arizona* still lay in the water. The memorial was completed in 1962. One feature of the memorial is a marble wall on which are engraved the names of all the men who died when the Japanese sunk the ship. The images below show the USS *Arizona* Memorial. The images on the following page were taken at a Remembrance Day ceremony in 1991 on the fiftieth anniversary of the Pearl Harbor attack.

Pearl Harbor, Hawaii
USS Arizona *Memorial*

Pearl Harbor, Hawaii
Pearl Harbor Remembrance Day, 1991
Left: Crew Members of the USS Arizona *Who Survived the 1941 Pearl Harbor Attack*
Right: U.S. Senator Daniel Inouye of Hawaii Addresses the Crowd

Reactions to Pearl Harbor

The day after Pearl Harbor was attacked, a man named Alan Lomax who worked for the Library of Congress had the idea of conducting interviews of everyday citizens across the country to find out what people were feeling and what kinds of thoughts were running through their minds. He and several others interviewed people from a variety of social, economic, and educational backgrounds. Below are excerpts from a few of the interviews that were made in Minnesota soon after the Pearl Harbor attacks. The photos on the following page show Minnesota residents working for the war effort.

> *My great-grandparents came to this country seeking religious freedom and they found it here and I feel that this is an opportunity for me at the present time in this emergency, this national crisis, to show my thankfulness and my gratefulness for the privileges and opportunities that this United States of ours has given me. . . . So I think that now in this crisis is time for us all to come to the aid of this great United States of ours and that no sacrifice is too great to make.*
>
> *— Reed Erickson*

> *I am a housewife. In this time of crisis I feel that every housewife should budget her time and her money so that she may help our national defense. Budget her time so that she may sew or knit for the Red Cross, and budget her money so that she may buy defense bonds and stamps. I also think it's the duty of every wife and mother to keep her home as pleasant and as cheerful as possible. Children don't understand this crisis and I feel that we shouldn't upset them continually by having them surrounded by an atmosphere of excitement. . . . Like everyone else, I didn't want this war, but now that it has been thrust upon us I pledge myself to do everything in my power to win it.*
>
> *— Mrs. Dorothy Fisher*

Minneapolis, Minnesota
Left: Working in a Factory for the War Effort, 1942
Right: Church Members Baking Cookies for a Servicemen's Center, 1942

I'll be all right to serve my country just as I can. I'll try to do anything I can do to help Uncle Sam win this war. It has been said that George Washington was the father of our great country and I think it's just as hard to run a house after it is built as it is to build it. I think President Roosevelt has done a good job of running our country and I wish him all the luck in the world. All I can say is "Keep up the good work, Pop." Thank you.

— *John Leo*

Learning from Our Elders

Moses wanted the younger Israelite generations to learn from the older ones. He knew that the older men and women had a lot to pass on to them. The same is true for us. If we are willing to ask and to listen, we can learn much from the generations who have lived before us.

Remember the days of old,

Consider the years of all generations.

Ask your father, and he will inform you,

Your elders, and they will tell you.

Deuteronomy 32:7

Family Activity

As a family, act out "A Date Which Will Live in Infamy." Instructions are on page 497.

BILL OF RIGHTS DAY

December 15

In August of 1941, Congress made an appeal to President Franklin Roosevelt to establish a day to commemorate the Bill of Rights in honor of its one hundred fiftieth anniversary. Roosevelt is pictured below. In November of that year, Roosevelt issued this proclamation:

By the President of the United States of America

A Proclamation

Whereas a Joint Resolution of the Congress, approved August 21, 1941, authorizes and requests the President of the United States "to issue a proclamation designating December 15, 1941, as Bill of Rights Day, calling upon officials of the Government to display the flag of the United States on all Government buildings on that day, and inviting the people of the United States to observe the day with appropriate ceremonies and prayer":

President Franklin D. Roosevelt, 1939

Now, Therefore, I, Franklin D. Roosevelt, President of the United States of America, do hereby designate December 15, 1941, as Bill of Rights Day. And I call upon the officials of the Government, and upon the people of the United States, to observe the day by displaying the flag of the United States on public buildings and by meeting together for such prayers and such ceremonies as may seem to them appropriate.

Roosevelt's proclamation went on to talk about how it was appropriate to remember the adoption of the Bill of Rights (the first ten amendments to the Constitution) since the United States had been able to enjoy the freedoms guaranteed in it for one hundred fifty years. These freedoms include freedom of speech, freedom of the press, freedom of religion, freedom of assembly, and the freedom to petition the government. Roosevelt said that it was fitting for the anniversary of the Bill of Rights to be remembered and observed by "the free schools, the free churches, the labor unions, the religious and educational and civic organizations of all kinds which, without the guarantee of the Bill of Rights, could never have existed."

When Roosevelt issued his proclamation, World War II was being waged around the world, but the United States had not yet joined the fighting. The photographs on this page show American citizens enjoying their freedom in 1941. In his proclamation Roosevelt also said:

> Those who have long enjoyed such privileges as we enjoy forget in time that men have died to win them. They come in time to take these rights for granted and to assume their protection is assured. We, however, who have seen these privileges lost in other continents and other countries can now appreciate their meaning to those people who enjoyed them once and now no longer can. We understand in some measure what their loss can mean. And by that realization we have come to a clearer conception of their worth to us, and to a stronger and more unalterable determination that here in our land they shall not be lost or weakened or curtailed.

Caldwell, Ohio
Children Waving Flags, 1941

Micala, Minnesota
Meeting, 1941

Rutland, Vermont
State Fair, 1941

White Plains, Georgia
Church Service, 1941

A celebration for Bill of Rights Day was planned at the luxurious Waldorf Astoria Hotel in New York City, pictured at right. Actress Helen Hayes was to be there, along with First Lady Eleanor Roosevelt. Just nine days after President Roosevelt issued his proclamation, however, the Japanese attacked Pearl Harbor and the United States declared war. Suddenly a grand celebration at a fancy hotel seemed out of place. America's focus shifted to defending itself so that no one could take away the freedoms that the Bill of Rights had established.

Free to Tweet

Bill of Rights Day has never gained a place of prominence on the American calendar, but some people are trying to change that. The John S. and James L. Knight Foundation is an organization that works to inform and engage the citizens of America. The foundation believes that a democracy cannot prosper unless the citizens are informed and fully engaged in the life of their communities. They seek to help communities figure out solutions and take action to solve the problems that they face. The foundation wants people to feel that they belong in their community and also to care about it. One large focus of the foundation is encouraging youth leadership.

New York City, New York
Waldorf Astoria Hotel,
c. 1901 and 2010

In 2011 the Knight Foundation funded a contest called "Free to Tweet" in honor of Bill of Rights Day. The contest was organized by 1 for All, a program that seeks to encourage a better understanding of the First Amendment freedoms among Americans. "Free to Tweet" was open to students aged 14 to 22. It was a celebration of the Bill of Right's First Amendment, which guarantees Americans freedom of speech, freedom of the press, the right to assemble peaceably, and the right to petition the government. To enter the contest, a student had to tweet or e-mail a message to the foundation saying what they thought of the importance of the freedoms outlined in the First Amendment. Students were permitted to enter essays, poems, videos, photos, and graphics to express their views. They could also send in just a single sentence.

A panel of educators, journalists, and experts on the First Amendment read and watched the 17,000 entries and chose twenty-two winners. Each of the winners received a $5,000 scholarship. The winning entries included some one-line tweets, a poem, and several videos. One of the

Washington, D.C.
First Amendment Engraving on the Newseum

videos showed a boy in front of a fireplace decorated with Christmas stockings reading a rap he wrote about the First Amendment.

Newseum

A museum about the news industry opened in Washington, D.C., in 2008. Inside the seven level museum, named the Newseum, visitors can explore the history of the media from the earliest days of printing to the digital age. Fifteen theaters, fourteen galleries, two broadcast studios, and over 130 interactive stations educate museumgoers on how and why news is made.

One of the special aspects of the Newseum building is the 74-foot-high stone monument pictured at left. The words of the First Amendment are engraved on the stone. The picture below shows the monument under construction the year before the Newseum opened. The First Amendment is what has made it possible for newspapers and broadcast companies to exercise their freedom of speech throughout America's history.

First Amendment Engraving Under Construction, 2007

On Bill of Rights Day in 2011, the Newseum hosted a conference for educators that explored how to use social media to teach about freedom of expression. The event included a panel discussion about the future of the First Amendment and a choral performance of "The Bill of Rights: A Musical Celebration."

Freedom of Speech Wall

On Bill of Rights Day and on the other 364 days of the year, people in Charlottesville, Virginia, have a special way that they can express their freedom of speech. In front of Charlottesville City Hall, a 54-foot-long monument made of slate stands seven and a half feet high. It is a giant chalkboard where people can write or draw whatever they want. The words of the First Amendment are permanently engraved on one part of the wall. A quote about the First Amendment by U.S. Supreme Court Justice Thurgood Marshall is engraved on another section. Other than those quotes, the words and pictures on the monument are always changing. Sometimes people write messages to members of the city government. The slate is cleaned twice a week, but anyone can erase what has been written and write or draw something else any time. Near the slate wall is a podium where anyone can stand and exercise their freedom of speech.

Charlottesville, Virginia
Freedom of Speech Wall

Words from Presidents On Bill of Rights Day

Below are portions from Bill of Rights Day proclamations made by Presidents during the second half of the twentieth century.

On this day I hope that citizens throughout our land will renew in their hearts and minds a devotion to these freedoms and a determination to defend them against all forms of attack. Let us also highly resolve to continue to strive for a peaceful world in which all mankind will share them.

— *Dwight D. Eisenhower, 1955*

Let us shoulder our responsibilities, as trustees of freedom, to make the Bill of Rights a reality for all our citizens. Let us reach beyond the fears that divide nations to make common cause for the promotion of greater understanding of right and justice for all, and in so doing strengthen our faith in the reason and conscience of men as the basis for a true and lasting peace.

— *John F. Kennedy, 1962*

It is with sincere thanksgiving that we reflect on the successful efforts of those wise patriots of two hundred years ago who laid the political foundations of our beloved Nation, and also to those millions of citizens ever since who have cherished and defended the Constitution and the principles it embodies. Many have given their lives on the field of battle so that freedom and human dignity might live both at home and abroad; let us never forget our debt to them or fail to honor their sacrifice and courage.

— *Ronald Reagan, 1985*

Save us, O Lord our God,

And gather us from among the nations,

To give thanks to Your holy name and glory in Your praise.

Psalm 106:47

Family Activity

Create a Freedom of Speech Driveway. Instructions are on page 500.

CHRISTMAS DAY

December 25

Christmas Day is celebrated from coast to coast in rural communities and big cities. Our nation's Capital has many Christmas traditions that are a special part of each year.

The National Christmas Tree

The tradition of a National Christmas Tree began in 1923 when Calvin Coolidge was President. That year the president of Middlebury College in Vermont, Coolidge's home state, donated a 48-foot Balsam fir tree to be used to decorate the White House grounds. There was a simple ceremony on Christmas Eve when Coolidge turned on the tree's lights by pushing a button. Music was provided by a local choir and a quartet from the U.S. Marine Band. Both cut trees and live trees have served as the National Christmas Tree since then. A Colorado spruce was planted in 1978 on the Ellipse, a large open area near the White House. This tree was decorated every year until it was damaged by a storm in 2011 and had to be replaced. The new tree soon died of transplant shock and had to be replaced again in 2012.

The lighting ceremony now takes place earlier in December, instead of on Christmas Eve. General Electric has designed and donated the lighting for the tree each year since 1963. Various groups sing and perform on a stage near the tree throughout the weeks leading up to Christmas. The photos below show the National Christmas Tree in 2007 and 2008.

Washington, D.C.
National Christmas Tree, 2007 and 2008

White House Christmas Trees

President Benjamin Harrison began the tradition of having a Christmas tree in the White House in 1889. There was no electricity in the White House at that time. The tree was lit with candles attached to the branches, the way most people lit their trees in that era. Electricity was installed in the White House two years later. Electric lights were first strung on a White House Christmas Tree in 1895 during the presidency of Grover Cleveland. The photo at right shows the White House Christmas tree from 1990.

Jacqueline Kennedy began the tradition of First Ladies choosing a special theme for the White House Christmas Tree decorations each year. Read the words on the Christmas balls below. Each one shows the year, First Lady, theme, and description of a particular White House Christmas Tree since 1961.

White House Christmas Tree, 1990

1961
Jacqueline Kennedy
Nutcracker Ballet

toys, birds, and angels inspired by the ballet

1966
Lady Bird Johnson
Early America

nuts, popcorn, fruit, and gingerbread cookies

1969
Pat Nixon
Fifty States

velvet and satin balls featuring state flowers

1974
Betty Ford
Thrift and Recylcling

patchwork decorations on swags

1977
Rosalynn Carter
Victorian

dolls, hats, fans, tapestries, and laces

1987
Nancy Reagan
Music

miniature instruments, notes, and sheet music

1989
Barbara Bush
Family Literacy

miniature books, eighty book character sculptures

1998
Hillary Clinton
Winter Wonderland

snowmen, knitted mittens and hats

2001
Laura Bush
Home for the Holidays

miniature replicas of historic homes and churches

2011
Michelle Obama
Shine, Give, Share

military medals, badges, and patches

Sometimes the First Lady chooses a special group of people to make the Christmas ornaments. For example, when Mrs. Ford chose the theme of Thrift and Recycling, she had the ornaments made by Appalachian women and senior citizen groups. Nancy Reagan had people in a drug addiction treatment program make the ornaments three of the years she was First Lady. Artists from all fifty states made the replicas of historic buildings that hung on Laura Bush's tree in 2001.

The White House Christmas Tree is an annual gift from members of the National Christmas Tree Association. Each year a tree that is the perfect height and shape is chosen to be cut down and delivered to the White House by a horse-drawn carriage. Christmas tree growers Eric and Gloria Sundback had the honor of donating a White House Christmas Tree four times over the span of thirty years. They delivered winning trees to Rosalynn Carter, Nancy Reagan (twice), and Michelle Obama.

White House Gingerbread Houses

Another Christmastime tradition at the Executive Mansion is to have on display an elaborate gingerbread White House made by the White House Pastry Team and other members of the White House staff. The gingerbread houses are so large and intricate that the pastry team needs the assistance of carpenters, plumbers, and electricians! Constructing the gingerbread houses can take as long as five months.

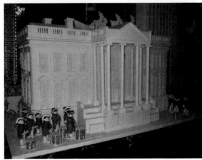

White House Gingerbread Houses, 1993 and 2008

The team uses up to 150 pounds of gingerbread to make each house. It is baked so thick that it takes a band-saw to cut through it. The chef and his crew have been known to use over 250 pounds of white chocolate for one creation! The image at right above shows the Clintons' cat Socks next to the 1993 gingerbread White House. The image at right below shows the house made in 2008.

White House Christmas Parties for Children

Through the years, Presidents have invited children to the White House to enjoy a memorable Christmas party. Andrew Jackson hosted a party for children in 1834, complete with an indoor "snowball" fight. Their snowballs were actually made of cotton.

Five hundred children attended a Christmas carnival at the White House in 1903 when Theodore Roosevelt was President. The children enjoyed ice cream molded to look like Santa Claus and other Christmas shapes.

The Christmas party in the White House State Dining Room pictured at left took place in December of 1961. It was hosted by President John F. Kennedy's sister-in-law Ethel Skakel Kennedy. The party was held for children from St. Ann's Infant Asylum and Junior Village, a nearby children's home.

The photo at left below shows First Lady Betty Ford and Santa leading a group of children of the Diplomatic Corps through the White House at a party in 1975. The Diplomatic Corps is made up of men and women from other countries who work in Washington, D.C., for the governments of their homelands.

At right below is a photo of President George W. Bush and his wife Laura hosting children of military families at the White House in 2005.

Christmas in the Military

Americans serving in the military often have to celebrate Christmas far away from their families as they are stationed across the country and around the world. Sometimes a business or individual will donate Christmas

White House Christmas Party for Needy Children, 1961

*First Lady Betty Ford and Santa with
Children of the Diplomatic Corps, 1975*

*President George W. Bush and First Lady Laura Bush
with Children of Military Families, 2005*

464

gifts for a needy military family as a way to show their appreciation for the sacrifices the family is making for our country.

The military tries to boost the morale of the men and women in uniform with special meals, programs, and events during the Christmas season. Sometimes the soldiers themselves spend time during the holiday season to serve others. The photos at right page show military personnel celebrating Christmas around the world in 2010. In the top left photo, a soldier in Iraq gives a thumbs up as he displays his Christmas dinner. The second photo shows U.S. Marines participating in a Holiday Fun Run at their base in Japan. Participants were encouraged to dress in holiday costumes for the event. In the third photo, soldiers are singing Christmas carols at a hospital in Afghanistan.

Sometimes the President makes Christmas phone calls or visits to people in the military to encourage them and thank them for their service. President Barack Obama visited a Marine Corps base in Hawaii in 2010. He is pictured at left shaking hands with the officer in charge of the base's dining hall.

Christmas Across America

Big cities and small towns across America celebrate the Christmas season by hanging lights across streets and around public buildings, putting up banners on streetlights, hanging wreaths on lampposts, and holding concerts and parades. Some towns put a nativity scene in front of the courthouse. The

Christmas in the Military, 2010

Kaneohe Bay, Hawaii
President Obama Shakes Hands with a Marine, 2010

465

Huntington Park, California
Christmas Decorations Strung Across the Street, 2010

decorations pictured at left are strung across a street in Huntington Park, California.

Immigrants began bringing Christmas traditions to America hundreds of years ago, and they are still bringing them today. Some immigrants are used to celebrating Christmas as many in America do, but our customs are strange to others. Some newcomers to America quickly embrace the American customs of putting up a tree and giving gifts, things that are not as common in their homeland. Others tend to hold onto the traditions of their native countries and have a very simple Christmas celebration. They might attend a church service, have a special meal with other immigrants, and let that be all. Some immigrant communities hold competitions and give prizes on Christmas Day, a custom they were used to before they came to America.

While many American Christmas traditions have become increasingly commercial over the past several decades, the spirit of giving and light and hope is going strong. The photo at right shows members of the U.S. Army Corps of Engineers holding hands before their Christmas dinner in Iraq. They come from different parts of the country and different religious backgrounds, but they are united by their belief in God and their desire to promote peace on His earth.

Praying Before Christmas Dinner in Iraq, 2007

Gathering with family and friends and remembering when Jesus came to earth as a little baby is a beautiful way to end each year. With the story comes a message of peace and joy that we can carry with us every day.

Do not be afraid; for behold,

I bring you good news of great joy which will be for all the people.

Luke 2:10

Family Activity

Decorate a Christmas tree with a special theme. Instructions are on page 501.

NEW YEAR'S DAY

January 1

America is full of New Year's Day traditions from parties to watching football to eating black-eyed peas. Many people like to gather with family and friends and stay up until midnight on New Year's Eve to welcome the new year. "Auld Lang Syne," an old Scottish ballad, has become a sort of New Year's anthem sung around the world when the clock strikes midnight and the new year begins. The tradition of the song being sung on New Year's Eve in America is attributed to Guy Lombardo. Lombardo sang the song at midnight on January 1, 1929, in a New York City radio broadcast. His orchestra continued to play this song every New Year's until 1976. Since then a recording of the orchestra's rendition of the song is played at the annual New Year's celebration in Times Square in New York City.

New Year's in Times Square

New York City has hosted a New Year's Eve extravaganza since 1904. The first celebration was in honor of the official opening of the new headquarters of the *The New York Times* newspaper. The area around the new headquarters had recently been renamed Times Square. The party lasted all day on New Year's Eve and ended with a fireworks display. It was reported that the cheers made by the 200,000 attendees could be heard thirty miles away. The pictures of Times Square at right show how much the area has changed since *The Times* building was built over one hundred years ago.

The New York Times decided to make the party an annual tradition. The city banned the fireworks display in 1907, but

New York City, New York
Times Square, c. 1905 and 2012

Alfred Ochs, owner of the newspaper, came up with a replacement. He had a large illuminated ball made of iron and wood lowered from a flagpole at midnight. The ball weighed seven hundred pounds. An illuminated ball has been lowered every year since then with the exception of only two years during World War II. The city was in a wartime dimout so that it would not be an easy target for possible enemy attack. Crowds still gathered in Times Square in 1942 and 1943, but at midnight they welcomed the new year with a moment of silence.

New York City, New York
Members of the U.S. Army Corps of Engineers Prepare for New Year's Eve, 2011

Hundreds of thousands of people gather in Times Square on New Year's Eve each year. An estimated one billion more watch the celebration on television around the world. The photo at left shows members of the U.S. Army Corps of Engineers getting ready for the big event. They are installing metal panels over the entrance and lower windows of an Armed Forces Recruiting Station in Times Square for protection during the big party.

Different balls have been used through the years for the celebration. The modern ball that is lowered is 12 feet in diameter. It weighs 11,875 pounds and is covered with 2,688 crystal triangles. The ball is lit by 32,256 LEDs of varying colors. As the ball is lowered beginning at 11:59 p.m., hundreds of thousands of voices join together to count down the seconds to the new year until the ball reaches the bottom of its descent precisely at midnight.

At the Times Square Museum and Visitor Center, anyone can write a message on a small piece of tissue paper and pin it up on the Wishing Wall, pictured at right. All the messages that are written throughout the year are added to two tons of tissue paper confetti that are dropped on Times Square at

Wishing Wall in Times Square Museum and Visitor Center, 2010

midnight on New Year's Eve. It takes about 175 Sanitation Department employees to clean up the streets after the event. Among their cleaning equipment on New Year's Day in 2010 were 23 mechanical sweepers, 21 collection trucks, and 36 leaf blowers. In 2009 they hauled away almost 40 tons of debris that was left over from the celebration. The cleanup that year cost over $50,000.

New Year's Messages from the President

Sometimes leaders from around the world send each other goodwill New Year's messages. The messages below were sent by President Herbert Hoover in late December of 1929.

To His Majesty Vittorio Emmanuele III, King of Italy, Rome

I THANK Your Majesty for your cordial new year greetings. May the coming years bring to Your Majesty health and happiness, and to the great nation over which you preside, continued peace and prosperity.

HERBERT HOOVER
December 30, 1929

His Excellency Chiang Chung-cheng, The President of the Chinese Republic, Nanking, China

I THANK Your Excellency in my own name and on behalf of my fellow countrymen for your courteous new year greetings which are most heartily reciprocated.

HERBERT HOOVER
December 28, 1929

New Year's With the President

Franklin and Eleanor Roosevelt usually had a White House dinner for family and friends on New Year's Eve. Sometimes they watched a movie together or enjoyed some live entertainment. At midnight they liked to gather in the President's study and listen to the radio. Then the President raised his glass of eggnog and made a toast to the United States of America. The Roosevelts' celebration was interrupted in 1939 when two uninvited Washington teenagers showed up, trying to get the President's autograph. The White House staff let the teenagers in because they thought they were just latecomers to the party. Even though they weren't supposed to have been there in the first place, the teens left the White House with the signatures of the President, the First Lady, and their youngest son, John.

When President Jimmy Carter asked his wife Rosalynn how she wanted to spend New Year's Eve in 1977, Rosalynn said she would like to spend it with the Shah, the leader of Iran, and his wife. The trip was planned and the Carters rang in the New Year on the other side of the world.

At the end of December in 1992, President George H. W. Bush left the United States for a meeting with Russian Prime Minister Boris Yeltsin in Russia. On his way, Bush stopped in Somalia where he had a New Year's Day lunch with U.S. troops who were deployed there. Bush is pictured with the troops he visited at right. Later in the day Bush visited a Somalian orphanage where more than seven hundred children clapped their hands and chanted, "Welcome, Bush! Welcome, Bush!"

President George H. W. Bush Visiting U.S. Troops in Somalia on New Year's Day, 1993

On New Year's Eve in 2010, the Obama family was on vacation in Hawaii and celebrated with a private party. Their celebration included their own tradition of a talent show.

New Year's Day Receptions

George Washington began the tradition of holding a New Year's Day reception during his first term, when New York City was the U.S. Capital. President and Mrs. John Adams hosted the first New Year's Day open house in the White House in 1801.

The first New Year's receptions were primarily for public officials and other prominent people, who bowed to the President instead of shaking his hand. Thomas Jefferson began the practice of opening the receptions to the general public and shaking hands with visitors. The New Year's Day reception was held elsewhere after the White House was burned by the British in 1814, but it returned to the White House in 1818.

On January 1, 1863, President Lincoln shook so many hands that he was concerned that his signature on the Emancipation Proclamation later that day might appear shaky and uncertain. Herbert Hoover shook an average of 9,000 hands during the receptions that were held when he was in office. The usual hours for the New Year's Day reception were from noon until 3:00 or 3:30 p.m. People lined up outside the White House for hours for the chance to shake hands with the President. The tradition continued almost unbroken through January 1, 1932, which was the last time it was held. The photo at left shows only part of the line of people waiting to shake hands with President Warren Harding in the White House. The building shown is the Old Executive Office Building. The White House is barely visible in the distance!

Washington, D.C.
People Waiting to Shaking Hands with President Harding on New Year's Day, 1922

Serenading the Commandant

Near the United States Capitol in Washington, D.C., stands the Home of the Commandant. The house was completed in 1806, and since then it has been the residence of each successive commandant of the United States Marine Corps and his family. It is said to be the oldest public building in Washington, D.C., that has been continuously occupied.

A tradition began during the Civil War of the U.S. Marine Band standing outside of the house to serenade the commandant and his wife on New Year's Day. The name of the band is "The President's Own." The band plays patriotic songs such as "Marine's Hymn" and "Stars

and Stripes Forever." After the concert, the commandant invites the band members in for brunch. The photo above shows "The President's Own" playing for the commandant on New Year's Day in 2006. The photo at right shows band members being welcomed into the house on New Year's Day in 2010 by Commandant of the Marine Corps General James T. Conway and his wife Annette.

Washington, D.C.
New Year's Day at the Home of the
Commandant of the Marine Corps, 2006 and 2010

The Rose Parade

One American New Year's Day tradition goes back to 1890 in Pasadena, California. An elite club there wanted to promote people visiting their part of the country. They invited people from the East Coast to an event where they could watch chariot races, jousting, foot races, polo, and tug of war. They decided also to hold a parade featuring carriages decorated with flowers. One of the club members commented on how citizens of New York were buried in snow on New Year's, but in Pasadena the flowers were blooming and the fruit trees were about to produce. "Let's hold a festival to tell the world about our paradise," he said.

Over time the parades came to include marching bands and motorized vehicles. Sporting events included ostrich races and a race between a camel and an elephant. The Tournament

Pasadena, California
Rose Parade Floats, 2009

of Roses Association was formed in 1895 to manage the annual event.

The association decided to add a football game to the festivities in 1902. The first football game was a disaster, however, and ended in the third quarter when Stanford University gave up to the University of Michigan, who was winning 49-0. Football did not return to the Tournament of Roses until 1916. Soon a new stadium was needed to hold the New Year's Day crowd and the first great modern football stadium was built. The first New Year's game was played there in 1923 and it soon came to be called the Rose Bowl.

The traditional parade and football game continue to be held in Pasadena every year and the event is televised around the world. The images at left show two of the floats from the parade in 2009.

Starting Fresh

Each New Year is a time to start fresh. It is a time to reflect on a year that has gone by and to look forward to what might be coming in the year ahead. Even if we made mistakes in the previous year, we can learn from them and press on toward the goal of becoming who God wants us to be.

> . . . forgetting what lies behind and reaching forward to what lies ahead,
> I press on toward the goal for the prize
> of the upward call of God in Christ Jesus.
> Philippians 3:13-14

Family Activity

Have a Home of the Commandant Brunch. Instructions are on page 502.

THE CONVENING OF CONGRESS

January 3

Section 2 of the Twentieth Amendment to the United States Constitution reads as follows:

The Congress shall assemble at least once in every year, and such meeting shall begin at noon on the 3d day of January, unless they shall by law appoint a different day.

Frequently either January 4, 5, 6, or 7 has been designated for the convening (or coming together) of a new Congress instead of January 3. One reason is that January 3 sometimes falls on a Saturday or Sunday and another day is more convenient. Both the Senate and the House of Representatives convene in the Capitol building, pictured below.

Before the Twentieth Amendment was passed in 1933, Congress typically did not convene until December of the year after the election—over a year after the new members were elected! This was because of the slow travel and communication of the time. By the 1930s, telegraphs, telephones, radios, railroads, automobiles, and airplanes had made it possible for newly-elected officials to take office sooner.

Washington, D.C.
United States Capitol

Each time a new Congress convenes (which happens every odd-numbered year), the Senate and the House of Representatives have a routine of how to begin the new session. Some aspects change from year to year, but there are many things that take place in a particular order and in a particular way.

The Senate Convenes

Usually the Vice President is in charge when the Senate first comes together. The Senate chaplain opens the session with a prayer. The Vice President makes an announcement about the certificates and credentials of election of the newly elected Senators. It would take a long time to read each of these documents, so instead they are printed in *The Congressional Record*. A Senator's election certificate is a document that is signed by the Governor and the secretary of state of the state from which the Senator was elected. Sometimes this documentation is not ready by the time Congress convenes. When that is the case, Congress may decide by unanimous consent to allow the Senator-elect to be sworn in anyway. The photo below shows the United States Senators of the 111th Congress seated in the Senate chamber in 2010.

Senators in the Senate Chamber, 2010

Swearing In

The first item on the agenda after the certificates and credentials of election are taken care of is swearing in the newly-elected Senators. Sometimes before the swearing in, the Majority Leader shares a brief history of the oath of office. The Majority Leader and the Minority Leader sometimes give a brief welcoming speech.

Newly-elected Senators are called to the front of the chamber in alphabetical order. Four Senators are sworn in at a time. Each one is escorted down the center aisle to the front. Traditionally the other Senator from a Senator-elect's state serves as the escort.

When Senators take the oath they each raise their right hand. They are permitted to decide whether they want to "swear" or "affirm" an oath as required by Article VI of the Constitution. The oath that is used now dates from the Civil War. Each Senator who is being sworn in raises his right hand and repeats the words after the Vice President says them. Senators are not required to hold anything as they repeat the oath, but many decide to place one hand on a Bible. Some place their hand on another religious text.

Senator Elmer Thomas Takes the Oath of Office, 1939

Sometimes Senators also hold a special family heirloom or another meaningful object while they take the oath. Photography is usually forbidden on the Senate floor; but at the convening of a new Congress, photographers are allowed to come in and take pictures. The photo above shows a Senator taking the oath of office on the opening day of Congress in 1939.

Here is the oath that every Senator-elect must take:

> *I do solemnly swear (or affirm) that I will support and defend the Constitution of the United States against all enemies, foreign and domestic; that I will bear true faith and allegiance to the same; that I take this obligation freely, without any mental reservation or purpose of evasion, and that I will well and faithfully discharge the duties of the office on which I am about to enter. So help me God.*

Each newly sworn-in Senator then signs his or her name on a specific page in the Senate Oath Book. This is a tradition that began during the Civil War.

Sometimes after the formal ceremony, a Senator will choose to reenact the swearing-in inside the old Senate chamber where she can have a photo made with her family gathered around her. Representative Diane Black from Tennessee's sixth congressional district is

Congressman Diane Black with Her Family and Speaker of the House John Boehner, 2011

pictured at left with her family and Speaker of the House John Boehner when Congress convened in 2011.

Notifying the President

After everyone is sworn in, the Senate clerk calls the roll. Someone notifies the House of Representatives that a quorum is present. Then the leaders of the House and Senate telephone the President to let him know that they are ready to begin their work.

Electing a President Pro Tempore

The Senators elect a President *pro tempore* to preside (or be in charge) of the Senate when the Vice President is not there. Usually this position is filled by the Senator from the majority party who has been serving for the longest continuous period. When the President *pro tempore* is away, he appoints another Senator to take his place.

Other Business

One other item that must be taken care of is for the Senate to decide when it will come together each day during the current session of Congress. The Majority Leader is usually the one to propose a time.

Some business that takes place when Congress convenes does not happen every time. If a presidential election has just taken place, for example, there is extra business for Congress to

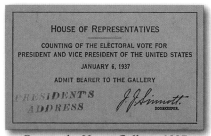

Pass to the House Gallery, 1937

do. The Senate must agree to hold a joint session of Congress with the House to count the electoral votes and to authorize the use of the Capitol building for special events related to the inauguration. The image at left shows a pass that admitted the bearer to the gallery of the House of Representatives to watch the electoral vote be counted in 1937.

After the initial work is completed, the Senators begin routine business such as introducing bills and resolutions. Sometimes it is necessary to appoint new officers. The Senate officers include the secretary of the Senate, the sergeant at arms and doorkeeper, and the chaplain.

Opening Day in the House

When a new Congress convenes, the Clerk of the House from the previous Congress is in charge until the Speaker is sworn in. The chaplain says a prayer and everyone recites the Pledge of Allegiance. Since the House has so many members, a roll call is not made out loud. Instead, each member-elect shows that he or she is present by using an electronic voting card.

The next item of business is to elect a Speaker. Each party usually nominates one person for the position in meetings that are held before the opening day. Generally everyone votes for the nominee from his or her party, so the nominee from the party who is in the majority is most likely to be elected. The Minority Leader introduces the new Speaker to the House. The Speaker often replies with a few comments and then takes the oath of office. Traditionally the longest-serving member administers the oath to the new Speaker. The oath is the same as that which is used in the Senate. The Speaker then administers the oath to all the Representatives.

Other Business in the House

Other business that takes place in the House of Representatives on the opening day of Congress is similar to proceedings in the Senate, such as electing officers and deciding when they will convene each day during the current session of Congress. The House adopts rules pertaining to how day to day operations will be carried out. Members are usually allowed to debate on suggested rules for an hour. In recent years, the set of rules suggested by the majority party always goes into effect. The chamber of the House of Representatives is pictured at right.

Daily Business in the House of Representatives, 2010

Out of the Ordinary Opening Days in the House

1855: This session of Congress opened just six years before the Civil War began. There was a great deal of tension in Congress between Representatives who supported slavery and those who opposed it. With so much division, Representatives had the longest battle in history to elect a Speaker. They tried four times on opening day, but all of their attempts were unsuccessful. Twenty-one Representatives were wanting the position. After voting on 133 ballots, Nathaniel Banks was finally elected as Speaker two months after the House convened.

1895: When the 54th Congress convened, it was not known who would fill 38 of the seats. That's how many contested elections there were in the 1894 election! Three committees worked hard to figure out who the winner was in each case, but some of them were undecided for more than two years after the election.

1929: In this year, Speaker Nicholas Longworth decided to change the tradition of swearing in new members by state to swearing in all members at the same time. This of course made things go much more quickly. The decision was made because in years past when separate groups were sworn in, the remainder of the House tended "to be in pretty complete disorder," as Speaker Longworth put it. The other Representatives approved of Longworth's decision. When he made the announcement, applause went up in the chamber.

1931: The Republicans won a majority in the election of 1930. Between election day in 1930 and the convening of Congress in 1931, however, fourteen of the Representatives-elect died. In the special elections that were held to fill those seats, more Democrats were elected, giving that party a majority.

1947: The first time there was a live television broadcast from the House chamber was during the opening session of Congress in 1947. The opening was broadcast in Washington, D.C., Philadelphia, and New York City. President Harry Truman watched the opening on a ten-inch television set in the Oval Office. Three days later, Truman's State of the Union address was the first to be broadcast on television.

The Senate and the House of Representatives have many customs and traditions to help things run smoothly and efficiently. When Paul wrote to the church at Corinth, he wrote about how they needed to conduct their gatherings in an organized way so that things would not get out of hand and so that the gathering would be beneficial for everyone there.

But all things must be done properly and in an orderly manner.
1 Corinthians 14:40

Family Activity

Write letters of thanks to one of the U.S. Senators from your state or your
U.S. Representative. Instructions are on page 503.

INAUGURATION DAY

January 20

George Washington was inaugurated as the first President of the United States on April 30, 1789, at Federal Hall in New York City, the first Capital of the newly-formed country. The inauguration was originally scheduled to take place on March 4, but the winter of 1789 was a hard one that made travel difficult. Enough Congressmen had finally arrived in New York City by April 6 that they could count the electoral votes and announce that George Washington had been elected. Washington was notified several days later and he then made his way to New York, traveling by coach and horseback. The illustration at right shows Washington's reception by the American people as he passed through Trenton, New Jersey.

Trenton, New Jersey
George Washington on His Way to the First Presidential Inauguration, 1789

On April 30, church bells rang and guns were fired to greet the morning. The swearing-in took place at noon. Washington placed his right hand on a Bible and repeated the words of the oath that were outlined in the Constitution:

> *I do solemnly swear that I will faithfully execute the office of President of the United States and will, to the best of my ability, preserve, protect, and defend the Constitution of the United States.*

At the end of the oath, Washington added the words, "So help me God." Every President since has carried on that tradition.

The Inauguration Moves to D.C.

The United States Capital was soon relocated to Washington, D.C. In 1801 Thomas Jefferson became the first President to be inaugurated there. The ceremony took place in the Senate chamber of the U.S. Capitol. The Marine Band played at the 1801 inauguration and has played at every inauguration ceremony since.

Most of the early D.C. inaugurations took place inside the Capitol building, in either the Senate or House chamber. Andrew Jackson's inauguration in 1829 was the first one held on the East Portico of the Capitol. This was the location of most inaugural ceremonies until Ronald Reagan became President in 1981. His first inauguration, pictured at right, was held on the West Front of the Capitol because that side can accommodate more people.

The Twentieth Amendment to the U.S. Constitution established the date for the inauguration as January 20. This was the same amendment that made January 3 the official day for Congress to convene. The temperature at Reagan's first inauguration was 55°F, the warmest on record for a January presidential inauguration. The temperature on the day of Reagan's second inaugural ceremony in 1985 was the coldest on record. With a temperature of 7°F and a wind chill between -10°F and -20°F, the ceremony was moved inside the Capitol.

For each modern inaugural ceremony, a wooden platform is constructed from scratch outside the Capitol. Each platform project is begun with a First Nail Ceremony, when several

Washington, D.C.
Ronald Reagan's
First Inauguration, 1981

people connected with planning the inaugural ceremony drive nails into a board to symbolically represent the start of the preparations. The 2009 platform was built strong enough to hold 1,600 people, including the President-elect and Vice President-elect and their families, Senators and Representatives, Cabinet members, Supreme Court Justices, former Presidents, and other dignitaries from the U.S. and other countries. Another 1,000 choir members and other guests gathered on a terrace above. An estimated one to two million people stood below and watched. Millions more in America and around the world watched on television and online.

When Franklin Roosevelt began his fourth term as President on January 20, 1945, World War II was raging in Europe and the Pacific. The United States was facing many challenges, including the rationing of many goods such as gasoline. Roosevelt decided it would be appropriate to have a simple ceremony at the White House. For the first and only time, a President began a regular term with no parade or official celebration.

Inauguration Receptions

For his second inauguration in 1805, Thomas Jefferson began the practice of hosting a reception at the White House where he greeted visitors. In 1829 the reception for newly inaugurated President Andrew Jackson, pictured at right, became unruly. An estimated 20,000 people entered the White House to celebrate Jackson as "the people's President." The crowd crushed in around

"All Creation Going to the White House"
Illustration of President Andrew Jackson's 1829 Reception

Jackson, while others stood on furniture to catch a glimpse of Old Hickory. White House staff took refreshments out onto the White House lawn to encourage the crowd to go back outside. Because of the chaos, Jackson spent his first night as President at a Washington hotel.

After his second inaugural in 1865, Abraham Lincoln shook hands with an estimated six thousand people. The practice of holding an inauguration reception ended with Grover Cleveland's first inauguration in 1885, when the new President reviewed troops outside of the White House instead of having people come in.

Inauguration Day Traditions

The morning that Franklin Roosevelt was sworn into office in 1933, he and his wife Eleanor attended a church service at St. John's Episcopal Church near the White House. This set a pattern that has been followed by almost every President since of attending a public worship service or a private prayer service the morning of Inauguration Day.

Each inaugural ceremony since 1901 has been planned by the Joint Congressional Committee on Inaugural Ceremonies (JCCIC). Before 1901 the ceremonies were planned by Senators only. The Senators and Representatives on the JCCIC are appointed by the current Vice President. After the morning worship service, members of the JCCIC escort the President-elect and Vice President-elect to the White House. The President-elect and the outgoing President hold a short meeting and then head to the Capitol. They traditionally ride to the Capitol together in the same vehicle. Outgoing President Herbert Hoover and President-elect Franklin Roosevelt are pictured at right on Inauguration Day in 1933.

Outgoing President Herbert Hoover and President-Elect Franklin Roosevelt, 1933

In former times, the Vice President was sworn in at a separate ceremony in a different location from that of the President. Today, however, the Vice President is sworn in on the inaugural platform just before the President-elect takes the oath of office. The photo at right shows Al Gore being sworn in as Vice President. Vice Presidents who have been inaugurated since World War II have each

Al Gore Takes the Vice Presidential Oath of Office, 1993

been permitted to choose a friend or associate to administer to them the oath of office. The Chief Justice of the Supreme Court is almost always the one who administers the oath of office to the President.

George Washington began the tradition of delivering an inaugural address (or speech) on Inauguration Day. In these addresses Presidents usually outline their goals for America in the coming years. Inaugural ceremonies traditionally end with a prayer called a benediction.

George W. and Laura Bush Depart from the Capitol After Barack Obama's Inauguration, 2009

After the ceremony is completed, the outgoing President and First Lady leave the Capitol to begin their new lives. Since 1977 the President and First Lady have left in a helicopter unless the weather was too bad. The Marine helicopter pictured at left is carrying former President George W. Bush and First Lady Laura Bush away from the Capitol after Barack Obama became President in 2009.

Many countries around the world have faced fighting and bloodshed when there has been a change in political power. The United States of America has been blessed to enjoy peaceful transitions from one President to the next since our country was founded.

Inaugural Luncheon

From the mid-1800s until the mid-1900s, Presidents traditionally went to the White House after the inauguration ceremony to enjoy a luncheon hosted by the outgoing President and First Lady.

The luncheons became more and more elaborate throughout the 1900s. The JCCIC began their current tradition of hosting the Inaugural Luncheon in 1953 when Dwight D. Eisenhower became President. The luncheons often feature foods from the home states of the new President and Vice President. Speeches, gift presentations, and toasts are also a part of the luncheon programs. The luncheons serve as an official welcome from Congress to the new President and Vice President. Since 1981 the luncheons have been held in National Statuary Hall inside the U.S. Capitol. The luncheon for George H. W. Bush held in 1989 is pictured at right.

Inaugural Luncheon for George H. W. Bush, 1989

When Jimmy Carter became President in 1977, he wanted to make it clear that he was a plain man of the people. He and his family walked from the Capitol to the White House instead of riding in a limousine. President Carter also requested that the fancy Inaugural Luncheon be cancelled.

Inaugural Parade

After the Inaugural Luncheon, the new President and Vice President head toward the White House down Pennsylvania Avenue. Behind them comes the Inaugural Parade with military regiments, special groups of citizens, marching bands, and floats. The new President and Vice President watch the parade from a specially-built reviewing stand. The first organized Inaugural Parade took place in 1809 when James Madison became President. A float from the 1989 parade in honor of George H. W. Bush is pictured below. Also pictured below is the U.S. Army Old Guard Fife and Drum Corps that participated in the 2009 Inaugural Parade.

African American groups joined the Inaugural Parade for the first time when Abraham Lincoln began his second term in 1865. The first time women joined the procession was in 1917 at Woodrow Wilson's second inauguration. The largest Inaugural Parade on record was in 1953 after Dwight D. Eisenhower was sworn into office. That parade had so many people that it lasted over four and a half hours. Today the number of participants is limited to 15,000.

Eagle Float in the Inaugural Parade for George H. W. Bush, 1989

U.S. Army Old Guard Fife and Drum Corps in the Inaugural Parade for Barack Obama, 2009

Inaugural Ball

The first ball given in honor of a U.S. President was held in New York City one week after George Washington became President in 1789. Twenty years later, when James Madison became President, his wife Dolley hosted four hundred guests at a fancy party the night of the inauguration. That party was the beginning of the Inaugural Ball tradition. The balls were held after almost every inauguration until Warren Harding became President in 1921. Harding wanted to promote thriftiness and simplicity and requested that the ball be canceled. In its place, the chairman of the Inaugural Ball committee held an extravagant party at his house.

President and First Lady Obama at an Inaugural Ball in Downtown Washington, D.C., 2009

Charity balls became the fashion for the next several years until President Harry Truman brought back the fancy balls in 1949. One ball came to be insufficient for the number of guests who wanted to attend, so the tradition began for multiple balls to be held. The new President is expected to make an appearance at each one. Bill Clinton's second inauguration was followed by a record-setting fourteen balls! An inaugural ball from 2009 is pictured at left.

Righteous Leaders

Presidents who serve our country well are long remembered and respected. People visit their homes, read their memoirs, and quote phrases from their speeches. Each American voter has the opportunity to help elect people who will lead America with integrity and righteousness.

Loyalty and truth preserve the king,

and he upholds his throne by righteousness.

Proverbs 20:28

Family Activity

Plan an Honor Ceremony for someone you know. Instructions are on page 504.

FAMILY ACTIVITIES

Each of these activities goes with one of the lessons on American holidays. Have fun creating, eating, laughing, talking, and making memories together as a family. Please keep in mind that children should be supervised when using scissors or knives, using the stove or oven, looking up information online, and visiting public places or the homes of others.

INDEPENDENCE DAY

"HAPPY BIRTHDAY, AMERICA" POSTER

Create a nighttime scene of Washington, D.C., lit up by glittery fireworks!

Supplies:

black poster board

white construction paper

pencil

scissors

glue stick

liquid glue

glitter

white crayon or colored pencil

Instructions:

★ Use a pencil to draw simple outlines of the Washington Monument and the Lincoln Memorial on white construction paper as shown at right.

★ Cut out the buildings.

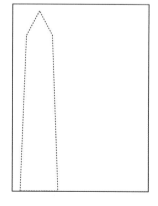

★ Glue the buildings on the black poster board as shown above. The bottom of the Washington Monument should be glued just under the top of the Lincoln Memorial so that it goes almost to the top of the poster board.

★ Squeeze liquid glue onto the poster board in the shape of fireworks. Sprinkle glitter over the wet glue. After the glue is completely dry (don't be impatient!), hold the poster board over a trash can and shake off the excess glitter.

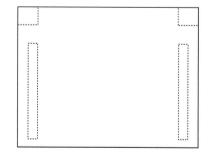

★ Write "Happy Birthday, America!" across the top of the poster using a white crayon or colored pencil.

National Aviation Day

Private Spacecraft Model

Make a 3-D model of a private spacecraft designed by you!

Supplies:

empty cardboard and plastic containers

scissors

glue

tape

wrapping paper and/or other types of paper

aluminum foil

markers, crayons, colored pencils, and/or paint

Instructions:

★ Let your imagination run wild as you create a spacecraft model. Look at the picture below to help get your creative juices flowing. Cut, glue, tape, and color to your heart's content. You can paint the empty containers or cover them with aluminum foil or wrapping paper. Everybody in the family can make one alone, or you might like to make one together. If there are young children in your family, you could make a model big enough for them to play in. You might be able to obtain a large box from an appliance store to use as part of your creation.

LABOR DAY

LABOR CHARADES

Give everyone in the family a turn to play this lively game!

Supplies:

small slips of paper

two empty baskets or bowls

pen or pencil

timer

Instructions:

★ Divide the members of your family into two teams. Have one person from Team A write each of the occupations from Occupation List B (on the next page) on a separate slip of paper. Cover up List A while this is being done so that the player will not see what is on that list. Fold the papers and drop them in an empty basket or bowl. Have one person from Team B do the same thing with Occupation List A. (The writers are making slips that the other team will use, so be sure they do not see them ahead of time.)

★ To play Labor Charades, set the timer for one minute. The first player on Team A draws a piece of paper out of his team's container and acts out the occupation written on it. The other members of Team A try to guess what the occupation is. The actor may not use any sounds. He may not point to or pick up anything in the room to help his team guess. He may only mime the actions of the occupation. If his team guesses correctly, the actor draws another piece of paper and acts out that occupation. If the team guesses correctly again, he may draw a third piece of paper, but three is the limit for his turn. After one minute, his team receives one point for each occupation he was able to get his team to guess (from 0 to 3 points). The first player from Team B then has a turn. Play continues until one team has used all of their papers, as long as both teams have had the same number of turns. The team with the most points at the end of the game wins.

Occupation List A

plumber

artist

taxi driver

landscaper

electrician

engineer

lawyer

preacher

construction worker

ballet dancer

fireman

doctor

veterinarian

coach

chef

mechanic

dentist

farmer

astronaut

animal trainer

mail carrier

bus driver

photographer

chiropractor

computer programmer

laundry worker

secretary

miner

musician

optometrist

tour guide

Occupation List B

teacher

reporter

writer

factory worker

truck driver

soldier

judge

waiter

janitor

clown

actor

police officer

nurse

football player

carpenter

cashier

archaeologist

real estate agent

accountant

pilot

scientist

barber

babysitter

fisherman

fashion designer

librarian

locksmith

maid

detective

security guard

carpet cleaner

PATRIOT DAY
A SPECIAL THANKS

Show the first responders in your community that you appreciate what they do.

Supplies:

patriotic stationery (bought or homemade)

pen or pencil

homemade treat such as cookies or brownies

red or blue paper plates

plastic wrap

Instructions:

★ Make or buy some patriotic stationery. If you chose to make it, you might create it on the computer and print it out, or you might draw your own design. Write a note of thanks to the police department, fire department, rescue squad, and ambulance service center in your community. Handwritten notes are usually even more appreciated than typed ones, so use your best handwriting and write your notes by hand. Thank the workers for all they do for your community. Tell them how much you appreciate the way they risk their own safety so that you can feel safe. You might want to include a Bible verse.

★ Make some cookies or brownies. You might like to use a star-shaped cookie cutter. When the cookies are done and cool, put some on four paper plates and wrap them in plastic wrap.

★ Make it a family outing to deliver the notes and cookies to the offices of the first responders in your area. When you make your deliveries, smile, look the workers in the eye, and tell them you appreciate the work they do. If your family likes to sing together, you could choose a patriotic song such as "America the Beautiful" or "God Bless America" to sing for the workers.

CONSTITUTION DAY AND CITIZENSHIP DAY

IMMIGRANT DINNER

Imagine that you are an immigrant who has just become a U.S. citizen.

Supplies:

all-American or international foods (see instructions)

table decorations to match dinner theme

Instructions:

★ Have everyone in your family pretend to be an immigrant. Everyone should choose a country of origin for themselves and an appropriate imaginary name from that country. Imagine that you have all just gone through a naturalization ceremony and are brand new American citizens. You are having a dinner together to celebrate. Everyone should dress nicely for the dinner. Immigrants who attend naturalization ceremonies are advised not to wear "jeans, shorts, or flip-flops."

★ You could choose to have an all-American dinner of chips and hotdogs, hamburgers and french fries, or macaroni and cheese. Or you could have an international meal with foods from one or more of the different countries your family is pretending to represent.

★ Set a nice table to match your chosen theme. If you are having an American meal, you can decorate the table with red, white, and blue. If you are having an international meal, you could set a globe in the middle of the table. Another idea is to pretend you are at a fancy restaurant and use a nice white tablecloth, cloth napkins, and china.

★ As you are eating your dinner, go around the table and give everyone a turn to ask the following questions to the person on their right. When asked, each person should make up imaginary answers.

- What is your name?
- What country are you from?
- Why did you decide to emigrate?
- What do you do for a living?
- Why are you excited to be a U.S. citizen?

LEIF ERIKSON DAY

NORDIC CENTERPIECE

Embroidery is an Icelandic craft that goes back many centuries. The traditional designs are mostly geometric. Make a centerpiece for your family's table using this traditional Nordic embroidery pattern.

Supplies:

one piece of white poster board

scissors

ruler

92 popsicle sticks

markers, crayons, or paint

Instructions:

★ Cut the poster board down to 22" x 22".

★ Have everyone in the family work together to color or paint the popsicle sticks. You will need 36 dark green, 20 medium blue, 20 golden yellow, and 16 light grey. You will need to break in half four of the popsicle sticks that are going to be blue. Break them before you paint them. To break them neatly, mark the center of the four sticks. Firmly hold each stick (one at a time) so that the center is directly over the edge of a table. Gently push down on the end that is hanging off to break it in half. Carefully smooth the edges and pull off any wooden splinters. The edges might be sharp, so be careful not to poke yourself. The pattern for one of the blue areas is shown enlarged above.

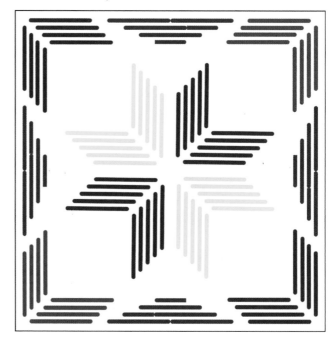

★ Glue the popsicle sticks onto the poster board as shown at right.

COLUMBUS DAY
ITALIAN HERITAGE MEAL

Celebrate Italian heritage with a pasta meal and Italian decorations.

Supplies:

spaghetti, lasagna, or pizza dinner

green, white, and red construction paper

scissors

ruler

tape

recorded Italian music

Instructions:

★ Prepare a meal of spaghetti, lasagna, or pizza. If you decide to have rolls with your meal, you could toss them to each other like the Orlando Bread Company does at the Italian Heritage Parade in Cleveland (if it's okay with Dad and Mom, of course!).

★ Make Italian flag placemats. For each placemat, cut one piece of green, one piece of white, and one piece of red construction paper down to 5″ x 10″. Tape the three sections together as shown above.

★ Make an Italian flag table runner. Tape one piece of green, one piece of white, and one piece of red construction paper end to end as shown below.

★ Play some Italian music while you enjoy your Italian heritage meal!

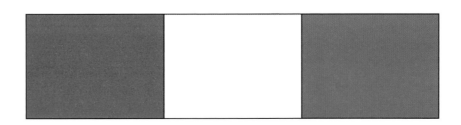

Veterans Day

Veteran Memory Book

Honor a veteran you know by preserving some of his memories in a special book.

Supplies:

audio or video recording device (optional)

computer

scanner (optional)

camera

stapler

Memories of Charles L. Boyd

Instructions:

★ As a family, visit a veteran you know. When you set up your visit, tell the veteran that you would like to hear stories about when he or she served in the military. Tell them about your project and make sure it is something of which they would like to be a part. Many memories that veterans have are painful and they do not like to talk about them. Sometimes, however, a veteran enjoys having people around who are good listeners and want to hear about their experiences.

★ When you are visiting, take notes about what the veteran is saying. On the next page is a list of suggested questions to ask. Different people in your family can be responsible for asking the various questions. You might want to use an audio or video recording device. Be sure to listen attentively to what the veteran is saying. Take a picture of the veteran while you are visiting. You might ask the veteran to loan you a few pictures of his life before, during, and after his military service. You might also take photographs of any uniforms, medals, or memorabilia the veteran has. These things might be hard to find, so be sure the veteran doesn't feel that he needs to go to any trouble to get them for you. Before you leave, make sure you tell the veteran how much you appreciate the service that he gave to our country.

VETERAN MEMORY BOOK (CONTINUED)

★ Use a computer to make a short book about the veteran you visited. Include the picture that you took while you were visiting. If you borrowed any pictures, scan them in and use them in your book as well. Create a patriotic cover for the book. Print off the pages and staple them together. Make one for your family and one for the veteran. You might also want to make books for other members of the veteran's family.

★ Go back to visit the veteran and take him his copy of the book you made. Thank him for sharing his memories with your family. Thank him again for his military service.

Suggested Questions

1. Where and when were you born?

2. What made you decide to join the military?

3. When did you join?

4. What process did you have to go through to join?

5. What happened at boot camp?

6. Where were you stationed?

7. What were your duties?

8. How was the food?

9. What is something funny that happened while you were in the military?

10. What is something scary that happened?

11. What is a time you were able to help someone else?

12. What is a time someone else helped you?

THANKSGIVING DAY
PARADE FLOAT MODEL

Design your own float for the Macy's Thanksgiving Day parade!

Supplies:

shoebox lid, cereal box, or some other material to use for a base

buttons, sequins, beads, artificial feathers, artificial flowers, stickers, tissue paper, etc.

miniature toys or furniture

wrapping paper

glue

scissors

Instructions:

★ Wrap the base in wrapping paper. Use a variety of craft supplies to create your model. You might want to incorporate miniature toys or furniture in your design. Look at the photos on this page to get some inspiration. Have fun!

★ Alternate idea: Use a toy construction set (such LEGOs) to create your float model.

Pearl Harbor Remembrance Day

"A Date Which Will Live in Infamy" Play

Act out this short play to get a feel for what Americans experienced on December 7, 1941.

Supplies:

script (pages 498-499)

Bible

costumes (optional, see instructions)

Instructions:

★ Decide who in your family will play each of the roles in the play. If you have more people in your family than there are roles, you can add more children to the family in the play and let them say some of Susan's or Jimmy's lines. You can also change Susan to Rick or Jimmy to Nan if you need a different number of male or female characters.

★ You don't have to have an audience when you act out the play, but if you would like to put it on for grandparents or other family or friends, they would surely enjoy it.

★ If you would like your characters to wear costumes, here are some suggestions:

○ Father: dress pants and dress shirt

○ Mother: dress and apron

○ Jimmy: jeans or overalls and T-shirt or plaid button-down shirt

○ Susan: dress or plaid skirt and white blouse

A Date Which Will Live in Infamy

Scene 1

Susan is sitting quietly reading a book. A Bible is lying on a table nearby. Jimmy rushes into the room.

Susan: What's wrong?

Jimmy: The Japanese attacked Hawaii this morning!

Susan: Are you kidding?

Jimmy: No, I'm not kidding! They did!

Mother enters.

Susan: Mother, Jimmy just said the Japanese attacked us this morning!

Jimmy: It's true! Sam Howard just called over the fence that he heard it on the radio.

Susan: Did people die?

Jimmy: Thousands of them!

Susan: Oh, Mother! I'm scared!

Mother: It's going to be okay, Susan.

Susan: Where is Daddy?

Mother: He took a walk. He'll be back soon.

Jimmy: Is Daddy going to have to fight?

Mother: I don't know, Jimmy.

Father enters.

Mother: Have you heard?

Father: Yes. Mr. Howard met me on the sidewalk and told me.

Jimmy *(pauses)*: Are you still going to take us to the air show this afternoon after church?

Father: No. The air show was canceled. I saw several of the planes flying off when I was outside.

Susan: But why can't they still have the show? I was looking forward to it.

Father: The pilots have to get back home so they can get ready to defend our country. This is war. War changes a lot of things. I know it's frightening, but God is still in control. Jimmy, read to us from Psalm 112.

Jimmy (*picks up the Bible, turns to the passage, and reads*):

> Praise the Lord!
>
> How blessed is the man who fears the Lord,
>
> Who greatly delights in His commandments.
>
> His descendants will be mighty on earth;
>
> The generation of the upright will be blessed.
>
> Wealth and riches are in his house,
>
> And his righteousness endures forever.
>
> Light arises in the darkness for the upright;
>
> He is gracious and compassionate and righteous.
>
> It is well with the man who is gracious and lends;
>
> He will maintain his cause in judgment.
>
> For he will never be shaken;
>
> The righteous will be remembered forever.
>
> He will not fear evil tidings;
>
> His heart is steadfast, trusting in the Lord.

Mother: That's right. We don't have to fear these evil tidings as long as we are trusting in the Lord. That will be a good verse to remember while we are getting ready for church. It's almost time to go.

Father, Mother, Susan, and Jimmy exit.

Scene 2

Father, Mother, Susan, and Jimmy are sitting around the living room.

Father: What happened at school today?

Susan: Everyone was talking about the attack yesterday. The principal called an assembly and we all listened to President Roosevelt give his speech to Congress.

Father: We listened to it at work, too.

Mother: I listened to it here.

Jimmy: I'd say just about the whole country listened to it.

Father: Children, I want you to remember well what has happened the last two days. When you are old and grey, people will still be talking about the attack on Pearl Harbor. They might ask you to tell them what you were doing when you heard the news. Like the President said, December 7 is a date which will live in infamy.

BILL OF RIGHTS DAY

FREEDOM OF SPEECH DRIVEWAY

Let everyone in the family exercise their freedom of speech with chalk!

Supplies:

sidewalk chalk

Instructions:

★ Go outside with enough sidewalk chalk for the whole family. If you do not have a paved driveway, you might ask a friend or relative if you can use theirs.

★ Everyone should use words or pictures to communicate things that they want other American citizens to know. Topics might include sayings or proverbs, things you like about America, things you believe should be different, or political candidates you support.

★ Remember that even though as Americans we have freedom of speech, as Christians we must choose our words carefully and be kind and considerate of other people.

CHRISTMAS DAY
THEMED CHRISTMAS TREE

Choose a special theme for a Christmas tree in your house.

Supplies:

Christmas tree (live or artificial)

themed decorations

Instructions:

★ Work together as a family to decorate a Christmas tree in your house with special decorations that center around a certain theme. Gather or make the decorations and put them on the tree while you listen to Christmas music. You could choose one of the themes that a First Lady has chosen for a White House Christmas Tree, or you can come up with your own. Here are some additional theme ideas:

- ◦ your state

- ◦ your family

- ◦ red, white, and blue

- ◦ things of nature

★ When you are finished, pretend Dad and Mom are the President and First Lady and take a picture of them standing in front of the tree as is typically done in the White House each year.

New Year's Day

Home of the Commandant Brunch

Welcome the new year with a special meal and some patriotic music.

Supplies:

brunch menu items (see instructions)

patriotic music

Instructions:

★ You can make your brunch for just your household, or you can invite other family and friends to join you. Here are some suggested menu items:

- Main Dish: quiche, french toast casserole, sausage biscuits, scrambled eggs

- Sides: hashbrowns, fruit salad, roasted potatoes, fried apples, grits

- Bread: muffins, quick bread, biscuits

★ Play patriotic music as you enjoy your meal together.

★ When "The President's Own" serenaded the commandant and his wife on New Year's Day in 2012, one of the songs they performed was "Bless This House" by May H. Brahe. Have someone in your family sing or read the lyrics of this song as you pray for God's blessings on your home in the coming year.

THE
CONVENING OF CONGRESS
LETTERS OF THANKS

Let a member of Congress know that you appreciate what they are doing.

Supplies:

stationery

pens or pencils

Instructions:

★ Have everyone in your family write a letter of thanks to one of the U.S. Senators from your state or the U.S. Representative from your district. Thank the Congressman for their service. Tell them a little bit about yourself and your family. Let them know that you homeschool. Write about issues that are important to you and things you think should happen or should not happen in America. Write your letters by hand on nice stationery. Be sure that your letters are kind and respectful. Younger children can draw a picture of an American flag or of the U.S. Capitol.

★ Put all of your family's letters and pictures in one envelope and mail them to your Senator or Representative.

★ Pray together for the member of Congress you chose. Pray that God will give him or her wisdom and guidance. Pray that this person will stand for what is right.

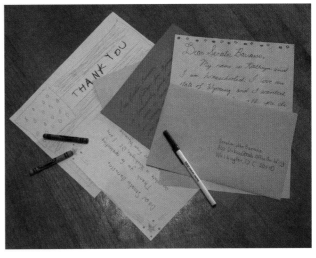

INAUGURATION DAY

HONOR CEREMONY

Give honor to someone you know in a very special way.

Supplies:

decorations

special meal

Instructions:

★ Choose someone your family knows and respects and would like to honor. It could be Mom or Dad, Grandma or Grandpa, a neighbor, a relative, or a friend. Plan a special ceremony to honor this person. Decorate your porch or a room in your house for the ceremony. You could choose a patriotic theme, or you could put a vase of flowers on a table with a pretty tablecloth. Everyone should dress up for the occasion.

★ Plan the ceremony. Here are some suggestions:

   ◦ Have different members of your family write a paragraph to read during the ceremony about why the honoree is special and why the family respects him or her. Younger children can draw a picture and present it to the honoree.

   ◦ Select one or more songs to sing or play during the ceremony. Hymns, folk songs, and patriotic songs are some possibilities.

   ◦ Have one person say a prayer, thanking God for the honoree and asking for God's blessing on the honoree's life.

★ Eat a special meal together.

★ If you would like, you could enjoy some dancing after the meal. You might look up some instructions for simple folk dances that would be fun for the whole family.

SOURCES

Articles

"Bilingual Voting Ballots Ordered in 25 States for 2012," *Alaska Journal of Commerce*

"Interview with a US Ambassador," www.jobshadow.com/ interview-a-with-us-ambassador/

"Joey Chestnut wins 6th straight hot-dog-eating title, downing 68 dogs," *Los Angeles Times*, July 4, 2012

"Matamoras to hold annual duck race July 4," *Times Herald-Record* (Middletown, New York), June 6, 2012

"Pony Express: Romance Versus Reality," Smithsonian National Postal Museum

"Sanitation plans massive cleanup after Times Square New Year's Eve celebration," *Staten Island Advance*, December 31, 2009

"The Busiest Man of His Age in the World," *New York Times*, Nov. 20, 1910

"Where have You Gone, Miss Columbia?" *Voice of America*, October 27, 2009

Amer, Mildred L. "The First Day of a New Congress: A Guide to Proceedings on the House Floor," Congressional Research Service of the Library of Congress.

Amer, Mildred L. "The First Day of a New Congress: A Guide to Proceedings on the Senate Floor," Congressional Research Service of the Library of Congress.

Baker, Richard A. "Traditions of the United States Senate," www.senate.gov

Ballhaus, Rebecca. "July 4th Fireworks: 15 of the Biggest Shows in America Ranked" AOL Travel, June 28, 2011

Berg, Ellen, "Where Is Miss Columbia?" Library of Congress.

Bumiller, Elisabeth. "Inside the Presidency," *National Geographic*, January 2009. http://ngm.nationalgeographic. com/print/2009/01/President/bumiller-text, retrieved July 11, 2012.

Chosick, Amy. "Bigger, Brighter, Louder," *Wall Street Journal*, July 3, 2009

Coleman, Kevin J., Joseph E. Cantor, Thomas H. Neal, "Presidential Elections in the United States: A Primer," Congressional Research Service of the Library of Congress.

Dang, Dan Thanh. "City Fees Push 'American' Parade to Dundalk," *Baltimore Sun*, September 9, 1994

De la Garza, Paul. "Mission Completed: Veteran's Persistence Leads to Perpetual Remembrance Day of Pearl Harbor Attack," *Chicago Tribune*, December 7, 1994

Gailey, Phil, "Democrats and Republicans Form Panel to Hold Presidential Debates," *New York Times*, February 19, 1987

Hart, Alexander C., "Pardoned turkeys off to Disneyland," *Los Angeles Times*, November 26, 2009

Haygood, Wil. "Eugene Allen, White House butler for 8 Presidents, dies at 90," *Washington Post*, April 2, 2010. http://www.washingtonpost.com/wp-dyn/content/ article/2010/04/01/AR2010040103444.html, retrieved July 12, 2012.

Jackson, David, "Obamas stay in on New Year's Eve," *USA Today*, December 31, 2010

Johnson, Haynes, "1968 Democratic Convention: The Bosses Strike Back," *Smithsonian Magazine*, August 2008

Korch, Travers. "The Explosive Costs of Big Firework Displays," *FOX News Network*, June 27, 2012

Lacitis, Eric. "Leif Erickson statue refuses to budge for the third straight day," *Seattle Times*, March 1, 2007

Lobel, Michael. "John Sloan: Figuring the Painter in the Crowd," *Art Bulletin*, September 1, 2011

Maskell, Jack. "Beginning and End of the Terms of United States Senators Chosen to Fill Senate Vacancies," Congressional Research Service of the Library of Congress.

McGeehan, Patrick, "Spurned by Lady Liberty, Macy's Fireworks Show Stays Put," *New York Times*, July 1, 2011

Perkes, Courtney. "Star of Disney Parade is a real turkey," *Orange County Register*, November 9, 2009

Pontius, John S., and Faye M. Bullock, "Congressional Staff: Duties and Functions," www.llsdc.org, retrieved June 25, 2012.

"The Role of Congressional Staff," www.sgim.org, retrieved June 25, 2012

"Roles of Congressional Staff Members," www.geron.org, retrieved June 25, 2012

Seidenberg, Steve. "The View from the Hill: Working as a Congressional Staffer," www.lawcrossing.com, retrieved June 25, 2012

"Who's Who in a Congressional Office," www.nann.org, retrieved June 25, 2012

Robbins, Liz. "Schools Spend on Debates, but Gain Prestige," *New York Times*, October 15, 2008

Schneider, Judy and Michael L. Koempel, "The First Day of a New Congress: A Guide to Proceedings on the Senate Floor," Congressional Research Service of the Library of Congress.

Thomas, Robert McG. Jr. "Lillian Parks, 100, Dies; Had 'Backstairs' White House View," *New York Times*, November 12, 1997, http://www.nytimes.com/1997/11/12/ us/lillian-parks-100-dies-had-backstairs-white-house-view. html, retrieved July 12, 2012.

Trescott, Jacqueline. "Newseum to Open April 11," *Washington Post*, February 7, 2008

Books

Boutell, Lewis Henry. *The Life of Roger Sherman*, 1896

Holanda, Ray. *A History of Aviation Safety: Featuring the U.S. Airline System*, 2009

Keogh, Edward A. "A Brief History of the Air Mail Service of the U.S. Post Office Department" from *Saga of the U.S. Air Mail Service*, 1927

McCullough, David. *Truman*. New York: Simon and Schuster, 1992.

Nichols, Frederick D., and James A. Bear Jr. *Monticello: A Guide Book*. Monticello: Thomas Jefferson Memorial Foundation, 1982.

Sprague, Donovin Arleigh. *Images of America: Rosebud Sioux*, Arcadia Publishing, Charleston, SC. 2005.

Business and Tourism Organizations

Carol M. Highsmith Photography, Inc.
Discovery Communications
Frankenmuth Chamber of Commerce
Good Worldwide, LLC
Independence Chamber of Commerce
Louisville Area Chamber of Commerce
Metropolitan Council of St. Paul, Minnesota
Morris Communications Company, LLC
Nathan's Famous, Inc.
Nauvoo Grape Festival Association
New York City Tourist
Orlando Baking Company
Santa Cruz County Fair and Rodeo Association
Scholastic, Inc.
Scripps Networks, LLC
Seattle Convention and Visitors Bureau
Seattle Foundation
Times Square District Management Association, Inc.
U-Haul International, Inc.

Civic, Historical, and Other Organizations

1 for All
American Battle Monuments Commission
American Democracy Project. "The Importance of Constitution Day: Constitution Day Planning Guide" by Katheyn Kolbert
Arbor Day Foundation
Blue Angels Association
British Museum
Calvin Coolidge Memorial Foundation
Camp Sherman Memorial Museum & Campus
Carter Center
Carter Presidential Library
Chicago Historical Society
Commission on Presidential Debates
Fair Vote
Family of Amelia Earhart
First Amendment Center
Ford Presidential Library
Franklin D. Roosevelt Presidential Library and Museum
Gold Coast Railroad Museum, Miami, Florida
Greis, Gloria Polizzotti. "Vikings on the Charles or, The Strange Saga of Dighton Rock, Norumbega, and Rumford Double-Acting Baking Powder," Needham (Massachusetts) Historical Society
Italian Heritage Parade, San Francisco, California

John S. and James L. Knight Foundation
Knights of Columbus
League of Women Voters
Leif Erickson International Foundation, "The Saga of Seattle's Leif Erikson Statue" and "Leif the Lucky" by Kristine Leander.
Massachusetts Historical Society
Museum of London
National Constitution Center, "Celebrate Bill of Rights Day: Tweet for Freedom," by Ken Paulson.
National First Ladies' Library
National Geographic Society
New York Avenue Presbyterian Church
Newseum
Nordic Heritage Museum, Seattle, Washington
Ohio Historical Society
Pacific Historical Parks
Pasadena Tournament of Roses
Republican National Committee
Republican Party of Iowa
Runestone Museum
St. John's Episcopal Lafayette Square
The American Presidency Project
The Charles A. and Anne Morrow Lindbergh Foundation
Thomas Jefferson Center
Thomas Jefferson Foundation, Inc.
Tuskegee Airmen National Historic Museum
White House Historical Association
White House Museum
X Prize Foundation

Government Agencies

Air Force Material Command, Media Gallery
Alaska Aviation System Plan
Alaska State Division of Elections, "Election Procedures for Bilingual Election Workers and Translators"
Architect of the Capitol
Biographical Directory of the United States Congress, U.S. Congress
California Secretary of State
Center of Military History, United States Army
Citizenship and Immigration Services
Communications-Electronics Command Historical Office, United States Army
Congressional Budget Office
Connecticut State Library
Federal Aviation Association
Federal Election Commission
General Services Administration
Government Accountability Office
Government Printing Office
Library of Congress
Mackinac Bridge Authority
National Aeronautics and Space Administration
National Archives and Records Administration
National Park Service, Liberty Bell Center
National Portrait Gallery
Naval History and Heritage Command, United States Navy.
Tennessee State Library and Archives
U.S. Capitol Police
U.S. Census Bureau
U.S. Centennial of Flight Commission
U.S. Congress, Joint Committee on Printing
U.S. Department of Defense
U.S. Department of Homeland Security

U.S. Department of Justice
U.S. Department of Labor
U.S. Department of State, Bureau of Public Affairs, Office of
  Public Communication
U.S. Department of Veterans Affairs
U.S. House of Representatives, Office of the Clerk
U.S. Marine Corps
U.S. Senate
White House
Wisconsin Courts

Magazines and News Organizations
ABC News
Boyd, Andrew. *Engines of Ingenuity*, Episode 2756, KUHF-
  FM, Houston, Texas
CBS News
Cleveland Live, LLC
Des Moines (Iowa) Register
Desert Turtle Productions
Folkenflik, David. "For Election News, Voters Still Turn to
  Old Media," NPR, Feb. 8, 2012
FOX News 2, Detroit, Michigan
KTNA Talkeetna (Alaska) Community Radio
Seabrook, Andrew. "GOP's Birthplace: A Wisconsin
  Schoolhouse," NPR
Smithsonian Magazine, Smithsonian Institution
Stars and Stripes
The Atlantic
Time
Washington Post
Xenia (Ohio) Citizens Journal

Reference Websites
www.britannica.com
www.history.com
www.merriam-webster.com

Universities
Cornell University Law School Legal Information Institute
Georgetown University, Berkley Center for Religion, Peace,
  and World Affairs
Marist College
Pennsylvania State University, Pennsylvania Center for the
  Book
University of Arizona Library
University of Iowa Department of Computer Science, Voting
  and Elections web pages, Douglas W. Jones
University of New Hampshire
University of Virginia, American Studies: The Capitol
  Project, The City Beautiful Movement
University of Virginia, George Washington Papers
University of Virginia, Miller Center for Public Affairs,
  "American President: A Reference Resource," Warren
  Gamaliel Harding

Videos
American Experience: Theodore Roosevelt, PBS
Becoming American: The Chinese Experience, PBS/Bill Moyers
  special
Destination America, PBS
The Duel, PBS
God in America: Frontline/American Experience, PBS

IMAGE CREDITS

Notgrass Family

Charlene Notgrass, 2 (all except t), 4, 5m, 6t, 7, 11tr, 16t, 20bl, 27, 42, 48, 50, 57tl/tm, 58tl/bm, 62br, 63, 64r, 66, 77b, 82b, 83b, 89r, 90b, 99t, 100, 102, 156, 168, 193, 197b, 199t, 295 (Carter marker), 310br

Mev McCurdy, front cover (bottom five portraits), 54, 409r, 485b, 488, 501, 504

Notgrass Family Archive, 3, 495

Library of Congress

Carol M. Highsmith's America, Library of Congress, 5t/b, 6b, 8, 9, 11br, 12, 14, 15, 16b, 17, 20m/br, 23, 24, 26, 30, 31 (top three), 33t, 34, 44b, 47, 55 (Capitol, Hoover Building, Lighthouse), 56 (OH, FL, WI), 57br, 58tm/br, 61t, 62mr, 76b, 89tl, 95, 121t/m, 123tl, 127ml, 136, 157, 177, 178b, 180tl, 181, 182, 217br, 230b, 237t, 238b, 242t, 249 (top three), 250b, 251t/m, 252m, 256b, 258 (top five), 259tr/bl/br, 260, 261 (top three), 267 (top four), 276t, 298m, 301b, 310bl, 316, 320t, 329, 341, 347m, 348b, 354tr, 358t, 361tr/bl/br, 362, 363, 364, 365, 366t, 370m, 387, 388 (all except bl), 389, 390, 391 (all except bottom three), 394tl/bl, 401b, 406, 433b, 483bl

Library of Congress, 18, 38 (top three), 44t, 45, 51, 67, 68m, 70, 72, 74m/b, 75 (Halterman, Kennedy), 76m, 77 (Knudsen, draft), 83 (GA flag), 84, 86t, 88, 90t, 94, 97, 103br, 106b, 109t, 113tr, 116tr, 120ml, 125t/m, 133t, 134, 135, 137, 138, 140, 141t/m, 142, 145, 146, 147t/m, 148, 155b, 167, 171, 178t, 180tr/mr/br, 184, 185t, 186tr, 189, 190, 191ml/mr, 197t, 199 (all Carter Campaign), 200, 201, 202, 204, 205, 208t, 212tl, 223tl, 224, 229, 232, 247, 248, 249b (Jack E. Boucher), 250t, 251b, 264, 265tl, 271b, 282, 298t/b, 300tr/br, 324t/b, 331b, 336t, 339, 355, 360, 388bl, 391 (bottom three), 401t, 402t, 403, 404t, 407, 408, 410t, 419, 420, 425, 429, 431, 432, 437, 438, 439 (top four), 441tl, 443, 444, 445, 449, 450, 454, 455, 456, 457t, 464bl, 467t, 470, 475, 479, 481

Other Libraries

Bush 41 Library (Flickr, CC BY 2.0), 126 (party/cake), 295 (Bush ladies)

Bush Library, 128t, 272t, 274m (Bush), 276bl/bm/br, 277 (top three), 278 (three George H. W. Bush), 279 (George H. W. Bush), 280t/b, 281, 291 (Bush), 293t, 295 (Bush reading, Johnson/Bush, Bush/Robb), 300 (Shari Lewis), 303, 304 (Christmas m), 305tl, 307, 330tr, 462t

Clinton Library, 279 (Clinton), 463t

Cornell University Library, ii

Jimmy Carter Library, 291 (Carter)

John F. Kennedy Presidential Library and Museum, Boston, 302t (Robert Knudsen/White House Photographs), 464t/m (Abbie Rowe/White House Photographs)

National Archives, 29, 30bl/br, 32t/b, 33m/b, 36, 37, 38bl/br, 39, 40, 42t, 46, 62tr, 73l, 77 (Clinton), 92tm, 103tr, 160t, 263, 265tm/tr/br, 267b, 268b, 269, 270m/tr, 271tr/ml, 272ml, 273, 274b, 277b, 278b, 279t/b, 284t/b, 285t, 287, 291 (Kennedy, Clinton, Ford, Reagan), 292 (Girl Scouts/Mother Teresa), 293 (Clintons/Carters), 294 (bottom three), 295 (Bess Truman, Johnson/Trumans), 299, 301t, 302 (Reagan, Ford), 305ml, 309, 310 (Truman in office)/(Carter photo by David Valdez), 330tl/tm, 357, 358m/b, 359t, 369, 422

Reagan Library, 292 (King Fahd), 295 (home of Senator Kennedy, Bushes/Reagans), 300 (Dave Brubeck Quartet), 304 (Christmas t/b)

Seattle Municipal Archives (Flickr, CC BY 2.0), 409l

U.S. Military

The California National Guard (Flickr, CC BY 2.0), 415t (Spc. Eddie Siguenza)

Chairman of the Joints Chiefs of Staff (Flickr, CC BY 2.0), 107, 127t, 441tr

DVIDSHUB (Flickr, CC BY 2.0), 79, 93br, 109b (Mass Communications Specialist 2nd Class Julia A. Casper), 114tl (Tech. Sgt. Jerry Morrison, Navy Visual News Service), 411b (Pfc. Donald Watkins)

Georgia National Guard (Flickr, CC BY 2.0), 295 (Carter/National Guard)

isafmedia (Flickr, CC BY 2.0), 150t (Sgt. April Campbell), 333bl

The National Guard (Flickr, CC BY 2.0), 280 (soldier salute), 286b, 380

NYCMarines (Flickr, CC BY 2.0), 80b (Sgt. Randall A. Clinton)

Official U.S. Navy Imagery (Flickr, CC BY 2.0), 127mr (Mass Communication Specialist 3rd Class Joshua D. Sheppard), 283br, 452tl (Mass Communication Specialist 2nd Class Ben A. Gonzales), 452tr (Mass Communication Specialist 3rd Class Michael A. Lantron), 375

RDECOM (Flickr, CC BY 2.0), 343 (military leaders meet with staffers)

Secretary of Defense (Flickr, CC BY 2.0), 236b

U.S. Air Force, 414 (Senior Airman Jonathan Steffan)

U.S. Army (Flickr, CC BY 2.0), 126m (Sgt. 1st Class Kevin McDaniel), 147b (Jay Mann), 150b (Mollie Miller, 1st Infantry Division Public Affairs), 212tr/bl, 268t/m, 270l, 415b (Leslie Benito), 466b (Van Williams, USACE), 343t (D. Myles Cullen), 359br (Senior Airman Andrew Lee), 378b

U.S. Army Africa (Flickr, CC BY 2.0), 271mr

U.S. Army Corps of Engineers (Flickr, CC BY 2.0), 413, 468t (Chris Gardner, New York District)

U.S. Army, 32b (Staff Sgt. Teddy Wade), 447t (Spc. Edward A. Garibay)/m (Spc. Karah Cohen), 464br (Samantha L. Quigley), 465tr (SPC Angel Turner), 465 (carolers/Spc. Kristina L. Gupton)

U.S. Department of Defense (Flickr, CC BY 2.0), 452bl/br, 453, 480, 482t/b (Mass Communication Specialist 1st Class Chad J. McNeeley), 483br (Mass Communication Specialist 1st Class Mark O'Donald, U.S. Navy), 484 (Tech. Sgt. Suzanne Day, U.S. Air Force)

U.S. Marine Corps, 447b (Lance Cpl. Patricia D. Lockhart), 465 (men in boxes/Lance Cpl. Jody Lee Smith), 465br (Cpl. Colby W. Brown), 471t (Sgt. Christopher M. Tirado)/b (Cpl. Erin A Kirk), 503 (Cpl. Erin A. Kirk-Cuomo)

U.S. Navy, 112m, 416 (Seaman Christopher Hall)

UNC - CFC - USFK (Flickr, CC BY 2.0), 422br

USACEpublicaffairs (Flickr, CC BY 2.0), 359mr

USACE-Sacramento District (Flickr, CC BY 2.0), 326t

West Point Public Affairs (Flickr, CC BY 2.0), 165 (Giuliani), 394m, 417

Government Agencies

Architect of the Capitol, 35, 139, 315, 317, 318 (all except 2nd), 319, 320 (bottom four), 321, 323, 326 (bottom four), 327, 328, 330bl/bm/br, 331t, 332, 333tr/mr, 334, 335, 338, 342, 343bl/br, 344bl/br, 345bl/br, 346, 347t, 350, 351, 352, 353, 354 (all except tr), 356, 359bl, 361bm, 473

Collection of the U.S. House of Representatives, 476b

Grand Canyon NPS (Flickr, CC BY 2.0), 20t, 424

Idaho National Laboratory (Flickr, CC BY 2.0), 286t

Metropolitan Transit Authority of the State of New York (Flickr, CC BY 2.0), 404b

Montana Legislative Services Division/Montana State Library, 153b

NASA Goddard Photo and Video (Flickr, CC BY 2.0), 451

NASA, 55tr, 74t

National Atlas, 151, 152

National Park Service (Flickr, CC BY 2.0), 255tm/tr

National Park Service, 11tl (John F. Mitchell), 55 (Craters), 120t (Betty Agati), 120mr, 122t, 123tr, 244t/m, 253tm

nigeria.usembassy.gov, 75b

Office of the Speaker of the House, 360l (Caleb Smith)

Oregon DOT (Flickr, CC BY 2.0), 57bl

U.S. Department of Agriculture, 55 (Owl/Bear), 257t (Lance Cheung)

U.S. Department of State, 295 (Clinton/Krishna), 367, 370t/b, 371 (all except astronauts), 372, 381, 382, 383, 384 (all except Ireland), 385, 392

U.S. Fish and Wildlife Service, 55 (Wildlife Refuge, Fish Hatchery), 89bl (Roy Lowe)

U.S. Mission Geneva (Flickr, CC BY 2.0), 285m

U.S. Senate Collection, 114bl, 483t

U.S. Senate Photo Studio, 324, 474

USDA (Flickr, CC BY 2.0), 62bl (Lance Cheung), 64l

USDA Forest Service, 82 (MT)

USDAgov (Flickr, CC BY 2.0), 284m, 293b

USFWS Pacific Southwest Region (Flickr, CC BY 2.0), 62ml (Bigger),

White House Photo, 128bm/br, 198t (Pete Souza), 280 (Obama with advisors), 292t (Chuck Kennedy), 300t (Pete Souza), 304t (Eric Draper), 360r

Other Sources

~MVI~ (goes miorror-less!) (Flickr, CC BY 2.0), 238bl

adactio (Flickr, CC BY 2.0), 220t

adamentmeat (Flickr, CC BY 2.0), 99b

aflcio (Flickr, CC BY 2.0), 187bl, 188tl/tr

akasped (Flickr, CC BY 2.0), 91 (AR)

Alex E. Proimos (Flickr, CC BY 2.0), 306

alvesfamily (Flickr, CC BY 2.0), 262

American Federation of Government Employees (Flickr, CC BY 2.0), 439b, 440b

AmericanSolutions (Flickr, CC BY 2.0), 165 (Gingrich)

amslerPIX (Flickr, CC BY 2.0), 195b

Ann Kite (Flickr, CC BY 2.0), 221b, 418b

Anthony Quintano (Flickr, CC BY 2.0), 393

Arden (Flickr, CC BY 2.0), 461bl

arianravan (Flickr, CC BY 2.0), 141b

Austen Hufford (Flickr, CC BY 2.0), 274t

Balalities (Flickr, CC BY 2.0), 457b

Ben Novakovic (Flickr, CC BY 2.0), 467b

Bernard Pollack (Flickr, CC BY 2.0), 394br, 410bl

Beth Rankin (Flickr, CC BY 2.0), 187tr

Bethany Poore, 119 (map)

Beverly & Pack (Flickr, CC BY 2.0), 411t

big mike – DC (Flickr, CC BY 2.0), 349 (motorcycle)

Bill Jacobus (Flickr, CC BY 2.0), 409m

Bob Mical (Flickr, CC BY 2.0), 459

bosc d'anjou (Flickr, CC BY 2.0), 58bl

Boston Public Library (Flickr, CC BY 2.0), 400

bradleygee (Flickr, CC BY 2.0), 81 (CO)

braveheartsports (Flickr, CC BY 2.0), 82 (soccer)

Bryan Alexander (Flickr, CC BY 2.0), 217tl, 219mr (no people)/br

bsabarnowl (Flickr, CC BY 2.0), 240bl

BU Interactive News (Flickr, CC BY 2.0), 164 (Romney/Sarah Mongeau-Birkett), 175t (Sarah Mongeau-Birkett), 186bl, 191bl, 192t

Cam Vilay (Flickr, CC BY 2.0), 49

Celso Flores (Flickr, CC BY 2.0), 93mr

ChadoeKyll (Flickr, CC BY 2.0), 56 (NE)

Charles Atkeison (Flickr, CC BY 2.0), 405t

Charleston's TheDigitel (Flickr, CC BY 2.0), 217tr

Chas Redmond (Flickr, CC BY 2.0), 428

chefranden (Flickr, CC BY 2.0), 98t

chmeredith (Flickr, CC BY 2.0), 91 (MS)

Christopher Macsurak (Flickr, CC BY 2.0), 62tl

cliff1066™ (Flickr, CC BY 2.0), 92br, 113bm/br, 114bm, 115, 116bl/bm/br, 118bm/br, 119bl/bm/br, 120bl/bm/br, 121bl/br, 122bl/bm/br, 124bl/bm/br, 125bl/br, 126bl/bm/br, 127bl/bm/br, 128bl, 158tl/ml, 185bl/br, 188br, 222b, 225tr, 252b, 254, 255tl, 256t, 261ml, 278m, 333br

cloud2013 (Flickr, CC BY 2.0), 441mr

509

Also Available from Notgrass History

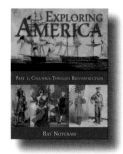

Exploring America by Ray Notgrass

Your child can earn one year of credit in American history, English (literature and composition), and Bible. Engaging history lessons, combined with primary sources, provide a rich understanding of our nation's past. High school.

Exploring World History by Ray Notgrass

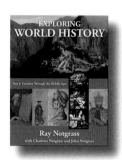

Engaging lessons, combined with primary sources, survey history from Creation to the present. Your child can earn one year of credit in world history, English (literature and composition), and Bible. High school.

Exploring Government by Ray Notgrass

This one-semester course provides a half-year credit in government and English (literature and composition). Learn about the operations of government and about issues facing our nation today. High school.

Exploring Economics by Ray Notgrass

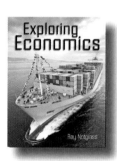

This one-semester high school course provides one half-year of credit in economics and an optional one half-year of credit in English. Your student will take a fascinating and relevant guided tour through the world of economics. High school.

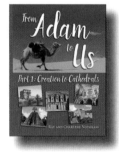

From Adam to Us by Ray and Charlene Notgrass

This one-year world history and literature course combines narrative lessons, full-color photographs, primary sources, literature, and hands-on activities to help the student connect with world history in a personal way. Ages 10-14.

America the Beautiful by Charlene Notgrass

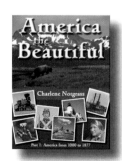

This one-year American history, geography, and literature course combines the flexibility and richness of a unit study with the simplicity of a textbook-based approach to history. Engaging, fascinating, and fun. Ages 10-14.

For more information about our resources, call 1-800-211-8793 or visit notgrass.com.